SCHOOL EMPOWERMENT

SCHOOL EMPOWERMENT

Michael D. Richardson
Georgia Southern University

Kenneth E. Lane
California State University-San Bernardino

Jackson L. Flanigan
Clemson University

TECHNOMIC
PUBLISHING CO., INC.

LANCASTER · BASEL

School Empowerment

a **TECHNOMIC**®publication

Published in the Western Hemisphere by
Technomic Publishing Company, Inc.
851 New Holland Avenue, Box 3535
Lancaster, Pennsylvania 17604 U.S.A.

Distributed in the Rest of the World by
Technomic Publishing AG
Missionsstrasse 44
CH-4055 Basel, Switzerland

Printed in the United States of America
10 9 8 7 6 5 4 3 2 1

Main entry under title:
  School Empowerment

A Technomic Publishing Company book
Bibliography: p.

Library of Congress Catalog Card No. 95-60051
ISBN No. 1-56676-269-3

*To Leah Richardson,
Roselyn Flanigan, and Maury Lane.*

Contents

Foreword

The chapters in this book offer a number of insights and perspectives about the notion of empowerment in schools. Particular emphasis is placed on dimensions of leadership in schools, with an appeal for a wider range of participation and more broadly defined school communities. Discussions range from defining empowerment and implications for creating environments that promote involvement to examples of what empowerment is and could be under certain circumstances. Having thought about what the authors suggest, it seems to me that *empowerment* is synonymous to *enabling,* with one distinct difference. That is, the root word in empowerment is power, and the concept of power is most often affixed to positions of authority, is in some way official, and is viewed as a commodity. Enabling broadens the concept of empowerment through providing opportunity, making things possible, and enlarging capacity, coupled with sharing power, authority, and responsibility.

Carson and Cairns (Chapter 7) provide an overview of the historical antecedents of disempowerment in society at large and in schools focused on democratic principles of social organization and the untenable nature of decision making by an "expert elite." The point is made that stakeholders have a moral obligation to participate in decision-making processes that affect their lives. Yet the profound acquiescence of these responsibilities is reflected in "sacred" communities where tradition and status quo prevail, within and outside school walls, where too many remain disenfranchised and marginalized.

Superficial dialogue and lack of debate are hallmarks. Lindle (Chapter 12) examines the Kentucky Education Reform Act (KERA), which legislated implementation of school-based decision making (SBDM) councils intended to empower constituents. The composition of councils and areas in which policy decisions were legally authorized to be made by SBDM councils were delineated in KERA. However, principals, teachers, and parents found themselves unprepared for the unfamiliar roles and relationships that emerged. In addition, autonomy was threatened in schools that had viable and representative community involvement by mandates concerning the configuration of councils and policy parameters. Smith and Cairns (Chapter 11) address empowerment in rural schools, and Greer (Chapter 15) discusses empowerment and school autonomy, suggesting that even the most honorable of intentions have unintended consequences. Altering or constructing new mental templates for empowerment is, at best, difficult, given perceptions and expectations rooted in traditional bureaucratic principles of standardization and routinization.

Two assumptions guide my thinking about empowering and enabling stakeholders, schools as human enterprises, and why some schools are disempowering and dysfunctionally enabling institutions. First, life in schools is potentially meaningful under any conditions. And second, it is not freedom from conditions, but freedom to take a stand toward conditions, that is of fundamental importance in creating empowering and enabling cultures. Before the concept of meaning and meaningfulness can be discussed, it is important to examine what guides our thinking about schools and the people in them. Assume that one of the primary purposes of schools is to enhance human growth and development. Growth and development for whom? By whom? To what end? Many would probably agree that our efforts should be directed toward providing opportunities and experiences that enhance learning and living in schools for our learners (birth to death); that, as educators, we are ultimately held responsible for providing opportunities and experiences; and that, through these opportunities and experiences, the learner will make significant contributions to self and others. The process of growth means achieving, realizing, emerging, fulfilling, and becoming. We know that changes can and do occur in people at any age even though human beings may not be infinitely malleable. There are some who view the potential for growth as fixed and limited, particularly for adults. I am convinced, however, that, in order to provide meaningful opportunities for learners, meaningful growth opportunities must be provided for those who serve as stewards of student learning.

Certain conditions impede or encourage opportunities for growth. Classic examples are inservice activities that have little or no relevance and meaning for recipients (the term *recipients* is operative since, too often, participation is restricted or nonexistent in the design, development, or delivery). In many, if not most, cases these are a far cry from growth-oriented professional development activities. Sources that limit growth opportunities must be removed. Basic correlates in making conditions meaningful are trust and reduced fears. Three critical aspects must be considered in creating conditions for growth—time, information, and resources. As many of the authors imply, rational models of decision making in schools have severely restricted access to these, elevated distrust, and perpetuated a prevailing sense of fear. Choosing to participate, to be empowered and enabled, is more than a choice between "yes," "no," or "maybe." The assumption that life in schools can be potentially meaningful under any conditions suggests that being left alone to do whatever it is that we envision as our primary function can be meaningful. Greer points toward school culture, and particularly norms of behavior, as a critical aspect of whether change occurs or the status quo is preserved.

Considering what the authors offer, I observed how the concept of anomie (meaninglessness and normlessness) is played out in environments of uncertainty and complexity. How are norms of behavior developed, chosen, and assessed in such environments? As Charles Hampden-Turner* indicates in his treatise, an anomic refrains from engaging in activities for renewal, and the ability to create meaning is severely limited by doubting the capacity to influence events in any significant way, by narrow perceptions, by stagnant identity, by a sense of helplessness, and by lack of investment and risk taking. The "me" is more important than "we," and great barriers exist between "us" and "them." How do we become empowered in order to empower and enable others such environments? Leadership is a void without followership.

The chapters that follow suggest that we must have a firm understanding of the descriptive and normative aspects of schools as organizations, schools as human enterprises, and schools as communities of learners. This means having hindsight, insight, and foresight—what has been, what is, and what could and should be in an increasingly diverse society.

L. NAN RESTINE, PH.D.
*Department of Educational Administration
and Higher Education
College of Education
Oklahoma State University*

*Hampden-Turner, Charles. 1971. *Radical Man: The Process of Psycho-Social Development*. Garden City, New York.

Preface

This book results from needs expressed by practicing school administrators, teachers, community members, and university professors for a book that could plainly and succinctly document both the conceptual and practical essentials of empowerment. This book is designed for multiple audiences: teachers, practicing administrators (who need concrete, practical advice), potential administrators (who need to understand the theoretical and practical aspects), parents, potential teachers, community members, and school board members. This would be an ideal supplementary text in graduate educational administration courses. Every superintendent and school board member should read this book.

The book contains seventeen chapters divided into four sections, each devoted to a separate aspect of the empowerment process. Section 1 addresses what is meant by empowerment. Chapter 1 by Flanigan and Gray provides a practical and conceptual look at the changing role of the school principal in empowered schools. In Chapter 2, Wayson provides the consummate review of the literature related to empowerment and its various subcomponents. Schmieder and Townley follow up in Chapter 3 with a review of the different definitions of empowerment and what it means to various constituent groups. Chapter 4 outlines very clearly the concept of the school becoming a community of learners by utilizing empowerment.

Section 2 outlines a means for creating a climate that permits empowerment to take place. Chapter 5 by Keaster discusses the need for problem solving in empowerment situations. In Chapter 6, Moffitt and Baldwin examine the role of staff, parents, and community members in empowered schools. The concept of community is further developed in Chapter 7, where Cairns and Carson examine the larger community to be served by education. Whitson, in Chapter 8, defines the roles of practitioners who are involved in empowerment projects. Finally, Chapter 9 by Grady explores the perceptions of superintendents and school board members toward empowerment.

Section 3 provides examples of empowerment at work. Chapter 10 by Hoyle describes the new roles for a principal in empowerment schools. Smith and Cairns, in Chapter 11, explore the unique attributes of rural school administrators in empowered schools, while Lindle, in Chapter 12, examines legislated mandates for change in Kentucky. Chapter 13 by Smith, Ruhl-Smith, and Richardson calls for a supervisory model that empowers teachers. The concluding Chapter 14 by Van Berkum specifies the need for empowering students in schools.

Section 4 investigates the future of empowerment. Chapter 15 by Richardson and Lane delineates a model for empowerment, which can be used by practitioners. Greer, in Chapter 16, describes the autonomous school as one where everyone has a voice in decision making. Chapter 17 by Kirby concludes the discussion with a moving analysis of the future of empowerment.

Several unique features highlight this book. A list of references is contained at the end of each chapter, which makes documentation easy and thorough for the reader. As a side note, this volume is extensively referenced. Although not intended to be simply a scholarly contribution, but a practical guide as well, nonetheless, the extensive documentation was a direct result of the authors' in-depth research into the topics covered by the book. It also provides the reader with an exhaustive list for further reference or, at the least, a place to start more discussion. Secondly, the extensive background of the various authors contributes immeasurably to the usefulness of the work. The editors are grateful to all the authors for their time, expertise, and commitment to the topics at hand.

Acknowledgements

The authors wish to thank the numerous people who have helped to make this work possible—Barbara DeLorenzo, Brenda Stiteler, and Patsy Greene for their help in translating our rough draft to the finished product; Dr. Joe Eckenrode and Susan Farmer at Technomic Publishing Company for their continued confidence in our ability to deliver; Dr. Dennis W. Van Berkum at North Dakota State University for his review of the manuscript and valuable suggestions for improving the quality of the work; and our wives for their enduring willingness to allow our pursuits, often at their expense. We extend a special thanks to all those students who have helped shape and stimulate our thinking about educational leadership and the various component parts of the discipline, particularly the concept of empowerment and how it impacts everyone in education.

Our particular thanks to Dr. Gordon W. Gray, former Dean of the College of Education at Clemson University, for his support and encouragement during the completion of this project. Numerous individuals contribute to such a work as this in a variety of ways and to any that we failed to recognize, our thanks for your help.

Introduction

This introduction contains some material that was originally part of a presentation by the authors at the *Annual Meeting of the American Association of School Administrators* in San Diego, California, in February 1994, entitled "The Value of Participatory Decision Making: A Collaborative Approach."

BACKGROUND

America faces a multitude of challenges as we approach the 21st century. Among these challenges are maintaining our competitive position among world markets, expanding the notion of "the American dream" to all groups of people, and bolstering the moral fiber of the nation (Baer et al., 1989). With the exception of our public school system, there is no single institution in the country that is so broad in its mission or that addresses the range and depth of challenges facing our nation (Shor, 1992). Our nation's schools impact all dimensions of life, whether this impact is felt directly or tangentially (Larson, 1992).

Unfortunately, at the present time, some evidence suggests that our system of public education is not adequately addressing our nation's challenges (Lunenburg, 1992). Students who drop out of our school systems are represented disproportionately among the unemployed, welfare recipients, and the incarcerated (Nel, 1992). Clearly, a large percentage of students are not only at risk for dropping out of school, but they are also at risk of failing in life. These students, along with an equally large population of students who complete school without sufficient skills to achieve in today's demanding society, will experience significantly reduced life chances (Schorr, 1992).

There remains a wide gap between our school and the communities in which they reside (Zeichner, 1991). With almost 50 percent of today's students coming from nontraditional homes (e.g., single-parent), it is increasingly important that school personnel build partnerships within the community, including the home (Garcia, 1986). Evidence suggests that few contacts with the school are initiated by the community (Hughes, 1993). For many members of the community, the schools remain an enigma or an intimidating place to avoid because of previous experiences (Hess, 1992). These attitudes, along with the concern about what schools are presently doing for the community, are reflected in the lack of public support for schools across the nation (Fine, 1993). It appears that these feelings are echoed by students who, themselves, report a low level of participation in school activities and often exhibit a poor self-esteem related to school achievement (Cuban, 1989).

This lack of interaction with the community results in the perception of schools as places where the curriculum is not responsive to the needs of society, where facilities are underutilized, and where faculty are not willing or able to address the most basic problems of the community. Certainly, these perceptions have contributed to the relatively low status assigned to teaching and to the educational process in our nation. As long as these perceptions, true or false, continue to exist, recruitment of the most capable from our society for teaching will be difficult (Eisner, 1992).

Business and industry have repeatedly voiced the concern that today's high school graduates are lacking the necessary skills to fill positions in the work force and to create the scientific innovations that have, in the past, positioned our nation as the world's industrial leader. For the first time in the history of this nation, we are importing large numbers of foreign professionals and other workers to assist in making our industries competitive (Boysen, 1992). Amidst the growing competition among the world's industrial leaders, institutions once considered to be immune to foreign competition are struggling to produce competitive products (Grenier and Hogler, 1991). Industry claims that this situation will not improve unless the products of our schools are sufficiently prepared to compete on the international market (Wilson and Schmoker, 1992).

The current school reform movement has grown out of an increasing awareness of the inadequacies of a school system that has its origins in the preindustrial period (Buchmann and Floden, 1992). As our nation moves into the 21st century, our system of education must reflect the demands of a high technology society. Employers must expect to have available a work force that is highly literate (McDaniel, 1989). To a large degree, the geographic location of new industries will be determined in the future by the availability of this highly literate work force, as opposed to past considerations of resources and transportation (Kozol, 1992). Therefore, the expectation for literacy has great impact on the quality of life in terms of the earning power of the community and the ability of the community to take advantage of health and nutritional, energy, and social-cultural advancements in our society (Katz, 1992). Clearly, the call to bring our nation's schools into the 21st century, to increase their effectiveness for all students, and to make them a positive center of life for communities is possibly the most critical challenge that we face as a nation (Heck, 1992).

Our nation responded to this call for educational reform in a number of ways. Following the release of the report entitled *A Nation at Risk*, states immediately formed blue-chip committees on excellence in education to study reform in their respective states. These committees, heavily influenced by political entities, often promulgated regulatory measures to increase graduation requirements, establish teacher certification testing, and revise teacher certification programs in institutions of higher education. Some states have promoted singular or combinations of instructional strategies as remedies to our nation's school problems. These attempts at school reform have often been labeled "tinkering," as contrasted to more systemwide approaches to change, which may take many years to implement and to evaluate (Boysen, 1992).

RESPONSE THUS FAR

American education is currently experiencing the fourth wave of reform, which is a direct result of the 1983 release of *A Nation at Risk* (Lipsky, 1992). This report was a warning from the National Commission on Excellence in Education "that our deteriorating public schools were awash in 'a rising tide of mediocrity'" (McDaniel, 1989, p. 16). *A Nation at Risk* found many problems with our educational system, including illiteracy, decline in graduation standards, decrease in student mastery of basic skills, rising student dropouts, the teacher shortage, and disciplinary problems (Cohen and Honetschlager, 1988). Between

1983 and 1985, as a direct result of *A Nation at Risk,* state legislatures enacted more than 700 statutes stipulating what should be taught, how it should be taught, and who should teach it (McDaniel, 1989). This reform was done from the top down, from legislators to school boards, from school boards to principals, and from principals to teachers (Ogletree and Schmidt, 1992). The catchword of the time was *accountability.* This top-down type of reform overlooked the values and concerns of teachers and students (Wilson and Schmoker, 1992). To change people, it is necessary to change their beliefs—not just alter the environment (McDaniel, 1989). Mandates from above tend to bring about fear and resentment from those at the bottom. One of the results of the "accountability" movement was the development of empowerment as not only a concept, but as an actual practice within our schools (Aronstein et al., 1990; Moore and Eselman, 1992).

While the intent of our nation to improve our system of education has been laudable, age-old traditions governing teachers and teaching systems still stand as formidable barriers to substantive reform (Harrington-Lueker, 1992). In many cases, the changing demands of our work force, as well as new technologies in education itself, have rendered ineffectual the old traditional approaches to education. The educational community is beginning to collect a body of knowledge about effective teaching and effective schools. The work of Goodlad and his associates at the University of Washington, as well as many other researchers in education, are providing direction in school reform (Hughes, 1993). However, this information will not have the desired impact unless barriers to school improvement are removed (Larson, 1992). One of the techniques being utilized to reduce these barriers is *school empowerment.*

INTRODUCTION

Here we attempt to demonstrate why empowerment is a viable alternative to traditional bureaucracy as a decision-making model used in many public schools. John Steinbeck in his great novel *The Grapes of Wrath* wrote about power and ownership and what he called "the little screaming facts that sound through all history." An attempt to paraphrase Steinbeck in the current vernacular of power and decision making might sound like this:

And the current leaders, who must share their power in the restructuring process, the leaders with access to history and to knowledge, those who know the great fact: When power accumulates in too few hands it is taken away. And that companion fact: When the majority of the people are powerless they will assume power through force. And the little screaming fact that sounds through all history: that repression of knowledge and power merely serves to strengthen and knit those deprived of knowledge and power. These same leaders ignored the cries of history and their every effort was directed at limiting access to knowledge and power. The effort that might have gone to growth and improvement was spent to control and intimidate in an attempt to protect their power. Change was ignored, and plans for change ignored: and only personal power was considered, while the powerless hungered—the causes of revolt continued. (Free, 1990, p. 1)

DEFINING EMPOWERMENT

Empowerment in education has drawn considerable attention, but what does it mean and what is involved? Empowerment means different things to different people (Heller, 1993). Empowerment could mean everything and nothing simultaneously; i.e., restructuring, site-based management, participatory decision making, and empowerment are often used interchangeably, but each has a distinct definition within its context of use (Kanpol, 1990).

One principal stated that empowerment meant the release from the constraints the central office placed on him (Harrison, et al., 1989). For another principal, empowerment meant the official power to make decisions that affect the school, rather than depending on central administrators to set up the rules (Harrison et al., 1989). For others, it meant the freedom to hire the personnel they wanted (Harrison et al., 1989). Overall, empowerment means bringing the responsibility for decision making to the lowest possible level, which specifies that the administrator does not make all the decisions (Liontos, 1993). Empowerment creates ownership for those responsible for carrying out decisions by involving them directly in the decision-making process (Harrison et al., 1989). Consequently, empowerment could be defined as a form of decentralization that places decision making and accountability at the lowest level (Kanpol, 1990).

What is involved in empowerment?

1. Empowerment implies a reevaluation of curricular and instructional efforts for students.
2. Empowerment means advocating participatory decision making and more leadership from teachers, students, and the community.

3. Empowerment specifies an appropriate and supportive environment for students and adults.
4. Empowerment requires new partnerships and networks.
5. Empowerment articulates the increased participation of parents and community members (Liebermann and Miller, 1990).

Empowerment refers to a process or philosophy to improve education by increasing the autonomy of teachers, principals, and staff to make school-site decisions. Empowerment is a decentralized system where decision-making is shared by all who have an interest in the decision. Empowerment emphasizes increased authority of teachers (Zeichner, 1991), students (Neely and Alm, 1993), parents (Delgado-Gaitan, 1991), and community members (Mercado, 1993) to make decisions outside the confines of traditional structures of authority (Dixon, 1992). Empowerment creates new relationships among teachers (Heller, 1993), administrators (White, 1989), parents (Delgado-Gaitan, 1991), and students (Nel, 1992). Empowerment actually gives certain powers to principals (English, 1992), teachers (Chapman, 1988), parents (Glenn, 1992), students (Short and Greer, 1993), and community members (Cochran and Dean, 1991), which demands more involvement in improving education.

Empowerment sounds like a great idea, but how does it work? The backbone of empowerment is autonomy; without autonomy, shared decision-making within schools has little meaning. Typically, school autonomy involves decision-making authority in three critical arenas: budget, staffing, and curriculum (David, 1989). Empowerment increases authority and responsibility in an attempt to improve accountability and productivity (Duke et al., 1989). Empowerment is viewed as a way to transform schools into effective learning environments by providing school staff with authority, flexibility, and the resources they need to implement change and to solve the educational problems particular to their schools (David, 1989).

Should everyone be involved in every decision? We believe that teachers and others should be involved in a decision if it is important to them, if they are interested in the area under discussion, and if they have the ability to act on the decision (Lewin, 1947; Stein and King, 1992).

IMPLEMENTATION

The largest obstacle to empowerment is implementation (Bhasin, 1991). Huddleston et al., (1991) stated that empowerment implementation involved three basic steps: 1) sanction by leaders, 2) training for all involved, and 3) development of a support system for those involved in empowerment.

SANCTION BY LEADERS

Sanction by leaders involves the school board, the administration, the faculty, and the community in developing a common definition of what empowerment means at the school site or at the school district (Watkins, 1986). The terms *teacher empowerment, site-based management, participatory management, decentralization, shared decision making,* and *school-based management* are all included under the general rubric of empowerment. Sanction by the leaders is the most critical element of empowerment (White, 1992). In many past educational innovations, leadership has given lip service to the change, and the consequences were less than satisfactory. Without leader buy-in, empowerment will go the way of the Edsel, a great idea with no ownership (Bredeson, 1992; Vann, 1992). Leaders at the district level, school site, and in the community must participate in empowerment and be committed to the ideal of involvement in decision making (Taylor and Levine, 1991).

TRAINING IN DECISION MAKING

Decision making at its best is a complex structure with many complicated tasks involved; at its worst, decision making is an arbitrary act of autonomy (Smith and Peterson, 1988). If the organization is to be efficient where a myriad of decisions are made, people and programs are coordinated, communication channelled, positions allocated, staff recruited, schedules developed, and resources obtained and utilized, then decision making must be shared (Garcia, 1986).

Administrators and teachers must examine how decisions are made in the schools and who is involved in making those decisions (Prestine, 1993). Research indicates that one of the real weaknesses of empowerment has been the inability of teachers to understand how decisions are made (Persing, 1989). Teachers make as many as 5,000 instructional decisions per day, but instructional decisions are different from administrative or management decisions, which often involve other people—peers, for example. Instructional decisions are made about such things as "Do I continue to teach addition now or should I stop and go on to language arts?" or "How can I best get this particular student to understand this math concept and what multiplication really means?" or "How can I better help this student understand how to spell phonetically?" All are examples of instructional decisions that teachers make constantly in the classroom (Walberg and Lane, 1989).

With school empowerment, decisions are moved out of the classroom and into peer relationships (Lincoln, 1992). For example, Who is responsible for bus duty this week? How do we decide who is responsible for bus duty? Should aides be hired to handle bus duty rather than teachers? Should bus duty be a decision involving the faculty, or is that an administrative decision? How should personnel resources be allocated? How should teachers be assigned to classrooms, to grades, to subjects? Those are curriculum or personnel decisions that teachers have to understand before empowerment will function effectively and efficiently (Lifton, 1992). Teachers need training in how to process information, how to collect data, how to examine different alternatives available, and then, ultimately, how to make a decision (Walberg and Lane, 1989).

Another problem teachers confront in work groups is a lack of experience with debating issues and building consensus (Wood and Caldwell, 1991). Working on group dynamics and the art of compromise early in the transition period may be time well-spent and critical to group decision making and consensus (Rummler, 1989). It will also be helpful if teachers learn the essential relationship between autonomy and accountability (Reed, 1988). Making decisions can lead to conflict and mistakes; even when the group finds a solution to a problem, often a new set of challenges appears (Reitzug, 1992).

SUPPORT SYSTEM

This decision-making process also implies one other important facet: accountability. If teachers are to be involved in making decisions, then they must be held accountable for those decisions, just as administrators are held accountable (Hughes, 1993). Principals often ask the question, do teachers really want to be involved in making decisions? Teachers talk about empowerment, about making decisions, but do teachers really want to take the time, the effort, and the energy that is required for participatory decision making? According to Richardson and Long (1991),

> Can . . . teachers who are burned out or turned off be enlivened to become productive teachers again? Some of the best researchers say yes. They indicate that much of the "dry bones" effect is due to undesirable teaching climates, that many good teachers are simply suffocated by an unsympathetic system: good teaching goes unrewarded; poor teaching goes unnoticed or unpunished, and system survival is the functional philosophy of the school. (p. 22)

For empowerment to work effectively, support must be given to teachers, administrators, parents, and students (Romanish, 1993). This support must include more than the training necessary to function efficiently in groups; it should include 1) time to participate in decision-making activities, 2) an adequate reward structure, and 3) an enlightened approach to personnel decisions (Orlich, 1989; Romanish, 1991; Reep and Grier, 1992).

DEFINING ROLES AND CONCERNS

There are numerous issues involved in empowering schools; however, one of the first that must be addressed is the changing roles for participants in the process. Smith and Peterson (1988) define role as "a label for the set of expectations about an individual's behavior" (p. 73). Role definition means that, in an empowered school, roles must be altered (Mitchell, 1990).

THE TEACHERS

The teacher's role undergoes many changes as a result of empowerment. In empowerment situations, teachers are actively encouraged to become involved in leadership roles (Romanish, 1993), which increases tensions between teachers and administrators. Teachers' customary relationships with students has provided personal and professional satisfaction; however, in empowerment situations, teachers are required to step out of the classroom environment and assume new roles with principals, staff, students, and parents (Strodl, 1992).

Many teachers perceive that empowerment activities take time away from instructional endeavors, i.e., preparing lessons, grading papers, counseling students, advising extracurricular activities, and handling routine teaching tasks. Empowerment requires teachers to spend more time in decision-making activities and, ultimately, in instructional activities (Streshley and Bernd, 1992).

In addition to concern over time, teachers often fear that empowerment may cost them a measure of autonomy (Clouse, 1989). Teacher involvement in empowerment permits teachers to gain a greater voice in determining how schools are operated, but often at the expense of individual teachers (Casner-Lotto, 1988). Teachers may have reason to fear that involvement in school decision making is not a pathway to collegial respect (Cornett, 1991).

In actual practice, empowerment could be seen as a substitute for delegated authority, which contributes to the blurring of labels between school improvement programs, shared decision making, empowerment, participatory decision making, and school-based management (Cunningham and Gresso, 1993). When the authority and resources to take action are not provided in empowerment situations, the best efforts of teachers and administrators can create controversary (Hallinger and Murphy, 1991). Asking people to participate in decisions about which they have little or no information and little or no authority creates frustration, not empowerment (Jones, 1992).

THE PRINCIPAL

If any role is perceived to be vulnerable with the onset of empowerment, it is the building principal (Gursky, 1990). Empowerment at the building level could have an adverse impact on the principal's already misunderstood authority and role. Historically, there is probably no more difficult role to perform in a school district than that of a building principal, who is given responsibility for total operations of the building without the resources necessary to perform the functions adequately, because most discretionary resource authority resides with the district office (English, 1992).

The administrator's role is critical to empowerment because empowerment will only work in those situations where administrators allow it to occur (Goldman, 1992). Initially, administrators must abdicate the perceived power they have held over students, faculty, and staff (Reitzug, 1992) and must articulate empowerment and teacher involvement in decision making as a positive measure for school improvement (Vann, 1992).

IMPLICATIONS

AVOIDING MISTAKES

In order to gain the support of those affected by empowerment, school personnel must avoid the mistakes most often associated with empowerment efforts (Orlich, 1989). The first mistake administrators should avoid is the tendency to focus on the "here and now" and not on the future (Phillips, 1989). A clearly defined, desirable end result must be plainly stated early in the change process so that all parties understand the nature of the change (Romanish, 1991).

Not addressing adequately the role changes of teachers and administrators is a second common mistake (White, 1992). With a shift from centralized management to empowerment, the roles of the district office staff, school staff, administrators, faculty, parents, community, and students change (Meadows, 1990). Lack of training and support for the redefined roles blocks many empowerment efforts (Harrison et al., 1989). The principal's role must change from a dictator to a leader of leaders (Hallinger and Murphy, 1991). Empowerment forces administrators to work more closely with teachers in schoolwide decision making than in the past; however, many administrators are reluctant to give up their role as controller (Lifton, 1992). Consequently, "districts should carefully delineate the parameters and conditions for responsibility and authority before implementation" (Harrison et al., 1989, p. 56).

A third mistake made in implementing empowerment efforts involves the failure to provide training for all school personnel (Foster, 1990). Suddenly, teachers and principals are being asked to work together and share their decisions when they are accustomed to working alone (Sagor, 1992). Districts can avoid unnecessary frustrations by providing the necessary training and support services to school personnel in the early stages (Harrison et al., 1989).

The fourth mistake concerns the lack of preparation for the realities of change (Fullan, 1991). Conflict is not always negative, but it is a signal that change is occurring (Holloway, 1992). Administrators should be conscious of the impact of change on individuals (Gresso and Robertson, 1992) and make sure to offer a wide variety of intervention strategies and have in-house personnel available to assist individuals or groups as conflicts arise (Harrison et al., 1989).

ISSUES IN EMPOWERMENT

The first major issue in empowerment concerns the attitude of school leaders toward such an endeavour. If the leaders are not willing to actively endose and participate in empowerment activities, then there is little need to attempt a substantive change (Epp, 1992). A second issue in empowerment deals with the dilemma of process versus content (Kanter, 1983). Empowerment as a process must have some focus or vision that drives the individual and collective actions of the group (Maeroff, 1988). Third, the needs of students and teachers should be appropriately balanced (Deal, 1990; Glenn, 1992). Empowerment activities should focus on students and their success in school by creating conditions that allow teachers to accomplish desired outcomes (Cherry, 1991). A fourth issue involves balancing action and reflection. There are no road maps for empowerment; the process involved is neither predictable nor orderly, and everyone must be aware that problems will occur along the way (Liebermann and Miller, 1990). The fifth, and most overlooked, issue concerns evaluation. Empowerment activities must be evaluated to ascertain their relative impact on both teachers and students. These evaluations should be conducted from both a formative and summative approach to give administrators reliable and accurate data (Bhasin, 1991).

RESULTS FROM EMPOWERMENT

"The banner word of the restructuring movement is empowerment" (Glickman, 1990, p. 69). When teacher empowerment occurs, Glickman notes that at least seven ironies occur:

1. The more the empowered school improves, the more apparent it becomes that there is more to be done. The people involved come to understand that education is a humbling enterprise that can never be perfected.

2. The more an empowered school is recognized for its success, the more non-empowered schools criticize it. Jealousy may occur between schools because of lack of recognition for some schools and over recognition of others. Also, teacher and administrators in schools that are to empowered may feel pressured to make changes on their own.

3. The more the school works collectively, the more individual differences and tensions between the staff become apparent. These differences will occur because everyone will have a say in decision and be allowed to express their opinion.

4. The more an empowered school becomes a success, the less the school becomes a practical model to be copied. "People need to understand that these programs work, not because they are so meticulously crafted and engineered, but because the faculty in these schools will not let them fail."

5. The more a school becomes empowered, the more it hesitates to act. It is easier to complain than it is to act. The area of empowerment moves schools from the known and comfortable to the unknown and uncomfortable. Risk will be a key word in this movement on the part of teachers and administrators.

6. The more an empowered school has to gain, the more it has to lose. When school make gains quickly, they will feel pressure to keep making gain. We have to remember that "education is a long-term proposition." The important thing to focus on is the long-term goals of the school, which may not occur for years down the road.

7. The more an empowered school resembles a democracy, the more it

must justify its own existence to the most vocal proponents of democracy. "It is inconsistent to endorse democracy in society but to be skeptical of shared governance in our school."

CONCLUSIONS

Empowerment is not a fixed set of rules; in fact, empowerment is the opposite of prescription. By definition, empowerment operates differently from one school to the next and from one year to the next because the goal is to empower school staff by providing authority, flexibility, and resources to solve the educational problems particular to their schools (Epp, 1992). Empowerment should create conditions in schools that facilitate improvement, innovation, and continuous growth for everyone in the school. However, empowerment takes a long time to implement and requires commitment on the part of everyone involved (Streshley and Bernd, 1992).

Many schools and organizations around the country are successfully implementing empowerment; however, the concept is as perilous as it is promising (Holloway, 1992). Empowerment can help teachers and principals respond less randomly, but more cooperatively, to the thousands of decisions they make every day in the schools. Research indicates that schools are unlikely to change without increased autonomy and that, without district leadership and support for change, empowerment is not enough.

Decentralized decision making allows educational reform to be implemented through increased involvement, which allows the principals, teachers, and community members to take ownership in the educational process (Prestine, 1993). Therefore, empowerment promises greater flexibility, increased participation in decision making, and the ability to meet the specific needs of students and teachers.

REFERENCES

Aronstein, L. W., Marlow, M., and Desilets, B. (1990). Detours on the road to site-based management. *Educational Leadership,* 47 (7), 61–63.

Baer, S., Bakalis, M. J., Bast, J. L., and Walberg, H. J. (1989). Restructuring the nation's worst schools. *Phi Delta Kappan,* 70, 802–805.

Bhasin, K. (1991). Participatory development demands participatory training. *Convergence,* 24 (4), 5–15.

Boysen, T. C. (1992). Irreconcilable differences: Effective urban schools versus restructuring. *Education and Urban Society,* 25 (1), 85–95.

Bredeson, P. V. (1992). Responses to restructuring and empowerment initiatives: A study of teachers' and principals' perceptions of organizational leadership, decisionmaking and climate (ERIC Document Reproduction Service No. ED 346 569).

Buchmann, M. and Floden, R. E. (1992). Coherence, the rebel angel. _Educational Researcher,_ 21 (9), 4–9.

Casner-Lotto, J. (1988). Expanding the teacher's role: Hammond's school improvement process. _Phi Delta Kappan,_ 69, 349–353.

Chapman, J. D. (1988). Decentralization, devolution and the teacher: Participation by teachers in the decision making of schools. _Journal of Educational Administration,_ 26 (1), 39–72.

Cherry, M. (1991). School ownership–The essential foundation of restructuring. _NASSP Bulletin,_ 75 (537), 33–39.

Clouse, R. W. (1989). A review of educational role theory (ERIC Document Reproduction Service No. ED 314 824).

Cochran, M. and Dean, C. (1991). Home-school relations and the empowerment process. _Elementary School Journal,_ 91 (3), 261–269.

Cohen, M. and Honetschlager, D. (1988). The governors restructure schools. _Educational Leadership,_ 45 (5), 42–43.

Cornett, J. W. (1991). Earned powerment not empowerment of teachers: The role of teachers' systematic reflection in restructuring schools. _Social Science Record,_ 28 (1), 71–77.

Cuban, L. (1989). The "at-risk" label and the problem of urban schools. _Phi Delta Kappan,_ 70, 780–784, 799–801.

Cunningham, W. G. and Gresso, D. W. (1993). _Cultural Leadership._ Needham Heights, MA: Allyn & Bacon.

David, J. L. (1989). Synthesis of research on school-based management. _Educational Leadership,_ 46 (8), 45–52.

Deal, T. (1990). Reframing reform. _Educational Leadership,_ 47 (8), 6–12.

Delgado-Gaitan, C. (1991). Involving parents in schools: A process of empowerment. _American Journal of Education,_ 100 (1), 20–46.

Dixon, A. P. (1992). Parents: Full partners in the decision-making process. _NASSP Bulletin,_ 76 (543), 15–18.

Duke, D. L., Showers, B. K., and Imber, M. (1989). Teachers and shared decision making: The costs and benefits of involvement. _Educational Administration Quarterly,_ 16 (1), 93–106.

Eisner, E. W. (1992). Education reform and the ecology of schooling. _Teachers College Record,_ 93 (4), 610–627.

English, F. W. (1992). The principal and "The Prince": Machiavelli and school leadership. _NASSP Bulletin,_ 76 (540), 10–15.

Epp, J. R. (1992). Teacher participation in school government: A central element in educational reform (ERIC Document Reproduction Service No. ED 343 223).

Fine, M. (1993). A parent involvement. _Equity and Choice,_ 9 (3), 4–8.

Foster, K. (1990). Small steps on the way to teacher empowerment. _Educational Leadership,_ 47 (8), 38–40.

Free, W. (1990). The little screaming facts of history. Bowling Green, KY: Western Kentucky University. Unpublished paper.

Fullan, M. G. (1991). *The New Meaning of Educational Change.* New York: Teachers College Press.

Garcia, A. (1986). Consensus decision making promotes involvement, ownership, satisfaction. *NASSP Bulletin,* 70 (493), 50–52.

Glenn, B. C. (1992). Include parents and teachers in reform. *Social Policy,* 22 (3), 26–27.

Glickman (1990). Pushing school reform to a new edge: The seven ironies of school empowerment. *Phi Delta Kappan,* 72 (1), 68–75.

Goldman, J. P. (1992). When participatory management attracts no buyers. *School Administrator,* 49 (1), 15.

Gresso, D. W. and Robertson, M. B. (1992). The principal as process consultant: Catalyst for change. *NASSP Bulletin,* 76 (540), 44–48.

Grenier, G. and Hogler, R. L. (1991). Labor law and managerial ideology: Employee participation as a social control system. *Work and Occupation: An International Sociological Journal,* 18 (3), 313–333.

Gursky, D. (1990). Without principal. *Teacher Magazine,* 1 (6), 56–63.

Hallinger, P., and Murphy, J. (1991). Developing leaders for tomorrow's schools. *Phi Delta Kappan,* 72 (7), 514–517.

Harrington-Lueker, D. (1992). The next four years. *American School Board Journal,* 179 (12), 18–23.

Harrison, C. R., Killion, J. P., and Mitchell, J. E. (1989). Site-based management: The realities of implementation. *Educational Leadership,* 46 (8), 55–58.

Heck, R. H. (1992). Public school restructuring in Chicago: Indicator of another revolution in the politics of education? *Equity and Excellence,* 25 (2–4), 216–221.

Heller, G. S. (1993). Teacher empowerment—Sharing the challenge: A guide to implementation and success. *NASSP Bulletin,* 77 (550), 94–103.

Hess, G. A., Jr. (1992). Chicago and Britain: Experiments in empowering parents. *Journal of Education Policy,* 7 (2), 155–171.

Holloway, S. (1992). The potential wolf in sheep's clothing: The ambiguity of "cooperation." *Journal of Education,* 174 (2), 80–99.

Huddleston, J., Claspell, M., and Killion, J. (1991). Participative decision making can capitalize on teacher expertise. *NASSP Bulletin,* 75 (534), 80–89.

Hughes, L. W. (1993). School-based management, decentralization, and citizen control—A perspective. *Journal of School Leadership,* 3 (1), 40–44.

Jones, R. R. (1992). Setting the stage for change. *Executive Educator,* 14 (3), 38–39.

Kanpol, B. (1990). Empowerment: The institutional and cultural aspects for teachers and principals. *NASSP Bulletin,* 74 (528), 104–107.

Kanter, R. M. (1983). *The Change Masters,* New York: Simon and Schuster.

Katz, M. B. (1992). Chicago school reform as history. *Teachers College Record,* 94 (1), 56–72.

Kozol, J. (1992). Inequality and the will to change. *Equity and Choice,* 8 (3), 45–47.

Larson, R. L. (1992). Can the frog become a prince? Context and change in the 1990s. *International Journal of Education Reform,* 1 (1), 59–68.

Lewin, K. (1947). Group decision and social change. In *Readings in Social Psychology,* T. M. Newcomb and E. L. Hartley (Eds)., New York: Holt and Company, pp. 330–344.

Lieberman, A. and Miller, K. E. (1990). Restructuring school: What matters and what works. *Phi Delta Kappan,* 7 (10), 759–764.

Lifton, F. B. (1992). The legal tangle of shared governance. *School Administrator,* 49 (1), 16–19.

Lincoln, W. (1992). Shaping good decision makers. *Learning,* 21 (1), 63–65.

Liontos, L. B. (1993). Transformational leadership: Profile of a high school principal. *OSSC Bulletin,* 36 (9).

Lipsky, D. K. (1992). We need a third wave of education reform. *Social Policy,* 22 (3), 43–45.

Lunenberg, F. C. (1992). Introduction: The current educational reform movement – History, progress to date, and the future. *Education and Urban Society,* 25 (1), 3–17.

Maeroff, G. I. (1988). A blueprint for empowering teachers. *Phi Delta Kappan,* 69 (7), 472–477.

McDaniel, T. R. (1989). Demilitarizing public education: School reform in the era of George Bush. *Phi Delta Kappan,* 71 (1), 15–18.

Meadows, B. J. (1990). The rewards and risks of shared leadership. *Phi Delta Kappan,* 71 (7), 545–548.

Mercado, C. I. (1993). Caring as empowerment: School collaboration and community agency. *Urban Review,* 25 (1), 79–104.

Mitchell, J. E. (1990). Coaxing staff from cages for site based decisions to fly. *The School Administrator,* 47 (2), 23–24, 26.

Moore, W. P. and Eselman, M. E. (1992). Teacher efficacy, empowerment, and a focused instructional climate: Does student achievement benefit? (ERIC Document Reproduction Service No. ED 350 252).

Neely, R. and Alm, D. (1993). Empowering students with style. *Principal,* 72 (4), 32–33.

Nel, J. (1992). The empowerment of minority students: Implication of Cummins' model for teacher education. *Action in Teacher Education,* 14 (3), 38–45.

Ogletree, E. J. and Schmidt, L. J. (1992). Faculty involvement in administration of schools. *Illinois Schools Journal,* 71 (2), 40–46.

Orlich, D. C. (1989). Education reforms: Mistakes, misconceptions, miscues. *Phi Delta Kappan,* 70 (7), 512–517.

Persing, T. E. (1989). Your staff must learn decision processes. *The School Administrator,* 46 (3), 21–23.

Phillips, P. R. (1989). Shared decision making in an age of reform. *Update,* 20 (3), 30–37.

Prestine, N. A. (1993). Extending the essential schools metaphor: Principal as enabler. *Journal of School Leadership,* 3 (4), 356–379.

Reed, C. J. (1988). Site-based decision making: An implementation experience. *Collective Bargaining Quarterly,* 1 (3), 1–6.

Reep, B. B. and Grier, T. B. (1992). Teacher empowerment: Strategies for success. *NASSP Bulletin,* 76 (546), 90–96.

Reitzug, U. C. (1992). Self-managed leadership: An alternative school governance structure. *Urban Review,* 24 (2), 133–147.

Richardson, M. D. and Long, P. K. (1991). Restructuring school reform. *Clemson Kappan,* 10 (1), 14–15.

Romanish, B. (1991). Teacher empowerment: The litmus test of school restructuring. *Social Science Record,* 28 (1), 55–69.

Romanish, B. (1993). Teacher empowerment as the focus of school restructuring. *School and Community Journal,* 3 (1), 47–60.

Rummler, R. L. (1989). Turn to your teachers for curriculum improvement. *Executive Educator,* 11 (4), 30–31, 37.

Sagor, R. D. (1992). Three principals who make a difference. *Educational Leadership,* 49 (5), 13–18.

Shor, I. (1992). *Empowering Education.* Chicago, IL: University of Chicago Press.

Schorr, L. B. (1992). Commentary: Reason to hope. *Teachers College Record,* 93 (4), 710–716.

Short, P. M. and J. T. Greer. (1993). Empowering students: Helping all students realize success (ERIC Document Reproduction Service No. Ed 355 670).

Smith, P. B. and Peterson, M. F. (1988). *Leadership, Organizations and Culture.* Newbury Park, CA: Sage.

Stein, R. and King, B. (1992). Is restructuring a threat to principals' power? *NASSP Bulletin,* 76 (540), 26–31.

Streshley, W. and Bernd, M. (1992). School reform: Real improvement takes time. *Journal of School Leadership,* 2 (3), 320–329.

Strodl, P. (1992). A model of teacher leadership (ERIC Document Reproduction Service No. ED 350 253).

Taylor, B. O. and Levine, D. U. (1991). Effective schools projects and school-based management. *Phi Delta Kappan,* 72 (5), 394–397.

Van, A. S. 1992. Shared Decision-Making = effective leadership. *Principal,* 72 (2), 30–31.

Walberg, H. J. and Lane, J. J. (1989). *Organizing for Learning: Toward the 21st Century.* Reston, VA: National Association of Secondary School Principals.

Watkins, P. (1986). From managerialism to communication competence: Control and consensus in educational administration. *Journal of Educational Administration,* 24 (1), 86–106.

White, P. A. (1989). An overview of school-based management: What does the research say? *NASSP Bulletin,* 73 (518), 1–8.

White, P. A. (1992). Teacher empowerment under "ideal" school-site automony. *Educational Evaluation and Policy Analysis,* 14 (1), 69–82.

Wilson, R. B. and Schmoker, M. (1992). Quest for quality. *Executive Educator,* 14 (1), 19–22.

Wood, F. H. and Caldwell. S. D. (1991). Planning and training to implement site-based management. *Journal of Staff Development,* 12 (3), 25–29.

Zeichner, K. M. (1991). Contradictions and tensions in the professionalization of teaching and the democratization of schools. *Teachers College Record*, 92 (3), 363–379.

MICHAEL D. RICHARDSON
Georgia Southern University
KENNETH E. LANE
California State University-San Bernardino
JACKSON L. FLANIGAN
Clemson University

What Is Empowerment?

CHAPTER 1

The Transitional Role of the Principal in School Empowerment

JACKSON L. FLANIGAN[1]
GORDON W. GRAY[1]

INTRODUCTION

The current wave of education reform is producing several basic changes in school policies as related to the management process. The movement toward the accepted theory that schools work best when principals and teachers are more involved in problem solving at the building level, known as shared governance, is one of the results of this restructuring. Today, we find many of the reform proposals calling for increased teacher participation in decision making erroneously referred to as "teacher empowerment."

It may be necessary, however, to begin to delineate several of the often referred to generic terms of restructured schools. Until we begin to separate and unravel the elements of teacher empowerment and shared decision making, as well as those of school empowerment, these school management and policy concepts need to stand separately for better understanding. If schools are truly to restructure, a broad range of instructional, organizational, and curricular alternatives to the traditional operational procedures of the schools must be applied. If the two most prevalent alternatives were selected, teacher involvement in the policy development process and reevaluation of the decision-making process used in school management could be increased.

[1]Clemson University.

An unending stream of material about teacher empowerment within school empowerment has been written and expounded upon, but trying to find the significant literature necessary to define changes in the principal's role in the process of school empowerment is challenging. The principal can bring about management procedures that allow for limited decision making within the school, but only the district may develop policies that allow true school empowerment. Clearly delineated leadership roles at the school building level are necessary for effective staff participation in decision making, but one of the unchanged tasks of the principal's authority and perspective is to keep reform focused in the direction of instruction and student learning.

DECISION MAKING

Decision making at its best is a complex structure with many complicated tasks involved. If the organization is to be efficient where a myriad of decisions are made; people and programs are coordinated, communicated, and channelled; positions allocated; staff recruited; schedules developed; and resources obtained and utilized, decision making must be shared (Garcia, 1986).

According to one publication, one of the most frequently recurring issues in the theory of democracy is "determining the appropriate size of political units or the appropriate balance between centralized and decentralized decision making" (Amundson, 1988, pp. 16, 17). On one hand, centralization regulates the aspects of the environment that citizens want regulated, but on the other hand, by virtue of the size of the centralized unit of governance, centralization decreases the opportunity for citizens to participate in government decision making. Proponents of school empowerment (or site-based management) choose to give up some of the regulation offered by centralization in exchange for the opportunity implicit in decentralization to implement education programs by means of increased participation and involvement of principals and staff at the level of the school (Amundson, 1988). When principals, teachers, staff, parents, and community members become involved in decision making, the structure might best be described as decentralized decision making that is shared.

Shared decision making gives more responsibility to principals and teachers who are more familiar with students' needs and concerns than are central office staff. It also promotes the involvement of parents in their children's education, and it increases the likelihood that decisions will be effectively implemented because school-level personnel have been involved in making them (Lindelow and Heynderickx, 1989).

POLICY DEVELOPMENT

Successfully implementing shared decision making involves a complex process. One question immediately comes to mind: should the school begin shared decision making, or do they find ways to make everyone in the process feel a part of the ownership as they attempt to solve problems at the point closest to the source? The best way to allow all partners to become truly a part of the process and to be knowledgeable about their roles is to address the issue of shared decision making at the policy table, either at the school level or at the district level. Conley and Bacharach (1990) state that "only through the participation of all professional colleagues in the school can this type of management truly be successful" (p. 542). School administrators and teachers both have legitimate roles to play in the policy process, but we must not forget that the school board is also a crucial link to the community and must balance its role to ensure that authority is appropriately shared (Phillips, 1989). According to a publication of the American Association of School Administrators, "The school board will play a pivotal role in supporting school-based management" (p. 12).

Harris Sokoloff (1990) observes that "the single greatest inhibitor to entering a shared governance system is lack of knowledge about how to structure such a process" (p. 43). At the beginning of the process of policy development, it is crucial to the central administration and the board and to the building-level management to recognize the decision-making process at both the district and the building level. Before the school board considers shared decision making at the school level, it should study extensively what the effect will be on its present policy. Prior to beginning a shared decision-making process at the building level, the board needs to develop a policy identifying participants and setting guidelines (Phillips, 1989). According to Sokoloff (1990), this policy should consider "what decision areas should be included in the process, which groups will be represented and in what ways, and how differences of opinion will be addressed" (p. 43). Establishing such a policy can eliminate many problems resulting from groups attempting to negotiate positions.

PARTICIPANT RESPONSIBILITIES

When shared decision making is being implemented, teachers and principals are not the only personnel involved. Parents and community members contribute to the process, as do the central administration and the school board. All of these participants must work together to make shared decision making successful. First, staff support must be willing to commit time and energy. Second, all staff members, as well as parents and community members, must be trained in problem-solving and decision-making skills. Third, the central administration and the board of trustees must support the process, encourage initial efforts, and provide flexibility. Fourth, good communication with the board of trustees is essential to facilitate and encourage individual school efforts (Barnes, 1990).

Harrison et al. (1989), in an account of a Colorado school's experience with school empowerment, stressed the importance of clarifying the roles of the central office staff:

> Because of the lack of training and support for the redefinition of central office roles, many central office administrators actively blocked the practice of school-based decision making. They did not trust the ability of school personnel to make decisions, and they were reluctant to give up their role as innovators and controllers. (p. 56)

As a solution to some of these problems, "district-level administrators are receiving training in participatory decision making. In addition, the superintendent and other key central office administrators are consciously modeling collaborative strategies" (pp. 56, 57).

District staff, in turn, must provide training and support for building-level personnel. They should "provide training in site-based management for school personnel" and "offer the necessary on-site support to principals" (Harrison et al., 1989, p. 57). Without this training and support, teachers and principals in the Colorado school district were unprepared for the new roles that they were suddenly asked to play.

A significant concern that will arise, once the mechanics to facilitate the change to shared decision making are put into place, is the discomfort some participants will experience with their changed roles. This phenomenon may be a result of the "disturbing the way things are" syndrome. People often become distressed when a structure is altered—even an ineffective one.

TEACHER ROLES

Many teachers will be uncomfortable in their new roles, and this discomfort will complicate the process of implementing shared decision making. The first problem teachers will encounter is determining the role expectations for their participation in this new form of school governance. If the board has established some guidelines, the process of discovery will be less uncomfortable. Teachers' own perception of their roles and the perception of others, their preparation, their experience, and their fear of the unknown account for most of the problems they will encounter during implementation of the new policy.

Lieberman (1988) describes what she refers to as the "egalitarian ethic": "that a teacher is a teacher no matter how experienced, how effective or how knowledgeable" (p. 9). She points out the fact that many teachers perceive their roles on the basis of this ethic and that "part of the norm is that teachers must spend all their time with students in classrooms" (p. 7). The conflict of values in teachers themselves leads to tension during the implementation process (Lieberman, 1988). Additional tension comes from the way we look at teachers and how we perceive their roles and functions. Too often, teachers are seen only as classroom facilitators or participants; their function and source of respect are confined to the arena of the classroom. A solution to this problem comes from working in collaborative situations where they are exposed to new ideas from the people who best understand the complexity of the situation – administrators, colleagues, district staff, and parents.

Gomez (1989) identifies two other problems encountered by teachers in a pilot program for shared decision making. First, they were "unprepared to deal with schoolwide problems. Their job experiences had given them a limited view of school operations. Consequently, they often advocated simplistic solutions to school problems" (p. 22). Second, they were unprepared to deal with administrative issues, such as budget preparation, because their education did not provide the necessary background. Both of these problems could be ameliorated by inservice training programs.

Another problem encountered by teachers that would be lessened by additional training is lack of experience with debating issues and consensus building. Working on group dynamics and the art of compromise early in the period of transition to shared decision making might be time well spent and might prove critical to group decision making and consensus (Rummler, 1989).

As they begin to take part in decision making at the school level, teachers may find themselves uncomfortable with the accountability that comes with autonomy. They will find it necessary to understand the relationship between having the power to make decisions and being responsible for the outcome. Making decisions can lead to conflict and mistakes; even when the group finds a solution to a problem, often a new set of challenges appears.

PRINCIPAL ROLES

As part of the decision-making team, the principal will find it necessary to facilitate the implementation process. Providing support for the teachers while they adjust to role changes and guiding the school through the process of implementation will be only two of the many new roles the principal will assume. Like the teachers, the principal will be uncomfortable in his or her new roles and will have to face the adjustment problems that result from these roles.

Most principals are not comfortable with change that is not clearly defined and that leaves the chance for many unknowns, and most will admit that they were not trained to work with shared decision-making procedures. Robert Holzmiller, principal of Hopi Elementary School in Scottsdale, Arizona, says that he is not ashemd to admit that his district's movement to site-based decision making has left him scared (cited in Bradley, 1990). The distinct fact that principals are scared demonstrates that they are not prepared for the task of being a principal participating with a shared decision-making team. Preparing principals to facilitate the team is no easy job; principals and educators will have to determine what roles principals will be expected to play, and educators will have to assist principals in acquiring the skills and knowledge needed to fill these roles.

One problem experienced by principals during the transition to shared decision making is the lack of clearly established goals and directions. Chopra (1989) observes that the effectiveness of shared decision making can be determined only by the impact it has on student learning (p. 46). If school empowerment is to have this impact, the principal – as facilitator of the team – must have a direction, a mission, and a set of goals to work from. Many principals now involved in shared decision making feel that they originally did not have a direction or a set of goals to work from. The anxiety that these principals feel results from the lack of a clearly delineated definition of "restructuring." What is considered school empowerment in one district is far different from the formalized process in another district in which the teachers union contract spells out who will sit on the team and how the team will make decisions (Bradley, 1990).

As teachers, parents, and, in some cases, students are assuming additional responsibilities, principals are seeking to redefine their roles and their relationships with others in their school districts. The task is complicated by a lack of consensus among educators about what constitutes school empowerment. Occasionally, the problem is exacerbated by feelings of concern; principals are being forced too quickly into roles they have not been prepared for. Dale Mann, a professor at Columbia University Teachers' College, observes that principals find that the skills needed to be effective in working with a team are quite different from those that most principals were taught or that they have acquired on the job. Mann states, "They can no longer be old-style CEO's. Is their new role clear? Not at all." (cited in Bradley, 1990, p. 22).

Not all principals find the new roles of school empowerment troubling. These principals argue that the ideas and the involvement of teachers and other staff members in decision making are just good management practice, but most people with any exposure to shared decision making require a reorientation in the way they think and the way they operate their schools (Caldwell and Wood, 1988).

PRINCIPAL SKILLS

At some times during the transition period, principals will be challenged to address the problem of uncertainty. Experienced administrators will readily admit that one of the most significant strategies in a school is to prepare the institution to cope successfully with uncertainty (Conley and Bacharach, 1990). It is necessary for them to determine to what extent their subordinates control the process. The idea of leaving staff members in control of uncertainty is directly opposed to many administrators' desires for control and cooperation.

The process of change poses another problem for principals: the different expectations for principals and the lack of a mutually acceptable decision-making process can generate underlying feelings of hostility on the part of the staff. Trust among colleagues can disintegrate. Forcing teachers to use new skills that make them uncomfortable may create a challenge to the principal's leadership ability (Meadows, 1990). In this new role, the principal is likely to be the target of anger and criticism because, by definition, he or she must challenge some group norms. In essence, principals using shared decision making may challenge some faculty traditions. Gomez (1989) observes that shared decision making can "aggravate an existing conflict between teachers and a principal" (p. 22). Staff members may see shared decision making as "a means for challenging the principal. This attitude tends to escalate the conflict" (p. 22).

Related to the problem of conflict between the staff and the principal is the problem created by teachers and staff who perceive the principal as a blocker of successful shared decision making (Mitchell, 1990). Mitchell (1990) observes that "although the district is supporting shared decision making, and though it is represented in the master agreements, there are those individuals who will see the principal in the role of manipulating the process to still get what he or she wants" (p. 24). "Blocks," says Mitchell, "impede progress" (p. 24).

In an environment of shared decision making, communication among the participants is vital. Administrators must realize that they are dealing with professionals and that the success of the organization depends on cooperation and on the exchange of information with these professionals (Conley and Bacharach, 1990). Conley and Bacharach point out that the obstacle to implementation of shared decision making created by a failure in communication is "not structural but cognitive" (p. 540). In order to minimize this problem, principals must examine how their attitudes toward teachers affect communication.

School empowerment is such a complex form of school governance and depends on such a larger number of people that it is not surprising to discover the problems created by the demands of time. Marburger (1985) points out that, especially during the first year, principals will have to cope with the problems of added demands on their time. Allotting time for teachers to meet and participate with the team is a very real concern for principals. Ann Bradley (1990) finds that "one of the greatest obstacles to participatory decision making in school is the blue collar mentality among teachers who are not willing to work beyond school hours" (p. 24). Bruce Goldberg, co-director of the American Federation of Teachers Center for Restructuring, identifies as "a major obstacle" the need for principals to change the school schedule "to create a block of time in which teachers could meet" (cited in Bradley, 1990, p. 24).

PRINCIPAL LEADERSHIP

Shared decision making intensifies the need for leadership from the principal. Ultimately, the degree to which school-level authority is shared and the way in which it is shared are in the hands of the principal. This new leadership role puts the principal under pressure because it gives him or her additional accountability and responsibility while, at the same time, it requires him or her to share decision making with teachers, parents, community members, and, in some cases, students. This position will require that he or she establish a climate of trust in the judgment of participants. The pressure of accountability can also come when principals are given authority over staff. In the Chicago school system described by Etheredge (1989), principals are designated as school community leaders and have more authority over hiring teachers and managing school affairs. Etheredge (1989) points out that "principals are the key to developing and implementing school improvements. At the same time, accountability is ensured by the renewable four-year contracts" (p. 24). This school system has done away with the practice of granting tenure to principals.

Some of the problems principals encounter during the implementation phase of shared decision making point to roles principals must assume. Other roles evolve from the implementation process itself. Of principals' roles, one principal, Douglas Gowler, observes, "It is to the point that when the district opens a new school, the principal gets a shell and must design and develop everything in it" (quoted in Lindelow and Heynderickx, 1989, p. 121). Says Gowler, "Our superintendent sees principals as curriculum directors of finance, and so on, as well as principals" (p. 121). The roles principals play in shared decision making are many, and there are probably some that have not yet been defined.

FACILITATION

Bradley (1990) gives a general description of the principal's role as that of "facilitator." A publication of Tacoma Public Schools (1990) describes the principal as a facilitator and summarizes some of the tasks involved in this role:

> School-centered decision making is not replacing the principal with a committee. The principal's role does not change—from that of a person with "all the answers" to that of the person who facilitates making good decisions. The principal assures that there is a sound information base for decision making, knows how to use appropriate decision-making strategies, effectively makes a case for his or her point of view, and keeps a common vision before the school community. (np)

The roles that follow, for the most part, can be derived from this descriptive summary.

CLIMATE

Caldwell and Wood (1988) describe one role of the principal as ensuring "the positive climate necessary for gaining commitment to school improvement decision" (p. 52). Similarly, Blanton (1991) describes as a role "developing processes which encourage teachers to fully apply all their life experience and knowledge toward the advancement of personal, school, and community educational innovations" (p. 9). These roles support the faculty in their adjustment to role changes and motivate them to become involved in the decision-making process.

COMMUNITY SUPPORT

Principals also "involve their staffs and those clientele served by the school in developing goals and programs plans for improvement" (Caldwell and Wood, 1988, p. 22). They encourage this involvement by developing "community support for school and district programs by implementing a marketing plan" (Scarp, 1988, p. 15). Shared decision making cannot serve the community unless community members provide input about their goals and needs. Involving staff members in this goal-setting process helps them communicate their needs and exposes them to the ideas of others, giving them a perspective from outside of the classroom.

STAFF DEVELOPMENT

The role of ensuring "that staff development programs designed for their staffs are related to their school improvement goals" (Caldwell and Wood, 1988, p. 52) helps the staff to obtain the new skills and knowledge necessary for their involvement in school improvement. The principal's role also involves him or her in the staff development programs for faculty, enabling him or her to gain new skills and knowledge also. The principal's participation in these programs with the faculty can provide a common basis for communicating with them and can help in resolving some of the conflicts that implementing shared decision making can produce between the faculty and the principal.

SCHOOL IMPROVEMENT

Principals also might play the role of director of the school improvement team (Harrison et al., 1989). In this role they will "ensure that the design of the school improvement plan addresses the major educational problems in their schools" (Caldwell and Wood, 1988, p. 52). In a broader sense, the principal's role might be described as that of "instructional leader" (Amundson, p. 10). These roles are necessary to keep the decision-making team focused and to provide support for inexperienced participants.

Another role of principals listed by Caldwell and Wood (1988) is to "implement and evaluate school instructional improvement with their planning teams" (p. 52). In some cases, the principal's involvement in these processes can help the other participants to clarify the expectations of their roles.

TEACHER EVALUATION

As instructional leader, the principal may be responsible for evaluating teachers (Scarr, 1988) if the master plan designates this role. He or she may also be responsible for "establishing staffing patterns and developing educational programs to meet district-wide objectives" (Amundson, p. 11). In some districts these roles may be shared with the school improvement team.

Mitchell (cited in Bradley, 1990) sees the principal playing the role of "a coordinator and a source of information about where to find the proper resources, research, and materials to accomplish goals" (p. 24) The principal playing this role can provide support for teachers who need to obtain the skills and knowledge necessary for filling their new roles.

OTHER

In school-based management, principals may find themselves expected to fill some roles not previously alloted to principals: providing technology for teaching and classroom management (AASA, 1990, p. 12), assuming responsibility for the physical plant, and preparing the budget. In these cases, shared decision making may prove useful if the principal delegates roles to those participants closest to the areas involved.

NEW PRINCIPAL SKILLS

If shared decision making is to be successfully implemented, participating principals need proper preparation for the roles they will be asked to assume. Publications on shared decision making identify a number of skills principals will need to acquire through training.

Stimson and Appelbaum (1988) suggest that "principals need to find ways to receive and act on feedback from their teachers" because "if a principal reacts negatively to feedback from teachers, the communication flow quickly dries up." They recommend that school districts "train principals to build coalitions and to keep lines of communication open" (p. 316). If principals are to provide support for teachers during the transition to shared decision making, they need to be in touch with teachers' concerns and be open to their suggestions.

Harrison et al. (1989) describe training given to school personnel in the early stages of implementation: "The staff development department works with school staffs to define *collaboration* and determine what processes to use in making various decisions." The department also provides workshops for teachers and administrators in "facilitation, conflict resolution, communication skills, and participatory decision making." Principals and teachers may also request additional staff development "to meet their identified needs in carrying out their visions" (pp. 56, 58). In addition, the district offers a "resource guide for school improvement team facilitators that contains ideas and examples for carrying out their plans" (p. 58).

Sokoloff (1990) points out the need for schools to identify the skills that principals and teachers need in order to be more successful in implementing shared decision making. These skills include "conflict resolution, problem identification, problem solving, solution planning, data analysis, team building, and consensus building" (p. 43).

A publication of the AASA, NAESP, and NASSP (Amundson, 1988) also lists some areas in which principals should be proficient:

- instructional leadership and curriculum awareness
- business management
- personnel management
- facilities, maintenance, and property management
- security
- counseling
- communicating
- community relations (p. 11)

In order to implement shared decision making, the principal should be knowledgeable about as many areas of school empowerment as possible, so that he or she can understand concerns brought up by other participants of the decision-making team.

According to Caldwell and Wood (1988), several training programs are needed to accommodate changes in roles brought about by shared decision making. A "systematic professional growth program" should be provided to the administrative team—central office and school administrators—and to teachers in order to better prepare them to work together and to acquire "the skills and understandings needed to carry out the new roles in the decentralized management of school improvement" (p. 53). For principals, the professional growth program "should focus on school-based improvement and management, including training in one school improvement process" (p. 53).

PRINCIPALS' USE OF POWER

Professional growth for principals involves acquiring the skills they need to perform their roles effectively in the transition to shared decision making. Upon acquisition of these skills, principals, by virtue of their expertise, may change the way in which school personnel perceive their use of power to promote effective behavior. Power such as that used by the principal can fall into two broad categories: positional power and personal power. Stimson and Appelbaum (1988) define these types of power:

> *Positional power* draws on one's position in the organizational structure as its primary source; it tends to be hierarchical in nature, to be frequently combative, and to produce winners and losers. *Personal power*, by contrast, is derived from the personal characteristics of an individual. It relies largely on the relationship between superordinate and subordinate, and it tends to be horizontal in nature and cooperative and sharing in orientation. (p. 314)

One kind of personal power is that of the expert, which is based on the subordinates' perception of the special expertise or knowledge of the supervisor (Stimson and Appelbaum, 1988, p. 314). When the principal demonstrates his or her expertise as an instructional leader–or as a facilitator for shared decision making–teachers perceive him or her as using one form of personal power and tend to cooperate with him or her on the basis of their appreciation of his or her skills or knowledge rather than on the basis of his or her position in the hierarchy of power.

In a study of principals' use of power, Stimson and Appelbaum (1988) found that "teachers typically viewed their principals as relying on personal, rather than positional, power" and that "the median score for *expert* power was highest" (p. 314). They also found that "teachers were more satisfied with principals who relied on personal power than with those who relied on positional power" (p. 315). Teachers satisfied with principals using personal power

> . . . believed that their principals cared about their opinions and responded to their concerns. Principals who took the time to build coalitions–to plant ideas with key teachers and then slowly build support– were among the most effective in influencing change in their schools. (p. 315)

Principals who use personal power are basing their leadership on what Blanton (1991) refers to as "discretionary effort." According to Blanton, discretionary effort "is not coercion or bossing teachers into doing better, but a belief that people are capable of doing more than they have been asked to do and knowing they want to do it" (p. 9).

As principals acquire skills and knowledge and provide support for teachers, they increase their personal power and gain the support of the staff. Their use of personal power enables them to facilitate shared decision making more effectively than they would if they relied on positional power.

CONCLUSION

School empowerment is a new term for a very old management idea. Simply stated, it embodies the idea that the decision about a problem can best be made at the lowest level in the organization or at the position closest to the problem – preferably where the process can lead to a solution. Removing as many barriers as possible means that solutions can be initiated at the site of the problem.

The process of shared decision making involves much more than moving power around in school districts. The process means systematically creating more room at all levels for creative problem solving. The process helps to address excessive bureaucratic requirements that have hindered the creation of new ideas and approach. Shared decision making enables schools to address more effectively the teacher-student learning process.

The key to effective shared decision making is the school principal, who acts as a facilitator for the process. The principal should see that professional staff members have the widest latitude possible in determining the human material and time allocation needed for effective learning.

Before attempting to change the school environment, principals need to immerse themselves in the literature about shared decision making. They should allow adequate time to initiate dialogue about shared decision making. The principals must work out an agreement with the district administration and the board in which a framework of understanding is established. All involved must have a knowledge of this understanding to prevent veto of future decisions. Principals must also convince their staffs that they are providing larger spheres of autonomy and new approaches to effective education. Then they must provide the necessary training and find the time for the staff to function properly. They must also take advantage of training opportunities to increase their own knowledge and skills. The issue is not one of losing decision-making authority but rather offering initiative to the greatest number of people possible. In this way, principals can expand their power with diversity.

REFERENCES

American Association of School Administrators. (1990). *A New Look at Empowerment.* Arlington, VA: ASSA.

Amundson, Kristen, Jr. (1988). *School-Based Management: A Strategy for Better Learning.* Arlington, VA: American Association of School Administration, National Association of Elementary School Principals, National Association of Secondary School Principals, pp. 5–19.

Aronstein, L. W., Marlow, M., and Desilets, B. (1990). Detours on the road to site-based management. *Educational Leadership,* 7, 81–83.

Barnes, L. (1990). *School-Centered Decision Making.* Tulsa Public Schools, 6.

Blanton, C. (1991) A principal's vision of excellence: Achieving quality through empowerment. *Praxis,* 3, 1,2,9.

Bradley, A. (1990). Who's in charge here? *Teacher Magazine,* 1, 22–24.

Caldwell, S. D. and Wood, F. H. (1988). School-based improvements. . . . Are we ready? *Educational Leadership,* 42, 50–53.

Chopra, R. K. (1989). Synergistic curriculum development. *NASSP Bulletin,* 73, 44–50.

Clune, W. H. and White, P. A. (1988). *School-Based Management.* New Brunswick, NJ: Center for Policy Research in Education, pp. 19–23.

Conley, S. C. and Bacharach, S. B. (1990). From school-site management to participatory school-site management. *Phi Delta Kappan,* 71 (7), 539–543.

David, J. L. (1989). Synthesis of research on school-based management. *Educational Leadership,* 46, 45–47.

Etheredge, F. D. (1989) Reforming the public school – Chicago style! *Updating School Board Policies,* 20, 1–4.

Garcia, A. (1986). Consensus decision making promotes involvement, ownership, satisfaction. *NASSP Bulletin* (Nov):50–53.

Gomez, J. J. (1989). The path to school-based management isn't smooth, but we're scaling the obstacles one by one. *American School Board Journal,* 176, 20–22.

Harrison, C. R., Killion, J. P., and Mitchell, J. E. (1989). Site-based management: The realities of implementation. *Educational Leadership.* 48 (May).

Lieberman, A. (1988). Expanding the leadership team. *Educational Journal* (February), 4–8.

Lindelow, J. and Heynderickx, J. (1989). School-based management. In *School Leadership: Handbook for Excellence* (2nd ed.), S. C. Smith and P. K. Piele (Eds.), Eugene, OR: ERIC Clearinghouse on Educational Management, pp. 109–134.

Marburger, C. L. (1985). *One School at a Time: School-Based Management: A Process for Change.* Columbia, MD: National Committee for Citizen Education, pp. 35–37.

Meadows, B. J. (1990). The rewards and risk of shared leadership. *Phi Delta Kappan,* 71, 545–548.

Mitchell, J. E. (1990). Site-based management: Coaxing staff from cages for site-based decision to fly. *The School Administrator,* 47, 23–24, 26.

Phillips, P. R. (1989). Shared decision making in an age of reform. Update, 20, 2–3.

Pierce, L. C. (1980, June). School based management. *OSSC Bulletin,* 23, 6–21.

Pierce, Lawrence C. (1980). School based management. *Oregon School Study Council Bulletin,* 23, 10, 6–21. In *ERS Information Folio on Site-Based Management.* (1990). Arlington, VA: Educational Research Service.

Rummler, R. L. (1989). Turn to your teachers for curriculum improvement. *Executive Educator,* 11 (4), 30–31.

Scarp, L. E. (1988). Lake Washington master plan: A system for growth. *Educational Leadership,* 48 (2), 13–16.

Sokoloff, H. (1990). Ideas for making shared governance work. *The School Administrator,* 47, 43.

Stimson, T. D. and Appelbaum, R. P. (1988). Empowering teachers: Do principals have the power? *Phi Delta Kappan,* 70 (4), 313–316.

Tacoma Public Schools. (March 1990). "Schools-centered decision making." 9 pp.

CHAPTER 2

Empowerment: A Variety of Definitions

WILLIAM W. WAYSON[1]
LAWRENCE M. HOFFMAN[2]

MEANINGS OF EMPOWERMENT

The concept of empowerment has been explored in relation to numerous fields. In a literature search through ERIC and PsychLIT, we found articles dealing with empowerment in many different contexts. References in areas of formal education included outdoor education, special education, higher education, vocational education, art education, experiential education, adult/continuing education, library and media specialists, writing, literacy, supervision, and evaluation. References in other social sciences but connected to education included community, health, child care, the home, families, runaways, consumer issues, environmental action, technology, counseling, sexual orientation, feminism, the elderly, mediation, motivation, business organization, politics, developing nations, and minorities (including Native American, South African, Hispanic, Oriental). The list is not exhaustive. Having become a focus in so many fields, empowerment has been defined in many ways. It can be conceived as a process of taking or obtaining, a process of growing, a process of giving or giving up. It can be viewed as an end state or as a means of maintaining an end state. Kreisberg

---

[1]Synergetic Development Inc.
[2]The Ohio State University.

(1992), in his book on empowerment in education, says it involves mutual dialogue and shared work. The mutuality can be seen among peers or persons whose job titles connote hierarchical difference. Within the gemstone of empowerment are all of these facets.

MAJOR ARGUMENTS FOR EMPOWERING TEACHERS

Two major purposes for empowering school staff members have received too little attention: 1) if students are to become problem-solving decision makers, they must be surrounded by adults who model that behavior, and 2) school staffs, like all people, are more committed to and feel more responsibility for decisions they make.

ADULT MODELS FOR STUDENTS

The major argument for empowering teachers is seldom, if ever, discussed and is obviously not understood: *if we want children to learn to be fully functioning adults, we must surround them with fully functioning adults.* When industries wanted unthinking, obedient workers, their teachers had to be unthinking. The unthinking teacher is a perfect employee in a school designed primarily for social control. But if we want students who will learn to make decisions, to work with other adults (including authority figures), and to solve problems, their teachers must be heavily involved in making the decisions that affect their work and the life of the school [see Johnston et al. (1990)]. Such teachers, and such a curriculum, are essential for a nation dedicated to freedom with social responsibility.

The culture of empowering schools is radically different from other schools. One cannot work with their staff members, usually from the custodians to the principal, without recognizing that they think differently.

> The young vice principal from the restructured school told about spending his summer (with no pay) wiring the school in preparation for computers that he anticipated getting from the $66,000 the staff had raised.

> A principal in the audience asked, "What about the fire laws? Do they permit you to do that?" (Questions never heard as good schools plan their programs). The vice principal was not smart-aleck, merely oblivious to such questions, as he flipped his hand and answered, "We don't think about those things."

The next questioner pleaded, "Tell us how you raised $66,000. We want to get computers, too." He responded earnestly, "I can tell you that; our staff raises its own money all the time. But you need to know that, in our school, all decisions are made for the welfare of the student, and we voted last week to spend the money on day care because we felt they need that more."

These educators have learned to perceive the world differently from staffs in other schools. They are problem solvers and divergent thinkers. Probably more by example than by precept, they teach that way of thinking to their students.

My daughter went to Princeton, and you can spot a King kid anywhere. How? They are the first to see a problem. They think of more ways to solve that problem. They are the first to accept responsibility for doing something about it, and they have learned to stick to their choice until it is fairly tested. They are among the best at solving it to satisfaction (father of child who attended empowering elementary school).

Empowered individuals perceive quite differently from their traditionally focused peers. They simply don't see things the same way. Frequently, the empowered person is labeled by peers as "creative"—less complimentary than it may sound—or as a "risk taker." One can observe that most organizational or social risk takers see less risk in a situation than others do. From their perspective, little or no risk is involved in what they do. However, they seldom are rewarded; in the valley of the blind, the one-eyed person seldom is king; more often, like the central figure in H. G. Wells' *Country of the Blind* (1927), the empowered person is threatened with having his/her eyes removed. Often, they are seen as foolish and may be ostracized. Sometimes, they feel and are told that they are crazy as was the wise but ill-fated king in the parable of Gibran's *Madman* (1970).

The argument will go on forever regarding whether these individuals are born with different ways of perceiving and are attracted to certain schools or whether they become such perceivers as a result of experiences that can be provided by the school to create new ways of perceiving. Both are probably true, and transformation in perception, without doubt, is transactional. Powerful people *can* be made by powerful school cultures, or they can be disempowered in typical schools. Powerless people can be empowered in certain environments, or they can reduce a powerful organization to failure.

What is important for educators is that both educators and their students can be educated to greater efficacy, and forces for building their capacity can be designed and fostered in the schools they inhabit. These forces occur in schools that may be termed *empowering*. Such schools exist and are refreshing models of what education can mean for both staff and students.

In a district where the graded course of study listed dozens of pupil performance objectives in each subject at each grade level, Hoffman (1992) observed in an elementary classroom where two teachers, experienced at curriculum development, were permitted and encouraged by their principal "to interpret district objectives broadly, 'stretching' them somewhat" (p. 162). The teachers generally felt comfortable making interpretations they believed would not have been permitted in many other schools. Through curriculum webs in interdisciplinary units, they gave their children real curricular choices as to what tasks to do and when, where, with whom, and in what way to do them. In combination with a warm teacher-pupil relationship and other aspects of the incentive environment, the positive effects of choice on students' personal investment included persistence, intensity, high quality of work, eagerness, questioning, and continuation on their own.

The example shows that 1) when sanctioned to make important decisions about their curriculum, the teachers were willing and eager to work at it and that 2) autonomy for the teachers enabled them to provide choices for students who generally were willing and eager to carry it out. Events in which people are allowed to make choices in matters significant to them are *informational*. That is, they provide feedback about people's efficacy. This efficacy-related feedback fosters intrinsic motivation, a desire to invest oneself (Ryan et al., 1985; Maehr and Braskamp, 1986).

Wassermann (1991), based on the theories of Louis Raths, observed that freedom to choose is implicit in empowerment. People are empowered by having choices; they also better fulfill their own emotional, cognitive, and value-driven strengthening. Depending on others to make one's choices "diminishes" the individual.

While relevant to individuals, empowerment in the present context is especially relevant to groups such as school faculties who share a sense of purpose and responsibility to achieve that purpose. One result is a sense of collective efficacy. Bandura (1982) noted that "the strength of groups, organizations, and even nations lies partly in people's sense of collective efficacy that they can solve their problems and improve their lives through concerted effort." People who perceive that they can do something together to cope with external obstacles will mobilize their efforts, according to Bandura, but if they are convinced of their collective inefficacy, they will discontinue trying, even when changes are possible through concerted effort.

A second crucial argument for empowerment of teachers is that, when people make their own decisions, they are more likely to carry them out than if someone decides on their behalf. They are more likely to accept the responsibility—to act upon the responsibility—of carrying out the decisions (see Likert, 1961, 1967; Schein, 1980). Glickman (1990) wrote about empowered schools and described the value of having people close to the problem come to own the solutions:

> The theory of empowerment is that when given collective responsibility to make collective decisions in an information-rich environment, educators will work harder and smarter on behalf of their clients: students and their parents. (p. 69)

Because most organizations fear the consequences of bad decisions, they prohibit all members from making any decisions (Wayson, 1971a). As a result, vital decisions do not get made. Basic decisions should be made closer to the problem, and the *natural consequences* of the decision must be readily apparent to the person who makes it. Schools support a nonresponsible role for all personnel. At present, a teacher who wishes not to perform responsibly can get succor and solace from colleagues and superiors. Excuses are protected.

That conclusion was borne of research in twelve large cities. The solution seemed clear in view of the work published by Schein (1980), Coch and French (1948), and particularly Likert (1961, 1967) on participative management. Coch and French had shown in the pajama factory that workers who made more decisions and worked where they could see the complete job through to a finish were happier and more productive with fewer of the normal pathologies—absenteeism, rejected work, and dissatisfaction. Likert had demonstrated that people close to the problem who made decisions were more likely to see that they are carried out. Empowerment comes as much from making successful decisions as from any other source.

Blumberg and others (Blumberg et al., 1969; Blumberg and Feitler, 1972; Blumberg and Greenfield, 1980, 1986) documented the process through which a school (and others) conveyed empowerment through decision making. Most restructured schools [see, for example, Lightfoot (1981, 1983, 1990); Murphy and Hallinger (1985); Wilson and Rossman (1986)] and nearly every forecast of what schools will become in the future (The Holmes Group, 1986, 1990; Schlecty, 1991; Goodlad, 1984,

1990; Boyer, 1983; Sizer, 1984) predict that teachers will work in colle-gial teams to make decisions from which they were traditionally re-stricted.

SOURCES OF THOUGHT ABOUT POWER AND EMPOWERMENT IN EDUCATION

SOURCES IN THE MANAGEMENT FIELD

To understand forms and uses of power by school administrators, Ishida (1994) reviewed organizational and sociological literature. There, he found a number of salient perspectives. Power has been described as a basic social process (Russell, 1938; Nyberg, 1988). It is used as a framework to discuss political science (Lasswell and Kaplan, 1950) and politics and influence (Pfeffer, 1992); to clarify the phenome-non of social influence (French and Raven, 1959); to explain domination in social interaction (Abbott and Caracheo, 1988; Weber, 1947); to clas-sify organizations (Etzioni, 1961); and to discuss leadership (Burns, 1978; Gardner, 1990; Yukl, 1989). Power in business has been discussed from a female perspective (Follett, 1924; Kantor, 1977, 1989) as well. Ideas that these writers have expressed about power, its various sources, and ways of using it are summarized later in this section.

Later in the chapter, in the context of multiculturalism, we summa-rize several more conceptions of power: female perspectives in the social services area (Pinderhughes, 1989; McWhirter, 1991) and in the decision-making process (Helgesen, 1990; Shakeshaft 1989; Shake-shaft et al., 1991) and African-American views of power in managerial positions (Dickens and Dickens, 1982) and in education (Comer, 1980).

Whether for administrators or teachers or other members of the school community, these authors illuminate ways to gain and exercise power in social organizations, through either formal or informal chan-nels. Some of their categories are experienced more commonly than others in the education system, hence, are more familiar to educators. But for persons and groups to be empowered in any field, education in-cluded, it is useful to understand all varieties.

Russell

Russell (1938), writing in the context of rising Naziism in prewar Germany, discussed six routes to power. *Kingly power* is hereditary. Its possessors resolve conflict by violent confrontation and decide when to do so. It is maintained by habit and custom and can be lost when taken for granted. *Naked power* is characterized by oppression and forced compliance, often by police and the military. Its elimination requires a watchful public gathering facts at every opportunity. The Catholic church is an example of *priestly power.* This kind of power is advanced by piety, learning, and statesmanship. It commands moral respect, requires holding fast to principles, and holds impersonal aims. *Revolutionary power* occurs when a large group united by a new creed becomes strong enough to change an existing government or organization (Russell, 1938). The American Civil Rights Movement and the unionization movement for teachers are examples.

Russell's final two routes to power are quite apparent in the educational system today. Empowered school staffs will either exercise these or will contend with others who use them. The first is *economic power,* which induces action by granting or withdrawing economic reward. The second gains *power over opinion,* which utilizes what Russell called propaganda. Belief, when it does not emanate from tradition, results from three factors: desire, evidence, and iteration (Russell, 1938). To overcome these factors and maintain one's own opinions would seem to require (a) reflective understanding of one's desires, (b) access to diverse sources of evidence, and (c) consciousness of iteration.

Nyberg

Nyberg (1988) pointed out that power requires two parties or entities. One claims power and acts to exercise it; the other, to whom the power is addressed, gives consent. The actor must have (a) the intention to act and (b) a plan of action. The plan requires foresight, organization, and control of information. Consent entails acceptance of (a) organization (i.e., that there is something to be adhered to, rather than chaos), (b) hierarchy (ranked ordering of priorities), and (c) delegation (division of labor).

While a leader may delegate tasks or roles to a group, group members delegate—by their consent—power to a leader. This echoes Barnard's (1938) assertion that all authority arises from the subordinate's acceptance of an order. Withdrawal of consent is an act of power: power-over power (Nyberg, 1988; Ishida, 1994). Nyberg named five varieties of consent: 1) acquiescence under threat of sanction, 2) compliance based on partial or slanted information, 3) indifference due to habit and apathy, 4) conformity to custom, and 5) commitment based on informed judgment. Consent differs qualitatively according to (a) one's degree of willingness and (b) the quality of information one possesses.

Nyberg said that power holders obtain consent in four ways: 1) *force* demands obedience; 2) *finance* seems equivalent to Russell's *economic power;* 3) *fiction* seems equivalent to Russell's *power-over opinion,* and 4) power attained through *fealty* (comparatively stable) is based on "balanced trust, shared understanding, and a mutual plan for action" (Ishida, 1994). Nyberg held that "consent is enhanced when the plan has important meaning, and thus meaning becomes the moral basis of power" (Ishida, 1994).

Lasswell and Kaplan

Lasswell and Kaplan (1950) defined power as participation in decision making. The degree of power is determined by (a) weight, or the degree of participation in formal or informal decision-making; (b) values, which are shaped or enjoyed; and (c) the domain, over persons who support or suffer its exercise.

These authors held that power is control over one or more of eight social values: power itself, respect, rectitude, affection, well-being, wealth, skill, and enlightenment (Lasswell and Kaplan, 1950; Ishida, 1994). Control over those values in the education system determines, to a very large degree, what schools and classrooms will be like. In a school, as in larger society, persons can gain control over the forces that determine those values (Sarason, 1972). Control over rectitude, for example, influences what is considered right and appropriate as defined by the cultural norms (or Sarason's "regularities" and "constitution"). Some of the values are influenced by regulations and contractual terms. Skill and enlightenment can be controlled in a variety of ways ranging from gossip to formal staff development.

French and Raven

French and Raven (1959) described five types of power to explain why a recipient (Nyberg's consenting party) would accede to another's control or influence. Their typology invites comparison to the three social influence processes advanced by Kelman in his theory of attitude change (Insko, 1967).

Two types of influence, *reward power* and *coercive power,* are based, respectively, on a recipient's perception that an agent is able to mediate rewards and punishments to him/her (French and Raven, 1959). Kelman asserted that when one's means are controlled by another, changes in attitude are not the result of agreement with the person's or group's positions but of compliance—outward acceptance—to gain reward or avoid punishment (Insko, 1967). A third type of influence, *referent power,* is based on a recipient's identification with an agent (French and Raven, 1959). Kelman held that, when one adopts another person's or group's opinions because he/she associates them with a satisfying self-defining relationship, the attitude change process is one of *identification.* Like compliance, identification involves an external incentive (Insko, 1967).

A fourth type of influence, *expert power,* is based on the recipient's perception that the agent has special knowledge or expertise (French and Raven, 1959). In Kelman's terms, this type of influence springs from an agent's credibility, and changes in opinion or attitude are due to *internalization.* That is, one accepts a person's or group's opinion or attitude and integrates it into one's own value system. Consistency with one's own opinion is an internal incentive to accept the influence (Insko, 1967).

Finally, *legitimate power* is based on a recipient's perception of an agent's legitimate right to prescribe his/her behavior (French and Raven, 1959). Conceivably, legitimate power can influence a person in each of the three ways proposed by Kelman: 1) One might comply with a person because of the person's position in the organization, whether he/she controls reward or punishment or not. 2) One might want to be associated (i.e., identified) with a person who holds an important position in the organization. 3) One might follow that person's lead primarily because of shared beliefs. Indeed, Kelman held that none of the three types of influence are likely to occur alone (Insko, 1967).

When the persons to be influenced are teachers, power-based in internalization is usually more productive than compliance or identification. First, because teachers obtain the larger part of their gratification from successful work with their children, they internalize and tend to approve of efforts of administrators in their school, district, and state whose values and understandings seem consistent with their own. The administrators' ability to influence teacher rewards and sanctions may not result in more than token compliance by teachers whose conception of proper curriculum and instruction differs from that of the administration. The teachers' consent is far more likely to be attracted and held by shared beliefs and values. Second, referent power of administrators is strong when teachers willingly identify themselves with a school, district, program or union. But when teachers disagree with the organization on internal issues—the whats, whys, and hows of teaching—identification with leaders will fade.

Abbott and Caracheo

Abbott and Caracheo (1988) stated that the two bases of power are 1) authority and 2) prestige. *Authority* refers to power exercised by virtue of an established position within an institution. *Prestige* refers to personal attributes in the categories of 1) knowledge, 2) moral character, 3) physical attributes, and 4) human relations skills. Egon Guba made the same distinction and asserted that having one without the other renders a person "half-powerful."

The qualities that define *prestige* are similar to those that define *ethos* in rhetorical theory. Ethos is the "composite perception an audience has of a speaker" (Andrews, 1983). A constituent of the persuasive, or rhetorical, quality of an action, the ethos of the person whose text is intended to persuade includes his/her reputation and the content and manner of his/her communication.

Etzioni

Etzioni (1961) said that power is an actor's ability to induce or influence another actor to carry out his/her intentions or support any other norms he/she supports. Power entails an actor's use of any of three means to obtain compliance from another actor. *Coercive* and *remunerative* power are similar to those described by Russell and Nyberg. *Normative* means for obtaining compliance are based on manipulation of esteem, prestige, and ritualistic symbols. Coercive power elicits alienative involvement; remunerative power elicits calculative involvement, and normative power elicits moral involvement though the morality may, as in the case of a gang of thieves, be thought of as immoral by others. Etzioni classified organizations in terms of their specializing in one of the three means. The consent of teachers, students, and parents may be obtained by any of the three.

School districts hold remunerative power-over employees, but the common salary schedule eliminates most of a school district's ability to control behavior by manipulating remuneration. Merit pay may restore some of that power, though the power of calculative compliance has obvious limits. Schools operate with strong norms and traditions, which give them substantial normative power for good or ill.

Gardner; Burns

Gardner (1990) said that leadership is carried out by persuasion and/or by example. Burns (1978) distinguished between power and leadership: power is exercised when the holder's purposes are not consistent with those of respondents; leadership is exercised to carry out purposes held mutually by leaders and followers. Consequently, power holders strive to maximize leadership by exercising sources of power that are not sensed by the recipients as power, using some of the sources discussed by Russell, Nyberg, French and Raven, Gardner, and others.

Matching Incentives

Maehr (1984; Maehr and Braskamp, 1986) has said that students in classrooms and adults in employment will invest time and energy in their work when, among other factors, the incentives they perceive are consistent with their own personal motives (personal incentives), which differ with each person [see also McClelland (1985)]. Personal incentives are categorized by Maehr and Braskamp (1986) as task-related (involvement; striving for excellence), ego-related (competitive; striving to attain power), social (affiliative; concerned about the well-being of others), and extrinsic reward. Hoffman (1992) found evidence of several related types of personal incentives in children: task-related striving for adulthood, ego-related striving for exclusivity or individuality, future success, advancement to a higher level, and desire to teach others. These authors' findings about incentives are not unlike those of Herzberg's (1966) classic study of executive rewards.

Yukl

Yukl (1989) defined influence as the effect of one party (agent) on another (target). Power, then, is an agent's capacity to influence unilaterally the attitudes and behavior of target persons in a desired direction. This capacity can be 1) *position power,* 2) *personal power,* or 3) *political power.*

Position power is likely to be formal authority, with control over resources, rewards, information, physical environment, technology, and mode of organization of work. It is analogous to what Abbott and Caracheo (1988) have called *authority.* Personal power is derived from expertise, friendships, loyalty, and charisma. It is analogous to Abbott and Caracheo's (1988) concept of prestige and resembles the phenomenon of ethos in rhetoric (Andrews, 1983). Sources of political power include control over decision-making processes (such as how decisions are to be made and what items are to be considered), ability to establish and utilize coalitions to desired ends, and coaptation (i.e., undermining opposition by recruiting influential opponents into the decision-making process).

Position power is something assigned. Personal and political power, in contrast, would appear to be learned or earned. These two forms of power could, then, be developed through preservice or inservice education.

Kantor

Kantor defined power as the "ability to get things done, to mobilize resources, to obtain and use whatever a person needs for the goals he or she is attempting to meet" (Kantor, 1977; Ishida, 1994). Empowerment, according to Kantor, entails control over conditions that make it possible for one to act, which includes participation in decision-making and access to resources.

According to Kantor (1989), the power of an individual in an organization can be increased by doing things that are 1) extraordinary (such as by taking a major risk, making a successful change in the organization, or succeeding in a new position), 2) highly visible (often by straddling different parts of the organization or doing one's work with people inside and outside the organization), and 3) relevant to the solution of a pressing problem. George McKenna's power as principal of a Los Angeles high school can be attributed to his acting in these three ways. He attacked the pressing problems of achievement, self-discipline, and self-esteem of his students. Gangs and teacher grievances posed major risks to him. High visibility was a result of his working with the community, as well as with students and teachers.

SOURCES IN ORGANIZATIONAL DEVELOPMENT

The major technology for empowering school personnel is embodied in the literature of Organization Development (Huse, 1980; Schmuck and Runkel, 1972, 1985; Schmuck et al., 1977). A powerful and influential line of research and application has grown from the work of Kurt Lewin (1942, 1951; Lewin et al., 1939), who conceptualized learning as changed human behavior caused by transactions between the perceiving individual and the perceived environment, the "life space" in which the individual is an active part [see Levine (1989) for a recent study]. Research stimulated by his theory naturally led to studies of small groups as a basic context for human interactions that subtly and powerfully influence human behavior and learning (Homans, 1950; Bales, 1950, 1953); Lippett, 1949; Cartwright and Zander, 1968; Katz and Kahn, 1978).

Inasmuch as organizations create the groups in which so many modern individuals are socialized (educated), the study of groups strongly influenced social psychology and organization theory (Follett, 1924; Gulick and Urwick, 1937; Barnard, 1938; McGregor, 1960; Likert, 1961, 1967; Benne and Sheats, 1948; Schein, 1980, 1988; Leavitt, 1963; Argyris, 1957, 1960a, 1960b, 1964, 1976; Argyris and Schon, 1974, 1978; Bennis, 1966; Miles, 1959). Those studies led to organization development as a technology for involving whole systems in decision-making and change. The impact of the movement had far more influence on Japanese managers than on American during the period 1970–1985 (Ouchi, 1981; Deming, 1986), though the consequent results have transformed American management practices (Peters and Waterman, 1982; Peters, 1988; Peters and Austin, 1985; Covey, 1989).

Any attempts to develop empowered staff members will utilize knowledge and techniques rooted in the recognition that the forces of groups and organizations are powerful influences over human behavior (Bandura, 1977, 1982; Bennis et al., 1969; Guskey, 1986; Levine, 1989). All organizations, for good or ill, are "Learning Communities" (Argyris and Schon, 1978), and any attempts to have the learning be "good" will have to mobilize group and organizational forces to do it [Schmuck and Runkel, 1972, 1977; Schmuck and Schmunk, 1971, 1974; Joyce and McKibben, 1982; Levine, 1989; see also Ponticell (1994, p. 162) for a description of staff development that empowers].

CONTRASTING CONCEPTIONS OF POWER: POWER OVER AND POWER WITH

MARY PARKER FOLLETT

Prior to most of the writers already discussed, in the early decades of the 20th century, Mary Parker Follett wrote as an analyst and philosopher of American business. Although not a famous figure today, her work has not been ignored. Naisbitt (1982), for example, referred in *Megatrends* to her Law of Situation. Kreisberg (1992) cites Follett several times in his intensive probing of power in education. Sergiovanni and Starratt (1983) quote her in discussions of leadership and authority. Follett wrote, mainly in the 1920s, about the fallacies of positivism and objectivism in business. Her fields of reference included psychology, sociology, international politics, business, labor, and law. She valued conflict and diversity for the richness they can produce. She advocated judging a situation not by comparing it as a whole with another, but by comparing its parts with those of another.

Follett's contributions apply beyond business to the broader fields of organizational psychology and organizational development. While little of what she has said has been restated or updated by more recent theorists, it is worthwhile to view power and empowerment in education in light of her insight.

She drew a key distinction between two types of power—"power-over" and "power-with" (Follett, 1924). The task is not, she admonished, to "place" or "transfer" power but to "develop" it. "Genuine power," she wrote, "is not coercive control but coactive control. Coercive power is the curse of the universe; coactive power, the enrichment and advancement of every human soul" (p. xiii). This coercive power she referred to as "power-over" and characterized as "pseudo power." Follett said, "The only genuine power is over the self" (p. 186), and it is developed together with others. She called it "power-with." It involves neither granting nor grabbing power but evolving power. Kreisberg (1992) contrasted her two concepts of power this way:

> *Power-with* is not a zero-sum proposition where one person gains the capacity to achieve his or her desires at the expense of others. Rather, power-with is a developing capacity of people to act and do together. (p. 71)

Power-With: Resolving Differences in Interests

Essential to *power-with* is a conception of how differences in interests are resolved. Follett (1924) had these thoughts on the resolution of differences:

> Social process may be conceived either as the opposing and battle of desires with the victory of one over the other, or as the confronting and integrating of desires. The former means non-freedom on both sides, the defeated bound to the victor, the victor bound to the false situation thus created—both bound. The latter means a freeing for both sides and increased total power or increased capacity in the world. (p. 301)

Lightfoot (1981) shared the same values when she wrote that "empowerment of the weakest member enhances and supports (does not diminish) the authority of the strongest" (p. 19).

Integration as Opposed to Compromise

The process Follett (1924, pp. 184–186) referred to as integration is, today, the basis of a widely taught practice in mediation in which resolution is based on recognizing compatible interests rather than on relinquishing competing positions (Fisher and Ury, 1983; Fisher and Brown, 1989). When integration occurs, the parties find ways to fulfill their interests and desires without imposing on each other. The relationship between them has been characterized as co-agency (Kreisberg, 1992). It is not "coincidence of interests" but "union of interests" (Follett, 1924).

Follett viewed integration as a creative, inventive process and also referred to it as *progressive adjustment* (p. 127):

> Not all differences can be integrated. . . . But it is certain that there are fewer irreconcilable activities than we at present think, although it often takes ingenuity, a "creative intelligence," to find the integration. (Follett, 1924, p. 163)

Compromise, to Follett, was not a useful practice:

> Integration might be considered a qualitative adjustment, compromise a quantitative one. (Follett, 1924, p. 163)

> Compromise sacrifices the integrity of the individual, and balance of power merely rearranges what already exists; it produces no new values. No fairer life for men will ever be the fruit of such doctrine. By adherence to such a creed we bind ourselves to equivalents, we do not seek the plusvalents of experience. (Follett, 1924, p. ix)

Follett (1924) criticized majority control. "All pure majority control is getting power-*over*," she wrote. "Genuine control is activity between not influence over" (p. 186). In conflict she saw the possibility for enrichment:

> What people often mean by getting rid of conflict is getting rid of diversity, and it is of the utmost importance that these should not be considered the same. We may wish to abolish conflict but we cannot get rid of diversity. We must face life as it is and understand that diversity is its most essential feature. (Follett, 1924, p. 300)

In good schools, staffs do not decide by majority vote, but rather by consensus (Wayson, 1982). Consensus means that everyone agrees to do all they can to make the decided-upon action happen, not to keep others from making it happen, and to respect each other's positions (see Schmuck and Runkel, 1972, 1985; Schmuck et al., 1977). (Consensus is discussed later in this chapter.)

Power-with as a Benchmark for Other Formulations

Instances of power that have been categorized by other theorists can be associated with Follett's power-over or power-with, depending upon how the power has been developed and what relationships exist among

the parties. Regarding French and Raven's (1959) categories, for example, reward power and coercive power are clearly subsumed by power-
over. The satisfying, self-defining relationship that seems to
characterize the influence of referent power may be possible in a collaborative power-with relationship, but it may also be possible in a power-
over relationship, where one is comfortable defining oneself as a subordinate.

Follett (1924; Metcalf and Urwick, 1942) held that power is most productive when viewed not in terms of one's right to it, but rather how it
can be used to resolve problems. Thus, French and Raven's legitimate
power (involving the right of a person or group to prescribe behavior)
would seem to be excluded from power-with. In Follett's view, French
and Raven's expertise would be a more consistent basis for power-with
because it is not possessed solely by managers or administrators but is
held in a unique form by every participant.

Yukl (1989) said that attempts to influence can result in either commitment, compliance, or resistance. Educators who are empowered can
expect to elicit all three of these responses at one time or another. However, because empowerment implies power-with, its successful exercise
fosters commitment.

BLANKE'S THEORY OF POWER STRATEGIES

Blanke (1980) has synthesized and expanded the perspectives of
many of the contributors to the literature on power in his Power Strategy Style Theory. Blanke defined power as the ability to create and
maintain a dominant coalition (the one or group with the most power)
that articulates a vision, mobilizes resources, gets others to accomplish
a plan, prevents undesirable modification of the plan, and induces most
members to accept dominant coalitions' decisions as binding (Blanke,
1980; Mieres, 1990; Ishida, 1994). Ishida (1994) described the theory's
five basic power strategies, two of which have names identical to
Follett's, as well as similar conceptions.

Power-Over

Through fear of bodily harm, violence to property, and public humil-
iation, power-over forces compliance to achieve intended outcomes. The
dominant coalition is comprised of the privileged. Everyone else is
powerless. School administrators and teachers join the police and military as co-opted functionaries who keep the powerless in place. Power
over assumes—as does Theory X leadership (McGregor, 1960)—that

most people dislike work, must be coerced to do it, prefer to be directed rather than free to choose, and want security above all. To undermine this type of leadership, people may use a passive-aggressive strategy (Sergiovanni, 1987; Comer, 1980).

Power-Through

In the power-through strategy, organizations are highly structured, roles are specialized, and rules standardized. The dominant coalition is the managerial elite, bright and creative persons skilled in organization design and management. The powerless are individuals and subunits who cannot aggregate enough energy and authority to accomplish their own plan within the organization. Wealth, respect, and skill are major motivators that are dispensed unequally and competitively on the basis of productivity and efficiency. Given only partial and slanted information, the powerless are satisfied to comply with the power elite. In the name of efficiency and effectiveness, the hierarchy is maintained by (a) impersonal rules that make performance predictable, (b) record keeping that facilitates evaluation, and (c) systematic division of tasks and authority (Blanke, 1980; Mieres, 1990; Ishida, 1994). Of the five types of leadership force (human, educational, symbolic, cultural, and technical) that Sergiovanni (1987) has suggested are available to school principals, power-through is aligned with the last. Power through is less obvious in its violence and more insidious than power-over.

Power-With

The assumption behind power-with is that all people are created equal, hold inherent human rights, and have immense latent potential that can be harnessed for the good of society. Its strategy involves those affected by decisions in the decision-making process. The dominant coalition of bright, creative, skilled persons seek to utilize social relations and group dynamics within the organization to help individuals fulfill the need to grow and develop as individuals and as workers. Motivating factors include active participation in decision-making, a feeling of belongingness in groups, and valuing cooperation over competition (Blanke, 1980; Mieres, 1990; Ishida, 1994).

Ishida (1994) notes that "those who have used fear to motivate in power-over and the managerial elite in power-through will have less power." Those who expect equal power in decision-making but do not expect the extra work that their new responsibilities require also lose power. Two drawbacks of the strategy are the cost and time required for organizations to provide, and persons to partake of, professional growth opportunities. For power-with to be a successful strategy, participants must be committed to the organization and its process. Commitment results from informed judgment (Blanke, 1980; Mieres, 1990; Ishida, 1994). Consonant with Theory Y leadership, power-with holds that work can be a source of satisfaction and that commitment fosters self-direction (McGregor, 1960).

Power-Against

To disarm the dominant coalition by disconfirming their habitual uses of control and creating a change in relations with them, powerless people use the two power-against strategies: nonviolent confrontation and terrorism. Both tend to be publicized by the mass media. For groups committed to nonviolent confrontation, the prime motivator is equality and justice. As in power-through, partial information forms the basis for consent. In power-against, this information includes stereotypes of those against whom the group is committed (Blanke, 1980; Mieres, 1990; Ishida, 1994). School administrators have experienced nonviolent confrontations with parent, student, and teacher groups who have felt oppressed by such things as transportation policies, discipline practices, and duty schedules that are considered unjust. School administrators in Columbus, Ohio, engaged in a nonviolent confrontational strategy in 1990 when the superintendent voided their contracts (Ishida, 1994).

Power Created

Blanke (1980) theorized a fifth power strategy in which energy and resources are increased because people are convinced that they are more powerful than they thought they could be. This system assumes that: 1) the energy of capable people is likely to expand if their work is important, do-able, and moral and 2) people need an atmosphere that provides the opportunity to love and accept love. This second assumption is what Nyberg (1988) called fealty and is more likely to be found in informal organizations. Informal groups within the formal organization provide it with moral fiber. No class emerges powerless because members care for each other (Blanke, 1980; Ishida, 1994).

In power created, unconditional love requires that persons trust each other's competence (Blanke, 1980; Mieres, 1990; Ishida, 1994) therefore need to help each other maintain it. It requires one to act in another's best interest according to that person's values, even when the action seems contradictory to one's own values. It expects that group members will support each other in times of grieving (Blanke, 1980; Ishida, 1994).

EMPOWERMENT IN EDUCATION AS A MANIFESTATION OF POWER-WITH

Empowering teachers and students does not mean power-over. Neither does it mean taking powers away from administrators or from policymakers or hindering enforcement. It means creating synergy by creating power–recognizing teachers for the resources they are and including them in collective responsibility (Follett, 1924; Metcalf and Urwick, 1942) for education. Theorists who support the principles of power-with in-school leadership include Sergiovanni (1987) and Leithwood and Montgomery (1982). Perhaps on the way to attaining social entities in which Blanke's notion of *power created* is feasible, empowering teachers and students must embrace the values and practices of power-with (Follett, 1924; Metcalf and Urwick, 1942; Blanke, 1980; Kreisberg, 1992).

COLLECTIVE RESPONSIBILITY

Follett (Metcalf and Urwick, 1942, p. 80) wrote of the strong tendency in organizations for each person to take *individual responsibility*, which she defined as being responsible only for one's own work, for one's function *in* the whole. This tendency occurs when people do not feel, in any but the weakest sense, that the organization is their own. Persons who take individual responsibility may compete against each other, or they may help each other. But if they do a better job, it is "because of the golden rule" (p. 82) or because they share each other's interests, not the purposes of the organization.

What Follett recommended is a shift from individual responsibility to joint, "interpenetrating" responsibility: *collective responsibility*, in which every person is responsible for the functioning of the whole (Metcalf and Urwick, 1942). Follett (1924) was convinced that collective responsibility does not mean that the collective supersedes the individual:

> The first test of the productive power of the collective life is its nourishment of the individual. The second test is whether the contributions of individuals can be productively united. (p. xiii).

Glickman (1990) has written that, when teachers are empowered, thus participating in collective responsibility, their work no longer has to be "routinized, isolated, individual, and mindless" (p. 75). Thus, the most important benefits of collective responsibility for educators should be those that accrue to each participant, and the second most important benefits, which can only occur if the first do, are improvements to the quality of education for the children.

ORGANIZATIONAL DYSFUNCTIONS THAT HINDER EMPOWERMENT

Empowerment in schools is hindered by organizational dysfunctions that are natural, inevitable outgrowths but unanticipated consequences (Merton, 1957; Argyris, 1957); Jackson, 1992; Lieberman and Miller, 1984; Rosenholtz, 1989) of the normal operations of organizations. They allow the manifest purposes of schools to be overwhelmed by their latent purposes (e.g., giving custodial care, sorting potential workers, providing cheap labor). Many people do not recognize these dysfunctions because of the mythologies felt necessary for maintaining organizations. In school, the dysfunctions deplete an educator's power to achieve his or her purposes.

Pinnell and Wayson (1991) identified a number of organizational dysfunctions characteristic of failure-oriented schools. *Isolation* is one of them. Teachers can easily experience isolation from events outside their job responsibilities, from information, from pressures for change that characterize much organizational life, and from professional colleagues (Lortie, 1977; Stanford, 1994). They close their doors, take responsibility for the students only in their classrooms, use the faculty lounge just to chat, and decline to plan collaboratively with colleagues. A certain degree of isolation may be desirable to shelter them from distraction and interruption. Administrators may see it as their responsibility to buffer teachers from outside interference, and teachers may expect them to intercept parents and salespersons. However, the isolation often exceeds reasonable needs, cutting teachers off from vital information, direct access to resources, and opportunities to learn to behave powerfully.

In a power-with situation, status and power are earned through successful experience and negotiation. But when an organization is bound instead by role concepts that prescribe status, power, and what people should do, *role rigidity* occurs. Home visits, team planning, team teaching, and nonpunitive discipline are seen as someone else's obligation. Teachers who have never attended problem-solving faculty meetings not only lack problem-solving skills but feel that such meetings violate established roles. Obedience and loyalty to superior and subordinate relationships can deteriorate further into *childish dependency*, characterized by submissiveness, irresponsibility, and alienation (Argyris, 1957; Goodlad, 1984, 1990; Goodlad et al., 1990a, 1990b; Jersild, 1955; Wayson, (1966b, 1966c; see also Waller, 1965).

Credentialism is the substitution of seniority, grades, diplomas, credit hours, degrees, or certificates for observed ability and merit—the goals credentialing was originally established to assure. By granting power or authority to credentials rather than competence, schools tend to discount possible contributions of persons with multiple skills and informal, experiential knowledge in areas other than those in which they are certified. Thus, rather than feeling they can be an integral part of a collective effort to improve their school, personnel are constrained from contributing in any but their credentialed area. Closely related to credentialism is *hyperspecialization* (Wise, 1983), in which work is divided into units too small for persons to have a sense of what the whole is intended to accomplish. In schools, this aberration hinders a person's ability to attend to the whole child, with the result that many a student "falls between the cracks."

Powerlessness

Follett (1924) spoke of dysfunctional reasons for seeking power:

> People often like to keep or acquire power even when they have no immediate use for it, as . . . a reserve in the bank for emergencies. (p. 183)

She held that people who receive low pay or are looked down upon for the nature of their work seek compensation in other ways, such as withholding something desired by those more affluent or in a more respected position (Follett, 1924). Kantor noted a similar condition in which persons were accountable for their results but had no access to resources, sponsorship, or ways to demonstrate the extraordinary. She called their condition *powerlessness*. They dealt with it by being "bossy, critical, and controlling" (Ishida, 1994) with persons over whom they had a modicum of power. They also "jealously guarded their own . . . domain" and "demanded strict adherence to rules and policies." Such behavior is characteristic of some teachers and frequently of teachers' unions. These are situations that Blanke (1980) would characterize as instances of power-against, in direct reaction to power-over or power-through. All these dysfunctions occur where educators take *individual* responsibility but do not take *collective* responsibility.

MOVING FROM ISOLATION TO COLLECTIVE RESPONSIBILITY

As a step away from individual responsibility and toward collective responsibility, Follett advocated moving first to group responsibility (Metcalf and Urwick, 1942). When participants undertake responsibility for their group, the members monitor, make suggestions for, and seek to improve the work and the well-being of their group. In a school, a sense of group responsibility may be manifest among teachers at the same grade level, in an academic department, or in a multilevel or cross-departmental team. Group responsibility is one of the aims when a large school is subdivided into smaller, less impersonal, semi-autonomous "houses."

Alliances

One characteristic of group responsibility would seem to be what Kantor has called *alliances*. Kantor (1989) asserted that power can accrue to persons who nurture alliances with peers, subordinates, and sponsors. Teachers may form peer alliances, helping each other plan or carry out instruction. A teacher who wishes to approach an administrator with a request would tend to have more influence if he/she has arranged with other teachers to couch the request as that of a group. While parents and nonteaching school staff are not subordinate to a teacher, he/she may well find that to be allied with them enables things to be accomplished more effectively and efficiently.

Kantor characterized a sponsor as someone who will promote or fight for a person, help bypass the hierarchy and cut red tape, or send a signal to others that the person has the backing of someone influential. The sponsor could be a superior, a knowledgeable or respected peer (Huling-Austin, 1992; Levine, 1989; Loucks-Horsley et al., 1987; Zimpher, 1988), or someone in an auxiliary, helping role such as a secretary or custodian.

Children and youth also accrue power-through alliances (Brantlinger, 1993; Coleman, 1961; Farrell, 1990; Heath and McLaughlin, 1993; Takanishi, 1993; Waller 1965; Jackson, 1990, 1992). Antisocial peer alliances range from collaborative cheating to gangs. Perhaps schools can facilitate student alliances for prosocial purposes by having frequent meetings between students and counselor-advisors (Kammeraad-Campbell, 1987), tutoring and dispute mediation for peers and younger students, and student councils that deal with real issues.

Perceptions of favoritism toward a group can hinder the growth of power in a school. A study of innovative schools in Ohio (Wayson, 1993) reported a "We-They split" that threatened every one of the innovations. Unless a school staff has become a cohesive, problem-solving unit (a rarity in American schools), it will react to isolated teams or other innovations as siblings do in dysfunctional families. When an individual or group is seen as getting more attention or more resources, no matter how much more difficult the new work may be or how responsibly the recipients worked to get the extra resources, the "have-nots" set out to discipline both the "sibling" and the organization, which they see as giving disproportionate attention to the favored recipients.

> We have had to be real cautious about the impact upon the faculty as a whole. Not one other faculty member could be offended. The principal is careful that she doesn't build up this team as better than any other.

> Life was unpleasant with our peers. The lounge grew silent when we went in, so we stopped going. The team was isolated from the school and had no impact.

These behaviors are akin to "ratebusting." Those who feel shunned have sought to overcome their powerlessness (Kantor, 1989) by asserting power-against (Blanke, 1980). In so doing, they have destroyed many attempts to improve schools.

Of course, even as early as the proposal stage of the reform, planners can begin processes that prevent a "we-they" split. They can use nondivisive terminology before it becomes a major point of contention. They can include others in the planning and involve others in examining the problems they wish to resolve. The "we" are usually those who have information. Hence, planners should design information flows that do not rely upon formal channels that would make them susceptible to distortion or blockage by a single individual or group. Staff development experiences can be designed to prevent or reduce the division and "share the goodies." Most of all, staff development begins as problems are identified and proposals are written to help staff understand the culture of the school, the dynamics that control how people behave and think, and the value of having a shared vision and enough trust in one another to confront issues before they fester and corrupt the school.

Administrators need staff development for recognizing the causes and results of the we-they split and for dealing productively with it; union representatives need staff development to avoid being drawn into a destructive game fraught with rumors. The whole staff needs staff development to develop shared goals to discipline their own efforts and to respect others while gaining power to analyze behavior and develop more productive ways to help others responsibly in pursuit of students' welfare (Lieberman et al., 1988; Sirotnik and Clark, 1988). Administrators usually are trained to manage, not lead. Administrators need skills for fostering the teaming process, delegating authority, sharing, and becoming part of the instructional teams.

Glickman (1990) observed that educators in a district with an empowered school often criticize it. The reason is that the aggrieved staff either 1) feels jealous that their hard work is not appreciated by the public, 2) believes little change has occurred in the empowered school, or 3) feels pressure to engage in similar changes that the staff feels are not in their best interests. Wayson et al. [1982, see also Wayson (1971a)] also reported that principals in good schools are often under fire from colleagues and central administration [see also Fullan and Stiegelbauer (1991)].

DEVELOPING AND MAINTAINING EMPOWERMENT

Regarding development of power, Follett (1924) said,

> Our task is not to learn where to place power; it is how to develop power .... We shall certainly [be satisfied to transfer power] as long as we think that the transference of power is the way of progress. Genuine power can only be grown, it will slip from every arbitrary hand that grasps it; for genuine power is not coercive control but coactive control.... Coactive power [is] the enrichment and advancement of every human soul. (p. xii)

In 1925, in the age of Taylorism, Follett wrote that the jobs of workers and managers should be analyzed, the former to help workers understand what opportunities they have for managing, and the latter to determine which management functions can be done or assisted by workers: "That might have both a direct and indirect effect on production. Indirect because this might greatly increase the workman's self-respect and pride in his work, which is so necessary for the best results" (Metcalf and Urwick, 1942, p. 86).

Follett (1924; Metcalf and Urwick, 1942) said empowerment is not conferring power. She said that power is not something divided, transferred, conferred, or shared; it is generated by a method of organization. Those in authority can give others "opportunities for developing *their* power [emphasis in original]," which may well involve redistribution of functions. The activity can best be furthered not by dividing power, but by creating more of it. The aim should not be to equalize or balance power but to build up the total.

Lightfoot (1990) asserted that empowerment requires redistribution of power from the usual hierarchical organization, including participatory decision-making, trust, alliance and intimacy with those who are trusted, and understanding of the mutual shaping of person and context [see also Prawat (1991)].

An atmosphere or ethos of self-criticism, dialogue, and discomfort is necessary to lead to empowerment (Lightfoot, 1990). One source of discomfort is the tension between (a) individual will and choice and (b) requirements of community cohesion and commitment. Glickman (1990) found a number of paradoxical sources of discomfort for participants in empowered schools. The more they learn about themselves and the school, the more they feel a need to improve. Openness to each other enables conflicts to surface that would otherwise remain submerged. Pursuit of the latent purpose of showing off their success can conflict with manifest educational purposes.

RELATIONSHIP OF RESPONSIBILITY AND ACCOUNTABILITY

Having discretion is essential to empowerment. Follett said, "No amount of supervision can compensate for the absence of discretion" (Metcalf and Urwick, 1942, p. 85). [She referred to supervision in the autocratic sense of traditional scientific management, not the more modern sense of supervision as human resources development (Sergiovanni and Starratt, 1983)]. Because teachers are well-educated professionals, they should be expected to exercise a great amount of discretion, to act in the best interests of their students and the entire school community.

Follett's distinction between the effects of discretion and supervision is paralleled in Craig's (1982) discussion of the option between responsibility and accountability. The discussion is directly pertinent to teachers, who are increasingly being held accountable for their actions in their classroom. Craig said that, when one is held accountable, one is expected to act on the basis of a prespecified model. He held that the sanctions and controls implied by accountability are external. The method of accountability, as he defined it, is constant surveillance. The attitude fostered by this method of control is to do the minimum, and the work can be done mindlessly as long as the prespecifications are met. In contrast, responsibility implies deliberation, in which one assesses one's intentions and the consequences of subsequent action. The sanctions and controls implied by responsibility are internal: people are said to have a "sense of responsibility" but not a "sense of accountability" (Craig, 1982).

Popkewitz (1984) characterized accountability as a key to "management by precise standards and techniques that direct, predict, and control all the activities of the organization" (p. 171). Accountability, in this view, is a method of evaluation in support of a system that relies on measurable behavioral standards to determine the efficiency of instruction. Accountability systems in schools, developed since the late 1960s, have brought about increased specialization among school staff members (Popkewitz, 1984). This specialization has contributed to the organizational dysfunctions discussed above. Its emphasis on concrete, measurable objectives tends to reify existing practice and expert advice (Popkewitz, 1984), which, in turn, tends to stifle initiative among practitioners.

Craig (1982) wrote that accountability can interfere with responsibility:

> If individuals are left to act responsibly, some of them will act irresponsibly. But if individuals are held strictly accountable, they can act irresponsibly in order to meet the demands of accountability. In fact, accountability encourages irresponsibility, for the individual is not called upon to make choices. (p. 7)

On that basis he reasoned, "Teachers must be encouraged to exercise responsibility" (p. 7).

We would vary from Craig somewhat, holding that the sanctions for responsibility are not entirely internal. The freedom inherent in empowerment is not boundless. If educators and, in turn, students are to exercise power, they must be aware of the milieu in which they are operating. In a school, responsible action is bounded by the interests of all its stakeholders. Teachers, while acting out of their best judgment, must include in that judgment the interests not only of students, but of parents, colleagues, administrators, and community.

Teachers must sometimes decide between actions that foster the independence of individuals and those that promote the development of community (Lightfoot, 1990). Given increased latitude in curricular and instructional decisions, teachers are obliged to meet dual objectives of "equal access to knowledge for all students and accountability to the public for results" (Glickman, 1990, p. 69). Empowerment arises from meeting responsibility to others. Otherwise, educators are not taking part in collective responsibility. They are not exercising powerwith; instead, their actions resemble Blanke's (1980) strategy of powerthrough or power-over—and they risk losing public support, thereby diminishing their power.

While it can be argued that accountability may be accompanied by some internal sanctions, we would caution that accountability can indeed discourage responsible action *when enforced in certain ways*. Good schools are frequently led by principals who emphasize "accountability to students and parents above accountability to the system" (Wayson, 1971a, p. 12). An example illustrates this distinction. When the system has adopted achievement test scores as the most important means of evaluating a school's efficacy and when teachers are held accountable for raising the average score in their class, they may pay far too little attention to opportunities for their students to experience socialization and incidental learning [Craig, 1982; see also Wayson (1993)]. Parents hold teachers accountable for dealing appropriately with their children, whatever the average test scores.

Another example occurs when union contracts enforce time limits on staff meetings. Although teachers are saved (but not through their own assertiveness) from long, fruitless meetings, they can go or be forced to go home without tackling pressing problems that students and parents might have preferred they solve.

What Follett held for government and business seems equally true for schools: "To confer authority where capacity has not been developed is fatal" (Metcalf and Urwick, 1942, p. 111). Many teachers lack understanding and skills for acting responsibly beyond narrow classroom limits. When a person exercises discretion, the organization and its members benefit only insofar as the person has maturity of judgment. That maturity comes from having had opportunities to learn how to exercise discretion. Decision-making is a high-level learned ability. It seems that empowerment for decision-making derives from learning how to do it better.

WHAT KIND OF THINKING OR DISCOURSE DOES EMPOWERMENT ENTAIL?

Empowerment can involve one's ability to control or to deal effectively with nonhuman forces. A farmer gains a certain degree of power over the land and over the way natural disasters affect him/her. A teacher can gain certain power over the subject matter or the physical environment. However, in almost all current usage, empowerment involves gaining confidence and competence to deal with human beings and social institutions. All empowerment in interpersonal situations requires participation in group decision-making and relating effectively to groups. Decisions must be made with the collective in mind; consequently, group skills and "savvy" are imperative for true empowerment. The group skills include knowing that no group operates separately from the rest of the world. Follett pointed out that decisions are not made in isolation (Follett, 1924); others will react in some fashion, and others are affected. No decision-maker can afford to ignore persons in what Homans (1950) calls the "external environment," those who either supply needed resources or use or are affected by what the group does (Follett, 1924).

Locke and Schweiger (1979) present reasons people have low motivation to participate in decision-making: 1) Some don't want or expect group decision-making. They may lack independence and want to be told what to do (Berkowitz, 1953; Davis, 1963). 2) Some are not used to group decision processes and find them fearful or frustrating (Carroll and Tosi, 1973). 3) Group decision-making assumes that morale, satisfaction, and performance are enhanced by participation in decision-making; however, some people in an organization may have low need for achievement or low commitment to organizational goals; they may withdraw spontaneously from group discussion (Fein, 1976). Lock and Schweiger (1979) do not discuss another deterrent that can be observed in anarchic situations or in institutions such as universities or high schools with excessive degrees of freedom unconstrained by either purposes, authority, or empowered constituents. The people who have learned to manipulate such environments for their own purposes (hold power) will not participate or permit others to organize group decision structures over which they have no control.

Certain factors enhance motivation for involvement in group decision-making, and fostering those conditions seems important for empowering staff or students in schools. An individual's eagerness to participate in group decision-making is stronger if he/she can trust the group, feels included (belongingness), feels secure, can avoid a diffuse sense of anxiety toward the group, feels he/she knows something about the matter, and/or feels interested in or highly affected by the decision to be made (Turner, 1988).

Empowerment is enhanced through understanding group processes as more than random human activity (Homans, 1950). One becomes more empowered by knowing more about their systematic character (University Associates, 1972; Bales, 1950; Cartright and Zander, 1968). Knowing how to enhance group formation (Bales, 1950; Schutz, 1958, 1966) or to analyze their behavior contributes to empowerment. Knowing their effect upon human behavior and the way in which they effect values and attitudes (norms) is a powerful stimulant to learning; hence, it is a powerful instructional device. For example, group dynamics instructors for decades have used Stogdill's (1959) classic analysis of helpful and destructive roles in groups to help work groups and social groups analyze their corporate behavior and to improve upon their performance and satisfaction.

Maier [1963; also see Maier and Sashkin (1971)] codified several principles of effective group decision-making:

1. Success in problem-solving requires that effort be directed toward overcoming surmountable obstacles. Empowerment occurs as more and more insurmountable barriers are seen as surmountable, but that is a result of increasing group maturity.

2. Available facts should be used even when they are inadequate and incomplete. More complete data generally are associated with more effective decisions, but the decision-maker must know that the data will seldom ever be complete and must avoid paralysis by analysis.

3. The starting point of a problem is the richest place to focus solutions. Tackling generally yields greater results than tinkering with symptoms.

4. "Problem-mindedness" should be increased while "solution-mindedness" should be delayed. Rushing to solution seldom yields effective results, a common characteristic of problem-solving in school staffs, and it results in solutions looking around for problems.

5. The "idea-getting" process, which promotes greater contribution, should be separated from the "idea-evaluation" process, which inhibits members from expressing ideas. Delayed judgment enhances creative contributions.

6. Leaders should suggest few solutions, particularly early in the discussion. Doing so inhibits open communication.

Not all group activity is productive, and proponents have been warned to avoid dysfunctions such as "groupthink" [Janis, 1982; see also Asch (1946, 1948); Asch and Witkin (1948); Sherif and Sherif (1953)] or the corporate equivalent "senatorial courtesy." Nutt (1989) cites self-indulgence, self-protection, and self-deception as deterrents to effective group decision-making. High morale, once thought to equate with high productivity, has been shown to be independent of production; that is groups can have high morale that works against production, as in an inner-city school where staff may feel the children can't learn and their instructional efforts cannot be productive, but they enjoy working with the group in the school or displace academic goals with others (Wayson, 1966b, 1966c).

DISCOURSE IN EMPOWERING SCHOOLS

Empowerment requires a much different discourse from what is found in mediocre or poor schools. The discourse both contributes to and springs from wholly different perspectives upon self, school, others, and the world in general. Information that enhances mutuality and shared meanings must be as undistorted as is humanly possible and must be open to others' interpretations and perceptions. Habermas (1971) lists features of undistorted communications: 1) noncontradictory gestures, 2) public communication conforming to cultural standards, 3) actors who can distinguish between language per se and what it denotes and describes, and 4) communication that leads to shared meaning.

He also describes claims to validity that people make to strengthen their ideas and asserts that members must be in a situation in which they can accept or challenge those claims with each other in a rational discourse through which they negotiate those validity claims and arrive at some consensus about validity.

Since all effective problem-solving in groups entails conflicting ideas being freely and fully discussed, empowered individuals must learn to accept and manage conflict with their peers. These are five ways in which people approach that conflict: 1) bargaining (which Follett saw as disempowering); 2) problem-solving, 3) escalating the conflict, which reduces problem-solving; 4) withdrawal, which reduces decision quality and personal commitment; 5) triangulation, which draws outsiders into the fray and reduces the group's reputation; and 6) suppression, which denies that conflict exists.

Rubin (1984) described characteristics of discourse that promote consensual decision-making, which tends to enhance power for all members. Problems are thoroughly explored, and alternative solutions receive full hearing. Everyone participates, and no one hesitates to express true feelings. The group doesn't rush to judgment or solution, and different solutions are thoroughly explored. Participants are not afraid to criticize or to make sincere objections. Disagreements are not suppressed but are encouraged until all parties feel they have been fairly heard. No one dominates the decision or curtails opposing views. Participants care about the problem and want to be involved in its solution.

Collins and Guetzkow (1964) further describe the discourse one finds among highly empowered teachers, pointing out that consensus can be achieved in high-conflict problem-solving if members avoid forcing their selfish interests or needs on the group, if the needs that are expressed are satisfied (generally people want to be fairly heard more than they want to dictate the solution), if the atmosphere is pleasant and participants feel a need for unified action, if the groups' process for solving problems is understood and focuses on one issue at a time, if facts are available and freely used, if the chairperson (formal or informal) summarizes discussion and proposes acceptable solutions after due discussion, and if participants feel friendly to one another.

Such discourse is difficult in traditional educational settings [see, for example, Lortie (1977), Sarason (1982, 1983), Smith (1983), Wolcott (1973) and Waller (1965)] though it is common in schools that are exceptionally productive (see the "good schools" discussion below).

Reformers may be surprised to find that getting school staffs to care about or to "own" the major problems in the school and to accept personal responsibility for resolving them is one of the most difficult tasks in school improvement and in empowering the staff or other members (see the dysfunctions listed previously).

ROLE OF ADMINISTRATORS IN EMPOWERING TEACHERS AND STUDENTS

Lightfoot (1981) found that empowerment was facilitated most strongly by principals who resisted becoming stereotypical caricatures of their role. These principals were characterized by their 1) recognition of the importance of close alliance and intimacy with trusted colleagues, 2) understanding the dynamic interaction between the person and the context (history, values, culture), and 3) exceptional efforts to redistribute power. They relied not only on assertive, "masculine" qualities, but on their softer, "feminine" qualities such as listening, nurturance, and endurance. Nonconformity and idiosyncracy were valued and encouraged.

Teachers who were thus empowered could enjoy their students, appreciate the unevenness of their growth, and develop a repertoire of strategies to deal with them. The teachers fostered cohesive communities with clear, fair rules and consequences, "a strong view of human relationships and sense of collective responsibility" (p. 25). To Lightfoot (1981), an empowered school is a good school.

Administrators who have, in the past, held power-over others, must ask to what extent empowerment means that the school should become a pure democracy. Glickman (1990) points out that, since the President of the United States does not have absolute veto power-over all decisions of the federal government, it should not necessarily be appropriate for a principal to have it over all decisions in a school. Lieberman says that to have effective schools with empowered teachers, principals should be strong but not authoritarian or patriarchal [Brandt, 1989; see also Wayson (1971a, 1971b)]. Maeroff (1988a, 1988b) believes principals should have the final say. He is also wary that union agreements can constrain empowerment of teachers by constraining the teacher-principal relationship.

Principals play an important role in schools that empower teachers, as they do in schools that disempower. Until teachers are given broader preservice preparation and have greater experiences in empowering schools, the principal may well be the most important factor in school improvement, including the move to empower staffs (Frymier et al., 1984; Glasser, 1990; Sarason, 1982; Stanford, 1994; Denton, 1981; Blumberg and Greenfield, 1972, 1980; Bennis, 1976, 1989; Murphy and Louis, 1994; Bennis and Nanus, 1985; Maehr et al., 1992; Goldring and Rallis, 1993). Wayson (1971a, 1971b) principaled an exceptional school and has reported on many others (1975; Wayson et al., 1982, 1988a, 1988b; Grady et al., 1988).

> We had some workshops but they really didn't turn us on a lot. I think the one significant thing was a workshop that showed us how to take criticism from teachers. I didn't like taking criticism, wasn't even sure that a principal should permit them to criticize. But I tried it. What happened seemed to be that when I took criticism from them, they would accept it from me. (Principal quoted in Wayson et al., 1988, p. 187)

Of course, empowerment can be misunderstood and misused. Several authors have observed that many efforts to engage staffs in decision-making are not genuinely empowering (Ogawa, 1984; Grimmett et al., 1992; Smyth, 1991, 1992; Fullan and Stiegelbauer, 1991). Argyris described a "soft Theory Y" style among management that turned Mac-Gregor's Theory Y into a technique for controlling: many school administrators can feel that they hold power and must delegate it to teachers. Ball (1987) identified several styles of leadership among heads in British secondary schools and reported that all of the leaders regarded autonomy as a privilege that they controlled. If teachers did not act within the limits perceived by the administrator or if their decisions did not conform to the criteria he or she held, the privilege was withdrawn or curtailed. Rightfully so, Ball saw autonomy as "an illusion" (Ball, 1987, p. 122).

However, the illusion should not be seen solely as a result of short-sighted or manipulative administrators. Illusions, after all, are in the eye of the perceiver. Ball's observations may well have been sustained by teacher's perceptions. Any innovative administrator or teacher can describe how their attempts to develop a genuinely empowered staff are scuttled by the staff's accepting traditional role definitions or by its lack of skill for acting in empowered ways.

GOOD SCHOOLS HAVE EMPOWERED STAFFS

No one ever saw an outstanding, really good school in which teachers were not empowered. One suspects that Dewey's teachers in Judd Hall would find it ludicrous that scholars feel the idea is a new one. Empowered teachers place first priority on the welfare of their students and take personal responsibility for developing the best possible learning environment and greatest possible achievements for students. We have surveyed nearly a thousand quite good to outstanding schools (Wayson et al., 1982, 1988b; Grady et al., 1988), and teachers in those schools tended to make more decisions and interact with more adults than one finds in most schools. Teachers in good schools make decisions; they solve problems; they interact effectively with adults and their students; they are relaxed with authority figures and parents. They play hard together, and they work hard together. They are not dissuaded by bluster or unexamined folklore from pushing beyond traditional boundaries. They do not shrink from controversy and debate, and they do not engage in the childish and dependent interactions that mark life in most schools.

Most such teachers have to make their own staff development to learn the skills and attitudes that mark good schools. We have observed (Wayson et al., 1982, 1988b; Grady et al., 1988) in many good schools that teachers perform many functions that are never introduced or developed in preservice education (Wayson, 1994). These include working together with other adults to solve problems, customizing curriculum and instruction, teaching self-discipline, assuring their own professional development and the school's continuous staff development, working closely with parents and other community members, dealing with personal problems to prevent their interfering with learning, managing more of the physical and management environments of the school, and sharing authority while reducing status barriers (Wayson, 1994; Wayson and Lasley, 1984; Lasley and Wayson, 1982; Wayson et al., 1982).

Though they may exist, we read no studies dealing with the way in which colleagues infringe upon one another's empowerment; however, observations in many reforming schools clearly show that the most powerful deterrent to teachers engaged in school improvement or innovation is "the other teachers" [for example, see the "We-They" split described above (Wayson, 1993)]. Any attempt to create the empowering school must deal with that contingent, and most teachers have little skill for withstanding the pressure exerted from that group. Stanford (1994) has published a study in which twelve teachers reported the "appreciation of colleagues" as a major factor causing them to persevere in their careers; however, it sheds little light on the way in which colleagues impact upon empowerment. The matter deserves much more study if schools are to become empowering for staff and students.

IMPLICATIONS FOR PRESERVICE TRAINING

The educational system is a system; the problems are systemic both in cause and impact. Any design for improving schools must account for the ways in which subsequent layers of the system influence others (Wayson, 1972; Wayson et al., 1988b). Preservice preparation contributes much to the dysfunctional system now in place (Ford Foundation, 1972; McDiarmid and Price, 1993; Huling-Austin, 1992; Weinstein, 1988) and must itself be reformed if preparation for teachers and administrators continues to occur in universities (Clinchy, 1994, pp. 750–751).

Ultimately, all educators' power resides in their capacity to teach, to influence their students to higher levels of achievement than mere schooling has ever elicited. Heretofore, teachers have been trained one-fourth powerful for eliciting the best from their students (Wayson, 1985). For whatever reasons, teachers (and other education professionals) have been denied knowledge and skill that would have brought them greater efficacy.

Power to educate stems from a broader view of education, seeing it as the total of psychic capital a person gains from all the forces in life. The classroom is only one force in the student's education and a relatively less-effective one (Clinchy, 1994, p. 747). So, the new rhetoric of pedagogical empowerment opens the need to promote teachers' and administrators' capacities to influence whole new realms of the school and the community (Silberman, 1964, 1970; Wayson, 1971b, 1972; Comer, 1980) that have always supplemented the confined and relatively less important "instruction" that characterized life in traditional classrooms.

However, current rhetoric (The Holmes Group, 1986, 1990) is looking at teaching as far more than merely supervising students in classrooms and administering a dull and dulling curriculum and administrative structure designed to control immigrant populations and produce cheap obedient labor for factories and willing recruits for armies when they are needed. Schools and teaching patterned after the 1830 Prussian model to produce docile citizens and good soldiers does not serve an information-age nation well in the last decade of the 20th century.

The education system is seriously undermined when its major gatekeepers are chosen (or are self-selected) in ways that denigrate teaching (Goodlad et al., 1990a; Clinchy, 1994; Sirotnik, 1990, pp. 314–320; Judge, 1982). They want to leave the classroom and distance themselves from children. Whether they are administrators, counselors, state department personnel, or professors, they strove to "get away" and the system rewards their doing so. Not only professors, as reported by Judge (1982) [see also Sirotnik (1990)], but most gatekeepers – though not all, to be sure – are torn between the desire to distance themselves from a low-status profession and align themselves with higher status groups. Perhaps none are so strategically placed for systemic effect as professors.

> Teachers will always dislike us. We are the chosen, the ones who have gotten away. They dislike us because we have freedom they don't, and we hold the keys to their careers. I want the students who are too good for teaching. (Professor of supervision and curriculum)

> She is a professor with a doctorate; she is much too valuable to be working with children. (Department Head of Teacher Education about a professor in a program requiring her to teach a child each week)

Without doubt, teacher education is undergoing a revolutionary change, at least at the rhetorical level. Teacher educators have seized power in many colleges of education and are engaged in great debates over the nature of teaching, its status in the world and in the university, and the content and process for developing teachers. The rhetoric echoes somewhat hollow in a university where the status of pedagogy is at its lowest point in half a century and colleges of education are struggling to maintain a slim hold on status. While pedagogy is lauded in literature written by associate professors of education, teaching and program development are denigrated by a promotion system dominated by status-seeking professors who hold archaic notions about the university's role [Clifford and Guthrie, 1988; see also Clinchy (1995)].

Though no teacher education program has yet produced a model, new developments in teacher education hold promise for empowering teachers when they cultivate teachers' talents for utilizing all of the educative forces in a school and community to empower students in greater numbers than the nation ever before wanted.

Others have written about the revolution in broad perspective, but this discussion will be confined to developments that seem to empower teachers to take more control and responsibility for their students' learning in the fullest sense of educating, rather than schooling them.

The purpose of this discussion is not to create the new curriculum nor to design the new strategies through which more powerful educators are to be prepared for professional practice. Though most of the discussion will be on teachers, the same principles apply to preparation for all educators, especially school principals and superintendents.

Whatever the conceptualization of teaching and the design of the new school (or other educative mechanisms) of the future, some new dimensions seem absolutely essential for empowering educators for the future: 1) greater group efficacy, 2) capabilities for effective interaction with other adults, 3) advanced knowledge of the dynamics of organizations, 4) ability to accept cultural values other than one's own, 5) ability and disposition to critically analyze traditionally hallowed practices, and 6) ability to utilize educative experiences beyond the classroom.

GREATER GROUP EFFICACY

Bandura (1982) spoke to the importance of collective efficacy—a pervasive confidence among members of a group or community that they can make progress. To achieve it in schools, as in any collective, factional interests must be related to shared purposes. Unifying purposes must be explicit, and they must be attainable through concerted effort. When success is expected to take a long period of time, subgoals must show evidence of progress and provide incentives along the way. Collective efficacy requires skill for participating in groups and skill for using group forces to achieve important educational purposes.

Interestingly, one of the most thorough treatments of group process in training for educators may be found in Barr et al. (1947). The "human relations" movement gave rise to much interest in group processes but fell prey to fair-weather advocates, inadequate understanding, and short-term faddism that characterizes much adherence to potentially powerful ideas in the profession. However, groups are the most powerful medium for teaching both concepts and behavior; therefore, teachers must have group skills and knowledge (see discussion in previous text concerning discourse and group bases for empowerment).

Recently, Griffin (1994) sees value in teaching teachers *in* groups if not about groups. Though his discussion does not seem to reflect a deep understanding of the necessity to empower teachers with greater efficacy in groups and greater power to use group processes to enhance learning, he argues that

... teacher candidates would be well-served if teacher educators focused more learning opportunity toward groups than is typically the case. (p. 238)

If teacher educators were more self-conscious about instruction that fosters group learning, promotes the value of exchange and negotiation of ideas, and creates ideas for students to work together to devise responses to complex problems and dilemmas, it appears to me that their students would benefit. . . . (p. 239)

EFFECTIVELY WORKING WITH ADULTS

Empowered professional efficacy requires educators to learn how to work effectively with other adults. A great portion of those in practice fear adults. They do not visit one another in classrooms. They fear having the principal or parents in their room. They have few skills for group planning or decision-making or problem-solving—all essential for personal and professional empowerment.

Not until a school culture becomes collegial will teachers begin to build meaningful partnerships with one another and become empowered to create and sustain educational change in their classrooms. (Dana, 1994, p. 11)

The rationale for enabling future educators to work effectively with adults as an essential new dimension of preprofessional preparation is stated throughout this chapter.

UTILIZING ORGANIZATIONAL DYNAMICS

Staff members in schools seldom understand the dynamics of organizational life; hence, they have few skills for mobilizing those forces to achieve educational purposes or to correct those that inhibit education (Wayson et al., 1982; Wayson and Lasley, 1984; Lasley and Wayson, 1982; see also discussion of the learning organization in the previous text).

[Preparation programs] do not consider the complexity of schools as organizations, the authority that the organization's normative structure has on teachers, or the ways that schools do or do not change and improve. Serious students of teaching need to be helped to move beyond acceptance of the school as an intractable and simple organization to understanding of the myriad ways that the school organization has to influence what goes on within boundaries. (Griffin, 1994, p. 236)

Preparation programs for teachers and others, except possibly administrators,* ignores organization as an educational force; consequently, educators are more frequent victims or passive receptors of organizational forces than creators of more educational environments
(see previous discussion of organization dysfunctions).

Empowered educators will need much understanding of the forces
within which they work and must be able to exercise influence over
those forces as they create more powerful educational experiences for
themselves and their students.

MULTICULTURAL EFFICACY

Educators are now called upon to teach multicultural populations in
schools throughout the nation. Former havens of mono-ethnicity, even
in rural and suburban areas, now are home to many ethnic groups
(Henry and Vilz, 1990; Lewis, 1985). Empowered teachers must acquire
skills and insights that are not commonly found in the profession and
are not conveyed through conventional wisdom (see Cox-New and
Wayson, in press).

Though one may too easily exaggerate and stereotype the findings,**
research on gender and ethnic perspectives on power can inform any
discussion of empowerment. However, the research merely generates
hypotheses about individual behavior that must be viewed through an
objective lens before they are accepted.

Shakeshaft (1989) and her colleagues reported that female school administrators were more likely than male counterparts to involve their
teachers in the decision-making process, though not unanimously so.
Women's collaborative approach to decision-making described by
Shakeshaft is similar to power with as described by Follett. Helgesen
(1990) studied successful female business leaders who also used power-
with. They shared decision-making, shared information, and solicited
information. Shakeshaft also concluded that women's collaborative
style is evaluated as "weakness" in systems that stress individualism
and personal achievement, but its success leads eventually to their
gaining recognition.

---

*Several studies indicate that administrators learn little about organizations and not
  enough to use them as educational tools rather than educational containers.
**One must never forget that anything said about a group tells nothing about a particu-
  lar individual. "Scientific facts" about social class or ethnic groups tend to become
  stereotypes that do more harm than good in schools. "All Indians walk single-file, at
  least the one I saw did," is no more false an assertion than "Many African-Americans
  come from single-parent families, and this one must."

Pinderhughes (1989) and McWhirter (1991) dealt with power and empowerment in the context of cross-cultural helping relationships. Ishida (1994) summarizes their recommendation that helpers (who could be teachers) should "empower clients by using strategies that enable them to act as competent, valuable, and worthwhile, both as individuals and as members of their cultural group." McWhirter (1991) cites sources who argue cross-cultural counseling is best conceived as a process for empowering communities as individuals. McWhirter says that the process of empowering minorities in counseling includes 1) analysis of power dynamics in the life context, 2) developing skills to gain some control, 3) exercising control without harm, and 4) helping others become empowered. The last three – if not all four – qualities are similar to those Follett describes as achieving collective responsibility or power with.

Dickens and Dickens (1982) determined that black managers, in order to be promoted could use four types of power: 1) *position power,* bestowed by authority; 2) *expert power,* gained through a reputation for expertise or competence; 3) *interpersonal power,* attained by influencing people via aggressiveness, assertiveness, tenacity, and ability to reason; and 4) *charismatic power,* resulting from personality, social skills, and appearance. None of these four types of power necessarily entail power-with. The researchers report that African-American administrators and managers (teachers and principals, for example) are often challenged (resisted) by subordinates, peers, and superiors. They recommend that charismatic power is the most reliable source of influence until position power is secure.

Comer (1980) described three bases of power as he examined ways to improve urban schools: 1) economic; 2) spiritual, psychological, and social; and 3) educational. Educators can gain power to help urban populations by fulfilling spiritual, psychological, and social needs, but, failing to do so, school personnel in typical impersonal schools often concede power to gang members and drug dealers.

Much of that concession is rooted in poor preparation. A study of 700 graduating teachers at Ohio State University [Ohio State University College of Education, 1988; Wayson, 1988; Moultry, 1988; see also Contreras, (1988), report from Indiana University)] showed that graduating teachers were poorly prepared for working with multicultural students, particularly African-American students. That echoes findings reported by Baker (1973), Grant and Koskela (1986), McDiarmid and Price (1993), and Irvine (1985).

Studies of faculty in higher education give little hope of improving the situation. Few studies have been done in higher education on

faculty attitudes about multicultural populations, but studies of preparation programs show that faculties do little and often oppose efforts to
do more, to improve future teachers' capacity to work effectively with
diverse populations (McDiarmid and Price, 1993; Grant and Koskela,
1986; Davidman, 1990; and Holm and Johnson, 1994). The Ohio State
study revealed that the college, by 1987, had dropped all but one of
twenty-one activities it had reported to NCATE in 1984 as meeting the
accrediting agency's thrust toward better multicultural preparation,
and at least one other institution dismantled its multicultural center
shortly after the NCATE visit.

Small wonder that preparations programs are notoriously deficient
in helping future educators work with populations whose culture differs from their own. For example, Holm and Johnson (1994, p. 86) report
a study revealing that 1) preservice teachers had a keen desire to
become multiculturalists; 2) preservice teachers were seriously under-
prepared to shape cultural partnerships; and 3) preservice teachers
identified two kinds of experience that were critical components in
their multicultural preparation but were scarce in their program of
study: carefully guided participation with model teachers who were
skilled and insightful in their work with diverse student populations,
and multicultural courses tied closely with their field experiences.

Experience shows that educators can be empowered to teach multicultural students and serve their communities (Banks, 1988; Willie,
1982; also see volumes of work done at Johns Hopkins University).
Power in African-American or Appalachian (or Ozark) neighborhoods
often is expressed by ministers and school principals skilled at inspiring with their rhetoric, teachers who can settle disputes peacefully and
fairly, and social service workers who facilitate access to services. According to Comer [1980; see also Ishida (1994) and Silberman (1970)],
parents and teachers' power to affect children results from an emotional bond between adult and child. Empowering school personnel to
serve low-income minority communities requires that educators learn
how to fulfill spiritual, psychological, and social needs for students and
their families (Wayson, 1966b, 1966c, 1971b, 1972, 1975; Passow, 1967;
Silberman, 1964, 1970; Reitzug, 1994).

Holm and Johnson quote Nieto (1992) and support his assertion that
teachers who have the power to "thoughtfully shape" better multicultural learning must have knowledge of the diverse cultures s/he serves;
be committed to pluralism; be able to shape learning settings that
foster respect, trust, and confidence; cultivate critical thinking; affirm
diversity; encourage solidarity; and provide avenues for constructive

criticism and conflict resolution within and among different cultural groups.†

CRITICAL ANALYSIS OF EXISTING PRACTICE

Numerous articles and books have been devoted to inquiry-based practice and inquiry-based teaching and related topics such as reflective teaching—too many to review in this review. However, the concepts are implicit in teacher empowerment and should become standard fare in preparation programs.

Problem solving, organizational renewal, and improving learning would seem to be part of ordinary, daily responsibility and practice in any but the most moribund institutions. Constant improvement is considered a routine part of the work in schools seen as outstanding.

Any empowering school must redefine what education is and what educators' roles are. Educators cannot continue to define as "extra" everything except existing practices and roles that have produced failure. Effective teachers refuse to be limited to functions associated with impotent, dull, classroom-bound, teacher-directed activities that depersonalize both teachers and students.

Yet many educators are unable to *see* how common practices harm students or truncate educational results. Others who do see feel that they should not discuss the problems or that they have no responsibility for solving them or that they should not solve them.

Every school has an "organizational culture" made up of norms, traditions and habits, values, and established routines. Though each school has its unique version, much of the culture is part of the educational system, and it is reflected in all schools. Some of the culture is "good." For example, the culture presses teachers to have something for students to do when they come to school; in very good schools the press is to have something engaging and highly educational. The culture can also be harmful.

The unexamined culture gives credibility and acceptance to structures and processes that inhibit learning among students and retard productivity for teachers [see Thomas (1990); Kozol (1967, 1991); Kauffman, 1964; Hentoff, 1966; Postman, 1969; and Kohl, 1967). That is one reason why reforms are needed: to change nonproductive culture and create new habits and values. However, the culture attributes fail-

---

† We have not attempted here to fully document what is known in the area of multicultural education. The material is voluminous and can inform the serious researcher, instructor, or reformer. Discussing it here would open a whole new category for review.

ures and shortcomings to other factors—usually the student or the family or other factors outside the teachers' influence—and blinds members to any need for change. Consequently, organizational causes for poor education seldom are examined, and they are seldom seen as causes. In that way, the system's failures are rationalized, explained, excused, and buried.

For example, Hoy and Rees (1977) posited that teachers each hold an ideology about controlling pupils [see extensive work by Willower and his students (1974)]. They found that student teachers moved away from a humanistic acceptance—i.e., trust and optimism about their self-discipline and responsibility—to a custodial orientation—i.e., distrust, maintenance of order, a punitive moralism. They felt that a process of bureaucratic socialization pulls newcomers toward custodial functions. In this process, formal and informal procedures, mechanisms, and sanctions induce individuals to adjust their beliefs, values, and norms to fit the organization culture. They contend that teacher education programs are unlikely to succeed until public schools alter their bureaucratic tendency, thereby expressing a classical institutional excuse—blaming last year's teacher.

Poor practices contaminate the educational system from earliest grades through graduate school. They are inherent in

- the historical relationship between schools and the nature of community life
- the relationship between the learner's personal respect for the teacher and what the teacher can induce the learner to learn
- the commonplace depersonalization of life in most schools
- the weaknesses of educator preparation programs
- the waste of staff development resources, including graduate programs
- the pervasive destruction and loss of productive relationships between children (particularly adolescents) and adults in all phases of their lives.

Almost all forces in the system reinforce traditional practices. Lack of critical analysis restricts problem identification and solution. Educators have little training, small skill, and practically no predilection to question the credibility and viability of longstanding traditions. Forces throughout the system reinforce older forms and inhibit adoption of new ones.

A recent book on the moral dimensions of teaching (Goodlad et al. 1990a) has no listing in the index for "critique," "improvement," or "problem-solving," an omission reflecting some cultural blindness.

However, the authors point out the need for educators to ". . . identify conditions that inhibit children from developing the skills needed to become participants in a self-forming public." But moral responsibility for continually improving practice or the school's influences is all but obscured by immediate reference to "other institutions":

> . . . The quality of other institutions, such as the media, the courts, and the instruments of income distribution, have much to do with the quality of the public discussion. Thus, the responsibility of teachers must extend beyond the school to a collective critique of the institutions that contribute to the quality of the public-forming process. (Feinberg, 1990, p. 183)

The juxtaposition could justify grousing in the lounge while achievement declines or students are being unfairly suspended from school for trivial misdemeanors arising from the organizational culture.

Another author in the same volume (Strike, 1990) concludes, "A serious dealing with the ethics of teaching requires that we connect the characteristics and behavior of teachers with the moral purposes (and the overall purposes) of education" (p. 206), but he seems to confine ethics to personal rectitude while ignoring professional practice and school improvement.

Sockett (1990), writing in the same book, also seems to confine his argument to individual teacher behavior while ignoring corporate irresponsibility, but he comes closest to the issue when he says,

> Really bad teaching is "bad" in a moral sense; really good teaching is "good" in a moral sense. No amount of technical virtuosity in instruction can compensate for or excuse morally flawed, irresponsible behavior. (pp. 263–264)

"Bad teaching" reflects badly upon the whole profession and the institution of education itself; hence, it should be seen as a problem for every professional. But endemic indisposition toward critical analysis of the existing system heightens many obstacles to more effective education. One group of teachers involved in school innovation reported a number of practices that limited their trying new ideas or methods:

- testing programs
- proficiency tests
- schedules
- traditional reporting mechanisms
- administrative restrictions
- untested fears about liability and legal restrictions
- time constraints

- curriculum guides and graded courses of study
- grading systems (Wayson, 1993, pp. 80–81)

Education was as much harmed by the staffs' acceptance as by miseducational practices:

> The surprising feature of this litany is that most teams accepted them, and took no proactive steps to change them. In fact, most teachers tried to conform to them even as they complained of their negative impact. (Wayson, 1993, p. 81)

The culture that suppresses critical analysis gives poor practice inordinate control over improvement and lays groundwork for poor morale and poor public support. Imperatives in the school culture may force everyone to be on the same schedule and to do the same things. The culture may convey that participants are not "real teachers" if they do not use textbooks or give grades or teach discrete facts. When those pressures are not examined or are not recognized, even the teacher most interested in change feels constrained to continue poor practice.

Lack of critical analysis exposes reformers to attack because they cannot explain their reforms to opponents by demonstrating a need. Participants or observers who know that failures among the bottom third of the students are more attributable to common practices and values in the system than to students' shortcomings would not so easily be persuaded to withdraw support for new practices.

Blindness or inaction contrasts sharply with what one finds in highly effective schools where "creative insubordination" is an expected response to poor practice (Hentoff, 1966). Those educators affect the culture; they do not let it dictate their program. A small rural school may request waivers from restrictive policies, or a school in Manhattan reports a common practice of changing the regulations they can, ignoring others, and passively and weakly complying with those they cannot change in the huge bureaucracy of New York City. Certainly, school staffs would be more empowered if members were prepared to think and act proactively to see and to modify the school culture.

Unfortunately, many writers reaffirm what Thomas (1990) has called the "isolate loner" (p. 294, n.15) whose teaching is an individual act in a closed classroom. Teacher preparation, especially for secondary teachers, must recognize that students' education takes place in the entire school:

> The course may be about algebra or art or history or English, but in [inclusive teaching] schooling is also about collectively initiating, creating, and sustaining an inclusive learning community. In the long

run, this community-building feature of inclusive teaching may be of as much social, developmental, and educational value as are the learning and remembering of academic content (Sockett, 1990, p. 263).

Continuous improvement can become a normal part of daily practice if the *whole* school staff feels the duty and has the skills to critically analyze the existing culture and its effect upon students' achievement and staff roles. Learning to make such an analysis would help every member of the school and not just those few who have been called "trailblazers" and pioneers (Schlechty, 1991).

Of course, staff development can be directed toward developing a proactive stance toward problem-solving, but the most efficient way to make it part of professional life is to incorporate problem identification and solution into preservice preparation.

Calling for preparation programs that legitimate and empower professional critique of both corporate and individual practice seems to call for a cultural reconceptualization of what teaching is, as well as a cultural revolution to make constructive critique a fundamental moral responsibility of practitioners. Nevertheless, it seems important for true empowerment and should be included in preparation for effective professionals.

> The final prerequisite [for teacher growth during the Eight-Year Study] was a habit—that of analysis and synthesis: the "co-ordination of study and doing . . . or . . . a working combination of the habit of thought and action—which we call scientific—and another combination which we call art." (Thomas, 1990, p. 285, citing Giles et al., p. 218)

Developing a propensity toward continuous analysis and improvement is directly related to empowerment. The suppression of creative problem-solving among professionals

> . . . underscores the moral bankruptcy latent in systems whose neatly scaled hierarchies . . . advance in place and gain in power . . . commensurate with distance from the classroom. . . . The sordid history of such systemic incoherence begins with the disempowerment of the teacher. Disempowered teachers cannot revise school practice to meet either new social or student needs. (Thomas, 1990, p. 281)

The corollary is also true: teachers who will not take action or who cannot see the need to revise school practices to meet either new social or student needs are disempowered.

> The teacher was understood to be central [in the schools that participated in the Eight-Year Study]; the purpose of the schools was as much to nur-

ture the development of teachers as it was to nurture students, for
without the one there could not be the other. (Thomas, 1990, p. 281)

The inquiry-mindedness that empowers teachers admits to introspec-
tion (Nash, 1973; Jerslid, 1955) but also recognizes that the real instruction in schools is conveyed through the entire school culture and
even the community the school serves (Rutter et al., 1979; Rutter,
1980). Consequently, legitimate critical practice must encompass the
ability to analyze *all* of the forces bearing upon the child's education
and a commitment to improve upon as many of them as the educator
can influence—school organization and process, district policies and
practices, union contracts and interpretations, community relations (or
their lack), and even community services and practices affecting students' welfare and learning. The preservice teacher could be socialized
toward inquiry by requiring him or her to analyze and improve the
preparation program itself.

Most teacher education programs profess to be value neutral, ignoring that neutrality itself is a powerful, and potentially destructive,
value. But most observers agree that they disproportionately serve
powerful interest groups (Anyon, 1980; Reich, 1988) and teach values
that serve those interests (Neff, 1985). Program norms reflect the
norms of society.

Preservice teachers tend to perceive what they learn as universal.
For example, they feel that approaches that work in suburban schools
are appropriate in most schools. They are not sufficiently discouraged
from doing so. Within the technocratic rationality, the socialization of
prospective teachers is seen as a problem of transforming raw material
into good workers (Raebeck, 1994; Funk and Brown, 1994). Few professors or students significantly question the quality of the society that
the schools support (Giroux, 1980, 1981).

Few future educators discuss how ideological and social conditions
shape and constrain pedagogy (Giroux, 1980). Students are not given
the "conceptual tools" to help them see that knowledge is socially constructed, based in history, and problematic. Those tools include concepts such as 1) culture as a structure that perpetuates the existing
economic and political system and 2) hegemony, which limits discourse
because certain ideas come to be seen as natural and universal—hence,
are beyond questioning. Giroux lauds teacher education faculties with
enough autonomy to "find the political space" to develop innovative approaches (p. 20).

Beyer (1984) described a teacher education program with four main
objectives. The first was to help students recognize that knowledge is

socially constructed. A second was to have students analyze and debate practices and attitudes normally considered matters of "common sense." For example, students analyzed curriculum materials for hidden values and bias. A third objective was to have students understand how school, social, and economic practices mutually influence each other. Students did an abbreviated ethnographic study of a classroom (but not their college classroom) from a critical socioeconomic perspective, a step essential to seeing beyond one's own perspective (May and Zimpher, 1986; Combs, 1962, Chap. 6; Rosenthal and Jacobson, 1968). Students chose from among viewpoints of groups considered "different," such as that of a female, a member of a minority group, or of the working class.

The fourth objective Beyer (1984) described was to have participants develop "alternative principles and approaches" (p. 38) to guide their practice. Students constructed their own approaches to curriculum, pedagogy, and evaluation. They built a curriculum project on a topic such as the history of science, local history, global wealth and poverty, or mass communications. In addition to the sociopolitical critique, the program featured close contact between university and schools, forming a network with socially critical cooperating teachers and principals.

UTILIZING BROADER EDUCATIONAL CONTEXTS‡

Education is more than what schools used to do. Education is the full supply of psychic capital that persons carry between their ears to enable them to live successfully and to participate fully in the world they inhabit. It is empowerment itself.

When American schools were created, families and communities provided the bulk of education while schools provided social control and academic skills for a few students selected to fill professional and administrative roles (Cremin, 1961). Children engaged in or observed the work-world firsthand. Extended families gave children all manner of tutoring for successful living, and close-knit communities implanted thousands of out-of-school lessons that completed their education (Good and Brophy, 1973, 1978; Cremin, 1979).

Those informal educational conditions changed markedly after World War II as families were reduced to the nuclear family and then to present-day status. Only 7 percent of American homes now fit the

‡Much in this section borrows from more comprehensive discussions in *Up from Excellence* (Wayson et al., 1988b). We are grateful to the authors and to *Phi Delta Kappan* for the original work.

school's image of a "good" home. Four-fifths of the population now live in cities or relatively impersonal suburbs, and only 3 percent are farming. Work is now far removed from homes and bedroom communities (Anyon, 1980; Neff, 1985).

The education formerly provided through enormous expenditures of human capital has gone; the average American teen has no significant contact with an effective adult (Glenn, 1977; Wayson et al., 1988b, Chap. 6). Out-of-school education for many is provided by MTV and the peer group; its effects confound the educational process, frustrate educational personnel, and impede educational improvement.

Pressures are mounting for greater professional skill among educators (Lewis, 1985). Schools are now challenged to provide much of the education formerly provided by family and community (Coleman, 1990). Schools seem the best social agency to find ways to do what formerly was done through long and continuous contact with adults in families and in the community. But they can't do that if they continue doing what they did when they provided schooling and left educating to others.

However, since 1957 American teachers have been trained for exceptionally narrow roles, primarily to be "walking textbooks." As Sputnick opened space, it narrowed the American educational agenda to what have been perceived as the basics of schooling. So teachers (and other educators) suffer "trained incapacity" for truly educating students for the next century.

Educating students for successful living in the future requires more than mere schooling. Present conceptualizations of the curriculum are too narrow to educate students. They constrain improvement, both by dictating too narrow a role for teachers and by blinding most participants to new and creative potentials. Of course, teachers can gain power-through mastery and love for their subject matter (Maeroff, 1988a, 1988b; French and Raven's concept of expertise, 1959). However, teaching conveys more than subject matter.

Empowering more citizens requires expanding the concept of what education is and how it is best brought to learners. The attitudes, values, and skills of fully functioning citizens often are learned best from informal contacts with mature tutors in hallways, playgrounds, gymnasia, and other places less structured than classrooms. Educators cannot assume that all education occurs in courses taught in classrooms by adults who pretend to special competence in the subject or skill (Sarason, 1983).

The focus is on topics rather than concepts. Subjects are covered; little is uncovered or mastered. Moreover, schools do not design learning activities to connect students with the structure and ways of thinking that characterize a field of inquiry. Students, in other words, are not learning how to learn. . . . [They] have not learned to think no matter how many years of subject matter they have taken, how many credits they have, or how high they score on standardized tests. (NCAS, 1985, pp. 50–51)

Any description of what occurs in good schools shows that teachers engage in many activities beyond direct instruction (Frymier et al., 1984; Rutter, 1979, 1980; Wilson and Rossman, 1986; Wayson et al., 1982, 1988a, 1988b; Lightfoot, 1981). Many things are learned easiest through "coaching" when a knowledgeable adult (or other student) seizes the teachable moment to improve the student's ability to make effective decisions, shoot baskets, read, converse, or develop strong moral character. Instruction in good schools emulates the powerful learning that occurs during dinner table conversation, drives through the countryside, fishing expeditions, breaking in "greenhorn" workers, mother and daughter conversations, shopping expeditions, or discussions before the prom.

These models are more effective ways to influence children's lives than most methods employed in schools. They are difficult, but not impossible, to emulate in modern schools but they depend upon changing the role adults are prepared to play.

For example, relieving teachers of routine duties in halls, lunchrooms, and playgrounds seems a logical way to free teachers. Yet, in good schools, informal contacts during those "routine" functions are valued as opportunities to reach children who cannot be reached in formal settings. During those contacts, teachers and students develop mutual trust that enhances formal instruction. Sharp reductions in achievement probably are an unanticipated (and unstudied) consequence of relieving teachers of extra classroom tasks (Powell et al., 1985).

Too often, students interact with adults only through impersonal, subject-centered, walking-through-the-paces instruction that they and their tutors mistake for education. Such instruction does not prepare them for the higher level participation necessary for maximum success and personal power after graduation.

REFERENCES

Abbott, M. G. and Caracheo, F. (1988). Power, authority, and bureaucracy. In *Handbook of Research on Educational Administration*, J. J. Boyan (Ed.), New York: Longman.

Andrews, J. R. (1983). *The Practice of Rhetorical Criticism.* New York: Macmillan.

Anyon, J. (1980). Social class and the hidden curriculum of work. *Journal of Education,* 162 (1), 67–92.

Argyris, C. (1976). *Increasing Leadership Effectiveness.* New York: Wiley.

Argyris, C. (1964). *Integrating the Individual and the Organization.* New York: Wiley.

Argyris, C. (1960a). *Understanding Organizational Behavior.* Homewood, IL: Dorsey.

Argyris, C. (1960b). Individual actualization in complex organizations. *Mental Health,* 44, 226–237.

Argyris, C. (1957). *Personality and Organization.* New York: Harper and Row.

Argyris, C. and Schon, D. A. (1978). *Organizational Learning: A Theory of Action Perspective.* Reading, MA: Addison-Wesley.

Argyris, C. and Schon, D. A. (1974). *Theory in Practice: Increasing Professional Effectiveness.* San Francisco: Jossey-Bass.

Asch, S. E. (1948). The doctrine of suggestion, prestige, and imitation in social psychology. *Psychology Review,* 55, 250–276.

Asch, S. E. (1946). Forming impressions of personality. *Journal of Abnormal Social Psychology,* 41, 258–290.

Asch, S. E. and Witkin, H. A. (1948). Studies in space orientation. *Journal of Experimental Psychology,* 38, 455–477.

Baker, G. (1973). Multicultural training for student teachers. *Journal of Teacher Education,* 24, 306–307.

Bales, R. F. (1953). *Small Group Theory and Research.* New York: Basic Books.

Bales, R. F. (1950). *Interaction Process Analysis: A Method for the Study of Small Groups.* Reading, MA: Addison-Wesley.

Ball, S. J. (1987). *The Micro-Politics of the School.* New York: Methuen.

Bandura, A. J. (1982). Self-efficacy mechanism in human agency. *American Psychologist,* 37, 122–147.

Bandura, A. J. (1977). *Social Learning Theory.* Englewood Cliffs, NJ: Prentice-Hall.

Banks, J. (1988). *Multiethnic Education: Theory and Practice* (2nd ed.). Boston: Allyn & Bacon.

Barnard, C. (1938). *The Function of the Executive.* Cambridge, MA: Harvard University Press.

Barr, A. S., Burton, W. H., and Brueckner, L. J. (1947). *Supervision; Democratic Leadership in the Improvement of Learning* (2nd ed.). New York: Appleton-Century-Crofts.

Bendix, R. (1960). *Max Weber: An Intellectual Portrait.* Garden City, NY: Doubleday.

Benne, K. D. and Sheats, P. (1948). Functional roles of group members. *Journal of Social Issues,* 4, 41–49.

Bennis, W. G. (1989). *On Becoming a Leader.* Reading, MA: Addison-Wesley.

Bennis, W. G. (1976). *The Unconscious Conspiracy: Why Leaders Can't Lead.* New York: AMACOM.

Bennis, W. G. (1966). *Changing Organizations.* New York: McGraw-Hill.

Bennis, W. G., Benne, K. D. and Chin, R. (1969). *The Planning of Change* (2nd ed.). New York: Holt, Rinehart, and Winston.

Bennis, W. G. and Nanus, B. (1985). *Leaders: The Strategies for Taking Charge.* New York: Harper and Row.

Berkowitz, D. (1953). Sharing leadership in small, decision-making groups. *Journal of Social and Abnormal Psychology,* 48, 231–238.

Beyer, L. (1984). Field experience, ideology, and the development of critical reflectivity. *Journal of Teacher Education,* 35 (3), 36–41.

Biklen, S. K. and Pollard, D. (Eds.). (1993). *Gender and Education: The Ninety-Second Yearbook of the National Society for the Study of Education. Part I.* Chicago: National Society for the Study of Education.

Bissex, G. (1986). On becoming teacher experts: What's a teacher-researcher? *Language Arts,* 63, 482–484.

Blanke, V. E. (1980). *Power.* Unpublished manuscript, The Ohio State University, Columbus, Ohio.

Blumberg, A. (1980). *Supervisors and Teachers: A Private Cold War,* Berkeley, CA: McCutchan.

Blumberg, A. and Feitler, F. (1972). Participative decision making in the schools. *College Student Journal,* 6 (1), 61–66.

Blumberg, A. and Greenfield, W. (1986). *The Effective Principal: Perspectives on School Leadership* (2nd ed.). Boston: Allyn & Bacon.

Blumberg, A. and Greenfield, W. (1980). *The Effective Principal: Perspectives on School Leadership.* Boston: Allyn & Bacon.

Blumberg, A., Wayson, W. W., and Weber, W. (1969). The elementary school cabinet: Report of an experience in participative decision making. *Educational Administration Quarterly,* 4 (3), 39–52.

Boyer, E. (1983). *High School: A Report on Secondary Education in America.* New York: Harper and Row.

Brandt, R. (1989). On teacher empowerment: A conversation with Ann Lieberman. *Educational Leadership,* 46 (8), 23–26.

Brantlinger, E. A. (1993). *The Politics of Social Class in Secondary School: Views of Affluent and Impoverished Youth.* New York: Teachers College Press.

Brown, L. D. (1983). Managing conflict among groups. In *Organizational Psychology,* D. A. Kolb, ed., Inglewood Cliffs, NJ: Prentice Hall, pp. 225–237.

Burns, J. M. (1978). *Leadership.* New York: Harper and Row.

Carroll, S. and Tosi, W. (1973). *Management by Objectives.* New York: Macmillan.

Cartwright, D. and Zander, A. (1968). *Group Dynamics: Research and Theory.* New York: Harper and Row.

Clifford, G. J. and Guthrie, J. W. (1988). *Ed School: A Brief for Professional Education.* Chicago: University of Chicago Press.

Clinchy, E. (1994). Higher education: The albatross around the neck of our public schools. *Phi Delta Kappan,* 75, 744–751.

Coch, L. and French, J. R. (1948). Overcoming resistance to change. *Human Relations,* 1, 512–532.

Coleman, J. S. (1990). *Equality and Achievement in Education.* Boulder, CO: Westview Press.

Coleman, J. S. (1961). *The Adolescent Society.* New York: Free Press.

Collins, B. and Guetzkow, H. A. (1964). *A Social Psychology of Group Process for Decision Making.* New York: Wiley.

Combs, A. W. (1962). A perceptual view of the adequate personality. In *Perceiving Behaving Becoming: A New Focus for Education. Yearbook 1962.* Washington, DC: Association for Supervision and Curriculum Development.

Comer, J. P. (1980). *School Power: Implications of an Intervention Project.* New York: Free Press.

Contreras, A. R. (1988). Multicultural attitudes and knowledge of education students at a midwestern university 1987. In *Multicultural Education: Knowledge and Perceptions,* C. A. Heid (Ed.), Bloomington, IN: Center for Urban and Multicultural Education, pp. 65–78.

Covey, S. R. (1989). *The Seven Habits of Highly Effective People.* New York: Simon and Schuster, Inc.

Cox-New, J. and Wayson, W. W. (in press). *Walking Fine Lines.* Little Rock, AK: Winthrop Rockefeller Foundation.

Craig, R. P. (1982). Accountability and responsibility: Some fundamental differences. Paper presented at the *Meeting of the Midwest Philosophy of Education Society,* Detroit, MI.

Cremin, L. A. (1979). Family-community linkages in American education: Some comments on the recent historiography. In *Families and Communities as Education,* H. J. Leichter (Ed.), New York: Teachers College Press.

Cremin, L. A. (1961). *The Transformation of the School.* New York: Alfred A. Knopf.

Dana, N. F. (1994). Building partnerships to effect educational change: School culture and the finding of teacher voice. In *Partnerships in Education: Teacher Education Yearbook II,* M. J. O'Hair and S. J. Odell (Eds.), Fort Worth, TX: Harcourt Brace, pp. 11–26.

Davidman, P. T. (1990). Multicultural teacher education and supervision: A new approach to professional development. *Teacher Education Quarterly,* 17 (3), 37–52.

Davis, K. (1963). The case for participative management. *Business Horizons,* 6, 55–60.

Deal, T. E. and Peterson, K. D. (1993). Strategies for building school cultures: Principals as symbolic leaders. In *Educational Leadership and School Culture,* M. Sashkin and H. J. Sashkin (Eds.), Berkeley, CA: McCutchan Publishing Co.

Deci, E. and Ryan, R. (1985). *Intrinsic Motivation and Self-Determination in Human Behavior.* New York: Plenum.

Deming, W. E. (1986). *Out of the Crisis.* Cambridge, MA: Massachusetts Institute of Technology Center for Advanced Engineering Study.

Denton, N. P. (1981). The "principal" effect: The dialectic between macro and micro ethnography in school. Paper presented at the *Annual Meeting of the American Anthropological Association,* Los Angeles.

Dickens, F. and Dickens, J. B. (1982). *The Black Manager.* New York: AMACOM.

Etzioni, A. (1961). *A Comparative Analysis of Complex Organizations.* New York: Free Press.

Farrell, E. (1990). *Hanging in and Dropping out: Voices of At-Risk High School Students.* New York: Teachers College Press.

Fein, M. (1976). Improving productivity by improved productivity sharing. *Conference Board Record,* 13, 44–49.

Feinberg, W. (1990). The moral responsibility of public schools. In *The Moral Dimensions of Teaching,* J. I. Goodlad, R. Soder, and K. A. Sirotnik (Eds.), San Francisco: Jossey-Bass, pp. 155–187.

Firestone, W. A. and Wilson, B. L. (1993). Bureaucratic and cultural linkage: Implications for the principal. In *Educational Leadership and School Culture,* M. Sashkin and H. J. Sashkin (Eds.), Berkeley, CA: McCutchan Publishing Co.

Fisher, R. and Brown, S. (1989). *Getting Together.* New York: Penguin.

Fisher, R. and Ury, W. (1983). *Getting to Yes.* Harmondsworth, Middlesex, England: Penguin.

Follett, M. P. (1924). *Creative Experience.* New York: Longmans, Green.

Ford Foundation. (1972). *A Foundation Goes to School: The Ford Foundation Comprehensive School Improvement Program 1960–1970.* New York: Ford Foundation.

French, J. R. and Raven, B. (1959). The bases of social power. In *Studies in Social Power,* D. Cartwright (Ed.), Ann Arbor, MI: University of Michigan Institute for Social Research, pp. 150–167.

Frymier, J., Cornbleth, C., Donmoyer, R., Gansneder, B., Jeter, J., Klein, F., Schwab, M., and Alexander, W. (1984). *One Hundred Good Schools.* West Lafayette, IN: Kappa Delta Pi.

Fullan, M. G. and Stiegelbauer, S. (1991). *The New Meaning of Educational Change* (2nd ed.). Toronto: The Ontario Institute for Studies in Education.

Funk, G. and D. Brown. (1994). From dissonance to harmony: Reaching a business/education equilibrium. *Phi Delta Kappan,* 75, 766–769.

Gardner, J. (1965). The anti-leadership vaccine. *Annual Report to the Carnegie Corporation.* New York: The Carnegie Corporation of New York.

Gardner, J. W. (1990). *On Leadership.* New York: Free Press.

Gibran, K. (1970). The wise king. In *The Madman: His Parables and Poems.* New York: Alfred A. Knopf (Original work published 1918).

Giles, H. H., McCutchen, S. P., and Zechiel, A. N. (1942). *Exploring the Curriculum: The Work of the Thirty Schools from the Viewpoint of Curriculum Consultants.* New York: Harper and Row.

Giroux, H. (1980). Teacher education and the ideology of social control. *Journal of Education,* 162, 5–27.

Giroux, H. (1981). *Ideology, Culture, and the Process of Schooling*. Philadelphia: Temple University Press.

Glasser, W. (1990). *The Quality School*. San Francisco: Harper and Row.

Glenn, H. S. and Warner, J. W. (1977). *The Development Approach to Preventing Problem Dependencies*. Bloomington, IN: Social Systems Inc.

Glesne, C. E. (1991). Yet another role? The teacher as researcher. *Action in Teacher Education*, 13 (1), 7–13.

Glickman, C. D. (1990). Pushing school reform to a new edge: The seven ironies of school empowerment. *Phi Delta Kappan*, 72, 68–75.

Goldring, E. B. and Rallis, S. F. (1993). *Principals of Dynamic Schools: Taking Charge of Change*. Thousand Oaks, CA: Corwin Press.

Good, T. L. and Brophy, J. E. (1978). *Looking in Classrooms*. (2nd ed.). New York: Harper and Row.

Good, T. L. and Brophy, J. E. (1973). *Looking in Classrooms*. New York: Harper and Row.

Goodlad, J. I. (1990). *Teachers for Our Nation's Schools*. San Francisco: Jossey-Bass.

Goodlad, J. I. (1984). *A Place Called School: Prospects for the Future*. New York: McGraw-Hill.

Goodlad, J. I., Soder, R., and Sirotnik, K. A. (Eds.). (1990a). *The Moral Dimensions of Teaching*. San Francisco: Jossey-Bass.

Goodlad, J. I., Soder, R., and Sirotnik, K. A. (Eds.). (1990b). *Places Where Teachers Are Taught*. San Francisco: Jossey-Bass.

Goodman, L. V. (Ed.). (1976). *A Nation of Learners*. Washington, DC: U.S. Government Printing Office.

Gordon, C. W. (Ed.). (1974). *Uses of the Sociology of Education: The Seventy-Third Yearbook of the National Society for the Study of Education. Part II*. Chicago: National Society for the Study of Education.

Grady, M., Zirkel, P. and Wayson, W. W. (1988). *Research on Effective Schools: Implications for Preparing School Administrators*. Tempe, AZ: University Council for Educational Administration.

Grant, C. A. and Koskela, R. A. (1986). Education that is multicultural and the relationship between preservice campus learning and field experiences. *Journal of Educational Research*, 79, 197–204.

Griffin, G. A. (1994). Teacher education curriculum in a time of school reform. In *Partnerships in Education: Teacher Education Yearbook II*, M. J. O'Hair and S. J. Odell (Eds.), Fort Worth, TX: Harcourt Brace, pp. 224–245.

Grimmett, P. P., Rostad, O. P., and Ford, B. (1992). The transformation of supervision. In *Supervision in Transition: The 1992 Yearbook of the Association for Supervision and Curriculum Development*, C. D. Glickman (Ed.), Alexandria, VA: Association for Supervision and Curriculum Development.

Gulick, L. and Urwick, L. (Eds.). (1937). *Papers on the Science of Administration*. New York: Columbia University Press.

Guskey, T. R. (1986). Staff development and the process of teacher change. *Educational Researcher*, 15 (5), 5–12.

Habermas, J. (1971). *Knowledge and Human Interest*. Boston: Beacon Press.

Hargreaves, A. (1994). *Changing Teachers, Changing Times: Teachers' Work and Culture in the Postmodern Age.* New York: Teachers College Press.

Heath, S. B. and McLaughlin, M. W. (Eds.). (1993). *Identity and Inner-City Youth: Beyond Ethnicity and Gender.* New York: Teachers College Press.

Helgesen, S. (1990). *The Female Advantage: Women's Ways of Leadership.* New York: Doubleday.

Henry, S. and Vilz, J. (1990). School improvement: together we can make a difference. *Educational Leadership, 47* (8), 78–79.

Hentoff, N. (1966). *Our Children Are Dying.* New York: Viking.

Herzberg, F. (1966). *Work and the Nature of Man.* Cleveland: World.

Hoffman, L. M. (1992). Continuing motivation in elementary school children: A naturalistic case study. Unpublished doctoral dissertation, The Ohio State University, Columbus, OH.

Holm, G. and Johnson, L. N. (1994). Shaping cultural partnerships: The readiness of preservice teachers to teach in culturally diverse classrooms. In *Partnerships in Education: Teacher Education Yearbook II*, M. J. O'Hair and S. J. Odell (Eds.), Fort Worth, TX: Harcourt Brace, pp. 85–101.

The Holmes Group. (1990). *Tomorrow's Schools: Principles for the Design of Professional Development Schools.* East Lansing, MI: The Holmes Group.

The Holmes Group. (1986). *Tomorrow's Teachers.* East Lansing, MI: The Holmes Group.

Homans, G. C. (1950). *The Human Group.* New York: Harcourt, Brace, and World.

Horenstein, M. A. (1993). *Twelve Schools That Succeed.* Bloomington, IN: Phi Delta Kappa Educational Foundation.

Hoy, W. and Rees, R. (1977). The bureaucratic socialization of student teachers. *Journal of Teacher Education, 28* (1), 23–26.

Huberman, M. (1993). *Lives of Teachers* (J. Neufeld, Trans.). New York: Teachers College Press.

Huling-Austin, L. (1992). Research on learning to teach: Implications for teacher induction and mentoring programs. *Journal of Teacher Education, 43* (3), 173–180.

Huse, E. F. (1980). *Organization Development and Change* (2nd ed.). St. Paul, MN: West Publishing Company.

Insko, C. (1967). *Theories of Attitude Change.* New York: Appleton-Century-Crofts.

Irvine, J. J. (1985). Teacher communication patterns as related to the race and sex of the student. *Journal of Educational Research, 78*, 338–345.

Ishida, M. (1994). An analysis of school administrators' power strategy styles. Unpublished doctoral dissertation, The Ohio State University, Columbus, OH.

Jackson, P. W. (1992). *Untaught Lessons.* New York: Teachers College Press.

Jackson, P. W. (1990). *Life in Classrooms.* New York: Teachers College Press.

Janis, I. (1982). *Groupthink: Psychological Studies of Policy Decisions and Fiascoes.* Boston: Houghton Mifflin.

Jersild, A. T. (1955). *When Teachers Face Themselves.* New York: Teachers College, Columbia University.

Johnston, J., Bickel, W., and Wallace, R. (1990). Building and sustaining change in the culture of secondary schools. *Educational Leadership,* 47 (8), 46–48.

Joyce, B., Hersh, R. H., and McKibbin, M. (1983). *The Structure of School Improvement.* New York: Longman.

Joyce, B. and McKibben, M. (1982). Teacher growth states and school environments. *Educational Leadership,* 40 (3), 36–41.

Judge, H. (1982). *American Graduate Schools of Education: A View from Abroad.* New York: Ford Foundation.

Kagan, S. L. (Ed.). (1991). *The Care and Education of America's Young Children: Obstacles and Opportunities.* Chicago: The University of Chicago Press.

Kammeraad-Campbell, S. (1987). *Doc: The Story of Dennis Littky and His Fight for a Better School.* Chicago: Contemporary Books.

Kantor, R. M. (1989). *When Giants Learn to Dance.* New York: Simon and Schuster.

Kantor, R. M. (1977). *Men and Women of the Corporation.* New York: Basic Books.

Katz, D. and Kahn, R. (1978). *The Social Psychology of Organizations.* New York: John Wiley and Sons.

Kaufman, B. (1964). *Up the Down Staircase.* Englewood Cliffs, NJ: Prentice-Hall.

Kelsay, K. L. (1991). When experience is the best teacher: The teacher as researcher. *Action in Teacher Education,* 13 (1), 14–21.

Klein, M. F. (1986). The master teacher as curriculum leader. *Elementary School Journal,* 86, 35–44.

Kohl, H. R. (1967). *36 Children.* New York: New American Library.

Kozol, J. (1991). *Savage Inequalities: Children in America's Schools.* New York: Crown.

Kozol, J. (1967). *Death at an Early Age.* Boston: Houghton Mifflin.

Kreisberg, S. (1992). *Transforming Power: Domination, Empowerment, and Education.* Albany, NY: State University of New York Press.

Lasley, T. J. and Wayson, W. W. (1982). Characteristics of schools with good discipline. *Educational Leadership,* 40 (3), 28–31.

Lasswell, H. D. and Kaplan, A. (1950). *Power and Society.* New Haven: Yale University Press.

Leavitt, H. J. (1963). *The Social Science of Organizations: Four Perspectives.* Englewood Cliffs, NJ: Prentice-Hall.

Leithwood, K. A. and Montgomery, D. (1982). The role of the elementary school principal in program improvement. *Review of Educational Research,* 52, 309–339.

Levine, S. L. (1989). *Promoting Adult Growth in Schools: The Promise of Professional Development.* Needham Heights, MA: Allyn & Bacon.

Lewin, K. (1951). *Field Theory in Social Science.* New York: Harper and Row.

Lewin, K. (1942). Field theory of learning. In *The Psychology of Learning: The Forty-First Yearbook of the National Society for the Study of Education. Part II,* N. B. Henry (Ed.), Chicago: University of Chicago Press.

Lewin, K., Lippitt, R., and White, R. (1939). Patterns of aggressive behavior in experimentally created "social climates." *Journal of Social Psychology,* 10, 271–299.

Lewis, A. C. (1985). Young and poor in America. *Phi Delta Kappan,* 67, 251–252.

Lieberman, A., Saxl, E., and Miles, M. (1988). Teacher leadership: Ideology and practice. In *Building a Professional Culture in Schools,* A. Lieberman (Ed.), New York: Teachers College Press.

Lieberman, A. and Miller, L. (1984). School improvement: Themes and variations. *Teachers College Record,* 86 (1), 4–19.

Lightfoot, S. L. (1990). On goodness in schools: Themes of empowerment. *Peabody Journal of Education,* 63 (3), 9–28.

Lightfoot, S. L. (1983). *The Good High School.* New York: Basic Books.

Lightfoot, S. L. (1981). Portraits of exemplary secondary schools. *Daedalus,* 110, 17–38, 59–80, 97–116.

Likert, R. (1967). *The Human Organization: Its Management and Value.* New York: McGraw-Hill.

Likert, R. (1961). *New Patterns of Management.* New York: McGraw-Hill.

Lippitt, R. (1949). *Training in Community Relations.* New York: Harper.

Locke, E. A. and Schweiger, D. M. (1979). Participation in decision making: One more look. In *Research in Organizational Behavior,* B. Staw (Ed.), Greenwich, CT: JAI Press, pp. 273–280, 316–322.

Lortie, D. C. (1977). *Schoolteacher: A Sociological Study.* Chicago: University of Chicago Press.

Loucks-Horsley, S., Harding, C. K., Arbuckle, M. A., Murray, L. B., Dubea, C., and Williams, M. K. (1987). *Continuing to Learn: A Guidebook for Teacher Development.* Andover, MA: The Regional Laboratory for Educational Improvement of the Northeast and Islands, and National Staff Development Council (ERIC Document Reproduction Service No. ED 285 837).

Lunenburg, F. C. and Ornstein, A. C. (1991). *Educational Administration: Concepts and Practices.* Belmont, CA: Wadsworth.

Maehr, M. L. (1984). Meaning and motivation: Toward a theory of personal investment. In *Research on Motivation in Education: Vol. 1. Student Motivation,* R. Ames and C. Ames (Eds.), Orlando, FL: Academic Press, pp. 115–144.

Maehr, M. L. and Braskamp, L. A. (1986). *The Motivation Factor: A Theory: Of Personal Investment.* Lexington, MA: Lexington Books.

Maehr, M. L., Midgley, C., and Urdan, T. (1992). School leader as motivator. *Educational Administration Quarterly,* 28, 410–429.

Maehr, M. L. and Buck, R. M. (1993). Transforming school culture. *Educational Leadership and School Culture.* M. Sashkin and H. J. Sashkin, Berkeley, CA: McCutchan Publishing Co., pp. 40–57.

Maeroff, G. I. (1988a). *The Empowerment of Teachers: Overcoming the Crisis of Confidence.* New York: Teachers College Press.

Maeroff, G. I. (1988b). Teacher empowerment: A step toward professionalization. *NASSP Bulletin,* 72 (511), 52–60.

Maier, N. R. (1963). *Problem-Solving Discussions and Conferences.* New York: McGraw-Hill.

Maier, N. R. and Sashkin, M. (1971). Specific leadership behaviors that promote problem-solving. *Personnel Psychology,* 24, 35–44.

Mangieri, J. N. (Ed.). (1985). *Excellence in Education.* Fort Worth: Texas Christian University Press.

May, W. and Zimpher, N. (1986). An examination of three theoretical perspectives on supervision: Perceptions of preservice field supervision. *Journal of Curriculum and Supervision,* 1, 83–99.

Mayo, E. (1933). *The Human Problems of an Industrial Civilization.* New York: Macmillan.

McClelland, D. (1985). *Human Motivation.* Glenview, IL: Scott, Foresman.

McDiarmid, G. W. and Price, J. (1993). Preparing teachers for diversity: A study of student teachers in a multicultural program. In *Diversity and Teaching: Teacher Education Yearbook I,* M. J. O'Hair and S. J. Odell (Eds.), Fort Worth, TX: Harcourt Brace Jovanovich, pp. 31–57.

McGregor, D. (1960). *The Human Side of Enterprise.* New York: McGraw-Hill.

McWhirter, E. H. (1991). Empowerment in counseling. *Journal of Counseling and Development,* 69, 223–227.

Merton, R. K. (1957). *Social Theory and Social Structure.* Glencoe, IL: Free Press.

Metcalf, H. C. and Urwick, L. (1942). *Dynamic Administration: The Collected Papers of Mary Parker Follett.* New York: Harper and Brothers.

Mieres, A. (1990). An instrument to operationalize a theory of power strategy styles. Unpublished doctoral dissertation, The Ohio State University, Columbus, OH.

Miles, M. (1959). *Learning to Work in Groups.* New York: Teachers College, Columbia University.

Mintzberg, H. (1973). *The Nature of Managerial Work.* Englewood Cliffs, NJ: Prentice-Hall.

Moultry, M. (1988). Senior education students' attitudes about multicultural education. In *Multicultural Education: Knowledge and Perceptions,* C. A. Heid (Ed.), Bloomington, IN: Center for Urban and Multicultural Education, pp. 49–64.

Murphy, J. F. and Hallinger, P. (1985). Effective high schools: What are the common characteristics? *NASSP Bulletin,* 69 (1), 18–22.

Murphy, J. F. and Louis, K. S. (1994). *Reshaping the Principalship: Insights from Transformational Reform Efforts.* Thousand Oaks, CA: Corwin Press.

Naisbitt, J. (1982). *Megatrends.* New York: Warner.

Nash, R. (1973). *Classrooms Observed: The Teacher's Perception and the Pupil's Performance.* Boston: Routledge & Kegan Paul.

National Coalition of Advocates for Students. (1985). *Barriers to Excellence: Our Children at Risk.* Boston: National Coalition of Advocates for Students.

Neff, W. S. (1985). *Work and Human Behavior.* New York: Aldine.

Nieto, S. (1992). *Affirming Diversity: The Sociopolitical Context of Multicultural Education.* New York: Longman.

Nutt, P. C. (1989). *Making Tough Decisions.* San Francisco: Jossey-Bass.

Nyberg, D. (1988). *Power over Power.* Ithaca: Cornell Paperbacks.

Ogawa, R. T. (1984). Teachers and administrators: Elements of the information processing repertoires of schools. *Educational Administration Quarterly,* 20 (2), 5–24.

Ouchi, W. G. (1981). *Theory Z: How American Business Can Meet the Japanese Challenge.* Reading, MA: Addison-Wesley.

Ouchi, W. G. (1982). Theory Z and the schools. *School Administrator,* 39 (2), 12–19.

Ohio State University College of Education. (1988). *Results from a Survey of Multicultural Attitudes and Competencies among Students Completing Student Teaching from the College of Education at The Ohio State University, 1985–86.* Columbus, OH: The Ohio State University College of Education.

Passow, A. H. (1967). *Toward Creating a Model Urban School System.* New York: Teachers College Press.

Peters, T. J. (1988). *Thriving on Chaos: Handbook for a Management Revolution.* New York: Harper and Row.

Peters, T. J. and Austin, N. (1985). *A Passion for Excellence: The Leadership Difference.* New York: Random House.

Peters, T. J. and Waterman, R. H. (1982). *In Search of Excellence: Lessons from America's Best-Run Companies.* New York: Harper and Row.

Pfeffer, J. (1992). *Managing with Power.* Boston: Harvard Business School Press.

Pinderhughes, E. (1989). *Understanding Race, Ethnicity, and Power.* New York: Free Press.

Pine, G. (1986). Collaborative action research and staff development in the middle school. *Middle School Journal,* 18 (1), 33–35.

Pinnell, G. S. and Wayson, W. W. (1991). Helping children learn in failure-oriented systems. Paper presented at the *Eminent Scholars Seminar,* Martha King Reading Center, The Ohio State University.

Pipho, C. (1985). Testing the teaching profession. *Phi Delta Kappan,* 66 (9), 597–598.

Ponticell, J. A. (1994). Seeing and believing: Using college coaching and videotaping to improve instruction in an urban high school. In *Partnerships in Education: Teacher Education Yearbook II,* M. J. O'Hair and S. J. Odell (Eds.), Fort Worth, TX: Harcourt Brace, pp. 157–174.

Popkewitz, T. (1984). *Paradigm and Ideology in Educational Research.* London: Falmer Press.

Postman, N. and Weingartner, C. (1969). *Teaching as a Subversive Activity.* New York: Delacorte.

Powell, A., Farrar, E., and Cohen, D. K. (1985). *The Shopping Mall High School.* Boston: Houghton Mifflin.

Prawat, R. S. (1991). Conversations with self and settings: A framework for thinking about teacher empowerment. *American Educational Research Journal,* 28, 737–757.

Raebeck, B. (1994). The school as a humane business: organizing problems out; designing productivity in. *Phi Delta Kappan,* 75, 761–765.

Reich, R. (1988). *Education and the Next Economy.* Washington, DC: National Education Association Professional and Organizational Development/ Research Division.

Reitzug, U. C. (1994). A case study of empowering principal behavior. *American Educational Research Journal,* 31 (2), 283–307.

Roethlisberger, F. J. and Dickson, W. J. (1939). *Management and the Worker.* Cambridge, MA: Harvard University Press.

Rosenholtz, S. J. (1989). *Teachers' Workplace: The Social Organization of Schools.* New York: Longman.

Rosenthal, R. and Jacobson, L. (1968). *Pygmalion in the Classroom.* New York: Holt, Rinehart and Winston.

Rubin, J. Z. (1984). Introduction. In *Group Decision Making,* W. C. Swap & Associates (Eds.), Beverly Hills, CA: Sage.

Russell, B. (1938). *Power A New Social Analysis.* London: W. W. Norton.

Rutter, M. (1980). School influences on children's behavior and development. *Pediatrics,* 65, 208–220.

Rutter, M., Maughan, B., Mortimore, P., and Orston, J. (1979). *Fifteen Thousand Hours: Secondary Schools and Their Effects on Children.* Cambridge, MA: Harvard University Press.

Ryan, R. M., Connell, J. P. and Deci, E. L. (1985). A motivational analysis of self-determination and self-regulation in education. In *Research on Motivation in Education: Vol. 2. The Classroom Milieu,* C. Ames and R. Ames (Eds.), Orlando, FL: Academic Press, pp. 13–51.

Sarason, S. B. (1993). *The Case for Change: Rethinking the Preparation of Educators.* San Francisco: Jossey-Bass.

Sarason, S. B. (1989). *Letters to a Serious Education President.* Newbury Park, CA: Corwin Press.

Sarason, S. B. (1983). *Schooling in America: Scapegoat and Salvation.* New York: Free Press.

Sarason, S. B. (1982). *The Culture of School and the Problem of Change.* Boston: Allyn & Bacon.

Sarason, S. B. (1972). *The Creation of Settings and the Future Societies.* San Francisco: Jossey-Bass.

Sashkin, M. and Sashkin, M. G. (1993). Principals and their school cultures: Understandings from quantitative and qualitative research. *Educational Leadership and School Culture,* M. Sashkin and M. G. Sashkin (Eds.), Berkeley, CA: McCutchan Publishing Co., pp. 100–123.

Sashkin, M. and Walberg, H. J. (Eds.). (1993). *Educational Leadership and School Culture.* Berkeley, CA: McCutchan.

Schein, E. H. (1988). *Process Consultation, Vol. 1: It's Role in Organizational Development* (2nd ed.). Reading, MA: Addison-Wesley.

Schein, E. H. (1980). *Organizational Psychology* (3rd ed.). Englewood Cliffs, NJ: Prentice-Hall.

Schlechty, P. C. (1991). *Schools for the Twenty-First Century: Leadership Imperatives for Educational Reform.* San Francisco: Jossey-Bass.

Schmuck, R. A. and Runkel, P. J. (1985). *The Handbook of Organization Development in Schools* (3rd ed.). Palo Alto, CA: Mayfield Publishing Co.

Schmuck, R. A. and Runkel, P. J. (1972). *Handbook of Organization Development in Schools.* Palo Alto, CA: National Press Books.

Schmuck, R. A., Runkel, P. J., Arends, J. H., and Arends, R. I. (1977). *The Second Handbook of Organization Development in Schools.* Palo Alto, CA: Mayfield Publishing Co.

Schmuck, R. A. and Schmuck, P. A. (1974). *A Humanistic Psychology of Education: Making the School Everybody's House.* Palo Alto, CA: National Press Books.

Schmuck, R. A. and Schmuck, P. A. (1971). *Group Processes in the Classroom.* Dubuque, IA: William C. Brown.

Schutz, W. (1966). *The Interpersonal Underworld.* Palo Alto, CA: Science and Behavior Books.

Schutz, W. (1958). *FIRO: A Three Dimensional Theory of Interpersonal Relations.* New York: Holt, Rinehart, and Winston.

Senge, P. M. (1990). *The Fifth Discipline: The Art and Practice of the Learning Organization.* New York: Doubleday.

Sergiovanni, T. J. (1987). The theoretical basis for cultural leadership. In *Leadership: Examining the Elusive. 1987 Yearbook of the Association for Supervision and Curriculum Development,* L. T. Sheive and M. B. Schoenheit (Eds.), Alexandria, VA: Association for Supervision and Curriculum Development, pp. 116–129.

Sergiovanni, T. J. (1984). *The Principalship: A Reflective Practice Perspective.* Boston: Allyn & Bacon.

Sergiovanni, T. J. and Starratt, R. J. (1983). *Supervision: Human Perspectives* (3rd ed.). New York: McGraw-Hill.

Shakeshaft, C. (1989). The gender gap in research in educational administration. *Educational Administration Quarterly,* 25 (4), 324–337.

Shakeshaft, C., Nowell, I., and Perry, A. (1991). Gender and supervision. *Theory into Practice,* 20 (2), 134–139.

Sherif, M. and Sherif, C. W. (1953). *Groups in Harmony and Tension.* New York: Harper and Row.

Shumsky, A. (1968). *In Search of Teaching Style.* New York: Appleton-Century-Crofts.

Silberman, C. E. (1970). *Crisis in the Classroom.* New York: Random House.

Silberman, C. E. (1964). *Crisis in Black and White.* New York: Random House.

Sirotnik, K. A. (1990). Society, schooling, teaching, and preparing to teach. In *The Moral Dimensions of Teaching,* J. I. Goodlad, R. Soder, and K. A. Sirotnik (Eds.), San Francisco: Jossey-Bass, pp. 296–328.

Sirotnik, K. and Clark, R. W. (1988). School-centered decision making and renewal. *Phi Delta Kappan,* 69, 660–664.

Sizer, T. R. (1984). *Horace's Compromise: The Dilemma of the American High School.* Boston: Houghton Mifflin.

Smith, L. M. (1983). *Innovation and Change in American Education, Kensington Revisited: A Fifteen Year Follow-up of an Innovative Elementary School and Its Faculty.* St. Louis: Graduate Institute of Education, Washington University (ERIC Document Reproduction Service No. ED 243 195).

Smyth, J. (1992). Teachers' work and the politics of reflection. *American Educational Research Journal,* 29, 267–300.

Smyth, J. (1991). International perspectives on teacher collegiality: A labor process discussion based on the concept of teachers' work. *British Journal of Sociology of Education,* 12, 323–345.

Sockett, H. (1990). Accountability, trust, and ethical codes of practice. In *The Moral Dimensions of Teaching,* J. I. Goodlad, R. Soder, and K. A. Sirotnik (Eds.), San Francisco: Jossey-Bass, pp. 224–250.

Stanford, B. H. (1994). A spirit of partnership: Qualities conductive to career perseverance and high morale in teachers. In *Partnerships in Education: Teacher Education Yearbook II,* M. J. O'Hair and S. J. Odell (Eds.), Fort Worth, TX: Harcourt Brace, pp. 192–202.

Stogdill, R. M. (1959). *Individual Behavior and Group Achievement.* New York: Oxford University Press.

Strike, K. A. (1990). The legal and moral responsibility of teachers. In *The Moral Dimensions of Teaching,* J. I. Goodlad, R. Soder, and K. A. Sirotnik (Eds.), San Francisco: Jossey-Bass, pp. 188–223.

Takanishi, R. (Ed.). (1993). *Adolescence in the 1990's: Risk and Opportunity.* New York: Teachers College Press.

Thomas, B. R. (1990). The school as a moral learning community. In *The Moral Dimensions of Teaching,* J. I. Goodlad, R. Soder, and K. A. Sirotnik (Eds.), San Francisco: Jossey-Bass, pp. 266–295.

Tolstoy, L. (1967). *Tolstoy on Education* (L. Wiener, Trans.). Chicago: University of Chicago Press.

Tomlinson, T. M. (Ed.). (1993). *Motivating Students to Learn.* CA: McCutchan Publishing Corporation.

Turner, J. H. (1988). *A Theory of Social Interaction.* Palo Alto, CA: Stanford University Press.

University Associates (1972). What to look for in groups. *The 1972 Annual Handbook for Group Facilitators.* University Associates Inc.

Van Til, W. (Ed.). (1976). *Issues in Secondary Education: The Seventy-Fifth Yearbook of the National Society for the Study of Education. Part II.* Chicago: National Society for the Study of Education.

Waller, W. (1965). *The Sociology of Teaching.* New York: John Wiley & Sons (Original work published 1932).

Wassermann, S. (1991). Louis E. Raths: Theories of empowerment. *Childhood Education,* 67, 235–239.

Wayson, W. W. (1994). *Teaching Skills Inventory.* Plain City, OH: Synergetic Development Inc.

Wayson, W. W. (1993). *Assessing the Future: A Report to the Superintendent of*

Public Instruction, Ohio Department of Education. Plain City, OH: Synergetic Development Inc.

Wayson, W. W. (1988). Multicultural education in the College of Education: Are future teachers prepared? In *Multicultural Education: Knowledge and Perceptions,* C. A. Heid (Ed.), Bloomington, IN: Center for Urban and Multicultural Education, pp. 39–48.

Wayson, W. W. (1985). Opening windows to teaching: Empowering educators to teach self-discipline. *Theory into Practice,* 24, 227–232.

Wayson, W. W. (1975). Good multi-racial and multi-ethnic inservice programs for urban schools. Paper presented at the *Annual Meeting of the American Association of School Administrators,* Dallas, TX (ERIC Document Reproduction Service No. ED 111 837).

Wayson, W. W. (1974). Developing the teachers of teachers. *Theory into Practice,* 13, 177–186.

Wayson, W. W. (1972). Educating for renewal in urban communities. *National Elementary Principal,* 51 (6), 6–18.

Wayson, W. W. (1971a). The new breed of principal. *National Elementary Principal,* 50 (4), 8–19.

Wayson, W. W. (1971b). Organizing urban schools for responsible education. *Phi Delta Kappan,* 52, 344–347.

Wayson, W. W. (1970). The new principalship for the last third of the 20th century. *New York State Secondary Education,* 8, 14–17.

Wayson, W. W. (1966a). The political revolution in education, 1965. *Phi Delta Kappan,* 47, 333–339.

Wayson, W. W. (1966b). Expressed motives of teachers in slum schools. *Urban Education,* 1, 223–238.

Wayson, W. W. (1966c). Sources of teacher satisfaction in slum schools. *Administrator's Notebook,* 14 (9), 1–4.

Wayson, W. W., Achilles, C., Pinnell, G. S., Cunningham, L., Carol, L., and Lintz, M. N. (1988a). *Handbook for Developing Public Confidence in Schools.* Bloomington, IN: Phi Delta Kappa.

Wayson, W. W., DeVoss, G. G., Kaeser, S. C., Lasley, T., Pinnell, G. S., and the Phi Delta Kappa Commission on Discipline. (1982). *A Handbook for Developing Schools with Good Discipline.* Bloomington, IN: Phi Delta Kappa.

Wayson, W. W. and Lasley, T. J. (1984). Climates for excellence: Schools that foster self-discipline. *Phi Delta Kappan,* 65, 419–421.

Wayson, W. W., Mitchell, B., Pinnell, G. S., and Landis, D. (1988b). *Up from Excellence: The Impact of the Excellence Movement on Schools.* Bloomington, IN: Phi Delta Kappa.

Weber, M. (1947). *The Theory of Economic and Social Organization* (T. Parsons, Trans.). New York: Oxford University Press.

Weinstein, C. S. (1988). Preservice teachers' expectations about the first year of teaching. *Teaching and Teacher Education,* 4, 31–40.

Wells, H. G. (1927). Country of the blind. In *The Complete Short Stories of H. G. Wells,* London: Ernest Benn Ltd., pp. 167–192.

Willie, C. V. (1982). Educating students who are good enough: Is excellence an excuse to exclude? *Change,* 14 (2), 16–21.

Willower, D. J., Eidell, T. L., and Hoy, W. K. (1974). *The Pennsylvania State University Studies No. 24: The School and Pupil Control Ideology* (new ed.). University Park, PA: The Pennsylvania State University.

Wilson, B. L. and Rossman, G. B. (1986). Collaborative links with the community: Lessons from exemplary secondary schools. *Phi Delta Kappan,* 67, 708–711.

Wise, A. (1983). Why educational policies often fail: The hyperrationalization hypothesis. In *The Dynamics of Organizational Change in Education,* J. V. Baldridge and T. Deal (Eds.), Berkeley, CA: McCutchan, pp. 93–113.

Wolcott, H. (1973). *The Man in the Principal's Office.* New York: Holt, Rinehart, and Winston.

Yukl, G. A. (1989). *Leadership in Organizations.* Englewood Cliffs, NJ: Prentice-Hall.

Zimpher, N. L. (1988). A design for the professional development of teacher leaders. *Journal of Teacher Education,* 39 (1), 53–60.

CHAPTER 3

Empowerment by Any Other Name: If You Can't Define It, You Don't Have It!!

JUNE H. SCHMIEDER[1]
ARTHUR J. TOWNLEY[2]

INTRODUCTION

The term *empowerment* continues to be prominent in the educational reform movement of the 1990s. Its interpretation remains markedly diffuse, shaped by negative connotations associated with recent employee job actions in the educational sector. A brief overview of the history that precedes emergence of the term is presented. Four instruments are proposed that can initiate and focus discussion at the school site and help create a more robust link between that discussion and practical applications. Limitations of empowerment, as well as policy implications for the future, are studied.

> Never doubt that a small group of committed citizens can change the world. Indeed it is the only thing that ever has.
>
> —Margaret Mead

THE PROBLEM

A large percentage of Americans believe that public education is in crisis. The education establishment throughout the nation feels that

---

[1]Pepperdine University.
[2]California State University, San Bernardino.

its members are engaged in a war, a war for the very survival of public education.

This crisis was dramatized in California when citizens of that state placed on the ballot an initiative for "schools of choice." Had this measure been approved by voters, parents could have enrolled their child in a private school, and the school would have received a voucher from the state of approximately $2,500 for that child each school year. This action would have drained resources from an already underfunded state public education system.

Other results of dissatisfaction with public schools are found in Rochester, New York, where the district is administered by teachers rather than administrators, and in Massachusetts, where Boston University manages that city's public schools. The "choice" solution is already in place in Milwaukee, Wisconsin, where parents are allowed to send their children to any of 147 public schools, and in Minnesota, where parents may enroll their child in any public school in the state.

Proponents of schools of choice argue that if parents and students could choose from a range of schools, then public schools, forced to compete vigorously with each other and with private education to satisfy its consumers, would also inevitably improve. They argue that the public school, as it has operated in recent decades, is autonomous, answerable virtually to no one. They charge that the vast bureaucracies administering the school districts of most large U.S. cities are too removed from the realities of the schoolroom to address its basic problems. Public opinion polls confirm that parents believe that exercising a choice in the kind of education their children receive is the key to raising standards.

A major source of dissatisfaction in the public schools is the perception that local control of public schools has eroded. As established by the Constitution, primary responsibility for education in this nation rests with the fifty states. However, ever since the first public schools were established in the United States in the 1800s, forty-nine of our states have delegated to local communities the authority to run their schools.

Nevertheless, a trend over the past decade has been a shift in control of schools from local communities to the states, which has exerted increasing authority over budgets, instruction, and personnel. Demographic changes, federal legislation, and court cases all have contributed to this shift away from local community control. In addition, such factors as the need to transport students across town for integration purposes, the spread of violence in the schools, and problems associated with poverty and riot-torn inner cities have created additional district and state administrative positions whose incumbents are motivated to "get the system under control," while inevitably pushing parents and teachers into the background.

At the same time, while communities were experiencing an increase in the centralization of school systems, they were also enjoying an increase in the money spent on education. Educating elementary and secondary school-age children in the United States during the 1987–1988 school year cost over $184 billion. This 34.1 percent increase over 1983 expenditures compares with only a 0.3 percent increase in enrollment. However, increased spending has yielded little improvement in student achievement. As Americans ponder what went wrong with education, they surmise that the missing element is loss of control at the school site on the part of principals, teachers, and parents.

EMPOWERMENT: WHAT IS IT?

In the efforts of communities to recapture control of their schools, the catchword for the 1990s school reform movement has become *empowerment*. Will this concept really enable teachers, principals, and parents to regain power over their schools, or is the term *empowerment* simply another buzzword, soon to find its way into the slagheap of "in" words of earlier decades? Is it doomed to eventual burial, right next to *decentralization* and *participative management*?

Empowerment is a term that migrated to education from the world of business. Nevertheless, the word is similar to many earlier relatives: decentralization in the 1960s–70s; participative management in the 1970s–80s; and school-based decision making, site-based management and shared decision making in the 1980s and 1990s.

The education community has embraced this latest term, *empowerment* in hopes of returning control to the school site, anticipating that local control will lead, in turn, to better student performance. There are high hopes that empowerment, which takes many forms (collaborative problem solving, site-based management, career ladders, and differentiated staffing among them), offers new opportunities for teacher-leaders to emerge as a positive force toward school improvement.

Although the term empowerment is widely used in the restructuring rhetoric, it has, like so many buzzwords, multiple meanings. The central thesis of empowerment seems to be that the educational system should bestow more power upon those who help students most—that is, the practitioners, the teachers at the school-site level.

Thus, one may view empowerment as a means of eliciting teacher leadership. In this view, empowerment is assumed to be motivational (Conger and Kanungo, 1988). However, teachers must first feel empowered enough to participate in decision-making processes and must become dedicated to their new role. It follows from this concept that the principal's function in facilitating leadership is to structure empowering experiences for teachers in schools (Taylor, 1991). But principals themselves must feel empowered. If principals perceive that their own freedom of action is closely controlled, they may find it impossible to act freely to empower teachers or parents (Lucas, 1991).

Another widely accepted understanding of empowerment calls for the school site to control its budget policies, hire and fire personnel, and determine its curriculum. According to this concept, an empowered school is governed by a school council consisting of the principal and representatives of teachers, parents, students, and the community at large. Articles on empowerment imply that such a change is relatively easy to implement and quickly embraced by all participants. In reality, however, anyone who has attemped any form of site-level decision making knows that it is neither easy nor quick, nor is it warmly received by the entire school.

Promoting empowerment in an organization, and especially facilitating the leadership of others, is a complex task. It requires processes that enable leadership to emerge, rather than a focus limited to the *outcomes* of processes (Michael et al., 1991). Frequently, then, empowerment upon this elusive term is essential to its success.

DEFINITIONS

THE IDEAL: PLATO

The word *power* symbolizes capacity to accomplish positive social ends or to make decisions that influence the behavior of others for "the good," as one understands the good. The nature of this influence and of "the good" or "the end" must always be subject to critical examination. Plato saw power as having two dimensions: active and passive. He defined active power as the capacity to influence and passive power as the capacity to be influenced.

THE DICTIONARY: WEBSTER

Webster's definition of empower (*Ninth New Collegiate Dictionary*) is "to give official authority or legal power to." The prefix "-em" originates from a Latin root that implies that the object, power, is being placed upon another. Implicit is the sense that power is a commodity to be bestowed upon a previously unempowered group. This "bestowal" may cause some trepidation in itself, but the root word, power, causes administrators to quake in their boots.

THE REALITY: MITCHELL AND BEACH

Mitchell and Beach (1993) queried school superintendents in California regarding their opinions about teacher empowerment. They found that half of the small sample expressed strong reservations about the idea. Indeed, one superintendent indicated that, as a consequence of recent collective bargaining events, he found empowerment distasteful. He felt that empowerment would give teachers control over all educational issues. From his perspective, teachers should control the classroom, while management should control the direction of the district. This educator strongly urged management to "have the final say" and not let matters get out of hand.

This response is a typical reaction to empowerment in the beginning stages. Administrators fear that any transfer of "power" to another group reduces their own diminishing span of control. As a consequence, efforts toward empowerment often generate mixed signals. Teachers sense that it is only with great reluctance that the educational system recognizes that they are closest to the client and so "bestows" power upon them. So the dilemma!

THE CURRENT CONTEXT

Before exploring a working definition of empowerment, it is important to view this issue from a contextual viewpoint. Many authors have attempted to fit the term into current educational thought. David Tyack (1990) organized his discussion into six thematic strands. These strands help anchor the definition into the current literature. Tyack focused his six themes into two subsets: 1) *what* he felt should be restructured (the school site, the teachers, and the governance system) and 2) *how* he felt they should be restructured (student/parent choice, pedagogical strategies, and the mix of services to be provided).

Mitchell and Beach (1993), on the other hand, limit their exposition to "teacher empowerment," which, in turn, is a subset of the current restructuring movement in education. More in keeping with Mitchell and Beach, this chapter focuses on teachers at the school-site level and how to initiate discussions of a definition of empowerment that might be useful at the site.

THE WORKING DEFINITION

The working definition of empowerment in this chapter is possession of power by teachers at the school site with the purpose of improving outcomes from students and/or working conditions for teachers. Given this working definition, four conditions must be in place before empowerment can move forward. Specifically, teachers and administrators must

1. Understand and accept the benefits of empowerment and shared decision making
2. Know the roles each will play
3. Recognize discrepancies or gaps between what currently is and what could be
4. Take the risk of commitment to change (Curry, 1990)

In focusing on empowerment of teachers at the school site, the authors make the following assumptions:

1. Empowerment must be carefully identified and defined if it is to be utilized at the school site.
2. An assessment should be conducted to discover where groups perceive themselves to be on an empowerment continuum—and where they would like to be.
3. Any tasks assigned to groups should be accompanied by the degree of authority necessary to accomplish them.

APPROACHES TO A SITE DEFINITION

Several approaches might be taken toward defining empowerment in a useful way. One approach is to identify a theory that purports to encompass all possible directions of empowerment, then pinpoint actions of groups designed to improve student performance and teacher morale. The difficulty with this approach is that the link between group decisions and student output rests upon scantily documented research and is, therefore, tenuous at best.

A second approach is to review the literature on empowerment to try to elicit a commonality of terms and ideas. However, as yet, there exists only a small body of research on specific applications of empowerment, especially at the site level. Thus, although an ERIC search of the term yielded 406 journal citations, all but six of these dealt with nonschool issues.

A third approach–the method directing the thought in this chapter–is to take a cue from practitioners who feel that the term is useful in their own schools. To explore this approach, we tease a little of the mystique from the term and thus reduce its negative connotations. After clarifying the purposes of empowerment, the chapter will

1. Briefly review from a historical perspective how the term has emerged, describing the assumptions that support an educational view of empowerment
2. Focus upon the school site (Sirotnik, 1990) and provide samples of empowerment instruments that could act as a catalyst for preliminary discussion at that level
3. Briefly note several key issues that must be addressed before empowerment issues can be resolved at the school site

PURPOSE OF EMPOWERMENT

One cannot attempt to define empowerment without identifying its purposes. We suggest three purposes directly related to teacher empowerment. They are to

1. Improve student performance
2. Involve teachers in decisions so they remain committed to student performance and pleased with the group processes utilized for decision making
3. Encourage teachers to stay in the profession and convince talented young people that teaching will afford them advancement opportunities (Hart, 1987)

Since education is a mirror of society and has taken its cues from other institutions such as business, what importance has this term for education?

EVOLUTION OF EMPOWERMENT

Until the scientific management movement began with the impetus of Frederick W. Taylor, (1856–1915), there existed no systematic body of knowledge related to the control of complex business and other organizations. The Protestant ethic strongly influenced Taylor's views on organizations. He emphasized ideas such as task management, worker efficiency, planning, and standardization. Today, we would recognize this as a top-down approach, with the company responsible for specific guidelines for worker performance.

The key elements of the bureaucratic model were efficiency, control, and power—all invested in the management layer of the company. The assumption underlying this theory was that management should plan, control, and direct the activities of the work group. Organizations that adhere to the tenets of this movement still have placards on walls that exhort company employees to Supervise! Delegate! Check progress and efficiency!!

The scientific management movement was followed by the human relations industrial movement that began with the research of Elton Mayo (1880–1949). Mayo completed a series of studies at the Hawthorne plant of the Western Electric Company between 1927 and 1932. These studies showed an increase in worker production due to changes in social relations, motivation, and worker supervision.

The behavioral scientists who followed Mayo emphasized the importance of more democratic, less authoritarian, and less bureaucratically structured organizations. McGregor (1960) emphasized the importance of replacing the bureaucratic Theory X with the more democratic-participative Theory Y. Maslow (1962) further extended the theory of motivation by proposing that workers could achieve self-actualization within the organization.

In the 1960s, as management approaches moved toward integrating individual and group goals, management by objectives (MBOs) began to take hold. Peter Drucker (1974) emphasized this structure as a way to keep the organization's goals in mind while still considering the involvement of individuals in the process. Many companies adopted MBO programs complete to a system of control, feedback on work performance, and strategic planning.

In the last few years Japanese management techniques have received worldwide attention. An American theorist, William Ouchi (1981), compared high production companies in Japan and the United States to determine what they had in common. His major interest was the "culture" of an organization and how it was managed.

The most recent organizational technique derived from business and applied to schools is the fourteen points of W. Edwards Deming. With his background as a statistician, Deming utilized these points to minimize product defects. Noting the failure of traditional methods of reducing defects, his proposed fourteen points stress improvement of the process, training and retraining of the worker, and forward-thinking leadership.

EMPOWERMENT TRANSLATED TO A SCHOOL SYSTEM

Schools of today are characterized by conditions that deviate from conventional theories of business management. Even though the administration of bus schedules and cafeteria periods might be described as "tightly coupled," the central goals of education have often been indeterminate, and evaluating individual student performance is a very complex undertaking. In the "egg crate" design of schools that predominated until the 1950s, communication of individual teachers with one another and sharing of information on school district issues were minimal. Thus, schools and school districts, lacking the hierarchical structure that marks business organizations, have been characterized as "loosely coupled systems."

Karl E. Weick (1982) identified a set of actions that are necessary in managing a loosely coupled system. In such an unfocused atmosphere, the administrator must constantly articulate the theme of the enterprise and spread throughout the system a sense of shared vision. This task is not easy. It requires articulation and rearticulation of common themes. It takes reminding.

Before a school district embarks on a full-scale program to empower its stakeholders, several questions should be addressed:

1. How do school principals react to increased empowerment of groups at their schools?
2. Do principals accept this movement toward decentralization?
3. Do teachers and other groups wish to be empowered?
4. Do groups tend to feel that the principal should do it all?
5. Is there a difference inherent in the limits of empowerment?
6. What occurs if some parents at a particular school must work and cannot devote time to the school?
7. How can one prevent the manipulation of empowered groups?
8. Can the tasks of empowerment be passed on to these groups without corresponding authority?
9. How are expenses such as training funded in a system that depends heavily on the participants learning new skills?
10. Would self-managed groups work (Reitzug, 1992)?
11. What will be done about teachers who do not meet minimum standards?
12. How are the process needs of teachers (reaching consensus, problem solving, gathering expert information, conflict resolution, meeting deadlines, and other time requirements) to be met?

These issues must be addressed before empowerment can become solidified in an educational culture.

Turning from the district to the school site, Table 3.1 (which must be tentative, since as many definitions of empowerment exist as participants) compares a traditional school and an empowered school on several dimensions.

The three assumptions that support continued attention to empowerment are that

1. Decision making at the school-site level is most successful when those affected are participants in the decisions.
2. Restructuring efforts that are most successful and long-lasting actively solicit the support of those affected.
3. The theoretical underpinning for the importance of empowerment lies in the writings of Herzberg (1966), who identified satisfiers and dissatisfiers relating to employee satisfaction. Opportunity for employees to contribute to their own work environments relates positively to morale and satisfaction.

If these assumptions hold true, then planners must assess the degree of empowerment operating in a school or district. Table 3.2 is designed to assist planners to complete a self-appraisal of the degree of empowerment at their school site or in their department. Each school can be charted to indicate the degree of empowerment of each stakeholder group.

Table 3.1. Defining stakeholder roles: traditional versus empowered schools.

Issue	Traditional	Empowered
Participation	Limited	Encouraged
Time required for decisions	Principal's domain	Increased
Information to stakeholders	Centralized	Decentralized
Autonomy	Limited	Greater (e.g., waivers for charter schools)
Training	Limited	Encouraged
Decision making	Limited	Decentralized
Conflict resolution	Centralized	Peer-directed
Principal's role	Authority	Facilitator
Principal/teacher interaction	Hierarchical	Collegial

Source: June Schmieder, 1994.

Table 3.2. Continuum of site or school district empowerment.

Object/Subject	No Empowerment	In Progress	High Empowerment
Personnel			
Finance			
Student Personnel			
Curriculum			
Legislation			
Restructuring			

Table 3.3 presents a chart for analysis of the degree of empowerment possessed by each stakeholder group. The chart is completed with arrows showing the direction and magnitude of the change.

Table 3.4 is designed to assist the principal in assessing the degree to which s/he is assisting stakeholders toward empowerment.

SCHMIEDER/TOWNLEY EMPOWERMENT INSTRUMENTS

Various constituencies are likely to perceive empowerment differently. Therefore, as a preliminary step to a careful and practical definition of empowerment for her/his school site, the principal may wish to inquire into existing perceptions of the stakeholders. The surveys in Table 3.5 may be used by the principal to assess what *is* before determining what *should be.* Teachers are the primary group to be assessed on each of these instruments. Appendix A provides a guide for interpreting the responses.

Table 3.3. Change in relative power of each stakeholder under empowered governance.

Stakeholder Group	Low Level	High Level
Students	→	
Parents	→	
Principal		←
Teachers	→	
Senior citizens	→	
School board		←
Superintendent		←
Special interest groups	←	
State legislature		←

Table 3.4. New definition of principal's role.

Task	Low Level	High Level
Facilitate coordination Develop and maintain the vision Develop process skills for staff Encourage self-reliance of groups Determine training needs		

A TYPICAL SCENARIO OF SCHOOL EMPOWERMENT

Although several scenarios may be considered in defining school empowerment, a typical model would leave some tasks to the domain of the principal, place some tasks totally under the purview of the teachers, and list many tasks in a shared domain. A typical scenario of empowerment is illustrated in Table 3.6.

LIMITATIONS OF EMPOWERMENT

Empowerment is not a panacea for all of education's ills. Rather, it is a vehicle through which professionals at a school site achieve a feeling of control over day-to-day actions and ultimate outcomes. It offers a method for teachers to exercise their creativity and knowledge while increasing interaction with their peers.

Empowerment will not resolve all conflict—indeed, initially, it may create new frictions—nor can it overcome poor leadership or an inadequate vision of the organization. Furthermore, as this chapter illustrates, it must be clearly focused to be useful.

Teachers who view the weekly faculty meeting as an intrusion that detracts their attention from teaching will likely consider empowerment a waste of time. With increased paperwork, parent demands, and a more complex family life, many teachers will opt to let the principal do it. At a somewhat higher level of involvement, participating teachers may choose to formulate options to be forwarded to the principal for an ultimate decision. The pattern of governance must be adapted to the local situation.

Empowerment of teachers is at least one step removed from the technical heart of the teaching and learning interaction. As a result, time may pass before measurable results can be teased from data on student learning. Many districts are cautious about embarking upon a path

Table 3.5. Schmieder/Townley empowerment instruments.

Personnel/Hiring Empowerment Instrument

Please circle a number from 1 to 10 to indicate where you visualize yourself with respect to personnel/hiring empowerment:

Low   High
Level   Level

1	2	3	4	5	6	7	8	9	10

Please complete the following:

To feel empowered, I would like to give my opinion on:

_____

This would move my rating to number_____.

Financial Empowerment Instrument

Please circle a number from 1 to 10 to indicate where you visualize yourself with respect to financial empowerment:

Low   High
Level   Level

1	2	3	4	5	6	7	8	9	10

Please complete the following:

To feel empowered, I would like to give my opinion on:

_____

This would move my rating to number_____.

Student Personnel Empowerment Instrument

Please circle a number from 1 to 10 to indicate where you visualize yourself with respect to student personnel empowerment:

Low   High
Level   Level

1	2	3	4	5	6	7	8	9	10

Please complete the following:

To feel empowered, I would like to give my opinion on:

_____

This would move my rating to number_____.

Table 3.5 (continued).

Curriculum Empowerment Instrument

Please circle a number from 1 to 10 to indicate where you visualize yourself with respect to curriculum empowerment:

Low   High
Level   Level

| 1 | 2 | 3 | 4 | 5 | 6 | 7 | 8 | 9 | 10 |

Please complete the following:

To feel empowered, I would like to give my opinion on:

_____

This would move my rating to number_____.

Legislation Empowerment Instrument

Please circle a number from 1 to 10 to indicate where you visualize yourself with respect to legislation empowerment:

Low   High
Level   Level

| 1 | 2 | 3 | 4 | 5 | 6 | 7 | 8 | 9 | 10 |

Please complete the following:

To feel empowered, I would like to give my opinion on:

_____

This would move my rating to number_____.

Restructuring Empowerment Instrument

Please circle a number from 1 to 10 to indicate where you visualize yourself with respect to restructuring empowerment:

Low   High
Level   Level

| 1 | 2 | 3 | 4 | 5 | 6 | 7 | 8 | 9 | 10 |

Please complete the following:

To feel empowered, I would like to give my opinion on:

_____

This would move my rating to number_____.

Table 3.6. One definition of school empowerment.

Principal Domain	Shared Domain	Teacher Domain
Safety	Public relations	Curriculum
Maintenance	Discipline	Classroom management
Payroll	Staff development	Textbook selection
Staff dismissal	Staff evaluation	Materials selection
Purchasing	Budget development	Instructional strategies
	Budget allocation	
	Staff selection	
	Campus supervision	

Source: June Schmieder, 1994.

that might "stir the nest." Therefore, to reduce negative fallout, the current situation and readiness for restructuring must be assessed before empowerment is placed at the top of the reform agenda.

Finally, accountability for consequences is a troubling dilemma. Even though many educators believe in stakeholder input, they also feel that one entity must have the final say and ultimate accountability. The degree to which a principal subscribes to this view affects the energy with which s/he will encourage teacher empowerment, which, in turn, becomes a major determining factor in the extent to which empowerment can be instituted.

Principals may be comfortable with state- and federal-mandated school-site councils but may balk at councils presenting proposals on budget, hiring, and student discipline. Yet successful site-based management and teacher empowerment depend upon the readiness of principals to share their autonomy, however extensive or limited, with those whose commitment is necessary to make the educational program function at the highest degree of efficiency (Lucas, 1991). Consequently, districts typically spell out what can and cannot be decentralized.

SUMMARY

A large percentage of Americans believe that public education is in crisis. A major source of dissatisfaction with the public schools is the perception that local control of public schools has eroded. During the past decade, greater control of local schools has shifted to the state, leaving students, teachers, and parents feeling estranged from and powerless to control their schools.

Teachers, parents, and members of the educational community have seized on the concept of empowerment to regain control of schools at the site level. While the definition of this term is elusive, it is generally accepted that empowerment gives teachers, principals, and parents control over budget policies, hiring and firing, and curriculum decisions.

The authors developed four instruments to assist personnel and parents to define empowerment through discussion of local control and concurrent responsibilities. This process is intended to create a more robust link between teaching and student performance. Only by establishing such a link can enthusiasm for local control lead to higher student achievement.

APPENDIX A

PERSONNEL/HIRING EMPOWERMENT INSTRUMENT RATING GUIDE

Level	Explanation
1–3	I have no input into personnel or hiring decisions at the school site.
4–6	I am asked my opinion on some personnel issues and participate at times in hiring decisions at the school site.
7–10	I participate fully with other teachers on most personnel/hiring issues at my school site.

FINANCIAL EMPOWERMENT INSTRUMENT RATING GUIDE

Level	Explanation
1–3	I have no input into financial decisions at the school site.
4–6	I am able to make some decisions with the faculty on how to spend allotted funds for such items as books, supplies, and art supplies.
7–10	I participate with other teachers on most financial decisions at the school site.

STUDENT PERSONNEL INSTRUMENT RATING GUIDE

Level	Explanation
1–3	I have no input into student personnel issues at my school site.
4–6	I am asked my opinion on some issues of student personnel at the site level.

7–10   I participate fully with my colleagues in student personnel issues at the school.

CURRICULUM EMPOWERMENT INSTRUMENT RATING GUIDE

Level   Explanation
1–3   I have no input into curricular decisions at my school site. I am not asked for my opinion on textbooks, computer programs, or other supplies.
4–6   I am able to make some decisions with the faculty on selection of curricular supplies.
7–10   I participate fully with other teachers on the majority of curricular decisions at the school site

LEGISLATION EMPOWERMENT INSTRUMENT RATING GUIDE

Level   Explanation
1–3   I am not asked my opinion about legislative issues or waivers from existing law.
4–6   I am able to participate in identifying some issues that require waivers and/or to review legislation in some areas.
7–10   I participate with other teachers in lobbying the legislature and/or developing requests for waivers from existing law.

RESTRUCTURING EMPOWERMENT INSTRUMENT RATING GUIDE

Level   Explanation
1–3   I have no input into restructuring decisions at the school site.
4–6   I am able to make some decisions with the faculty on actions related to restructuring.
7–10   I participate with other teachers on most restructuring decisions at the school site.

REFERENCES

Conger, J. and Kanungo, R. (1988). The empowerment process: Integrating theory and practice. *Academy of Management Review, 13.*

Curry, B. R. (1990). What do you think . . . about teacher empowerment? *Centering Teacher Education,* 7 (2), 16–19.

Drucker, P. F. (1974). *Management: Tasks, Responsibilities, Practices.* New York: Harper and Row.

Hart, A. W. (1987). A career ladder's effect on teacher career and work attitudes. *American Educational Research Journal,* 24 (4).

Herzberg, F. B. (1966). *Work and the Nature of Man.* New York: McGraw-Hill.

Kanter, R. M. (1977). *Men and Women of the Corporation.* New York: Basic Books.

Lucas, S. L. (1991). Principal's perceptions of site-based management and teacher empowerment. *NASSP Bulletin,* 75 (537).

Maslow, A. (1962) *Toward a Psychology of Being.* Princeton, NJ: Van Nostrand.

Mayo, E. (1933). *The Human Problems of an Industrial Civilization.* New York: Macmillan.

McGregor, D. (1960). *The Human Side of Enterprise.* New York: McGraw-Hill.

Michael, R. O., Short, P., and Greer, J. T. (1991). Principals' perceptions of school empowerment: What we say is what we are. Paper presented at the *Annual Meeting of the University Council for Educational Administration,* Baltimore, MD.

Mitchell, D. E. and Beach, S. A. (1993). School restructuring: The superintendent's view. *Education Administrative Quarterly,* 29 (2), 249–274.

The Ninth New Collegiate Dictionary. (1991). Springfield, MA: Merriam-Webster, Inc.

Ouchi, W. G. (1981). *Theory Z: How American Business Can Meet the Japanese Challenge.* Reading, MA: Addison Wesley.

Reitzug, U. C. (1992). Self-managed leadership: An alternative school governance structure. *Urban Review,* 24 (2).

Sirotnik, K. A. and Clark, R. W. (1988). School-centered decision-making and renewal. *Phi Delta Kappan,* 69.

Schmieder, J. H. (1994, May). Keys to success: Critical skills for novice principals. *Journal of Educational Leadership,* 4(3):272–293.

Taylor, E. E. (1991). Implementing school-based governance. *School in the Middle,* 1 (12).

Taylor, F. W. (1947). The principles of scientific management. In *Scientific Management.* New York: Harper and Row.

Tyack, D. (1990). Restructuring in historical perspective: Tinkering toward utopia. *Teachers College Record,* 92 (2), 170–191.

Walton, M. (1986). *The Deming Management Method.* New York: Putnam.

Weick, K. E. (1982). Administering education in loosely coupled schools. *Phi Delta Kappan,* 63, 673–676.

CHAPTER 4

School Empowerment within a Community of Learners

ROBERTA D. EVANS[1]
JERRY M. LOWE[1]

INTRODUCTION

The concept of "school as community" is somewhat unique in that it examines teaching and learning within a social context where commonality of human goals, aspirations, and needs serve as the catalyst for developing a learning environment based upon trust, collaboration, sharing, and caring. A critical component of an effective community of learners is that a natural process of "empowerment" must be in place where faculty, staff, students, and parents enjoy a sense of ownership and collegiality. This chapter will attempt to examine the roles and perceptions of principals and teachers as they consider the dynamic parts they must play in this revolutionary process.

WHAT EMPOWERMENT MEANS TO TEACHERS

While few teachers are powerless, few are empowered. Ashby et al. (1989) reported that, when asked to detail the elements needed to nurture a climate conducive for empowerment, teachers listed as their top five conditions: good communication, higher salaries, professional sup-

[1]Department of Educational Leadership and Counseling, The University of Montana, Missoula, MT 59812.

port (networking), decision-making power at the classroom level, and recognition of teacher accomplishment. Interestingly, when asked to list elements needed for efficacy, the same sample identified administrative support, responsibility for meaningful tasks, control and decision making relating to curriculum, decisions on teaching assignments, input on policies and procedures in the school, and choice in determining staff development. These items characterize the empowerment agenda sought by teachers. It is ironic, then, that, even with these conditions intact, teachers in a school may not be truly empowered. Understanding this dichotomy requires a deeper analysis of the concept of empowerment.

Traditional usage of the term *empowerment* in educational literature, at best, views it as an outgrowth of an administrative approach most likely to foster organizational change. At worst, it is reduced to a mere strategy through which school administrators delegate tasks to teachers, thereby better managing their own workloads. In both instances, empowerment is perceived as a tactic utilized by the already empowered to elevate the status of the unempowered. Indeed, it is frequently cast as a benevolent gift.

During the course of the last several years, this same concept of empowerment has been the source of a raging debate by social workers concerned with the perceived failure of entitlement programs. Currently, critics of the status quo hold that empowerment as a gift is ineffective; instead, some argue that empowerment should be viewed as a process rather than an outcome. This process involves the development of attitudes that promote the following key values:

1. Mutual respect, in which diversity is valued by members of the group
2. Critical reflection, allowing each member of the group to assess his or her own circumstances in making plans for the future
3. An increased investment in caring by and for all members of the group (Clark, 1991)

Given these values, empowerment has been defined as "an intentional, ongoing process centered in the local community, involving mutual respect, critical reflection, caring, and group participation, through which people lacking an equal share of valued resources gain greater access to and control over those resources" (Cornell, cited in Clark, 1991). Maeroff (1988) agreed, calling empowerment "the power to exercise one's craft with quiet confidence and to help shape the way the job is done. Empowerment becomes inevitable when teachers have so much to offer and are so sure about what they know that they can no longer be shut out of the policy-making process" (p. 475). Viewing empowerment in this light may better clarify its purpose in an organization; that is, teachers "taking" the power may be the logical outgrowth of schools in which principals operate in a truly collegial and collaborative fashion. This does not mean that principals are no longer in charge, but that they must understand the organizational context in which empowerment is successful. It may well be that the best description of those organizations with effective empowerment models is to characterize them as "learning communities."

WHAT IS A COMMUNITY OF LEARNERS?

One definition of community is "a unified body of individuals—a body of persons having a common history or common social, economic, and political interests—joint ownership or participation" (*Webster's*, 1985). When this definition is applied to the learning community of the school, it supports the concept of a community wherein there is a recognition of the value of shared efforts in an environment safe for experimentation. It follows, then, that effective learning communities include those schools that provide teachers, students, parents, and all stakeholders decision-making opportunities. All are encouraged to develop and share ideas, collaborate, and interact within an environment of empowerment. It is here that risk taking is encouraged and expected. Since the notion of "empowerment within a community of learners" is the heart of the learning process, it is appropriate here to examine the perceptions held by those persons who are directly responsible for its effectiveness.

WHAT EMPOWERMENT MEANS TO PRINCIPALS

While principals and other administrators share many views on the process of American schooling, there appears to be some measure of divergent thinking in relation to the issues being washed about among the flotsam of educational reform. The notion of empowerment (one of the more promising issues, although probably a misnomer) has emerged as a component providing direct challenges to traditional school organization and control.

It goes almost without saying that even though school organization and control differ in a variety of ways throughout the country, there remain many similarities in the manner in which school principals administer their individual campuses. For example, the various theories and philosophies to which many school administrators adhere obviously reflect upon the nature and effectiveness of their job performance. Close examination, however, reveals that educational thinking among school leaders is fairly similar and generally falls within parameters established by the culture and value system. Leadership and managerial skill levels are obviously different, but practitioners remain linked in similarity by the very nature of the skills themselves. Preparation programs at colleges and universities throughout the country, by providing similar experiences for aspiring educational leaders, tend to further solidify the common strand that weaves throughout the practice of educational administration.

Although many similarities exist regarding administrative practice, important differences are evident in the way principals view their professional responsibilities. Currently, perhaps the most significant difference is the way in which principals perceive the notion of empowerment. Today, more than ever before, effectiveness may depend as much upon the manner in which they define and deal with the issue of empowerment as it does any other single component of their job.

Outside the affects of demographics and resource availability, the way school administrators view organizational leadership must be considered a major difference in the way schools are administered. Very simply stated, leadership styles manifest themselves under three basic headings: autocratic or controlling, humanistic, and a combination of both. As a result, administrators generally perceive the notion of empowerment in direct relation to their individual styles of leadership.

While the more controlling models of leadership may assume a variety of forms and definitions, they share, to some degree, the basic characteristics of direct supervision and centralized authority (Hoy and Miskel, 1991). Traditional bureaucratic leaders generally possess a strong sense of autonomy and are skeptical about relinquishing any measure of authority to others within the organization. They are satisfied with "top-down" control and feel threatened by the idea of shared decision making. Obviously, the term *empowered faculty* brings on visions of anarchy or loss of power and control for principals who operate within this traditional administrative mind-set. It is necessary to mention, however, that models of bureaucratic structure do successfully exist where the autonomy individual teachers have over their students, as well as their teaching, may be considered empowering to some extent (Mintzberg, 1983). Administrators in these somewhat empowering systems possess a more liberal view of organizational control and believe that teacher professionalism means recognition for having expertise in their subject areas, substantial autonomy over their teaching, and classroom organization and control. Teachers who work in these organizations report feelings of empowerment resulting in part from input (to include a small measure of shared decision making) they have into the management and organization of their teaching (Hoy and Miskel, 1991). It would be erroneous to assume, however, that empowerment as defined in current educational reform literature is a component of this model of bureaucracy; it is not. Although some measure of decision-making authority and other forms of empowerment may be found on several organizational levels, involvement of a majority of stakeholder groups is not part of the recipe. It should be pointed out here, as well, that some administrators find themselves in positions where their individual leadership styles do not "fit" within the organizational philosophy. For example, many principals who advocate shared decision making and other forms of empowerment may be caught in a bureaucratic web, compelled by district organizational structure to operate within a more autocratic leadership mode. Effectiveness of these principals is usually inhibited, and they should either be activists for change within the district or seek positions more compatible with their empowerment mind set.

School principals who practice a more humanistic or compassionate approach to organizational leadership generally view empowerment of faculty, students, staff, and other stakeholders as the very foundation upon which total quality education rests. Empowerment to these leaders means that teachers have the authority to teach—that they have control over their classrooms and can depend upon support and facilitation from the administration. Empowerment to these leaders means encouraging the professionalism of teachers by providing an educational atmosphere where collegiality and professional interaction is accommodated—where teachers have significant authority to share in governance and are expected to contribute their expert knowledge and abilities to the school in a variety of ways. Principals who demonstrate a genuine concern and understanding for the needs and feelings of all persons within their schools view empowerment of students as a vital component of a total quality program. These principals realize that, as students become more and more responsible for a portion of their own learning, they must have the autonomy to help make decisions to facilitate and enhance their individual learning styles. Just as they depend upon the advice and considerable talents of faculty and staff members within the school, empowering principals realize that students (not just members of the student council) have the desire and capability to participate in decisions that will impact them during their educational experience.

Administrators who have sincere consideration for people believe that paraprofessional employees should be empowered with the same decision-making opportunities regarding issues that concern their jobs and well-being as are teachers and students. These administrators contend that perceptions of pride and ownership in the mission of the school among auxiliary personnel are developed only through sincere, humanistic approaches, which empower them as critical members of the total school program, seeking their input in continuous improvement.

When any measure of consideration is given to the complexities of educational reform in this country, it should be evident that the role of the principal is undergoing significant change. The days of assessing principal effectiveness by how straight the lunch line is maintained or by the continual lack of wax build-up along the corridor baseboards are rapidly coming to a close. From the autonomous director of pupils, personnel, and programs to a facilitator of teaching and learning within an environment that is truly a community of learners, the principal's role as instructional leader of the school is rapidly becoming more complex and critical. As this role continues to evolve, effective principals will be those who truly support and utilize a collaborative leadership model and who believe that empowerment, to some extent, is essential for effective schooling to occur. For the principal, this means modeling and actively supporting the elements of empowerment. In so doing, effective principals create an atmosphere within the school in which teachers, students, and staff members understand that the empowerment they enjoy is not an award bestowed upon them by a benevolent administration, but rather autonomy and power they are able to assume as professionals and concerned stakeholders. While some principals have been able to "go with the flow" and move easily into the dynamic stream of change, others have found the waters to be far too swift and frightening. In traditional schooling environments, most people view change as redirecting them away from the paths of familiarity thereby threatening their confidence and security. It is essential to foster better understanding of the principal's role in shaping an organization wherein change and risk taking are central issues of the learning community culture.

BUILDING A COMMUNITY OF LEARNERS: THE PRINCIPAL'S ROLE

For effective community building to occur, it is imperative that certain components be in evidence. First, the principal must be a trusting person with the knowledge and skills necessary to develop a trusting atmosphere within the community. Next, the principal must be sincere in his or her belief about the importance of collaborative leadership. Finally, the principal must be a model for the community by practicing and promoting the building of trust and collaborative leadership among all school stakeholder groups. Building a community of learners where parents, students, community members, teachers, and administrators consistently come together in a collegial, trusting atmosphere is not easy under the best of circumstances. However, the task can be a most rewarding experience.

DEVELOPING TRUST

The very foundation of effectiveness for any school (or organization) is trust (Cunningham and Gresso, 1993). Without a sincere trusting atmosphere that serves as the hallmark of the day-to-day operation of the school, any attempt to develop an authentic community of learners will be futile. The beacon for the development of a trusting atmosphere on any campus is the principal. Indeed, this could very well be the most important role that she or he plays. The development and continuous support of an empowered faculty/staff must be considered one of the great tenets of total school quality.

Specific approaches to building trust include group collaboration and shared decision making, where success should be guaranteed and come quickly. Groups must feel from the start that they are making progress and that their efforts are paying off. Otherwise, they will likely become frustrated and lose trust and confidence in the principal's leadership. Developing trust is a difficult undertaking at best, especially in schools where trust has become a structural phenomenon, as evidenced in labor contracts, administrative regulations, and operating procedures. It is imperative in schools that trust be less structural and more relational. Unfortunately, the connecting tissue that allows these relationships to be energized is disturbingly thin in many schools and across levels in most districts (Murphy and Hallinger, 1993). A strategy that may be empowered by the principal to foster a trusting atmosphere is, first of all, to open the budget. One of the primary causes for lack of trust and a degenerating learning environment has been due to the manner in which campus budgets have been developed. At budget time, teachers traditionally have been asked to submit their lists of "needs and wants" to the principal, who edits them to make sure the dollar amounts fit within allocated parameters. Teachers have little or no knowledge, input, or understanding regarding how money is allocated and on what criteria campuswide spending and purchasing priorities are established. Opening the budget and allowing faculty and staff members the opportunity to become involved in development of priorities and allocation of allotted funds is a fairly simple way to foster ownership and a feeling of empowerment. It is important to note that moving to a collaborative budget-building process will facilitate trust to emerge quickly among faculty and staff.

Another way for the principal to help develop trust is to model trust. In modeling trust, the principal should be open in all dealings with stakeholders. He or she should never withhold information that can be shared, nor should "under the table" deals be made. These kinds of activities only serve to erode trust and the entire campus learning environment. School leaders must be open with parents, students, faculty, and staff members within the bounds of legality and common sense. The principal who is trying to build trust should model consistency.

Critical to fostering trust is an environment that promotes risk taking. Principals whose leadership characteristics foster a trusting learning climate usually support and encourage risk taking as an important component. Trust and empowerment are enhanced when faculty, staff, and students realize that they may be "risk takers" in teaching and learning, without the fear of reprisals for failure. In an environment where risk taking is encouraged, mistakes are expected and not considered failures; rather, they are considered building blocks for future successes.

A trusting environment is enhanced when an effective, proven clinical supervision program replaces the traditional summative evaluation system of teacher performance. Cunningham and Gresso (1993) note that trust develops as people expose themselves and share and take risks together and that those personal values of respect, confidence, and self-esteem come into play as people realize they do not have all the answers and will have to depend upon each other to achieve success (p. 121).

Trust is the adhesive that bonds together all the components of an empowering environment for teaching and learning. Without this most important component, effective schooling is impossible.

TOTAL QUALITY EDUCATION

Years of educational reform and restructuring (shuffling and sparring) in this country are gradually giving rise to a paradigm shift in the way we view teaching and learning. We are moving from a closed, autonomous structure saturated with traditional instructional delivery systems focusing upon the demonstrated comparative abilities of students, to an open environment of collaboration and empowerment where schooling occurs within a community of learners—where the focus of teaching and learning is on the cultural values of mastery, hard work, and improved academic achievement (Midgley and Wood, 1993).

At the forefront of this paradigm shift is the notion of Total Quality Education (TQE), which contributes to the idea of "community" by advocating the meaningful systematic empowerment of all employees in the school, including the principal. In order to operate under the principles of TQE, empowerment must be focused upon the school community, instead of a specific group of employees or individuals. In this light, it is important to note the significance of the term *total*. There is no such system as "Partial Quality Education." The entire community of learners is empowered through a cultural commonality that bonds them together (Sergiovanni, 1991). TQE stresses a commitment to *total quality* and *continuous improvement* in the way we teach and learn, using a variety of data to assess progress and make informed decisions in a process-driven approach aimed at 100 percent quality. The following is a good example of what can be expected by being satisfied with 99.9 percent quality (Brocka and Brocka, 1993):

- at least 20,000 wrong prescriptions per year
- unsafe drinking water one hour per month
- no electricity, water, or heat for 8.6 hours per year
- no phone service for ten minutes each week
- two short or long landings at each major airport per day
- 500 incorrect surgical operations per week
- 2,000 lost articles of mail per hour

Given the evolutionary nature of American education, the benchmarks for 100 percent quality are elusive. In truth, they must be site-driven. Nevertheless, the idea is this: if we become satisfied with what we have achieved and believe that we are doing all we can do, then the system is static and everything stops. There is no more effort, no research, and no more success—only maintenance. In contrast, TQE offers a system that is dynamic and committed to continuous improvement. Coupled with effective leadership and vision, there are specific principles of TQE that enhance the development of an authentic community of learners. Specifically, a total quality educational program will (Brocka and Brocka, 1993)

- require total commitment from the school board and top administration
- develop and maintain a culture committed to continuous improvement (continuous, daily assessment of administration, teaching, and learning
- focus on meeting the needs and expectations of students and parents
- involve each employee (not just teachers) in developing ways to improve work effectiveness
- develop sense of community through teamwork and constructive working relationships
- recognize that people are the most important resource
- utilize the best management and administrative practices, techniques, and tools available

It is important to realize that TQE is not a procedure that, once initiated, may be left to operate on its own. It is an ongoing process that must be managed and assessed continuously.

Another important component of TQE and the process of building community is through the involvement of stakeholders in the decision-making process of the school. The rationale for shared decision making has evolved from a body of research that implies decisions made by groups have certain advantages over those made by individuals, such as acceptance, quality, creativity, understanding, and accuracy (Lunenburg and Ornstein, 1991). It is important to point out, however, that some research findings are inconsistent with those stated above and indicate that the real advantages of group decision making are probably not directly related to quality decisions, but to the collaborative effort itself. Indications are that the real benefits of group decision making result from gains in morale and job satisfaction through participation and increased ownership and feelings of empowerment (Hoy and Miskel, 1991). Regardless of which research camp is on target, it is important for the principal to understand the process of group decision making as an important component in building an effective learning community. In considering the nature and resulting circumstances of all decisions that any group or committee might be called upon to make, the principal should understand that, in general, groups seem to perform better if they possess at least the following characteristics (Lunenburg and Ornstein, 1991): 1) members of the group have differing skills and areas of expertise (too much difference in this area could possibly cause inter-group conflicts); 2) members are representative of a variety of stakeholder groups (students, teachers, parents, administrators, business leaders, etc.); and 3) members have a genuine interest in overall school effectiveness and not just their own special interests.

Logistics should be major considerations for the principal in establishing group decision-making parameters. If consideration is not given to such important elements as meeting places, times, length of meetings, released time for group members, etc., the process may be sabotaged before it has a fair chance to evolve. The principal should understand, as well, that group decisions should be made by consensus. Group consensus may be defined as reaching a decision as a result of each individual member making a commitment to support the decision of the majority of group members. Voting should be discouraged as a method of reaching group decisions because it only serves to dissect the group into "yea's and nay's" with neither side ever supporting the other on the issue. Consensus, on the other hand, fosters total group support. Disagreements will surely occur during consensus, but these are expected and encouraged as a necessary dynamic component of the process.

Using TQE, there are a variety of strategies and skills the principal can utilize to help groups gather data, reach consensus, and enhance the planning process. Among the most popular and readily used are the following: 1) Nominal Group Technique (Delbecq et al., 1975) allows the group to generate ideas in round-robin fashion, which are recorded on a chalk board or flip chart. The ideas are then discussed in order of appearance on the chart and voted on silently by each individual in the group. The idea with the highest votes is selected. The nominal group format allows voters to maintain anonymity. 2) Brainstorming (Osborn, 1957) allows for the generation of many ideas of great variety without evaluation. Lunenburg and Ornstein (1991) provide the following rules for effective brainstorming:

1. Do not evaluate or discuss alternatives.
2. Encourage "freewheeling." Do not consider any idea as outlandish.
3. Encourage and welcome many ideas. The more the merrier.
4. Encourage "piggybacking." Encourage group members to combine or improve ideas.

Most people feel a need to evaluate ideas as they are presented; brainstorming is very effective in eliminating this tendency. Other popular strategies common to generating and developing group ideas include variations of the Delphi Technique (Dalkey, 1969), which utilizes participants' generation of ideas through a series of mail-outs and the Nominal Group Technique (Delbecq et al., 1975), which allows for the expansion of brainstorming ideas. The Nominal Group Technique also allows for participant anonymity when final selection of ideas is made. Surveys are useful for gathering a variety of information and in prioritizing problems and opportunities. Flowcharts can be an effective tool for group interaction, in that they display a process that can be developed from start to finish.

There are a variety of other techniques that may be utilized by the principal to foster effective group dynamics and consensus building. Lunenburg and Ornstein (1991), for example, provide an excellent resource for a more complete summary of group decision-making strategies.

SUMMARY

Sergiovonni (1991) writes that we must avoid the mistake of equating empowerment with freedom. He contends that empowerment is being able to make decisions based upon common values and that there is a certain amount of obligation and duty involved. It is this "commonality of values" that separates the community of learners from a traditional, ineffective school. Members of a learning community share a common culture and display a shared interest in the effectiveness of the learning environment in their school. Teachers offer invaluable expertise to all decisions that impact teaching and learning. Further, their involvement at the outset yields broad-based support for continuous improvement. Commonality of values and culture, coupled with shared decision making under the umbrella of TQE, provide the environment of empowerment that is integral to the success of a learning community.

As the role of the principal continues to evolve from autonomous leader to a TQE leader, the need for increased leadership skills is becoming more critical. A thorough understanding of the components of TQE and the decision-making tools that enhance it will be essential knowledge for the principal as he or she serves as a vital member of the community of learners in the 21st century.

REFERENCES

Ashby, S., et al. (1989). Empowering teachers: The key to school based reform, paper presented at the *Meeting of the Association of Teacher Educators,* St. Louis, MO.

Brocka, B. and Brocka, S. (1993). *Quality Management: Implementing the Best Ideas of the Masters.* New York: Irwin Professional Publishing.

Clark, F. (1991). An action plan for personal and community empowerment, paper presented to the Alumni College, The University of Montana, Missoula, MT.

Cornell, Cited in Clark. (1991). *Empowerment Definition.* Cornell University Empowerment Group.

Cunningham, W. and Gresso, D. (1993). *Cultural Leadership: The Culture of Excellence in Education.* Boston: Allyn & Bacon.

Dalkey, N. (1969). *The Delphi Method: An Experimental Study of Group Opinion.* Santa Monica, CA: Rand Corporation.

Delbecq, A., Van de Ven, A., and Gustafsen, D. (1975). *Group Techniques for Program Planning: A Guide to Nominal Group and Delphi Processes.* Glenview, IL: Scott-Foresman.

Hoy, W. and Miskel, C. (1991). *Educational Administration: Theory, Research, Practice.* 4th ed. New York: McGraw-Hill, Inc.

Lunenburg, F. and Ornstein, A. (1991). *Educational Administration: Concepts and Practices.* Belmont, CA: Wadsworth Publishing Company.

Maeroff, G. (1988). Teacher empowerment: A step toward professionalization, *NASSP Bulletin.*

Midgley, C. and Wood, S. (1993). Beyond site-based management: Empowering teachers to reform schools, *Phi Delta Kappan.*

Mintzberg, H. (1983). *Power in and around Organizations.* Englewood Cliffs, NJ: Prentice-Hall.

Murphy, J. and Hallinger, P. (1993). *Restructuring Schooling: Learning from Ongoing Efforts.* Newbury Park, CA: Corwin Press.

Osborn, A. (1957). *Applied Imagination.* New York: Scribner.

Sergiovanni, T. (1991). *The Principalship: A Reflective Practice Perspective.* Boston: Allyn & Bacon, p. 137.

Webster's Ninth New Collegiate Dictionary. (1985). Springfield, Massachusetts: Merriam-Webster, Inc.

Creating a Climate for Empowerment

CHAPTER 5

Problem Solving in School Empowerment Environments

RIC KEASTER[1]

INTRODUCTION

Solving problems is the heart of school principals' work. For most principals, the average school day is divided into numerous interactions with individuals who desire from them a decision or authority for some action. Much has been written concerning the decision-making and problem-solving behaviors that principals exhibit. Logically, this chapter fits within this book, focusing on the role of the school principal.

In an empowered school setting the traditional role of the principal, who has total control over its destiny, is de-emphasized. Within the body of literature concerning empowerment, one outstanding characteristic that persistently emerges is that of *shared* decision making. Sharing a responsibility and a role behavior with others that has traditionally been restricted to the individual in charge requires some major restructuring of the way school personnel think and work together.

Naturally, those who will, for the first time, be participating in the decisions within their schools deserve some attention and instruction. Current empowerment literature provides this information. For those school administrators who will be required to expand their perspectives upon how quality decisions are best made, a model for their role

[1]Southeastern Louisiana University.

change is now in demand. Some questions the school principal, who now surrenders various aspects of control over the decision-making process within the school, should consider are:

1. How does one share the all-important activity of making decisions within the environment of the school?
2. What is required of the school principal to ensure that the processes and the decisions made are appropriate?
3. How does the principal share responsibility for the decisions that are made for the effective functioning of the school?

[Portions of the information that follow are borrowed from the Louisiana Leadership in Educational Administration Development (LEAD) program. From 1987 to 1994 this model was used with novice school administrators to establish within their schools the appropriate collegial atmosphere and provide them with a proven model for school empowerment. These materials are used by permission.]

SCHOOLS AS PROBLEM-PRODUCING ENVIRONMENTS

One might ask initially, "Why do schools have so many problems to solve or decisions to make?" For a variety of reasons, schools have traditionally been fertile ground for conditions that produce problems. As schools have changed in recent decades, the fertility of the soil for producing problems has become richer and the "crop" itself has become more varied in content (Willower, 1971).

HIGH POPULATION DENSITY

Many schools are overcrowded; even those that are not struggle with the great variety of racial, social, political, and philosophical differences found within their walls. Thousands of interactions are taking place every minute of every school day. The hallways and the classrooms where these students mix and mingle provide multiple opportunities for problems to occur.

VULNERABILITY TO THE EXTERNAL ENVIRONMENT

If problems do not come from within the school, many are sure to arise from without. Most members of the public have attended school and are familiar with procedures found therein. They feel this qualifies them to criticize what goes on there for they are also the taxpayers who provide for the existence of that school. The general public feel that they possess a natural right to question the decisions and procedures that take place within school. Doctors, lawyers, and other professionals deflect such interference through a highly technical vocabulary and a somewhat more complex professional knowledge base. Education, however, lacks such buffers.

MANDATORY ATTENDANCE OF AN UNSELECTED CLIENTELE

Students are forced to attend school until the age of sixteen (in most states). Where some students have personally chosen a vocational/ technical future and are forced to participate in a college preparatory curriculum, it is logical that problems might occur. Additionally, public schools (at this point in history) are not allowed to discriminate among the students they must teach. In fact, it is becoming increasingly more difficult to move problem students out of the school environment, even when the disruptions they cause make it difficult for regular instruction to take place.

SCARCE RESOURCES

Supplying instructional materials, implementing state and district policies, feeding students, providing healthcare for students, and purchasing necessary equipment place a considerable strain upon the already strapped budgets of public schools. When individuals compete for scarce resources, problems and a competitively political atmosphere emerge.

LOOSE STRUCTURE

From the time a public school policy is made at the highest level of government to the time that policy is put into effect within a teacher's classroom, many individuals have had a hand in its implementation. Large amounts of autonomy are granted up and down the ladder of authority, especially within the classrooms where the implementation of policy reaches maturity. Coordination and communication under these conditions contribute to a structural "looseness" that makes monitoring and control difficult. Problems result.

More could be said concerning the problem-producing nature of contracts, negotiations, evaluations, finances, and many other aspects of public schools. This abbreviated list will suffice to illustrate this characteristic within educational environments.

"PROBLEM" DEFINED

The simplest, most straightforward definition that can be provided for the word *problem* might be "a state of affairs perceived with dissatisfaction." The state of affairs might range from a misplaced gradebook to a potential teacher strike. In order for a problem to exist, a state of affairs (circumstance or situation) must be present.

Perception comes into play because problems, as far as people are concerned, only exist after they are exposed or when they come to someone's attention. Problems may actually exist for a period of time undetected but will not be considered as such or addressed until discovered. In order for a state of affairs to be classified as a problem, it must cause discontent with someone or among some group. If it is not viewed with dissatisfaction, it is simply an acceptable condition or situation, certainly not a problem.

The potential of a teachers' strike implies that negotiations have broken down (a state of affairs), that both parties certainly have their versions of what is fair (perceptions), and that at least one of the parties is terribly unhappy (dissatisfaction) with the situation. An impending teachers' strike is certainly a state of affairs perceived with dissatisfaction. Most problems within schools are not this serious, although an extreme example serves to illustrate the definition well.

In fact, most problems within schools are very limited in scope and impact a relatively few individuals. Problems can be labeled according to the number of people affected by them and the number of individuals needed for a decision (Hemphill, 1970).

Individual problems have a very restricted impact. Only one or two individuals may be affected. They are, however, problems that must be addressed. The misplaced gradebook, for instance, initially affects only that teacher. Unless other teachers concurrently begin to miss their gradebooks (which might suggest a larger problem), the one gradebook being misplaced is viewed as an individual problem. It will require, more than likely, no more than the retracing of footsteps and looking in the places where the gradebook might have been left.

On the other hand, if other teachers begin to miss their gradebooks, a much larger problem has emerged, and more people are required to correct this state of affairs. Heads must be put together to arrive at a solution to this *group problem* that has arisen. An apparent conspiracy is afoot, and efforts must be taken to address the problem.

Although a planned, organized approach could be used to solve either of these situations, the latter (the group problem) is most appropriate for the model discussed below. Some problems can be or must be solved by an on-the-spot decision. What to do with an injured student is not something that can be delegated to a committee. A decision is required immediately by the one in charge, whether that person is a playground duty teacher, a school nurse, or the administrator of the school.

If that injury, however, was one of several recent accidents that had occurred on the playground, a more thorough approach to solving the problem might be required. Without too much delay, an analysis of the problem should occur and an appropriate solution should be put into effect. That solution should address the specific problem and be the best one available. A more deliberate approach might provide these conditions.

THE ROLE OF THE PRINCIPAL

In the injury case mentioned previously, the school principal might choose to arbitrarily close the playground during the times the injuries occurred, restrict the activities in which students engage during those times, or increase the number of teachers on duty. Each of these solutions would undoubtedly cause other problems and may not even solve the injury problem.

Without consulting those individuals most knowledgeable concerning the problem (teachers, playground supervisors, students, etc.), a knee-jerk reaction to the situation is not the best approach. Even a thoughtful, perceptive principal might not arrive at the best solution without some collaborative effort. The age-old maxim, "Two heads are better than one" has strong application in problem solving.

Traditionally, school principals, often in isolation from other school personnel, have made all major decisions concerning the instructional program and the day-to-day activities within their schools. In most cases, this was not considered atypical behavior for school administrators nor dictatorial in style. Principals have always been responsible for the school and its students and therefore expected to make decisions commensurate with that responsibility. This autocratic/authoritarian leadership style was even sought after by superintendents and school boards.

Recent managerial trends in education have made this type of school leader practically obsolete. Although many still maintain this traditional approach to running schools, a newer, more democratic school leader has emerged and is in greater demand as each school year passes. In the evolution of organizational management, the effective manager is one who leads through facilitating the emergence of leadership in others.

Implied in this approach is the fact that these facilitators will not only use the input from their employees, but will enlist them in the effort to make decisions concerning their work and the efforts to educate the students in their charge. This empowerment enables the organization to function at maximum capacity and contributes to a climate where teachers and students feel ownership in the enterprise.

More will be noted later concerning the benefits of this approach and the reasons why this shift has been made. First, a detailed explanation of the proposed model for incorporating shared decision making within schools is given.

A MODEL THAT WORKS

Changing a leadership style does not occur overnight. It could be that years of autocratic behavior will be difficult to modify in an effort to employ a more productive leadership style. In this case, a blueprint or step-by-step procedure is necessary to lead these individuals through a shared decision-making process.

What follows is an outline of a very thorough, deliberate process for solving a school problem (or any problem) with a quality solution. Where a major group problem will allow for this type of methodical approach, the process will produce a decision that will, in all likelihood, be superior to one made by any individual.

FOSTERING ENGAGEMENT—STEP ONE

School teachers used to functioning under an autocratic leader will be hesitant to engage in a more participative management initiative, especially if the leader has been effective. They tend to break various aspects of schooling down into teacher things and administrator things. An attitude of "We teach—you run the school" is often expressed. On the other hand, if the principal has been less than effective, it might be that the faculty and staff will be eager to get their chance to make a difference in the operation of the school.

In either case, certain perceptions must be cultivated among the individuals who will be assuming these new roles (Licata, et al., 1977). First, if faculty and staff are now going to participate in the decisions that affect the operation of the school, they will have to view this new role as being low in hindrance. School personnel, especially teachers, regularly experience busy and, often, hectic days. Their first response, with regard to working on school problems, will undoubtedly be "When?"

The answer lies within the first problem they will confront. In the earliest attempts to demonstrate the power they now have, the participants will be encouraged to decide for themselves how time can be found for this effort. The question, "How can we find time during the school day to work on school problems?" will be their first challenge. Once the sparks are ignited, creative faculty and staff will be surprised with exactly how many alternatives they can produce once they get started. When they see the variety of ways time can be set aside without affecting, to any large degree, their personal productivity, the hindrance factor will be negligible.

A second belief that faculty and staff must possess is that their participation in this new activity is nonthreatening. Teachers, especially, in schools across the country face what might be somewhat benignly called "challenges." In the earlier list of reasons why schools produce problems, a characteristic best labeled "stimulus overload" was omitted. Countless interactions with students, parents, other teachers, and administrators contribute to an environment full of frustrations. Participating in an exercise that has the potential to increase the number of confrontations in which they might engage would certainly be unappealing.

This potentiality is counteracted by establishing very early an atmosphere within the meetings of trust, openness, respect, and mutual support. If this is accomplished, ideas will flow freely and the energy produced will yield fruit. If these characteristics are absent, it will be difficult to get even minimal participation from either faculty or staff members.

Participating faculty and staff, thirdly, must perceive their involvement as consistent with their roles within the school organization. As noted above, school personnel face challenges throughout the school day. In their own worlds, they attempt to solve a number of problems that will ease the tensions they regularly encounter. Problem solving then is not a new experience.

Often, the problems they face are the result of coping with the effects of some larger school problem. For example, a student in a teacher's class is regularly tardy and thus disrupts instruction upon entering the classroom. The fact that this state of affairs exists in the first place might be attributable to the lack of a concise, consistent attendance policy. If the attendance policy could be improved and consistently supported, the teacher's individual problem would take care of itself.

The point is this: if teachers focus their energies on *school* problems, many of their *classroom* problems would disappear. Solving problems, whether the school's or their own, is an integral part of a teacher's day. Making the focus of these efforts the school instead of the classroom is, in reality, a very small step.

Brainstorming

One of the most effective methods of composing a relatively comprehensive list of things is to gather a group of knowledgeable individuals together and brainstorm. Though brainstorming has been used in a number of contexts and has produced usable lists for different groups, there are rules that should be followed if the process is to be used for maximum effectiveness.

An initial concern, since part of the emphasis in this approach is to engage a large percentage of the faculty and staff, is how to get widespread input. In this case, the leader might allow a minute or two for individual meditation upon the topic, suggesting that the participants write down their suggestions. When it is time for offerings, participants, in turn, can propose an item from their respective lists until each individual has had the chance to make at least one or two contributions. This method simply assures diversified participation.

Next, *all* ideas are solicited and accepted. The greater the number of suggestions, the greater the likelihood that an effective solution to the problem identified can be brought to light. If the group is exceptionally large, it might be wise to break up into smaller groups to allow more individuals to contribute. In either arrangement, participants should be encouraged to be creative.

Participants should be encouraged to avoid criticism, of either their own ideas or those of others. Criticism, both verbal and nonverbal, stifles creativity and inhibits the flow of ideas. "Far-out" thinking is encouraged in order to generate possibilities. Within organizations there are norms of expectations and behaviors. Brainstorming should encourage members to think beyond these boundaries and should emphasize creativity and innovation. Participants should not restrict their suggestions as a result of "we-could-never-do-that" type of thinking.

Participants should be encouraged to build on the ideas of others. One productive aspect of brainstorming is that individuals are not working in isolation of others and are not restricted to their individual perceptions. "Piggy-backing" on the ideas of others is a means of compounding creativity.

Refine, combine, and modify ideas as they are offered. There may be some overlap or duplication of suggestions. When this takes place, the owners of the suggestions should be briefly consulted for clarification before any combining can take place. Once similarities or distinctions have been established and refinement has resulted, brainstorming can continue.

Finally, brainstorming should have parameters. A time limit should be established prior to the commencement of the session. Depending upon the tempo of the activity, the leader may determine to cut off or extend this limitation. Leaders are encouraged to keep the session moving. This may require an interpretation upon their part for appropriate timing to end the session.

One other suggestion should be made at this point. In order for participants to (a) use the ideas of others to stimulate their own thinking and (b) feel an element of ownership in the process, all ideas suggested in the brainstorming activity should be made available for easy viewing. While overhead projectors are excellent tools for normal display of information, chalkboards in this case might be more advisable due to the potential amount of information to record. An even better idea might be to use newsprint and tape the completed sheets on the walls around the room. This will be useful during later steps in the problem-solving process.

Committee Formation

Another consideration that will, at some point, demand attention is that of deciding exactly who will comprise the committee assigned to work through the rest of the problem-solving model. Considering the unique interpersonal dynamics that occur within schools, committee formation has the potential to directly influence the degree of success of the entire problem-solving effort.

The first concern that comes to mind is the appropriate size of the committee. Naturally, using the entire faculty and staff is unwise. Because of its size alone, the group alone could prove to be unwieldy and might preclude their direct involvement. They will, however, need to be kept abreast of the committee's progress to maintain interest, provide input through committee members, and to continue to feel a part of the problem-solving process.

Though some practitioners suggest a range of five to twelve members, a more restricted range of seven to ten might be advisable or, at least, more ideal. This number seems to allow optimum input from individuals while providing for adequate variety. Naturally, context will determine decisions in this matter, and these numbers are only suggestions.

A second, and possibly more major, concern is that of committee composition. As mentioned above, those not selected for membership on the committee need to continue to feel a part of the process. This is best accomplished through representatives of various subunits who regularly interact with the groups they represent. The committee can be assembled through volunteering, assignment, election, or a combination of these three. A cross-sectional representation of groups within the school, however, is advised.

Though every subunit within an organization might not be represented due to size limitations, every effort should be made to report to all groups concerning the progress of the committee. Often-overlooked contributors are the noncertified personnel (maintenance, cafeteria, secretarial, etc.). Not only do these individuals have keen insight to the problems that plague the school, they and the school can benefit greatly by the enthusiasm these individuals exhibit when they realize that they are deemed important to the organization.

It has been mentioned above that an early problem the committee will face will be mutually acceptable meeting times. Faculty and staff within schools generally do not have large amounts of flexible time. A suggestion might be made, while considering committee composition, to organize this group with common off periods during the day. Though this is only one way that school personnel can be released during the school day to work on school problems, numerous other suggestions will undoubtedly be made. A potential list of suggestions is included in Appendix A.

One final point should be made concerning committee make-up. Every school has its "types," and each has its value concerning contribution to a committee. The "matriarch/patriarch" has experience, historical perspective, and a feel for the community. The "rookie" possesses a totally objective orientation, unfettered by years of organizational behavior, plus the enthusiasm and energy that others might lack. The "intellectual" might possess analytical or organizational capabilities. The "wallflower" might be able to represent the views of the silent majority. The "whiner" will have value as a devil's advocate when considering negative consequences, which are detailed in later steps.

Including some of these individuals might seem logical; including others might seem a hindrance to the process or even self-destructive. However, if individual value is considered, each part might possibly contribute to an effective whole. Also, when school personnel who are infrequently consulted for input are suddenly placed in an important role within the organization, leaders often emerge. Don't overlook a potential leader.

Committee selection is important. Time should be taken to make sure that the committee chosen for solving school problems has the best chance to develop quality solutions that reflect the feelings and input of the organization.

Some of these ideas will be revisited in sections to follow. If participants can embrace these preliminary suggestions as they enter a school empowerment endeavor, the stage is set to begin addressing school problems.

DEFINING THE PROBLEM—STEP TWO

Since schools are such problem-producing environments, an initial concern might be, "Which problem will we address first?" The process under consideration will help determine the problem that deserves the group's most immediate attention.

Brainstorming for Problems

At a faculty/staff meeting early in the school year, it is suggested that the school principal initiate the problem-solving process. The principal will announce that the school will attempt to address some of its problems, but help is needed to find out where all of the problems lie. Brainstorming (keeping in mind the rules discussed earlier) could then be used to develop a list of school problems.

A reminder and a caution are included at this point. The principal should remind the participants to focus on school or mutual problems for the present and should forgo suggesting those concerns that would fall into the individual category. The caution concerns the ego of the principal and the willingness of participants to venture into sensitive areas. Principals who ask for a list of school problems will receive one of two results. They will, if perceived as closed-minded, vindictive individuals, obtain a list of safe suggestions. The list will not contain problems related to the administration of the school, potentially the area of greatest impact for organizational improvement. Teachers will be hesitant to suggest that there are problems in this area if doing so will offend the principal or, in some way, bring retribution in their direction.

In order to obtain the best possible list of school problems, principals must convincingly establish an atmosphere of openness, honesty, and acceptance. Egos must be subliminated. Stating that anything is fair game and meaning it is difficult. Principals may have to swallow some pride during the exchange, but it will be more difficult for those who have never been open to criticism. These individuals will have to be especially convincing in laying this new foundation for trust and a mutual concern for improving the school, regardless of what changes need to take place.

Problems versus Problem Indicators

The list of problems generated by faculty and staff must now be converted into something that the group can handle. Undoubtedly, the list will be long and will cover a variety of areas within the school, especially if attempts were made to include input from diverse populations. It should be acknowledged that each of the suggestions is indeed a problem, but an attempt will be made to treat these problems as problem indicators of larger problems. Clustering indicators into common groups will facilitate the manipulation of these problem indicators and will, in addition, help identify larger and possibly more important problems.

With the help of the group, the principal will cluster those problem indicators that should go together. Avoid trying to label these groups for the present; once a label has been assigned, only those indicators that specifically fall under such will be clustered there. Others that are related to this larger problem the group is attempting to define might be relevant but will be excluded. An example will demonstrate and clarify this point.

Suppose the group has within its list the following cluster of related problem indicators:

- parental complaints concerning office procedures
- parents phoning teachers at home
- poor attendance at PTA
- board members calling the principal concerning parent complaints

With this group of problem indicators, it might be tempting to assign the label "parent problems" or "parent/school communication." Consider, however, that the following indicators are also present within the larger list:

- media concern over construction plans
- local businessman upset over proposed routing of traffic
- neighborhood concerned about impact of proposed year-round schooling

Attaching a "parent" label to the first list while attempting to cluster them would automatically restrict the second list from inclusion. In reality, they deserve to be considered under the umbrella of "school/community relations" should a label at some point be desired. The group must cluster to help avoid the exclusion of related indications.

Once the original list of problems has been converted into clusters of relevant indicators, the group is now ready to select one problem area for further attention. This will be the problem the group has chosen to address in the proposed problem-solving model.

(It should be noted here that, at some point, the details of the process will be turned over to the committee that has been or will be selected for that purpose. Exactly when this shift is made will be up to the principal. The faculty and staff, or the committee itself if it has been named, might be considered for input on this decision.)

Exactly how the group decides which problem to address will be up to the group itself. Naturally, there will be pet problems that will be forwarded for consideration. A more objective means might be to examine the number of individual indicators within a cluster. Larger numbers of indicators might suggest that this problem deserves greater or more immediate attention because the evidence shows that it was on the group's mind. However, numbers can be deceiving in the larger picture of things so the group should be encouraged to look objectively at the clusters.

If a decision is difficult in coming, the suggestion to consider the educational payoff might be made. Often, one portion of the group might be focused on a cluster that, if solved, would make their lives easier. Another group might be focusing on a problem that will help students. "What will be best for the students?" can be used to sway the argument in one direction when the group cannot decide. Few teachers will feel comfortable arguing against this tie-breaker.

Problem Definition

The group (committee, henceforth) will now need to define the cluster of indicators. The attempt will be made to appropriately capture the essence of the larger problem suggested by this group of problem indicators.

It is suggested that the problem definition be framed "How can we. . . ." This phrasing suggests, initially, that the committee is faced with a question or a dilemma. Notice also that the question is phrased positively using the word "can." The result of this approach may be psychological and may even operate at a subconscious level. The intent is to get the participants thinking creatively and positively about solving a school problem.

In the earlier example a list of problem indicators suggested some problems with parents. Assuming, for the moment, that the second related list was not a result of the brainstorming exercise, the problem definition might be "How can we improve relations with the parents of our students?"

Earlier, it was noted that the problem definition should appropriately capture the problem indicators. There should be a good fit between the definition and the indicators for the sake of validity (Zetterberg, 1966). If the participants address a problem that doesn't reflect the list that suggested it, then the process and, probably, the result will be invalid and a waste of time. There are two ways this might happen.

First, the problem definition might be too broad. Suppose the problem definition adopted were, "How can we improve the school?" Obviously, the scope of this definition includes numerous indicators other than those in the clustered list. An attempt at addressing this problem definition would be too global and may, or may not, address the more specific concerns.

On the other hand, the problem definition might be too narrow in scope. Suppose the definition were, "How can we improve attendance at PTA meetings?" One can see that this effort has the potential to improve communication with the parents of the students, but it might not address the other three indicators. In this case the definition is too limited or narrow in scope. There are indicators that lie outside the problem definition and have the potential of being overlooked. Again, validity is in question.

If there is a concerted effort to make the problem definition match exactly what the indicators suggest, not only will validity cease to be a concern, but the chances for solving the problem as proposed through the indicators will be much greater. One caution, however, should be included at this point. There might be the temptation on the part of some to include within the problem definition a solution. This should be avoided. Suppose the definition were, "How can we initiate a newsletter to improve communications with the parents of our students?" This sounds similar to the suggested definition above but includes the idea of a newsletter. The danger of allowing solutions to creep into the problem definition will limit the options available in the next step when the committee brainstorms for solutions. If the definition has restricted their efforts to working toward a newsletter, all other potential solutions will have been overlooked. It is advisable to keep the problem definition free of problem solutions and leave that concern for the next step.

CHARTING ALTERNATIVES—STEP THREE

Once the problem has been appropriately and accurately defined, it is the duty of the committee at this point to generate some possible solutions or alternatives. Brainstorming, once again, provides the most thorough and broad-based list of ways to solve the problem.

This second brainstorming session in the process can be enhanced through input from the faculty and staff at large. If various members of the committee have time to discuss the problem with other school personnel, suggestions from them can be brought to the brainstorming session. Spontaneity might suffer, but other committee members might be able to use these suggestions to stimulate their thinking. As always, creativity and free thinking are encouraged and adherence to the rules of brainstorming will aid the group's effectiveness.

Once the committee has created a list of possible solutions, an effort should be made to reduce them to a manageable number. Just what is manageable is subject to interpretation, but generally, between five and ten will provide an adequate selection. It should be remembered that common alternatives might possibly be collapsed into one.

Each alternative will now be considered independently and will be analyzed according to its intended benefits and its negative consequences. This process is used to ensure that the chosen alternative will be the best solution and to allow us to develop a management plan for implementation.

Intended Benefits

Beginning with the first alternative, the person who made the suggestion should be called upon to explain the reason it was proposed. What should result will be a list of intended benefits or advantages the alternative will provide. Once the author of the alternative has spoken to clarify purposes and intent, others in the group should be allowed to make additional suggestions concerning the proposal's effectiveness in addressing the problem.

"What do we hope to accomplish by this alternative?" should be asked of the group. As suggested above, the things listed at this point will provide for informal objectives during the stage where planning for implementation occurs.

Negative Consequences

Before moving on to the second alternative, the first should be examined from a different perspective. This is where the "Devil's Advocate" that was placed on the committee will prove to be beneficial. For individuals who spend much of their professional life finding fault with procedures or the system, looking for negative consequences of a proposed solution should be relatively easy.

The questions "What could go wrong?" or "Who/What will be adversely affected?" should be asked of the group at this point. Each member is asked to think critically and try to envision as many possible drawbacks of this proposal as they can. Members are encouraged to be objective, even if the proposal under consideration was theirs. An effective, thorough means of examining effects of an alternative is to scan the organization and its various component parts (see Appendix B) (Licata, 1989). This will reduce the chances that someone or something is overlooked in the process and will throw a roadblock into the process at a later stage.

Omission of this step, considering the negative consequences of an alternative, has the potential to totally derail an otherwise good plan. It is not that solutions will be perfect. The attempt, however, will be to reduce or eliminate as many of these problems as possible *prior* to implementation. The negative consequences, like the intended benefits, will be considered during the development of a management plan before the solution is actually put into effect.

Ranking Alternatives

Once the first alternative has been critically analyzed, laying out the intended benefits and the negative consequences, the committee is ready to do the same for the second, the third, and all of the remaining proposed alternatives. Because of the depth of analysis on each proposal, it is easy to see why the number of alternatives to be considered should be limited. Appendix C contains a sample of what the charting might resemble.

Again, as with brainstorming for problems, brainstorming for and analysis of the solutions should be displayed for all to see. This is most easily accomplished with newsprint, markers, tape, and plenty of wall space. When arrayed on the walls of the meeting room, the committee can weigh one solution against the rest, assessing each proposal's value and potential for solving the problem.

It should be noted at this point that it is not necessary to choose one solution to the exclusion of all the rest. It might be advisable to combine two or more solutions into one very thorough and effective plan. A two- or three-step plan of attack is much preferred to eliminating good suggestions for addressing a problem.

The final effort in this step is to rank the proposed alternatives in order of preference. Like the decision on which problem the group was to address, the ranking of solutions might consider various criteria. The most obvious might be to look at mere numbers: how many benefits versus how many consequences? On first examination the logical choice might be to choose the alternative possessing the greatest number of benefits and the fewest negative consequences. This may or may not be wise.

It may be that, despite the large number of benefits, very few of them are significant where improving the school is concerned. Conversely, it may be that, though the negative consequences are few, they may encompass insurmountable barriers. In these cases, sheer numbers might be misleading.

There is no magic formula for choosing the best solution. The committee, its knowledge of the school and its constituency, and the perceived quality of the proposals will be the determining factors for consideration. As every school is different, every set of solutions developed by problem-solving committees will be different; the correct choice will be determined largely by context.

If a tie-breaker is needed, it might be suggested that the committee employ the same criterion used by the faculty and staff when they selected one overriding problem area to address. Examining the educational payoff or what would be best for the students will sometimes cast a different light on the perceived value of one choice over another.

A final reason for ranking the alternatives could best be summed up by the Boy Scout motto "Be Prepared!" It might be that the number one solution, as designated by the committee, encounters a major roadblock. A negative consequence that cannot be reduced or eliminated will have the potential to ruin an otherwise excellent plan. The superintendent may simply say, "You cannot do this."

In this case it is wise to have a "Plan B" ready to develop for implementation. By critically analyzing all the alternatives and ranking them during the charting phase, it will be a relatively easy step to shift gears and direct efforts to the second choice on the list. Though possibly distasteful, this accommodation will not be as discouraging as having to return to square one and start over. Much of the work for developing the management plan has already been accomplished.

PLANNING FOR IMPLEMENTATION—STEP FOUR

The last step prior to implementation involves developing a management plan. This plan will be the program for putting the solution into effect. The effort will consist of developing a set of activities designed to accomplish each intended benefit and another set of activities designed to reduce or eliminate each negative consequence. Each benefit or consequence would be listed followed by its related activities.

In addition to listing these "en route" activities directed at the various benefits and consequences, the plan will detail not only who is responsible for the activity, but will also include when the activity is to be completed and how the committee will know the activity has been accomplished. In-hand evidence will demonstrate that this portion of the plan has been completed and requires no further attention. Appendix D is a chart for keeping track of the schedule and the work of the individuals responsible for various portions of the plan.

Once the plan has been completed, the school is now ready for implementation. Much effort has been expended to this point in preparation of this moment. However, it is exactly this degree of preparation that ensures that the implementation will be smooth and successful.

IMPLEMENTING AND EVALUATING—STEP FIVE

It should be understood that no amount of preparation will take into account all problems that might arise. It has been said that, with each solution, another problem is created. What must occur at this point is a process of working through each problem as it arises. The committee by now should be comfortable with the problem-solving process and may even be able to streamline it somewhat.

Implementing the Plan

Review the problem indicators (What tells us we have a problem?) and develop a problem definition. Brainstorm for solutions; chart them, looking at intended benefits and negative consequences. Rank the choices, develop a management plan for the preferable alternative, and implement.

As this process continues, there should be a refining of the solution in evidence. Fewer and fewer problems should now be surfacing, and solving them should become increasingly easier. Care should be taken not to overreact to these unanticipated negative consequences.

As noted above, no plan is perfect and not every possible thing that could go wrong can be foreseen. The approach to handling these new problems should be to "*mod*ify, not *mort*ify." Plans can be changed to accommodate unanticipated problems without killing or scrapping the entire solution. As also noted, much work has gone into making this plan very appropriate to the problem. The age-old advice should be heeded: don't throw out the baby with the bathwater. Save the good and get rid of the undesirable aspects of the plan.

Evaluating the Solution

Evaluation is an important component of any plan, especially when solving a problem is its intent. If a plan for solving a problem fails to, indeed, do exactly that, then the problem will still exist and continue to demand attention. An observation that the problem remains is evaluation enough.

If, on the other hand, the solution has been effective, it is considered profitable to measure (a) what parts of the solution proved effective and (b) how effective the solution proved to be as a whole. This is, in effect, the extent of the evaluation of the problem-solving model under consideration.

Quantifying the success of a solution to a school problem is possible. A committee might look at the percent reduction of referrals of discipline problems to the office following the implementation of a new discipline plan. A pre- and post-survey of teacher attitudes toward some problem-solving attempt might produce data that would accurately measure the effectiveness of a solution. It should be noted that, if measures such as these are to be used, they should be included in the management plan in Step four, not as an afterthought.

What might be a better method of evaluating the success of an implemented solution would be to look back at the management plan with a qualitative approach. The committee might examine each intended benefit and ask, "Was this realized?" or "Did the activities accomplish this?"

For the negative consequences the committee might ask, "To what extent was this consequence reduced?" or "How many of the consequences were totally eliminated?" Answers to these questions might require some discussion and interpretation on the part of the members of the committee. Conclusions might lie within the boundaries of feelings or opinions.

While this sort of feedback is considerably "softer" than those of a quantitative nature, it may, however, be all that is necessary to establish that the problem has been solved. That was, in reality, the original intent. Remember, too, that the definition of a problem adopted earlier was a state of affairs *perceived* with *dissatisfaction*. If the perceivers are satisfied, the problem ceases to exist, and the effort has been successful.

BENEFITS OF THE MODEL

The advantages of employing this model within schools has three primary advantages. Most apparent is that what has resulted is that a major school problem, identified through a rather objective (but subconscious) means, has been addressed and solved. Considering the amount of effort and detail that went into choosing and planning the solution, the parties involved can be confident that they have, undoubtedly, selected the best solution that could have been developed for their particular problem.

Management by crisis, where administrators jump to conclusions and solutions that simply address the brushfire of the moment, does little to extinguish the conditions that caused the fire in the first place. The effective doctor will try to discover the cause of the illness rather than simply treat the symptoms. These examples illustrate the wisdom of approaching problems that allow deliberation with a measured strategy designed for successful and complete problem solving.

A second advantage of this approach is that it employs the strategy that the best offense is a good defense. By confronting all the foreseeable barriers to implementation prior to putting the plan into effect, the group has practically assured itself of success. Refuting the naysayers before they get a chance to speak has won many a debate. This approach simply handles problems before they have a chance to arise.

Finally, the greatest advantage of this approach to solving problems lies not in the inherent wisdom of the strategy. The most beneficial aspect of this system is actually a by-product realized by every leader who ever considered using followers to help improve the quality of their decisions. Research is replete with the benefits of shared decision making from the human perspective. Teamwork, commitment, commonality, unity and ensemble are all images that emanate from such an effort that can only contribute to a positive, healthy school climate.

The principal of a school where school empowerment has been instituted cannot ignore the wisdom of adopting a shared decision-making approach to solving the school's problems. The model proposed above is a lock-step procedure for any leader who sees or would like to experiment with the benefits of such an approach. The philosophical approach of this shared decision-making model is best captured by the following quote:

> Quality is never an accident; it is always the result of high intention, sincere effort, intelligent direction, and skillful execution; it represents the wise choice of many alternatives.
>
>   –Will A. Foster

APPENDIX A

Scheduling Released Time*

1. Use teacher aides to supervise classes while teachers meet.

---

*Adapted from "Initiating Structure for Educational Change" by Licata, Ellis, and Wilson, *NASSP Bulletin,* April, 1977.

2. Use parent volunteers.
3. Shorten the school day for students (once a month/week).
4. Schedule a work day for teachers once a month.
5. Plan a schoolwide assembly and have the committee meet at that time.
6. Schedule committee meetings to correspond to the daily planning period of members.
7. Use a team-teaching approach so that one teacher may take two classes (or two teachers take three classes) and those not teaching meet.
8. Have a committee meet on a regular daily basis during the student milk break.
9. Hire substitutes to replace regular teachers who are meeting on a regular basis.
10. Schedule committee meetings to correspond with times when special teachers (art, music, etc.) have responsibility for students.
11. Have students such as FTA members, student council members, and other students help supervise classes while teachers meet in committee.
12. Have other personnel such as guidance counselors, assistant principals, and librarians supervise students.
13. Schedule meetings to correspond with student testing conducted by central office personnel.
14. Schedule districtwide inservice days once a month.
15. Have board members and/or central office personnel supervise students.
16. Shorten all periods during the day to develop a free period (once a month/week) and plan large-group activities while teachers meet.
17. Plan in-school activities such as football games, basketball games, or recreation for the students so teachers can meet.
18. Schedule meetings to correspond with student club meetings such as 4-H, Y-Club, and FHA.
19. Dismiss school a half-day early so that teachers can meet.
20. Schedule meetings during student recess periods.
21. Have students view films or educational TV in large groups.
22. While students are having lunch, plan a faculty luncheon and an extended lunch period.
23. Use community volunteers to cover classes of teachers serving on committees. In fact, this might be one benefit of starting a volunteer program.
24. Plan a career day using community volunteers to introduce students to their careers while teachers meet.
25. Have teachers meet for an all-day-Saturday planning session. Pay

them for their time by allowing them to take an extra day of professional leave of their own choosing.

APPENDIX B

SCANNING THE ORGANIZATION

Every organization has features and aspects that can be negatively affected by decisions that are made. Organizations have structural features and social science aspects that need to be considered when assessing the impact of implementing new programs or policies.

Structural Features

Sub-units: Grade levels, departments, nonclassified personnel, etc. "How will this decision affect the various groups of people within the school?"

Programs: Chapter 1, special education, counseling, drug prevention, etc. "How will this decision affect the various programs within the school?"

Policies: Substitution, faculty leave, discipline (district), etc. "How will this decision affect the various policies already in effect within the school?"

Roles: Positions, offices, or status, whether formal or informal "How will this decision affect the various roles individuals have either assumed or been assigned within the school?"

Social Science Aspects

Political: Power
"How will this decision affect the power structure among various individuals or groups within the school?"

Economical: Costs and budgets
"Is this decision affordable? How will it be paid for?"

Psychological: Self-esteem and individual worth
"How will this decision negatively affect the sense of value to the organization various people feel? Will anyone be hurt?"

Sociological: Interpersonal or inter-group relationships
"How will this decision impact the various relationships among groups or individuals within the school?"

APPENDIX C

CHARTING ALTERNATIVES

Alternatives	Intended Benefits	Negative Consequences
A.	1.	1.
	2.	2.
	3.	3.
	4.	
B.	1.	1.
	2.	2.
		3.

(continued)

APPENDIX C *(continued)*

CHARTING ALTERNATIVES

Alternatives	Intended Benefits	Negative Consequences
C.	1.	1.
	2.	2.
	3.	
	4.	
	5.	
D.	1.	1.
	2.	2.
		3.
		4.

APPENDIX D

MANAGEMENT PLAN

Intended Benefit	Activity	Who	When	Evaluation Criteria
A. _____	1. _____			
_____	2. _____			
_____	3. _____			
_____	4. _____			
B. _____	1. _____			
_____	2. _____			

(continued)

APPENDIX D *(continued)*

MANAGEMENT PLAN

Intended Benefit	Activity	Who	When	Evaluation Criteria
C. ___	1. _____	_____	___	___
___	2. _____	_____	___	___
___	3. _____	_____	___	___
___	4. _____	_____	___	___
___	5. _____	_____	___	___
D. ___	1. _____	_____	___	___
___	2. _____	_____	___	___
___		_____	___	___

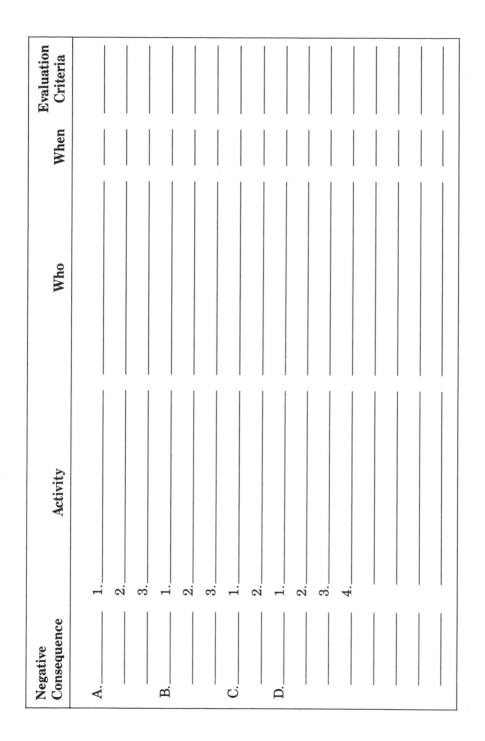

Negative Consequence	Activity	Who	When	Evaluation Criteria
A. 1.				
2.				
3.				
B. 1.				
2.				
3.				
C. 1.				
2.				
D. 1.				
2.				
3.				
4.				

REFERENCES

Hemphill, J. D. (1970). Administration as problem-solving. In *Administrative Theory in Education,* A. W. Halpin (Ed.), London: Collier-MacMillan Limited.

Licata, J. W. (1989). *Internship for the Next Generation of School Principals.* Baton Rouge, LA: Louisiana State University.

Licata, J. W., Ellis, E. C., and Wilson, C. M. (1977). Initiating structure for educational change. *NASSP Bulletin* (April):25–33.

Willower, D. J. (1971). Social control in schools. In *Encyclopedia of Education,* L. C. Deighton (Ed.), New York: Macmillan and Co. and The Free Press.

Zetterberg, H. (1966). *On Theory and Verification in Sociology* (3rd ed.). Tototwa, NJ: Bedminster Press.

CHAPTER 6

What Are the Roles of Teachers, Parents, and Community in a Restructured School?

BEATRICE BALDWIN[1]
JEANNE M. BURNS[1]
MICHAEL R. MOFFETT[1]
MARTHA H. HEAD[1]

INTRODUCTION

The significant and substantial restructuring of schools is implicit in the notions of "empowerment" and "participatory decision making." In most American school systems, traditional operating procedures, an institutionalized hierarchical culture, a high degree of role differentiation, and an emphasis on quantitative success require schools to operate in a top-down fashion. At the building level, longstanding bureaucratic norms exist in school cultures to support and institutionalize top-down processes.

Restructuring for empowerment impacts the political and social nature of the school. This view of restructuring is based on a social system perspective, that is, schools are units within a social hierarchy, and a social hierarchy exists within the school itself. The social system, however, can be changed to accommodate the needs of the individuals within the system.

The restructuring movement has dealt increasingly with governance and empowerment concerns and the issues of who should provide leadership for a school. Teacher groups are encouraging more decision making by teachers, administrators are promoting site-based management,

---

[1]Southeastern Louisiana University.

and the general public seems to be more willing to accept school decentralization.

What has not been addressed is the *how* of empowerment. How would teachers, parents, and the community participate in decision making in a restructured school? What would this type of school look like? Are there ways that a school administrator can support and encourage the meaningful participation of others in governing a school?

A FRAMEWORK FOR EXAMINING SCHOOL EMPOWERMENT

One way of examining the issue of school empowerment is to examine *themes*. These themes are derived from philosophical tenets that inform us of what schools are and what they can be. Numerous examples of empowered schools exist in the literature. These examples include schools like Jackie Robinson Middle School in New Haven, Connecticut, and the O'Farrell Community School in San Diego. Jackie Robinson is a "Comer Process" school (Payne, 1991; Elliott, 1992), and O'Farrell was restructured as a center for advanced studies for middle school students (Goren and Bachofer, 1990). In reading about these two schools, we discovered several key themes.

The first theme to emerge deals with *community*. Both schools are successful due to the united efforts of administrators, teachers, parents, students, and neighborhood residents (Stocklinski and Miller-Colbert, 1991). At Jackie Robinson a School Planning and Management Team includes parents and students, and at O'Farrell there is an emphasis on learning through community service and team teacher by teachers and peers through "educational families" that work, plan, and study together.

A second distinguishing theme of these schools is *unity of purpose*. Both schools operate under communally shared precepts that put students at the center of the school mission. Jackie Robinson's program focuses on the whole child by attending to children's psychosocial and academic needs (Zeldin, 1991). O'Farrell's restructuring plan was based on integrated curriculum and a vision of accelerated learning for all students. The schools promote their goals enthusiastically, and teachers, parents, and students alike can articulate how the programs work.

Innovation is the third prominent theme of these schools. At both institutions, the needs of students, parents, and community are addressed with novel approaches. Seeing a need to have entering middle schoolers focus more on learning than on socializing, Jackie Robinson's teachers experimented with single-sex fifth grade classrooms. Teachers at O'Farrell fulfill advocacy roles and spend part of every day listening to and responding to the socioemotional needs of students.

Another mechanism for examining empowerment issues is the analysis of *operational components*. By definition, a restructured school must involve alterations in four operational components—rules, roles, relationships, and results (Corbett, 1990). Restructuring by changing the power structure is thus a systemic activity and, by its nature, forces conjunctive and concurrent changes in all four components. For example, empowering teachers to make curriculum choices changes curriculum policy (the *rules*) while making simultaneous changes in the *roles* teachers play, the *relationships* between teachers, administrators, parents and students, and the assessment *results* that are used to judge the new policy's effectiveness.

Rules represent common understandings about what is and what ought to be—formal policy, as well as shared beliefs, assumptions, and protocols, make up the rules. Rules are the foundations of action as rules affect behavior and help to define relationships. *Roles* are regular, expected ways of acting and include what people are expected to do and what they are responsible for. Restructuring alters existing roles and creates new roles.

Relationships refer to how various roles interconnect. Both formal and informal relationships are present in schools. If roles change, then relationships must also change. Restructuring cannot be based on "hollow empowerment," that is, increasing the amount of time that staff and parents spend on decision-making activities without correspondingly increasing influence. The "right to decide" is not the same thing as the "right to advise."

Results are the products of rules, roles, and relationships. To gauge effectiveness, one must look beyond standardized test scores at a variety of student, staff, and parent outcomes. Results must be measured in terms of nontrivial differences.

By combining the examination of themes with the analysis of operational components, one can define twelve distinguishing characteristics of empowered schools (see Figure 6.1). To verify that these attributes adequately describe an empowered school, we studied a school known for being "empowered." Interviews with the principal, new and veteran teachers, parents, and children were conducted, and six hours of interview tapes were transcribed and reviewed. A description of what we discovered at this school follows.

OPERATIONAL COMPONENTS					
		Rules	**Roles**	**Relationships**	**Results**
T H E M E S	Community	Everyone must be involved	Bring together staff, parents, students, and community	Notion of partnership; division of labor	Increased participation
	Unity of purpose	Rules are shaped to fit the purpose	All parties involved have a job to do	Open, honest communication is the norm	Increased pride and morale; student achievement increases
	Innovation	Experimentation is encouraged; mistakes are acceptable	New roles created; old roles modified	Partners share vision and ideas; high level of enthusiasm	Recognition by others

Figure 6.1. A framework for examining empowered schools.

148

A CASE STUDY—AUDUBON ELEMENTARY SCHOOL

At Audubon Elementary School, a sign in principal Phyllis Crawford's office reads, "What today is impossible to do in education, but if it could be done, would fundamentally change what we do?" That outlook characterizes the operations of Audubon, a K–5 school of about 650 students and forty-five teachers in Baton Rouge, Louisiana.

Despite the fact that Audubon is located in a middle-class residential neighborhood, Audubon is a school that reflects the typical problems of urban schools. As the result of court-ordered desegregation, many of Audubon's students are bused in from the city's poorer neighborhoods, some as far as ninety minutes from the school. Approximately, 60 percent of the school's student population is from single-parent families, 55 percent could be described as "at risk," 53 percent receive free or reduced price lunch, and 35 percent are classified as minorities.

Audubon Elementary, however, is far from being a typical urban school. Consistently acknowledged for innovation, Audubon is one of the first schools that local educators mention when the discussion focuses on restructuring and empowerment. Audubon has been recognized on the national level by participating in research projects conducted by the Center on Organization and Restructuring of Schools at the University of Wisconsin and by Howard University. The school has also been honored by Panasonic Foundation, the Citizen's Education Center of Seattle (WA), *Learning* magazine, *Instructor* magazine, and the National Association of Elementary School Principals.

Upon entering Audubon Elementary, the immediate impression is that Audubon is a busy, bustling place. Audubon is crowded, both literally and figuratively. The halls of the school are lined with furniture, display cases, memorabilia, framed pictures, certificates, and newspaper clippings. The school building has some twenty-seven years of wear and tear, and there is the feeling that each piece has a story and a memory for the people who work there. Each teacher's classroom has a bulletin board or display area outside the door.

The school office is also packed with people, furniture, and sound. Everyone is moving—responding to a question, answering the phone, or solving a problem. Ms. Crawford's own office looks like the rest of the school—comfortable chairs are arranged around a nondescript, standard issue wooden desk. Framed certificates and awards are arranged on the walls next to children's artwork and mementos from former students.

The general description of Audubon Elementary School given above begins to answer the question, "What does an empowered school look like?" The responses of staff, parents, and students to our interview questions indicate the extent to which empowerment is the operational norm. Categorized by operational component (rules, roles, relationships, or results), the following perceptions and comments are compelling evidence that empowerment has fundamentally changed the school.

EVIDENCE OF NEW RULES

Everyone associated with Audubon reflects the spirit of empowerment. Parents, teachers, students, business partners, and staff possess a common vision for Audubon Elementary. The vision is to meet the diverse needs of every child in the school, and this common mission influences both formal and informal rule-making. New teachers are selected on the basis of holding this philosophy, and the philosophy is cultivated in staff and parents.

At Audubon Elementary, there is an explicit and implicit belief that everyone—parents, students, teachers, business partners, and staff—must do their share to create an atmosphere and environment that supports learning. They perceive that the expectations for students, parents, teachers, staff, and the principal are higher at Audubon Elementary than at other schools, and they strive to reach those expectations. They are also aware that the rewards are more plentiful because of the recognition that is received when risks are taken and success is experienced.

Parents, students, teachers, and staff understand that they are expected to abide by the school rules and policies. However, when the policies are curriculum related and fail to meet the needs of individual students, they know that they can approach the principal with new ideas that will be considered for implementation. Parents know that they are their children's primary advocates, but their priorities may be contrary to the principal's, who must consider the well-being of the whole school.

Students know that, while Ms. Crawford respects and loves them, she is also a disciplinarian. Children hate being called to her office—not out of fear—but out of concern that Ms. Crawford will be disappointed in their behavior. One student remarked, "She doesn't yell, but we know she means business." They know that she will attempt to meet their individual needs as long as she can remain within the policies that have been established for the good of the school.

Experimentation by students and teachers is supported. Teachers are encouraged to "use failures as fertilizer for success," as Ms. Crawford says, and if an idea does not work, students and teachers are urged to try again. New forms of collaboration are encouraged. For example, some teachers have combined two grades, and others have asked to stay with the same children for more than one year. Risk-taking has also been exhibited by Ms. Crawford, as Audubon has been one of the first schools in the school system to set up an Advisory Council, to fund a social worker to work with a newly created parent support group, and to utilize an interview team to select new teachers.

EVIDENCE OF NEW ROLES

Teachers, students, parents, and business partners are united in their belief that they have an important role in the decision-making process at Audubon Elementary. Stakeholders are aware of the fact that "no one person is THE leader," as one teacher put it, for there are many leaders at the school. Although Ms. Crawford makes some final implementation decisions by herself, all interested parties have input in the creation of recommendations.

In addition, parents, teachers, students, and administrators view themselves as an extended family. Teachers look out for each other and pitch in when help is needed. Families and teachers donate food, clothing, gifts, and other materials when a member of the "family" is in need.

Extensive efforts are made to bring together staff, parents, students, and members of the community. Art shows and school programs involving the students are held during the fall, winter, and spring of each year to encourage parents to visit the school. Parents are invited to eat with their children and watch their children perform during special student performances at a restaurant owned by one of the school's business partners. The restaurant provides the school with a percentage of the profits during these special evenings. Parents and teachers set up booths at a local amusement park, and parents are encouraged to bring their children to the amusement park on a designated date for a family night. Proceeds from the booths are used to fund school projects. Other business partners provide opportunities for students to visit their companies for field trips, and children reciprocate by creating works of art, which are framed and hung within the business partners' offices.

An open door policy is maintained at the school, and parents are encouraged to volunteer their time and energy to support teachers and students. Parents are provided a special area in the library where they may check out written materials that will assist them in better understanding the needs of their children. They are also invited to attend four parent seminars that have been designed to help parents interact with their children.

Teachers within the school are aware that they have freedom to plan activities in their classrooms that are best for the child, rather than best for the organization. Teachers provide opportunities for children to choose what they want to learn, and when students are working below grade level, teachers are expected to "push" the children at their own comfort levels. Parent involvement is important to the teachers, and they persevere to see that all parents attend parent conferences.

Parents are aware that Ms. Crawford expects them to give as much as they can give. As one parent said, "We know we have to do our part for our kids." If they are unable to spend time at school, the school is very accommodating and will "bend over backwards" to keep the parent informed about school activities. Parents are aware that the teachers expect more from their children, and their children have a responsibility to do their best.

Ms. Crawford provides her teachers with a supportive environment in which they can work. She trusts her teachers to make good decisions and holds her teachers accountable for their actions. She "taps into the interests" of her teachers and uses their expertise to improve learning and teaching at the school. Teachers describe Ms. Crawford as being "one of them—not above them." She is as actively involved in professional development as the teachers.

Ms. Crawford has been instrumental in creating new roles for parents, teachers, and students at the school. One new role that teachers and parents have assumed is that of selecting new teachers. Teachers, the principal, and, occasionally, parents are provided the opportunity to volunteer to serve on an interview team that is responsible for interviewing candidates for new positions. Interview questions are developed by the team, and the teacher candidates meet with the full team.

Once the interview process is completed, team members identify the best teachers and recommend that they be hired. Staff members report that they often bond with new teachers because of the personal and professional dialogue that takes place during the interview process. The teachers take ownership of the decision to hire new teachers and help ensure that new teachers succeed.

As mentioned previously, Audubon Elementary was one of the first schools in the district to establish an Advisory Council. Teachers and parents elect persons to serve on the council, and representatives from the community are included. The council is responsible for developing the school's action plan. The plan includes the mission statement with specified priorities for meeting the instructional and socioemotional needs of students and the annual goals. Objectives for each goal statement target enhancements in the language arts, mathematics, science, and art curricula as well as continued efforts in student assessment, parental involvement, marketing and community involvement, and program evaluation. Activities in the action plan hold parents and advisory council members, as well as principal and staff, responsible for satisfactory completion.

Among schools in Louisiana, Audubon Elementary has been a pioneer in child advocacy. Teachers made the decision to decrease the number of regular teaching positions at the school in order to have enough funds to hire a full-time school social worker. The social worker assists parents in both school and home settings and helps parents identify ways to communicate more effectively with their children. At-risk students see their parents in classrooms as parents observe teachers presenting new concepts. Parents report using the teachers' behavior as a model for their own behaviors when interacting with their children. Audubon staff also created a parent support group to assist parents of at-risk students in disciplining and motivating their children.

Students have even assumed new roles through their student council. Students are provided the freedom to recommend new ideas to the principal, and the ideas are implemented if approved by the principal. New ideas include selling lollipops as a fund-raiser, picking up trash, announcing the weather, and having teachers dress as kids on a designated day.

EVIDENCE OF NEW RELATIONSHIPS

Parents, teachers, students, business partners, and administrators work collaboratively through the Advisory Council, Student Council, parent support group, interview team, and business/education partnerships to support the vision for the school. This vision is communicated to students, parents, staff, and others through Open Houses ("the principal talks about how important children are"), memos to parents, phone conversations with teachers and the principal, home visits, parent newsletters, parent-teacher conferences, student conduct sheets, and letters from school to home.

Recognition of Rising Stars (students who have improved) and rewards to children for reading books with parents are just two of the ways that the staff foster better relationships with students. Openness and honesty characterize communication between the principal and the children. Students indicate that Ms. Crawford "talks TO us—not AT us," and "tells us everything that's going on."

Relationships with the community and with other schools have also benefited from the efforts of Audubon staff. Teachers came up with the idea of hosting a "Super Saturday" convention as a way to share new teaching strategies with other schools and as a way to raise funds. When they suggested to a national organization that "Super Saturday" could be a preconference institute for a professional meeting, Audubon teachers were told that there weren't enough teachers and other educators in the area who would be interested and dedicated enough to attend weekend workshops on topics such as whole language and using computers in the classroom. The teachers, however, were convinced that "Super Saturday" could be a worthwhile project. Banding together with community leaders and business partners, Audubon Elementary launched "Super Saturday," and the school now makes an average of $20,000 on the annual event. Teachers and principals from five states travel to Audubon to participate.

EVIDENCE OF NEW RESULTS

Parents describe the teachers at the school as being different from other teachers because of their commitment to education. One parent related, "I've never been in a school like this—at other schools, everyone knew there were teachers that, well . . . you just wouldn't want your child in that classroom. I haven't found that here." Students say that their teachers are "better than teachers we had at our old schools." Teachers describe the school as having a positive atmosphere in which to work and as being a place where they are treated as professionals— "not just teachers."

Faculty are kept informed about new happenings in education and are provided opportunities to directly participate in professional meetings and conferences. Expectations of teachers are higher at Audubon, and as a result, they push themselves further. Ms. Crawford has insight into what they can do, and she motivates them to extend their existing capabilities. Ms. Crawford encourages the teachers to take advantage of new opportunities and, as a result, about thirty instructional leaders at the school conducted workshops in Louisiana and in ten other states during the previous summer.

Teachers and students publicly celebrate what they do by hanging their awards in the halls and classrooms. Artwork of students is framed and placed in the halls and public buildings. A Student of the Month is selected for greatest gains during the previous month, and the student is honored at a luncheon with the principal.

Although test scores have increased at the school, they are not considered to be true measures of success. Instead, school personnel look at parents' feeling good about their children, children demonstrating better problem-solving skills, students thinking independently, library circulation and use statistics, parents saying "I'm so glad . . .," notes of appreciation sent by parents/students, and outside recognition of the positive accomplishments of the school as signs of success.

WHAT ARE THE BENEFITS OF "EMPOWERING" SCHOOLS?

The example of Audubon Elementary School suggests that there are numerous benefits to empowering teachers, parents, and community. The teachers at Audubon are more confident of their abilities to teach and to be leaders. They have high levels of job satisfaction despite the longer hours and more numerous work-related projects. They express pride in their accomplishments and the rewards and recognition that have come to them and to their students.

Students themselves have a higher sense of self-esteem. They recognize that teachers and the principal care for them. As one student said, "Ms. Crawford will listen to our ideas. . . . She does what's good for all the kids." Higher levels of pride manifest themselves in higher levels of participation and academic achievement. Audubon's school profile shows that only one child was suspended in all of 1992–1993, and the daily attendance rate is consistently over 96 percent. Criterion-referenced and norm-referenced results in the Louisiana Educational Assessment Program indicate that Audubon students outperform their peers in both language arts and mathematics.

Parents, likewise, have a higher level of involvement and satisfaction. The open door policy at Audubon encourages parents to express opinions and to consider Audubon as a family resource. Parents and teachers work shoulder to shoulder to provide the basics for students and their families in times of need. Parents trust teachers and the principal more when they feel that they are all on the same team.

Audubon has had a somewhat unexpected bonus from empowerment—more resources. As the school has opted for more nontraditional and innovative options for schooling, staffing, and governance, businesses within the community have supported the school. Businesses provide additional fund-raising opportunities for Audubon, as well as making direct contributions in the form of materials, manpower, and equipment.

Is there a downside to empowering a school like Audubon? The only negative aspect that Ms. Crawford and her teachers can identify is the perception that some outsiders have of the school—"When I first came to Audubon, I was told by other teachers at my old school that I would be worked to death," said one teacher. "They saw teachers' cars here late at night and heard stories about long meetings and inservice workshops." Ms. Crawford and her teachers acknowledge that there are some untrue rumors about the school and what it takes to make a school like Audubon successful; they attribute the negative impressions to the natural resistance that people often have to change.

WHAT IS THE ROLE OF THE PRINCIPAL IN EMPOWERING SCHOOLS?

LESSONS TO BE LEARNED

Our observations at Audubon Elementary School point to several fundamental lessons, which could be applied to other schools as they seek to become empowered institutions.

Lesson #1 is that *to empower others, the principal must institute a mechanism that literally and figuratively facilitates a transfer of power for an important decision-making process.* The changes that occurred at Audubon began when Ms. Crawford had veteran teachers participate in new teacher hiring interviews. She created a structure that gave staff more authority, as well as symbolically demonstrated that a new balance of power was to be instituted. This shift in authority for decision making resulted in new levels of trust and mutual respect between principal and staff.

A similar mechanism was instituted to bring a transfer of power between school staff and parents. The School Advisory Council was given the authority to set schoolwide objectives for curriculum and enrichment and to accomplish those objectives. Thus, by example and by constitution, parents and community were guaranteed a part in the decision-making process.

Lesson #2 is that *to empower others, the principal must ensure the grounding of a common philosophy.* Our observations at Audubon Elementary School showed that constituents must have a common philosophy that serves as the foundation for empowered action. Teachers, staff, parents, and students aid each other in moving forward, only when there is agreement on ultimate outcomes. By recognizing and focusing on their commonality, all parties enhance communication and avoid unnecessary conflict.

Lesson #3 is that *to empower others, the principal must view the school as a learning community.* By example, the principal in an empowered school demonstrates that education is a growth process for both the children and the adults who care for them. Professional development for principal and teachers is expected, and staff members often attend workshops and conferences together. Learning opportunities are also extended to parents.

Lesson #4 is that *to empower others, the principal must eliminate traditional role differentiation.* Phyllis Crawford, the staff, and the parents see the principal's role as being "a role model and mentor." A visitor to Audubon might have a difficult time identifying who's who. Ms. Crawford is most likely to be in the halls and in the classrooms, talking to children and helping them with their learning. At times, she may be filling the role of parent, arranging for a child's hearing aid or helping the social worker get the electricity turned back on in a child's home. Parents are active participants in classrooms and in the library, working with individual children and with small groups. The typical responsibilities of the principal, teachers, and parents are shared as all persons work for the good of the children. In addition, communication is enhanced by the perception of equitable status.

Lesson #5 is that *to empower others, the principal must make high expectations the new norm.* Instituting change to meet the needs of children is hard work. Staff members often work longer hours and make personal sacrifices to advance their professional objectives. The principal constantly encourages staff and students to do their best and to strive to reach their goals. Having high expectations, however, is a double-edged sword, for the principal must do everything possible to ensure that high expectations are met with success.

Lesson #6 is that *to empower others, the principal must critically evaluate his or her own personal characteristics.* When asked to describe Phyllis Crawford in one word, teachers and parents repeatedly used the same terms—"dynamic," "committed," and "energetic." Does this mean that to be effective principals in empowered schools, all principals must be cut from the same cloth? Not really. Phyllis Crawford at Audubon Elementary has a decidedly different style than, for example, "chief executive officer" Robert Stein at O'Farrell Community School (Stein and King, 1992). Our observations at Audubon, however, do seem to confirm that effective principals take stock of their own assets and then utilize those assets in high-energy endeavors. They accept their own limitations and collaborate with other high-energy individuals who have complementary strengths.

In conclusion, school administrators play powerful roles in supporting and encouraging the meaningful participation of others in governing a school. The principal leads, not by fiat, but by example. The principal facilities, inspires, and supports. In return, principals and schools gain much more than they ever give up.

REFERENCES

Corbett, H. D. (1990). *On the Meaning of Restructuring.* Philadelphia, PA: Research for Better Schools.

Elliott, I. (1992). A blueprint for tomorrow. *Teaching K–8* (Nov./Dec.): 34–38.

Goren, P. and Bachofer, K. (1990). *Restructuring: An Inside Look. The Evolution of the O'Farrell Community School.* San Diego, CA: San Diego (CA) Unified School District (ERIC Document Reproduction Service No. ED 334 709).

Payne, C. (1991). The Comer intervention model and school reform in Chicago: Implications of two models of change. *Urban Education,* 26, 8–24.

Stein, R. and King, B. (1992). Is restructuring a threat to principals' power? *NASSP Bulletin,* 76, 26–31.

Stocklinski, J. and Miller-Colbert, J. (1991). The Comer Process: Moving from "I" to "we." *Principal,* 70 (3), 18–19.

Zeldin, S. (1991). A matter of faith: The interpersonal aspects of restructuring in a "Comer" school. *Equity and Choice,* 7 (2–3), 52–57.

CHAPTER 7

Community Empowerment

ROBERT N. CARSON[1]
DONALD V. CAIRNS[1]

INTRODUCTION

This chapter will investigate the practice of community empowerment with respect to public schools and what theories of democracy,
political processes, and organizational behavior have to say about who
has the power to influence school policy and how it ought to be exercised.

An examination of the systematic disempowerment of communities
that occurred during the Progressive era and recent trends (spanning
both industry and education) aiming to reapportion decision-making
power will be explored.

Finally, some practices will be examined, whereby the school administrator may involve the community in determining the direction
that school governance will take without incurring a dissembling loss
of leadership. This means that school administrators need to understand the historical and philosophical concepts of democracy in a re-
publican form of government.

DEMOCRACY

Democracy is a wonderfully fluid term. It has taken on a variety of
meanings through the ages, even from the beginning of recorded social

[1]Montana State University.

history. To appreciate its flexibility, one has only to recall how, during the cold war, both sides evoked the banner of "democracy" in support of wildly divergent ideologies and political systems. Within our own society, each competing faction sees its policies and ideals as essentially democratic. If we are to use the term, then, we will need to identify which of its several meanings we intend to evoke.

At the dawn of the classical age in ancient Greece, Solon the Lawgiver was advised by an Athenian citizen to establish a democracy by his new laws. Solon retorted, "Try it in your own house first." Yet the constitutional laws he drafted did establish the first "democracy" to which our own system of governance traces its most distal lineage.

In Solon's day, as in our own, the term *democracy* spanned a wide range of meanings. The etymology of the term derives from the Greek *demos*, meaning "people." But the *demos* were, specifically, the disenfranchised mass of citizens whose interests were in contrast to the oligarchy, those land-owning families who actually held power in the ancient agricultural societies. Solon's interlocutor was asking if Solon intended to turn civic authority over to this faction. His answer was "no."

Democracy in classical Athens did not become the rule of the many but became the rule of law, based upon principles consistent with the cultural values of an emerging middle class. According to Aristotle's later account of the event in *The Politics*, Solon's task was to arbitrate the perennial conflict between *demos* and oligarchy at a time when that society was on the verge of civil war (McKeon, 1941). Each side assumed he would arbitrate on its behalf. Instead, he arbitrated on behalf of the middle class. Thus, begins that version of democracy known as "liberal democracy," which is not always to the liking of the *demos*.

Liberal democracy in government has not been rule by the many in modern times, but rule according to the values of the middle classes, especially those spearheading the conversion to mass production and corporatism as a form of social organization. How this rule was established and held against the competing interests of the disenfranchised is an intriguing story. Numerous accounts describe the effects on schooling as the industrial/corporate model was adopted (Spring, 1990; Tozer et al., 1993; Tyack, 1974).

Even within the restricted social context of middle-class preferences, the term *democracy* spans a range of meanings. There is, for example, a fairly wide breach between representative governance and participatory governance. Representative government only requires citizens to participate in the selection of representatives who then formulate policy, whereas participatory governance requires personal commitment to study and debate on policy issues. Another example is the difference between government that serves "the interests of society" and government that facilitates the rights of individuals. In our own history, in less than 200 years, we went from founding patriots who declared the inalienable rights of the individual to social scientists for whom "existential autonomy of the individual was considered dysfunctional" (Violas, 1973).

In most of America, the nation's public schools serve the interests of the dominant social group, as evidenced by the ethnographic studies of Vidich and Bensman (1968) and Iannaconne and Lutz (1970). However, this is changing across much of America, even within the traditional small rural American communities (Zlotkin, 1993; Kessler, 1992). We have arrived at a time in our own history where the dominant social group is having difficulty assessing where its interests lie, and its hegemony is being challenged by a rising tide of contention from the less enfranchised minorities. This is the realpolitik of democratic process—messy, contentious, and inherently out of balance. Whether power shall be violently wrestled away, gently conceded, or democratically shared, will be an interesting development to watch as the next century unfolds. The challenge for the leaders of our nation's schools will be how we develop strategies of inclusion for the disenfranchised in order to fulfill our educational mission.

In this chapter we will try to offer historical context and philosophical reflection, whereby the conscientious administrator might be assisted in seeing his or her own responsibilities against the backdrop of a widening democratic process. The practice of an "expert elite" issuing executive fiat on behalf of the untrained citizen is fast becoming untenable. The antagonism between labor and management, citizens and school administrators, and parents and the schools can be replaced by relationships that engage and utilize the intelligence and the constructive energies of the entire community. As a practical matter, Deming's fourteen principles offer a popular illustration of the meaning of democratic participation in the institutes of society (Walton, 1986).

The citizenry of the United States is becoming increasingly heterogeneous, increasingly strident, and defensive of individual and group rights. This creates a potential for greater conflict over the governance of schools than this turbulent profession experienced in the past (Conners and Reed, 1983). What, then, is the role of the administrator, and how does one share power without abdicating responsibility?

Community involvement in the governance of schools is indicative of a healthy democratic process, at least in theory. It will fall to the administrator to know how to cultivate the process within the community. In a democratic state, management of the public schools becomes not just an executive task for the administrative experts, but part of the critical substrate upon which an entire community educates itself. For where else, but with respect to the schools, do all of the critical questions concerning the very meaning of democracy and education converge? Where these issues are intelligently debated, a community gains critical insights by which democracy may be broadened and education more greatly appreciated. For this reason, the wise administrator seeks opportunities to host this debate and to inform it with professional understanding. In this broadened vision of the school's role in society, the administrator becomes an educator of and for the entire city. This describes an ideal, of course. The reality of American schools has been much different.

A BRIEF HISTORY OF DISEMPOWERMENT

From, roughly, 1870 to 1920, the United States went from being an agrarian society with few international entanglements to being the world's most dynamic urban-industrial power. Prior to this period, Americans were a reasonably homogeneous people, living fairly autonomous lives in rural circumstances. They were suspicious of government. They were willing and able to keep its interference in their lives to a minimum. Freedom was often associated with social atomism and a simple, unencumbered, agrarian lifestyle.

All of this began to change, as early as the mid-1800s, in those parts of the country that were becoming industrialized. Massachusetts had the first industrialized political economy, was the first state to undergo rapid and thorough urbanization, and the first to face the dilemmas of massive, ethnically diverse immigration. Not coincidentally, Massachusetts was also the first state to develop a system of state-funded and state-controlled public schools. From the point of view of the established citizenry, one of the main incentives was to ensure the Americanization of immigrant children and the inculcation of habits and attitudes conducive to the needs of the emerging urban-industrial order (Tyack, 1974; Spring, 1990).

To state it bluntly, schools were designed, in part, to serve as instruments of social control and cultural indoctrination (Karier, 1967). The "melting pot" was, in reality, a kind of drop-forge that worked with admirable certainty to ensure conformity to established cultural and social norms. Upon reflection, this should not surprise anyone, as education is indoctrination and induction into the ways of the tribe. But in a complex urban-industrial society having many and diverse "tribes" or social groups, the question of whose values prevail in determining the goals of schooling is an interesting one. It has been argued by Callahan (1962) and others that the goals of schooling during the Progressive Era were heavily influenced by the business community. This also makes a certain amount of sense, since one of the presumed purposes of education is to prepare people for their role in society, and businessmen were the people who understood most clearly where the evolving political economy was heading, since they were the ones pushing it in that direction. As a practical matter, their increased influence may have been inevitable, but the damage to democratic institutions was enormous. The very conditions under which most people lived and worked were created with very little input from the ordinary citizen.

There was nothing "natural" or inevitable regarding the evolution of the political economy of the United States—its outcome was a result of deliberate policies designed to serve the interests of the emerging corporate order (Braverman, 1974). The orthodox values of the United States were largely those of the cultural, political, and economic elite, self-assigned proxies of the predominant social group.

The very nature of human relations changed as industrialization, urbanization, and the rise of corporate forms of social organization reduced individuals to the status of cells within the larger social organism. As this process unfolded, the meaning of democracy was altered, and schools entered into practices that, in retrospect, were inimical to democratic empowerment (Karier, 1967).

One key feature of the Progressive Era was the centralization of decision-making power. Long ago, Plato had argued that the most competent thinkers ought to ascend to positions of leadership and render decisions on behalf of everyone in order to create the good society. This form of governance is known as a meritocracy—rule by those who have the greatest merit, especially intellectual merit. Plato assumed that these highly skilled thinkers would be the most virtuous people, would safeguard their own integrity, and would scorn material wealth and those base impulses associated with its accumulation. Political decisions would be rendered for the good of society. Similar arguments were evoked to justify centralization of power during the industrial era.

In contrast to the relative autonomy of an earlier age, individuals became as like cells within a larger organism, owing their existence to and taking their role from the form of the corporate whole (Lortie, 1969). Division of labor, task specialization, and a narrowly defined organizational purpose resulted in decision-making power being channelled up into the formal apparatus of an administrative bureaucracy.

Under these conditions, there is little incentive for those at the top to promote a liberally educated citizenry.

This was an age in which "the business of America" was business, and what was good for General Motors was also good for the United States. Or so went the rhetoric. "Educationists," to use Arthur Bestor's (1985) derisive term, proved ineffective in defending the inherent ethical obligations of the teaching profession. Instead, they moved lockstep to convert the schools to the model of organization utilized in business and undertook the task of supplying industry with its cadres of complaint workers (Karp, 1985).

Smaller school boards having city wide authority replaced the dozens of neighboring and smaller country school boards across America. By this means, control of the schools passed out of the locally defined neighborhoods and into the hands of the professional and business class (Tyack, 1974). Within the school itself, administrators took on the role of production managers, issuing orders and demanding accountability. The central office became a paper mill. Whatever autonomy teachers might have possessed was gradually eroded, replaced by the rule of an expert elite.

Students found themselves in school buildings architecturally reminiscent of factories, in which they were controlled by administrators, "rules," and regulations. The student body was subdivided into ability groups, which, predictably, tended to fall out along social class and ethnic lines. Black students were housed in separate schools of markedly inferior quality. Indians were shipped off of their reservations to boarding schools where their entire socialization process could be more fully controlled. While outright discrimination has been declared illegal and the most blatant abuses stopped, varieties of systematic disenfranchisement continue.

At present, school districts are still being consolidated, suggesting that the centralization of education has not been halted. As recently as 1947, there were 127,000 individual, autonomous school districts nationwide. By 1983 the numbers had been reduced to 14,700 (Burrup et al., 1988). During this time, as districts were consolidated, high school students from formerly discrete districts were gathered together into larger institutions where the corporate model could be more easily deployed.

The advent of a differentiated curriculum and tracking of students ensured that the experience within the school made the social arrangements outside the school seem quite natural. The tracks coincided with the social class divisions typical of an urban-industrial society (Karier, 1972).

Children in the upper track received a liberal education, which for twenty-five centuries has been the accepted standard leading to the empowerment of free citizens. Those in the middle track were subjected to practical "life-adjustment" courses (Bestor, 1985). Those in the bottom track career education, or vocational training, which did little to prepare them for positions on the cutting edge of technology (Grubb and Lazerson, 1975). The main effect seems to have been to ensure that all but the most incalcitrant students would eventually come to accept the new industrial arrangements as natural and would develop the dispositions needed to participate as directed (Violas, 1978).

All of the important decisions were made by a loose and informal consortium of professional education "experts" in the colleges and universities and practicing administrators who willingly took their cues from the business community (Callahan, 1962; Bestor, 1985).

Standards of efficiency, bureaucratic order, management, accountability, and productivity were lifted from the business world and applied, inappropriately, one might argue, to the public school. Unlike a democracy, in which the interests of the individual are promoted, the alleged needs of the society taken "as a whole" were preeminent.

At some point, a foundational analysis of schooling may be required to set things right. The standard foundations of educational theory are history, philosophy, psychology, and sociology. From these studies taken all together we enter into a detailed interdisciplinary analysis of the purposes, methods, and effects of educational policy. From these foundational disciplines, we may be able to return to a fundamental sense of what it means to be educated and how best to provide for effective education, who should control the schools, to what purpose or purposes does one become educated, and so forth.

History does provide some guidance, in both the uses and misuses of schooling. For example, there is a remarkably stable standard for what it means to be "educated." Ever since Plato and Isocrates worked out the basic configuration of liberal studies, the cultural effects of a liberal education have been known, at least to the privileged few. Regardless how intricate the public debate over vocational training, alternative education, various innovations, etc., people in a position of power have tended to educate their children to the standards of liberal education established long ago. A liberal education need not be grounded in the classics, necessarily, but the essential practice of equipping the mind to see the world through multiple lenses affects that liberating quality that allows individuals to master themselves and to resist mastery by others. This is the traditional meaning of education for democracy.

Classical liberal education by the beginning of the 20th century had decayed so badly that it was easily dismissed as irrelevant. It had lost the dynamic thrust of dialectic, of math studied as a style of reasoning, of literature as models of writing, and of history as the anatomy of civilizations. Instead, it had become a half-hearted worship of dead letters. "The classics" are not the only subject matter worth studying and may not be the best. However, there is some value in a shared cultural canon, which all people within a society can use, knowing that they are making references on the basis of a common allusionary pool. In late 20th century America, commercial television has assumed this role.

EDUCATION, DEMOCRACY, AND EMPOWERMENT

We know what it means to be "educated" and have known for over twenty-five centuries. People in power have seldom been confused about this—they have ensured a cultural education for their children that prepares them for positions of leadership and existential freedom. It is the education for everyone else that gets subjected to enervating debate. Are "they" really capable of receiving a cultural education? And do "we" really want them to receive it?

An institution that operates in a coercive and beguiling manner cannot prepare children for social responsibility. Yet democracy cannot ascend from its roots in anarchy without the necessary self-discipline of its citizens. It is for this reason and for the practical forum that it provides to the entire community that the school itself needs to function as a model of participatory democracy. While education ought to be going on within the school, the school itself ought, as well, to be the center of a democratizing process within the larger community. It has the unique characteristic of offering a needful focus for community empowerment.

Given our current level of political skills, full democratic participation within an open systems framework of school governance is not possible. As a people we have delegated much of our social responsibility to professional politicians and a cadre of experts, but that may be changing. The fact that decentralization of control is now occurring in business suggests that the business community itself may support the cultivation of responsible participatory democracy in the governance of schools, for it is there that the skills to participate must be learned.

There are several reasons why direct community participation in the running of schools might be considered worthwhile and defensible. The first, a kind of shareholder's argument, is the fact that schools are paid for by the community, and its members surrender their children to its care. Thus, the community has a right to be involved in the outcomes of schooling.

Secondly, with increased community involvement come opportunities for the school to acquire an extensive pool of resources. We can imagine that public education would be different, for instance, if schools had access to a large pool of individual tutors, such as senior citizens, or parents who have time available while their children are in school. So too would it be different if more people from the community shared their expertise and professional insights with students as an ongoing part of the educational process.

The third reason supporting community involvement in the schools is the notion that enough members of the community taking part in the way schools are run would make it difficult for the school to be used in cynical ways by any one group.

Fourth and importantly is the fact that the school is one of the central, defining institutions of a democratic society. The marketplace, the courts, and the halls of government also qualify as central institutions, but the school is unique in that it educates both students and adults in the ways of democracy. Any community that has gone through the difficult exercise of debating what it means to be educated will be better for it. Any community that debates the question of who is capable of being educated will look deeply into the meanness or the decency of its collective soul. And any society that actively participates in the provision of education for its children will harvest a bounty of betterment, both for its children and its adults.

In other words, community empowerment need not be seen merely as a concession to citizens who are prying into the business of the school. To the contrary, democracy by its very definition may require that mechanisms be established whereby citizens participate in a public discourse centered on the ways and means and the purposes of their schools.

There are some well defined, practical methods by which an administrator—the principal or superintendent—can invite participation in the running of the school without generating chaos or inviting a disaster. There are also ways of facilitating public debate or setting limits on the range of issues to which public debate will gain access. Still, influence over the outcome is subtle, indirect, and incomplete. A school leader, like the rudder, is but a small part of the ship—it only works well if it is correctly positioned. The role of the leader is to facilitate discussion. The leader hosts a public discourse and ensures that participants engage the issues in a timely and responsible manner. He helps to establish a mechanism for building consensus. But he cannot take people where they do not want to go.

During the Progressive era the educational elites decided the issues themselves and then went into the community for the purpose of engineering a consensus. This frankly cynical practice gradually eroded public interest in participatory government, and so we have arrived at our present state of indifference. The school administrator who tries to rekindle community interest will have to begin by overcoming the enormous inertia of indifference that exists in many communities and will likely attract a number of single-issue fanatics from the lunatic fringe before he is able to attract a more representative cross section of the citizenry to participate. Once the gate is open, it is necessary to get enough involvement that the centrists are in the majority. Adequate publicity through the local news media and a few carefully selected topics for initial debate will help get the process up and running. The wise administrator will not hold too vehemently to any particular agenda item. He or she will make use of the energy generated by one debate to launch into the next and will always make a point of urging people to think and study deeply on the issues. Schools will improve as the public interest increases. The process itself is the substance of democracy.

A REPRESENTATIVE CASE

Let us take a hypothetical situation—that of a community that is dissatisfied with its schools. Consider the scenario familiar to superintendents in which the previous superintendent has been squeezed out of office, caught unawares perhaps, in the political maneuvering between the community's old power elite and a minority whose power has grown large enough and vigorous enough to challenge the established order (Iannaconne and Lutz, 1970).

Demographic changes are a common cause of this kind of reshuffling, such as the migrations of African-Americans within the United States since desegregation or the influx of Hispanic and Asian immigrants over the past few decades. While the politics are dramatic when different ethnic groups are involved, they can be just as complex even where ethnic diversity is not the issue. Consider, for example, the influx of city people into the western mountain or farming communities or the invasion of southern towns by northerners. Even if the oldtimers and the newcomers are of similar ethnicity, they may have vastly different ideas concerning the role and methods, the purposes and curriculum appropriate for their children in the public school. If the new superintendent lacks political savvy, he will wind up the scapegoat for both groups.

Shifting demographics is not the only source of community dissatisfaction, of course, but it is an example easily visualized. If there is not a problem, then, of course, one need not try to fix it, and if there is a problem that is recognized and agreed upon by everyone, solutions should not be too difficult to come by. It is when a community is split in its thinking, especially when different groups have competing interests, that the situation becomes most complex. In such cases, it is risky to try to mediate the political controversy. It is also risky to simply play dictator and try to rule on behalf of everyone by executive fiat. Needless to say, it is political suicide to go marching blindly along, oblivious to the rumblings of discontent that emanate from the community. Most frequently, in communities that are dissatisfied with their schools, there has been a general failure to develop clear goals and a sense of direction. As Weick (1982) suggests, loosely coupled systems lack a general consensus on goals, policies, or inspection of those goals, often leading to a corruption of the educational mission with resultant conflict and confusion. This requires that the school administrator focus upon methods to empower the community to participate in some type of goal-setting process.

Community empowerment implies the establishment of public mechanisms for participation in the governance of the schools. The community already has power, but more often than not, it resides in concentrated pockets. Democratization of power occurs when appropriate mechanisms are established, but this cannot be done without first understanding the dynamics of power as it exists within the community. Every community is different, so there is no substitute for careful study of local conditions.

An administrator new to the community will face a learning curve, during which he will be especially vulnerable. The quicker he is able to diagnose the political matrix, the quicker he will be able to exercise effective leadership and begin moving toward a process of negotiated problem solving (Rada, 1989).

DIAGNOSING THE GOVERNANCE STRUCTURE

Most communities have a power elite. They tend to be conservative, in part because the status quo has already been established to their liking. Change is resisted by them because it can threaten the stability of current arrangements.

This power elite is generally reflective of an invisible government—the "power behind the throne" (Vidich and Bensman, 1968) being a few powerful families; an informal coalition of business and/or professional people; or the occasional individual who, by sheer pluck and persever-ance has become, like Benjamin Franklin, powerful in the governance of social institutions without actually holding office. This is not to evoke the image of conspiracies, but merely to recognize that political power does not always reside in official channels, nor does it operate ac-cording to the dictates of a civics class model. To look at an organiza-tional chart and assume that decision making necessarily follows those lines is simply naive. The trick is to figure out where power does reside and how it manifests influence.

In addition to the social oligarchy, the community and business leaders, the local political officials, religious leaders, and representa-tives of various ethnic and minority groups, the superintendent deals with an established governing body for the schools. School boards, over time, will tend to reflect the composition of the community. Very small factions may remain forever disenfranchised, but most groups having sufficient numbers will eventually acquire the political organization to gain representation on the board. As this is happening and a com-munity is undergoing change, the board itself can become a cauldron of discontent. The superintendent who sides with the weaker faction will likely wash out.

That said, it helps to recognize that the more general tendency of school boards is to try to present a united front in its public declara-tions. Once elected, board members realize they are less vulnerable in-dividually if their judgments appear to be made in a unanimous voice. Thus, it is worthwhile to help create conditions under which conflict can be negotiated and resolved, for at that point the board becomes a protective agency for the superintendent (Kerr, 1964).

Within the board, each member has a different philosophical orienta-tion. Some view themselves as trustees, some as delegates. A trustee is a caretaker, willing to approve the administrator's recommendations, provided these recommendations do not collide with his personal values or his perception of the community's values (Rada, 1989). At the other end of the spectrum is the delegate, who has his own agenda, which he has taken, he believes, from his "constituency." This person brings to the board meeting preestablished ideas, which he expects the administrator to implement. In order to work with the board, one needs to understand the orientation of each member, each member's particu-lar agenda, and the collective behavior pattern of the board of directors. One cannot predict group dynamics merely from a knowledge of the in-dividuals, so both forms of study are warranted—of the group and of its members.

DELIBERATE PROBLEM-SOLVING STRATEGIES

A good problem-solving protocol will help reveal the political matrix and, at the same time, will create the conditions under which political power will be channeled into some kind of rational process and structure.

Problem-solving protocols tend to include at least half a dozen distinct steps. We identify the problem, define it, brainstorm for solutions, sift the options, select a solution, execute it, and then analyze the results. If our first solution does not work, we go back into the loop, either generating additional proposals or engaging one of the ideas that was passed over previously.

Having understood how one solves problems in a systematic fashion, the next step is to figure out how to get an entire community of people, or its representatives, to adopt such an orderly approach. Again, there are numerous protocols available to serve as models.

As a representative example, let us examine the goal-setting protocol used by the Cashmere, Washington, school district. The Cashmere model is a way to set an agenda, a way to diagnose community dynamics, and a way to inculcate an orderly procedure for making progress on issues. Briefly, it works like this.

Each board member will be asked to bring to the next meeting his or her own selected team, consisting, for example, of a teacher, a noncertificated school employee, a senior citizen, a parent, perhaps a student, and a community member that is not necessarily a parent or senior citizen. The administrator can define the size and, to some extent, the make-up of these teams. If there are seven board members, and each team consists of one board member and five additional members as specified, then the plenary session will contain forty-two persons.

Each board member will act as a facilitator, providing leadership over his or her team. The team will brainstorm and focus on two topics:

1. Things I like about the school and the school district
2. Things I would improve if I had the power to do so

The first question sets a positive tone for the balance of the evening, and it tells you what people like about their school. These are the sacred cows, which the administrator will avoid tampering with.

The second question gives a measure of where and to what extent there is community dissatisfaction.

Each team member is asked to come up with, say, five items under each topic. Now the goal is to narrow this list to a manageable size, and to secure consensus on where to begin the work. Assuming a seven-member board, seven teams will generate both these lists. Now the results are compiled onto a master list, according to categories. Each participant is given, say, five gold stars, which he or she may then stick on the master list to indicate which items are most important. No one can put more than one star on any given item. This generates a rank ordering, from most important to least important, of issues that exist within a school district. Items that receive the most votes are the issues that are ultimately submitted to the board of directors for policy planning and potential action.

In addition, what emerges from the session in both the positive and negative are reported to the community at large, to the participants, and to the staff. Positive communications are maintained, encouraged, and facilitated in order to gain consensus on district- and/or school-level goals. The result is a distillation of concerns from a broad representative section of the community.

All of this has been done in one meeting. A limited number of items is presented to the administrative team to review and to develop a plan of action for prior to the next meeting. The administrator now has time to organize an agenda, assemble relevant information for the board to consider, contact any special consultants who might be needed (e.g., an attorney, a curriculum specialist, etc.) and begin preparing in advance for the next set of items.

This model gives an opportunity to analyze the nature and extent of community dissatisfaction. By observing who each board member invites to participate, it allows the administrator to understand the political sense each member brings to the occasion. It places some responsibility in the community, thus taking some of the focus, and some of the heat, off the administrator. And, relevant to democratic theory, it offers a limited forum for community involvement in the decision-making process. Any device similar to the Cashmere goal-setting process brings a controlled measure of decision making into the governance of school policy. Notice that all we have done in this case is to set an agenda for the board meetings. But it is an agenda that comes from the community by limited representation, rather than from a single administrator playing the role of sovereign over a community's schools. What has been instituted is a coping process for the open systems theory of school organizational behavior.

By asking each board member to bring together a team of participants from the community, the power of the board becomes more representative, and, with this many people involved, the influence of the lunatic fringe or the renegade board member may be effectively diluted. This process also has clear advantages over the "open town meeting" in which structure is inherently lacking. The open town meeting can work, but only in a community where democratic process is ongoing and habitual. If passions are running high, a town meeting over controversial topics is an invitation for disaster. While it is important to keep the community informed, it is also necessary to proceed by means of an orderly process. The Cashmere process can be done before a general audience, and, if desired, there can be consultation between members of the audience and those participants invited by the board members.

In this model the administrator plays only a facilitator role. He is a social host for a democratic decision-making process. He orchestrates this process but does not try to determine its outcome. Clearly, there are ways in which his expertise plays a role in this process, but it is primarily as an advisor to the process.

This is a goal-setting process only. After the goals have been set, the board has the opportunity, upon reflection, to accept, reject, or modify these goals. In this manner does the board control the degree to which the process is democratized with respect to the community.

COMMUNITY DISSATISFACTION

As long as the entire community is pleased with its schools, the superintendent's job and the jobs of other administrators will be relatively pleasant. It is when a community begins to experience dissatisfaction that the job becomes perilous. If the entire community is dissatisfied, all for the same reasons, then it should be possible to fix the problems without undue anguish. It is when a community is split that the administrator's role becomes most difficult. Trying to arbitrate between opposing factions is sometimes nasty business.

When the constituency of a community changes, there is a period of turbulence. This period may be short-lived or of a longer duration. For a period of time, the community will split—a bipolar power struggle emerges in which the established board does not represent the community.

If, for example, a new ethnic population moves into a previously homogeneous community, this group will feel its lack of representation and will begin to agitate, and from its midst will arise one or more challengers to seats on the school board. The election process will tend, in time, to create a board that better reflects the make-up of the community. But there is a "time warp" as this realignment takes place.

Superintendents who cannot understand the political complexities will not survive; under these conditions, superintendent replacement occurs within three years. The savvy administrators will avoid getting caught in the time warp.

Note that a community that is not in change and does not want change is like the "traditional" society described earlier in this chapter. The status quo is maintained to the satisfaction (or acquiescence) of the community. Innovators are generally not welcome, unless something causes a need or a desire for change. These are the so-called "sacred" communities in which tradition and the status quo prevail (Iannoconne and Lutz, 1970). Mechanisms to support change, such as the Cashmere process, can be used to keep a finger on the pulse of the community.

When a community is in the midst of rapid change, a deliberate and orderly mechanism to facilitate change is essential. Without it, the superintendent, rather than the community's real problems, becomes the focus of discontent. Each side comes to assume that replacing the superintendent will serve to strengthen its position, and the superintendent then becomes expendable in everyone's eyes. If the superintendent has, in fact, proven incapable of breaking the deadlock, then replacement may be a sensible option, but if the impending replacement is mere scapegoating, the problem will not get solved in this manner and the next superintendent will also be short-lived.

A new superintendent going into a community in turmoil must try to get it right the first time and must understand as deeply as possible the actual conditions and how people within the community have aligned themselves. More to the point, the superintendent need to enter this situation with a deliberate strategy for identifying problems, setting priorities, securing consensus, arbitrating compromise, and getting on with the business of providing for the education of the community's children. To understand a school system in its integral relationship with the surrounding community is to see the schools in the context of an "open systems" theory (Hanson, 1991). Problems of the school system, in this case, must be considered in concert with problems of the larger community. Democratization of the problem-solving process supplies the administrator with channels by which to understand what is happening out there in the community.

GROUPS TO CONSIDER

The squeaky wheel gets the grease, as the saying goes, but the wise mechanic knows the value of preventive maintenance. If properly maintained, the vehicle should not have any squeaks; thus, squeaks are indicative of a failed maintenance policy. The rest of the craft ought to be examined for signs of neglect as well.

Several components, or groups, of the educational nexus come to mind. Each community and its schools can be sifted into the community at large: special interests, parents, teachers, other school employees, the school board, and the students. Special interests might include the largest employer(s) in town or a particularly vigorous religious component. A superintendent who ignores any of these factions does so at his peril. Any of these factions can sabotage a plan that looks good on paper.

Site-based management has become one of the latest buzzwords. The practice reflects a shift away from centralized, bureaucratic control toward the greater empowerment of those people who are the most directly involved with a particular aspect of running an organization. The automobile industry, for example, has been experimenting in some factories with management teams that consist of managers, accountants, engineers, and the assembly line employees. Inclusion of the workers is the novel aspect here, along with the fact that the impromptu management team does its decision making on location, rather than at an office downtown. Decisions are made by all those who are most directly affected by the particular problem. Experience is beginning to show that worker satisfaction and output both increase as people become responsibly involved in the decisions that affect their professional lives. This simple adjustment is at the heart of recent organizational development models such as Total Quality Management, popularized by Edwards Deming (Walton, 1986).

While site-based management is not a panacea and might be ill-advised in some circumstances, it does show promise, and it does fit in with the general theme of this chapter, which is the enhanced democratization of public schooling.

CONCLUSION

Not everyone believes in the value of community empowerment. Many administrators may lack the skills or the temperament to make it work. The political climate in some communities may suggest a preference for strong, dictatorial leadership. Many communities will have to be schooled in the skills needed to participate in a responsible and cooperative fashion.

Political theorists often claim that the best governance is a benevolent dictatorship—a claim that has served to bolster the hegemony of a great many mediocrities. In this chapter we have tried to examine the philosophical defense of community empowerment, based on the traditions of liberal democracy. We have argued that, despite its inherent messiness, democracy is defensible because it functions as an ongoing mechanism of community improvement. We have also tried to bear in mind that this country made a constitutional commitment two centuries ago to the proposition that people need to participate in decisions affecting their lives.

We have argued that the school is one of democracy's central institutions. If we care about education, we will not wall the school off from the society it is supposed to serve but, instead, will make use of the school as a centerpiece of community discourse. This obviously requires capable, intelligent leadership by administrators who have some mastery of the philosophical complexities of government, education, and democracy.

We gave a brief, no doubt inadequate, account of the disempowerment that occurred in American society during the Progressive era. We hope this will spur anyone unfamiliar with the history of that time to look into some of the critical scholarship on that era.

Finally, we have tried to examine some of the cautions and some of the practical means by which an administrator can facilitate the participation of a community in the governance of the schools. We have tried to bring some degree of sober pragmatism to the occasion, in part to balance the optimism found in the chapter's opening sections. We described the Cashmere model for goal setting as a representative example of an orderly mechanism for group work.

Democracy is not a very well understood form of social organization. Its leadership principle is more difficult to understand than the neat hierarchy of despotism. It is an "organic" model, but, unlike the model of meritocratic specialization adopted earlier in this century, it is a model in which both leadership and intelligence are mysteriously dispersed throughout the community. If a society is predicated on a commitment to democratic forms of social organization, then mechanisms for community empowerment in the governance of its schools are a logical necessity.

REFERENCES

Bestor, A. (1985). *Educational Wastelands—A Retreat from Learning in Our Public Schools*. Urbana, IL: University of Illinois Press.

Braverman, H. (1974). *Labor and Monopoly Capitalism*. New York: Monthly Review Press.

Burrup, P., Brimely, V., and Garfield, R. (1988). *Financing Education in a Climate of Change* (4th. ed.). Newton, MA: Allyn & Bacon.

Callahan, R. (1962). *Education and the Cult of Efficiency; A Study of the Social Forces That Have Shaped the Administration of the Public Schools.* Chicago: University of Chicago Press.

Conners, D. and Reed, D. (1983). The turbulent field of public school administration. *The Executive Review,* 3 (4).

Grubb, W. and Lazerson, M. (1975). Rally 'round the workplace: Continuities and fallacies in career education. *Harvard Educational Review,* 45 (1).

Hanson, M. (1991). *Educational Administration and Organizational Behavior* (3rd ed.). Needham Heights, MA: Allyn & Bacon.

Iannaconne, L. and Lutz, F. (1970). *Politics, Power and Policy; The Governing of Local School Districts.* Columbus, OH: Charles Merrill.

Karier, C. (1972). Testing for order and control in the corporate state. *Educational Theory* (22).

Karier, C. (1967). *The Individual, Society, and Education.* Urbana, IL: The University of Illinois Press.

Karp, W. (1985). Why Johnny can't think. *Harper's Magazine* (June).

Kerr, N. (1964). The school board as an agency of legitimation. *Sociology of · Education,* 38, 34–59.

Kessler, R. (1992). Shared decision making works! *Educational Leadership,* 50 (1), 36.

Lortie, D. (1969). The balance of control and autonomy in elementary school teaching. In *The Semi-Professional and Their Organization,* A. Etzioni (ed.), New York: Free Press, pp. 1–53.

McKeon, R. (1941). *The Basic Works of Aristotle.* New York: Random House.

Rada, R. (1989). A political context framework for the study of local school governance. Unpublished manuscript.

Spring, J. (1990). *The American School, 1642–1990.* New York: Longman.

Tozer, S., Violas, P., and Senese, G. (1993). *School and Society–Educational Practice as Social Expression.* New York: McGraw-Hill.

Tyack, D. (1974). *The One Best System: A History of Urban Education.* Cambridge, MA: Harvard University Press.

Vidich and Bensman (1968). *Small Town in Mass Society; Class, Power, and Religion in a Rural Community.* Princeton, NJ: Princeton University Press.

Violas, P. (1978). *The Training of the Urban Working Class.* New York: Rand McNally.

Violas, P. (1973). *Roots of Crisis.* New York: Rand McNally.

Walton, M. (1986). *The Deming Management Method.* New York: Perigree.

Weick, K. E. (1982). Administering education in loosely coupled systems. *Phi Delta Kappan,* 63 (3), 673–676.

Zlotkin, J. (1993). Rethinking the school board's role. *Educational Leadership,* 51 (2), 22.

CHAPTER 8

A Guide for Practitioners to Lead Educators' Reform

JAMES E. WHITSON[1]

SCHOOL CULTURE

The most redoubtable charge assigned to the principal today is leading other educators and stakeholders through the change process. Schools are governed by regulations provided by the district, state, and federal government and national licensing agencies. Other regulatory forces are also imposed on schools by their own mores and values that tend to support those of the surrounding community. It is a unique culture that emerged from the combination of regulations and values, which dictates behaviors and problem-solving capabilities. The principal is attempting to reshape the way the staff conceptualizes the dilemma with the school functions. His/her plight is exacerbated because of an organization's success and value for the present methods of analyzing situations and solving problems.

Since it is the perception that educators are doing the best they can with the mounting perplexity of circumstances, changing by doing more will make little difference. Combining the perceptions with the fact that most educators are giving all of their time and energy just to maintain the level of competency we have reached, leaves little enthusiasm with stakeholders that educational reform is going to ameliorate the instructional program. The barriers to reform are too lengthy and

[1]Greenville County Schools, South Carolina.

complex to enumerate. Moreover, if one agrees with the assumption that school cultures are unique, then it is reasonable that barriers to change will have a related uniqueness. The suggestion that this chapter will serve as an exposé for the principal to follow exclusively is misleading. It can only deal with the principles of leadership, human behaviors, and suggested activities. Practitioners should guard against a universal remedy. What has worked in other schools and districts may not satisfy the conditions existing in your specific school culture.

SCHOOL EMPOWERMENT

Empowering the school staff is not a new concept. It has gained more notoriety in our country because it is so closely associated with the quality movement sweeping the business community. It is serving as a managing strategy used by organizations to reach their vision. *Empowerment* is a general term and does not have a concise meaning. It is important that everyone agrees with exactly what is meant by empowerment and how it will relate to each member of the staff. The principal's inability to communicate a concise meaning will result in frustration. Clear understanding of what is meant by empowerment and its purview is the responsibility of the principal. The initial step for the school leader is to remove an ambiguity in his or her own mind. A working definition will be offered for the purpose of bringing focus to this chapter. It will enable all stakeholders who implement decisions the opportunity to collaboratively share in the decision-making process and be held accountable for those decisions.

At first glance, it should be stated that educators have always shared the power with staff members by allowing them input. The difference is that the principal still assumes responsibility and controls all the resources and time allocated to any decision that met approval. Without question, this is a level of empowerment, but it has limitations and negatively impacts improvement. The reasoning for this point will be discussed as follows. When the principal asks a teacher or group of teachers to work on different school-related problems, it creates an unhealthy competition among staff members. The principal controls the boundaries of the decision and the resources to be committed. It becomes the responsibility of the staff members to convince the principal that their solution is not only workable, but that it should be supported with the resources available. The conflict occurs when other groups are vying for those same resources to fund their projects. Principals are left with the task of allocating what resources are available.

Rarely are schools replete with resources, and the result is that some stakeholders will not get what is needed to insure the success of their program. The result is: "For me to get what I need, then someone else must lose." Those not getting the resources consider themselves the losers and usually have difficulty with a principal's decision not to support their cause. An even worse scenario is to distribute resources equally. The result is that, usually, no one gets what is needed. Instead of one or two projects falling short of the expected outcomes, they all fall short. This is a lose situation for everyone.

MIXED DEFINITION

Empowerment is simple in concept and extremely difficult in practice. For a school to be empowered, the behaviors of the reformers must change. Expecting staff members to automatically make the transition from followers to empowered leader takes time, training, patience, understanding, and more training. This ability to use power, combined with the belief that they can change the future of the educational process, will determine the success or failure of empowerment. It would be naive not to recognize that external factors affect and influence our control. Keeping these external forces in perspective is vital to avoid the deep-seated emotions of futility. Once perceived that the external factors are beyond the reach of control, the seeds of frustration and hopelessness are sown. These factors must be approached with the same forethought as any other obstacles facing the reformers.

The principal must ask, "Where do I begin?" The simplest answer is asking, "Where do I want to lead?" and "What am I willing to commit of myself and others to get there?" His or her ability to persuade others that they must learn a new strategy in order to find ways to solve the significant problems is the place to begin.

VISION

"Where I want to go" or "what I want to be" is what is commonly referred to as vision. The vision is that dream of what one would like to be, but today is not. As the principal conceptualizes all the possibilities for the students, staff, and school, the first obstacles appear. It is not enough for the leaders to have a vision, but it must be shared by the stakeholders. As leaders, they should realize that not everyone shares that vision, and in many cases some have absolutely no vision. Patience and understanding are paramount for the practitioners. The principal should acknowledge that the system he or she has operated under for years has robbed the staff of the desire to dream. Dreams are connected with hope for the future and the power to make what is desired a reality. This power has not traditionally been in the hands of those assigned to implement decisions. Shared visions set the direction. The best way to find what visions staff members have for the school is to ask in a nonthreatening way.

The leader should avoid blurting out his or her vision to the staff. This approach only encourages others to paraphrase the leader's vision for no other reason than to give him or her what he or she wants to hear. Instead, a process should be followed so a collective dream will begin to take shape. The first rule is: "If the staff has no involvement in formulating a vision, it will have no commitment to it." It is better to allow all staff members to work in small groups to formulate their vision. Then, in a whole group setting, the vision can be juxtaposed with those of other groups. This makes it easier to select the things everyone can support. It may be necessary to break into small groups again and allow them to build on what has already been put together. Once again, the whole group will need to reconvene to build on the foundation. This process may take time and should be considered the cornerstone for change. The leader's skills and resolution will be tested. It is his or her responsibility to be on the lookout for the barriers that impede the process. Once identified, positive steps should be taken to eliminate them or at least abate their effect. These obstacles are people's resistance to change. Patience and understanding are important. Alienation of staff members will have a negative impact as the staff begins to work through each step of the change process. Once a consensus has been reached by the staff, it should be given a final test. This can be done by asking these simple questions:

- Who will benefit if we reach this vision? If a major benefactor is not the student, then it would be wise to revisit what attitudes the staff has about children and learning. This can be a painful moment because the staff can be confronted with the root cause of serious obstacles to learning in the school.
- Do we have to make changes in how we see problems and our behaviors to reach the vision? If the answer is no, then it is unlikely that the vision is really a vision, but rather a statement reaffirming the status quo. It is frustrating for everyone if the vision cannot pass the test; however, it is better to deal with it now than accept something that cannot direct the staff.

MISSION

The next critical step is helping the staff come to a consensus about its mission. There are many schools and districts that will argue that mission and vision are the same. This is not always true. Vision sets the direction, while mission states exactly what the purpose is. The question should be asked, "What is the reason I enter this school every day?" The leader will need to set some direction. As simplified as this may seem, it can result in fierce debate within the staff. Sometimes this can be approached by allowing a team of teachers to work on a statement of purpose. It is important to get input from everyone and share the team's progress with everyone.

The problem is how educators view themselves and what they really have control over. It cannot be denied that they are instruments to disseminate information and facilitate higher levels of thinking. The question is whether educators believe all students will learn and whether it is in their control to ensure this will happen. Convincing everyone that the purpose has not been met if students do not learn the right things can be difficult. If the staff can accept that there must be something that has not been tried to reach a wayward child, then much of your task has been accomplished.

Some children will be lost because there was not sufficient time to adjust what was being done instructionally to what was needed to help the child learn. Students' attitudes about themselves and the power thay have to control their own destiny is just as critical as anything we do in the school. This is the responsibility of everyone. This is truly an oversimplification of the obstacles to learning. It is only meant to start thinking about how important and difficult it may be to come to a consensus of purpose.

Oneness of purpose is critical and should not be taken lightly. The principal must market the mission to everyone in the school and community. It is this purpose that the leader inspects to ensure it is done by all. When the mission is accepted, then a tracking component should be developed. Principals can utilize the assistance of other administrators, lead teachers, or lead teams, but they cannot separate themselves from their duty. The purpose is the most important activity in the school and must be supervised by the leader.

TRAINING THE STAFF

As the practitioner works through the initial steps, it becomes more apparent that a major function for him or her is to support the staff through the resolution of conflict with the purpose of reaching a better end. Rapport building and training to help the staff with conflict resolution are slow processes. Leaders should not ask staff members to accomplish tasks when adequate preparation has not been taken. It is the leader's responsibility to take every measure to reduce the anxiety that occurs as individuals begin work as a team.

TRUST

The relationship among all staff members will greatly determine the quality and creativity of solutions reached by the staff. This relationship is often referred to as trust among the staff. An ambience of trust is a continuous process that is never ending and protected at all times. The best way to begin developing an atmosphere of trust is to give the staff opportunities to familiarize themselves with each other. Group socials are good because staff members become less formal in a relaxed atmosphere. Using luncheons, celebrations, or human awareness activities are a beginning. It is important to try to include all staff members as often as possible. Initiatives should be taken to demonstrate how everyone's performance affects the learning opportunities for children. A team consists of everyone—not just teachers. Clean rooms or good and positive support services should not be presumed to have little impact on learning. Dignity should be given to every staff member and every job function. Acknowledgement of a person's function helps to instill pride and will promote a positive self-esteem. Unfortunately, educators' attitudes have been jaundiced by the belief that only teachers and those in particular departments impact a child's education.

School systems have a bureaucratic culture that is defended with and without malice in their staff. The practitioner must help his or her staff realize its prejudices are barriers to trust and positive relationships. A staff member's trust of the leader will be measured by his or her skills in protecting him or her. The more a decision by the group affects an individual, the more confidence and feeling of safety must be present. It is good to begin by letting the staff make decisions that have low impact on individuals. The gradual approach permits the staff to practice decision-making skills and allows time to build the trust among each other.

SKILL DEVELOPMENT

There are skills that can be taught that will give an impetus to trust and collaborative decision making. Some skills are designed to give a better understanding of the leader and team members, while others are patterned for group dynamics. Unique individual differences will either act as a hindrance to collaborative decision making or as a strength. The dichotomy in this assumption is that individual differences will prevent creative decision making or it will not be a group decision. Instead, it will be a decision of those with the strongest will. Differences become an asset when they can be coordinated in such a way that each team member can use his or her strengths to share his or her experiences and ideas. To facilitate team members, it is good to help them understand that they all have differences in the way they learn, in personalities, in what motivates them, in abilities, and even in approaches to life. There are many instruments on the open market that will help educators better understand themselves. These activities should be shared to help break down the barriers that exist among members of the staff. It will not prove beneficial to the staff if this kind of training is a one-time event or is not developed in such a manner to be used as a tool for committee members.

Staff members need to be taught to use their individual differences as a strength. Since solutions and decisions will take more time to develop, this will require them to be more tolerant and patient. It means that the staff must move from one set of beliefs to another. As the facilitator, the principal should be alert to the emotional needs of the individual. Moving from one set of beliefs to another shatters the security people sense in their beliefs. The loss of security may be damaging to the staff member, and a strong demonstration of support and sensitivity will heighten the bond of trust and escalate self-confidence.

COMMUNICATION

Leaders should not assume that the skills of communication are understood or practiced. This basic assumption should be the first signal that productive communication does not exist among staff members. Some staff members may resent the implication that listening and communication skills are lacking. Ninety percent of what is communicated is done through the tone of voice or body language. Assuming the data is reasonably valid, it is paramount then to teach team members to be good listeners and communicators. As a listener, one needs to discipline himself or herself to focus attention on the speaker. Patience in listening is often uncharacteristic with team members. Once again, time must be taken to hear opposing points of view. Listening is impacted because, in most cases, minds have already been made up concerning an issue. Educators revert back to past habits that usually bring them to a most favored solution. Staff members should be taught to ask themselves the question, "What did I just hear?" and "Do I understand what was just said?" The better listeners will not only ask themselves the question, "What did I just hear?" but also "Why did the speaker say it?" There are some team assessment activities that will be discussed later in this chapter that will help instill active listening skills.

It is equally important for team members to be communicators. Team members can be taught to be concise and thoughtful while communicating their point of view. Good communicators are mindful of each team member and prepared to restate ideas or arguments in terms that are simple and unambiguous. The more lucid the speaker, the greater is the opportunity for solid team communication.

Poor listening and communication skills will erode the effectiveness of the team. Collaborative decision making insists that every team member be empowered with necessary information. To reach creative decisions, barriers to free information flow should be reduced to a minimum. The failure to train staff members to be good listeners and communicators will be a root cause of the frustration that team members are compelled to endure while working in a group.

CONFLICT MANAGEMENT

Collaborative decision making in its simplest form is a process in resolving conflict to reach a mutual decision with a commitment to implementation. Training staff members to recognize conflict and giving them the necessary coping skills result in a growth process for the individual. Developing conflict resolution skills takes practice by the participants on the team. The training should be divided into two categories: those stimuli that cause the individual to utilize self-control and those that cause the individual to respond to an external situation.

Teaching team members negotiating skills is a good place to begin. It causes everyone to understand that, to resolve conflict, two or more parties must be able to gather all the pertinent information for group analysis. Negotiation is the process that attempts to drive out emotion and intuition in favor of reasoning based on fact. For all the reasons previously mentioned, this is simple in concept, yet difficult in application. Helping the team member to deal with himself or herself is the first step in the training process. Until individuals are in control of their own emotions, they have little chance of defusing the emotions of another person. Moderating the anger in oneself can only be accomplished if the team member understands what causes it and what is his or her typical response. Self-awareness activities are helpful to instill the individual security required for a person to maintain his/her composure under duress. Staff members will question leaders on the value of spending time developing these skills. The logical explanation is that unfavorable behaviors exhibited during duress have long-term effects on trust levels that are essential among team members.

COLLEGIAL SUPPORT

It is not enough for the team members to be responsible only for themselves. Abating the agitation in others is equally important to the team. Identifying the emotionally unhealthy staff members and supporting them are the obligations of everyone. Principals can plan activities that are designed to give staff members the opportunity to assist those under duress. Collegial support teams will give team members an opportunity to express concerns with their peers. They provide a forum for sharing and emotional support.

Collegial support teams should be organized to allow maximum candor from all members. Principals should encourage staff members to vent frustration but should not allow the support teams to turn the meeting into complaining sessions. This is critical in developing a proactive and productive atmosphere in the school. When venting frustration, help is sought from others experiencing similar problems and circumstances. It is a time for sharing to lead to something positive. The positive results should take the form of either direct intervention of just a sympathetic listener.

Collegial support teams used as complaining sessions will prove to be destructive to the school because of their demoralizing effect on the staff members. Blaming, finding fault, and unproductive criticism add no value to the program. Unchecked, these emotions and feelings will prohibit the team and school from being able to reach a consensus.

School growth will depend on the support of the staff. Support means that a critical mass of staff members actively support the reforms being considered. The remainder of these staff needs are somewhere between "I'm not willing to take part until I see more evidence that this will work" and "I'm doing it because I want to support the school or team."

SABOTEUR ACTIVITY

A negative by-product of emotion or fear is the attempt to destroy the root cause of the distress or anxiety. The individual becomes a saboteur. Some individuals are open and actually easier to control because the leader knows where they stand on the issues and can take measures to moderate their attempts to undermine the program.

A much more difficult group of saboteurs is one whose members are not open, in which their actions are concealed or disguised as something else. These acts are usually associated with deep feelings of resentment by the individual. The leader has to be open to subtle signs that saboteurs are at work. Usually, it begins when staff members attempt to evaluate the program in a distorted point of view. They will acknowledge the shortcomings of not only the program, but staff members that actively support the reforms. Certainly, the attempts are to first create dissatisfaction, then gain support to their view. There are several ways to deal with the situation. One is an attempt to help the saboteurs see the program from a different point of view by actively getting them involved. This would be ideal if it worked; however, this should be monitored closely because the program is at risk.

It may become necessary to confront the saboteurs and demand that they move at least to a level of "wait-and-see" how the program is going to work. Albeit, when dealing with saboteurs, the leaders are just as responsible to protect them as they would their closest ally. If the leader doesn't, then the next best solution is to try to arrange a separation by mutual consent. The belief that these individuals can be isolated and that everything will heal itself in time is misleading and rarely results in a harmonious staff.

STAFF CONGRUENCE

The congruity of the staff is affected by the very nature of the process to which they are being subjected. It is important that teams move forward at their own pace of development. Principals and leaders with the staff need to be aware that groups work through stages. Teams begin with conceptualizing visions, situations, and ideas and progress to an implementation of plans. In between these ends, groups will debate the issues, identify their differences with each member, and resolve the points of agreement and disagreement. As team members become more skilled at understanding these stages, it is easier for staff members to be patient with each other. Too often, leaders assume that these stages will occur as a natural process. The truth is that a person's own impatience causes him/her to move too quickly, resulting in the previously mentioned attitudes and emotions.

Teams can be taught to recognize the steps and actually discuss how they are progressing. These open discussions will help flush out the anxiety that builds within the team. It builds trust and confidence that team members must share among themselves. It actually helps model for teachers how important it is to exercise restraint when their classes are not moving at their desired pace. It is in the debate stage that frustration is experienced.

Educators sometimes find their values and beliefs challenged. They perceive that what they have done successfully for years is no longer valued or being debased for something untried. It is in this stage that the most unhealthy and unproductive motivation will first appear. Simple discussions by team members about these natural human responses to conflict will prove to be healthy for group growth. In this stage strict team rules should be adhered to by team members concerning the dignity and worth of each member. Rules about worth and dignity will be discussed later in this chapter.

As emotional and combative as the debate stage is, the implementation stage can be just as rewarding. The team has been forced to go through such a demanding process that they should come out a transformed team of individuals. Team members will know more about each other at this point and will build on their trust within the group. If they can agree that they disagree without emotion, much has been gained even if the reform efforts do not produce the outcomes desired or expected. The more the principal can expose staff members to this process, the better. Once again, it is better to start slowly. Give staff members time to internalize the process. Leaders should select areas where, in the beginning, there is little disagreement. The avoidance of decisions that attack the core of the staff's long time value will allow the time for the team to mature to a level that such issues can be confronted.

When the teams get to the implementation stage, readiness becomes an issue. If the staff does not understand exactly all its responsibilities or have the means to accomplish them, then implementation should be delayed. At a time when the staff may have its most enthusiasm, the leader may have to call a halt until he or she is satisfied that everyone knows what needs to be done and how it will be accomplished. The staff must know how to communicate in exchanging the necessary information from individual to individual. This communication is vital to keep track of unexpected problems or to fine-tune the process that will occur in the implementation stage. It is equally important that the staff believe it can work collectively as individuals to reach the desired outcomes. If the team still needs direction or continues to debate, then a halt is better than jeopardizing what has been accomplished. There are several activities designed to give the principals and teams this information. Taking the time to find out if everyone understands what needs to be done and that he/she can make it happen once again models that the principal can be trusted. The objective is to succeed. If time has to be spent revisiting some issues, then it will be in everyone's best interest to show patience.

Once the implementation has begun, good leaders should prepare themselves, as well as members of the staff, for all systems having an impact on humans. In a reform process there is usually some anxiety in the individual and the staff as a whole. In the new process many of the beliefs and habits that were effective in the former system do not apply. It is a natural instinct to revert to old behaviors in times of distress. This instinct will erode the effectiveness of the new process and leave staff members confused and frustrated. It can result in a loss of self-confidence and doubts about an individual's abilities. This seems to affect the veteran teachers that experienced success in the old process but are experiencing problems in the new system. This situation is exacerbated when peers are reporting their success. This loss of confidence, once again, encourages some staff members to resist the new process.

Depending on the severity of discouragement, it is easy for frustrated staff members to lose the desire to work within the new system, and they may begin to sabotage the work that has been done. Other feelings may also occur that, in the scope of the entire process, may seem insignificant. Actually, failure to address these situations with support and comfort will have a long-term effect on the staff.

Reform is not a one-time event. If staff members feel they have lost the prestige and status they once possessed, they are not as willing to give their support or accept the next round of changes. The reform process is continuous, and leaders cannot afford to isolate staff members simply because systems have some negative effects on people. This is where collegial support teams can be most helpful. Leaders should exercise their best listening skills. Stroking is not enough. Leaders need to find out how things are progressing and be ready to provide whatever support is required until the staff member can cope with the situation. The change process is difficult, if not intractable, and it is best to keep emotional highs and lows to a minimum.

Leaders must monitor their own emotions. Being positive is a must; however, too much praise to individuals or small groups for early success can lead to frustration later when more difficult solutions cannot be reached. This happens when the team is trying to please the leader instead of working to solve problems. Praise is important for groups and individuals, but is harmful if it causes the team to lose its primary focus.

TEAM BUILDING

Teams will work with great intensity and diligence as they become more involved in the process. Combine this intensity with the difficult task of carrying on the daily operations, and new fatigue problems will begin to emerge. Fatigue will lead to anxiety and restlessness within the staff. Leaders need to train their staff in recognizing the absurdity in what is being done. Releasing stress and tension is a skill and should be taken very seriously. Leaders should model taking their work seriously but, at the same time, realize that their work is just one part of their selves. It is important to be on guard to note that either an individual's personality or that of his/her peers is changing as a result of work.

Leaders must help the staff members learn to laugh at themselves and the circumstances of the environment in which they are working. This is a maxim that has been preached for many years, yet it is one that is rarely practiced except by the more effective individuals or organizations. Dysphoria will detract from the performance of the individual, and assuming everyone is a link in the chain to learning, then the symptoms of the individual will propagate throughout the organization. Anxiety, restlessness, and depression are just as contagious as enthusiasm. The leader's failure to build into the process healthy degrees of silliness will have long-term effects on performance.

SITUATION STUDY

Emotionally healthy staff members are a result of planning and skill and not chance. Staff must be trained to use processes to insure the most efficient use of time and energy as the team begins its restructuring process. The beginning step is "how-to-do" situation studies. Normally, if staff members are asked what is wrong, they can tell who is at fault and why the situation exists. It is rare that individuals being questioned ever admit they are the problem or that things under their control have led to the current state of affairs. Albeit this statement is undocumented, it exists in most schools.

Positive situation studies and the collection of data will help to clarify exactly what is presently taking place. The emphasis is not seeking blame, but identifying all the factors that exist in the current operation of the school. Once the real situation can be separated from the perceived, then proper steps can be taken to improve.

Principals must help staff members to ask the right questions as they begin to do a self-study. It is easy to steer the research into the areas that are already believed to be a problem. Not controlled, the planners of this activity will design the study in one direction versus trying to understand all the processes and their relationship to each other. The more accurately and precisely a situation is examined, the more efficiently one can determine the influence the processes are having on learning. This tends to set the tone for understanding versus our own personal biases. If done improperly, the long-term effect of this step will cause leaders to be misguided in attempts to reform. This then will only strengthen the belief in the intractability of the educational process.

Once leaders have determined that everything that can be done has been done and nothing significant changes, then they are less likely to continue in the reform process. Leaders should be willing to return to this initial step if beginning action steps do not produce the desired outcomes for children. This will be frustrating to the staff; however, if it is the root cause of the problems, then it will continue to inhibit progress, or success will be a simple matter of chance. Even when successful, staffs should study how their solutions have impacted the functions as they existed at the time of the study.

PROBLEM IDENTIFICATION

Once the situation study is complete, the staff can begin to identify the problem that has caused the deviation between the vision and the real situation. An important step is to clearly state what the problem is. This will help the team maintain its focus on exactly what solution it is seeking. In many cases, the root cause of educational problems involves more than a single solution. This will make it difficult for the staff to analyze the impact of a single solution. Usually, educators are going to be asking themselves why their students are underachieving—whether they are the best students or those in danger of losing all hope of being successful.

It will be helpful if the staff can identify and test one solution at a time. This will not be possible if the solution will take a long time before the staff begins to see positive results. In those cases the staff may have to pilot or totally implement all solutions at once. Logical problem identification does not seek to blame. This point should continually be instilled in the staff.

If the trust level is high, the staff members will more likely take an active part in the problem identification process. To maintain the confidence of the staff, the process of problem identification should be communicated and followed. This serves several purposes. It allows everyone to understand how problems were identified, which permits the process itself to be evaluated. It will also add to the feeling of security that individuals need, especially in the areas where problems are associated with a particular department or grade level.

DECISION MAKING

When problems have been properly identified, a decision-making process should be used to sort through all the possible alternatives. A common technique is to list everything the solution must do, as well as everything wanted to be done. Resources should not be left out of the process. Teams may want to weigh the potential solutions in this way: one that best suits the needs with the present resources and others that would be more effective with greater resources. This systemic approach to decision making takes the emotion out of the process. It helps individuals realize that what they perceive as the best or only alternative may not be true.

Decision-making processes will make it easier to gain a consensus. The fact that decisions are made by a weighted system removes the winner and loser. The alternatives will stand on their own merit. It is even possible, after comparing alternatives, to modify the best solutions once it is realized that weaknesses exist. This will renew opportunities for staff members to be involved. It is a means to help generate creativity in group decision making. A decision-making process will create an audible trail for the team.

On the occasions that solutions do not work, the team can review what did not occur in the plan and then compare that to their process. This will be most helpful for the team to recognize what was wrong about the way they saw the problem. The team can now begin work to correct and improve. No fault is associated with anyone. It is simply part of the school's culture that needs refinement. This is not to imply that staff members are never the cause, but when that is the circumstance, then it is always best to work through those situations with facts. This helps the leader show the individual where he or she is out-of-step with the staff, and procedures can be made to take appropriate action.

IMPLEMENTATION

Once all of these steps have been taken, the staff will have to agree on an implementation model. A good model begins by comparing the plan with the desired outcomes. The staff should ask simple questions about the plan. "What will likely go wrong?" "How can we either avert the situation or minimize the impact?" This kind of thinking prior to actual implementation removes some of the anxiety the staff will feel. It recognizes that nothing is guaranteed. It says adjustments will likely have to be made, but that is natural and not something that should be feared. This final analysis is comforting to the staff because they know that little has been left to chance, and if the plan fails, then the cause is something that alluded the entire staff. When these simple questions have been asked, then a decision can be made to either pilot the plan or implement it on a full scale.

TRACKING

The next step is a tracking procedure. How does the staff know the implementations are doing exactly what they agreed were intended? It should be fully understood that this is not an evaluation of the plan nor the individual. It is an attempt to insure the credibility of the outcomes. Unfortunately, this step is often not included and is the root cause of the failure of more reform movements.

It a natural tendency to innovate plans to make them better. Certainly, innovation would not be discouraged. It is important that innovations be reported since the plan may appear to work successfully by one staff member and not by another. The variable then appears to be the skill of the individual when, in reality, it is not. The innovated system does not work the same for each individual. Few plans will have a reasonable chance of working if everyone is not doing his/her part. For teachers to revert back to their old ways once they return to the confines of their classroom is natural. If they revert back to the old ways, then the old results should be expected or something less than the anticipated outcome. The tracking component can be as burdensome as anything done in the entire process. Because it attempts to take away the means of retreating from something that is uncomfortable to do, it may cause anxiety. It also asks teachers to share what they believe will bring better results that, if shared, could deny individual personal recognition.

EVALUATION

Once the plan has been implemented, the staff should evaluate the plan based on the prior stated expected outcomes. Evaluation should serve several purposes. The staff needs to know if it met the stated objectives, and, if not, then using its problem identification technique, they should try to find out the causes. The plan should not be evaluated just for shortfalls. Were the outcomes set high enough? Does the plan have greater potential than originally anticipated? What effects has the plan implementation had on the staff? As a result of this, are there tasks that now can be eliminated? These last components of evaluation will improve the morale of the staff. It demonstrates a concern for the staff about its feelings and the value of the task it is doing.

Leaders will have to help staff members alter skills that have been previously avoided for continuity reasons. Team members should be made aware that doing all the planning, monitoring, and evaluation is an extremely time-consuming task. Principals should spend time helping staff members learn to hold meetings that are shorter and more effective. Establishing roles for committee members will help to improve meeting quality. These roles would include, but not be limited to, leader/facilitator, recorder, materials procurement, timekeeper, and sergeant-at-arms. By rotating and sharing these responsibilities, team members will increase their skills and relieve the burden that often falls on one or two individuals. Teams should take the time to assess their meetings. A simple means to accomplish this is to make team participation rules during the first meeting. These rules should include participation, listening, leadership, and those things that protect the value of all ideas and individuals. Quick assessments at the conclusion of each meeting with open discussion on how improvement can be made on group performance will condition teams to use their time judiciously. It will set the tone for future meetings that improve team performance.

CELEBRATIONS AND AWARDS

Principals will need to spend time and give thoughtful consideration to what should be celebrated and rewarded at the school. Assuming that the future of education will be to continue to improve all the processes that affect learning, then the reward system should be designed to support that end. Schools are like most other organizations in that most praise is intended for the people that demonstrate some measure of achievement. Recognition should be given for outstanding performance when all things are equal and when everyone has exactly the same opportunity to obtain the same results. In many districts this is not always the case. It should be kept in mind that good students tend to make outstanding educators. The task is to make all learners good students.

Good systems and processes create an environment that is favorable to help educators make learners good students. It has already been stated that outstanding performance should be recognized but not necessarily rewarded. The current thinking concerning reward is that the best performance is expected from everyone. The same reasoning is used when acknowledging systems and processes. When a school is practicing a process that works to help students, it must acknowledge that the needs of children are being met.

If mounds of praise on what we are doing are allowed, then our incentive to change will be retarded. This encourages acceptance of the status quo and leads to mediocrity. The schools that are most vulnerable to this syndrome are those experiencing success. Principals should acknowledge those practices that are already working; however, the celebration of that practice should be done when a new practice replaces the existing one. This is analogous to a retirement banquet. A person is honored and celebrated for what he or she has done for the organization; however, that person is not the future. Even though these persons have laid the foundation for the future, the leader must keep his or her vision of the future and the adaptability of the school processes to function effectively.

Rewards should be given to those who continually try to make the changes necessary to solve the problems the present practices and processes cannot. These individuals or groups should be rewarded whether they are successful or not. Certainly, every idea for improvement is not good; however, the commitment to give every proposal the dignity it deserves will encourage positive innovation. By rewarding the pioneering spirit, risk taking is promoted. The creativity required to develop systems that are not reactive must be cultivated. The best way to imbue the development of these systems is to reward what is valued. People and systems that give students the best opportunity to learn are valued. Students' needs continue to change, and the systems required to be effective must evolve prior to the old ones becoming deficient. The casualties suffered by using deficient systems will be people. First, the student will be lost; then frustration will take the educator.

BARRIERS TO THE EMPOWERED SCHOOL

Leaders can do all the things previously mentioned in this chapter and still not be effective. There are external influences that will create barriers to the empowered school. Some of those are school boards, the business world, and the community. Elaboration is not necessary on each of these, though community concerns are important. Communities are often fearful of change. The more radical the change, the greater the anxiety.

When it comes to children, safety always comes first. A child's education is his or her future. Parents know that, when educators fail to properly guide their children, they are then hurt for life. Few parents want educators experimenting with their children. Yet it is this conservative approach that will limit the opportunities for the quality education that enables a student to be productive and self-fulfilled in his present and future society.

Principals need to involve parents, students, and businesses. They must be open to the limitations of the educational systems and collectively work to eliminate those factors that retard the opportunities for students. This is an absolute oversimplification of the problem. Involving and educating parent and community groups are time-consuming endeavors and may or may not gain the school the support required to make significant changes. The leader should remember that no involvement means no commitment, and a community in opposition to changes will force the governing body to react to the proposed practices. If an abeyance of activities is called because of community pressure, it will be difficult to get the staff to give the same commitment to change again. The leader must not only be aware of the mood of the community but should also know who is providing the information that is shaping its frame of mind. It will serve the school and staff if the leader will deal with opposition in the early planning stages. Early intervention allows the leader to focus the attention of all stakeholders to the future using reason and not emotion.

CONCLUSION

In conclusion, it is the responsibility of leadership to provide the training and creative environment that allows a staff to be empowered. Significant change in learning will not occur unless all stakeholders change their behaviors and how they view problems. Principals must give people the opportunity to be successful and feel self-satisfied in their jobs. This will not happen as a natural course of events. It will happen because the leader has anticipated the needs of everyone and actively taken steps to provide maximum support. The price of leadership is tiresome and often lonely, but it can be exhilarating. Reforming the educator is simple. It is just not easy.

CHAPTER 9

Superintendents' and School Board Members' Perceptions of Empowerment

MARILYN L. GRADY[1]

INTRODUCTION

This chapter focuses on superintendents' and school board members' perceptions of empowerment. The literature is rife with descriptions of empowerment from the perspectives of principals and teachers. Little has been written about empowerment from the perspectives of superintendents and school board members. This chapter is based on interviews conducted with school board members and superintendents from four midwestern states, as well as available literature. The school board members and superintendents who were interviewed represent districts that have had experience with empowering their staff members. Using this information, the sections include administrators' roles, school board members' roles, impact on administrative roles, definitions of empowerment, and recommendations.

ADMINISTRATORS' ROLES

In examining administrators' roles and empowerment, it appears that the roles most affected by empowering staff members are those of the central office staff. In school districts that traditionally have had

---

[1]University of Nebraska–Lincoln.

many central office staff members, empowerment may lead to a reduction in staff.

CENTRAL OFFICE ROLE

In order for empowerment to occur, the central office staff may need to shed some of its legitimate authority and become facilitators, not dictators (Lindelow and Heynderickx, 1989). As authority is stripped from the central office staff, considerable power is also lost. Power is lost because functions change from that of control to that of service. Obviously, the central office staff may not be happy about the loss of authority and power (Lindelow, 1981).

In addition to losing authority and power, the central office staff frequently becomes smaller. A dramatic reduction in the number of central office staff members is typical. Although this downsizing may simply represent the reassignment of individuals to different roles in a district, the concomitant anxiety about job change can be stressful and even frightening for individuals.

The central office continues to oversee a number of district functions. Personnel is one of these areas. Personnel functions include recruiting employees, maintaining personnel records, and providing technical assistance to school sites. The central office staff may also retain responsibility for centralized preservice teacher training (Lindelow and Heynderickx, 1989).

Developing student and staff performance standards; offering technical assistance to schools; determining how much funding each school should receive; and carrying out systemwide planning, monitoring, and evaluation are other central office staff functions (Lindelow and Heynderickx, 1989). Districtwide, the central office monitors the district's effectiveness in meeting its goals, through both visitations and standardized tests.

In these new roles as district facilitators, the central office staff must learn to adjust to new and often ambiguous expectations. It is sometimes difficult to decide when to play the role of initiator (the transformed "director" role) and when to play the role of responder (more commonly known as the "facilitator"). Although both roles— responder and initiator—are important, it can be difficult for central administrators to find the appropriate balance between them (Delehant, 1990, p. 18).

SUPERINTENDENT'S ROLE

The superintendent, however, is in a unique position. The superintendent may be the initiator and facilitator of empowerment within a district, or the superintendent may be a blocker. Whatever course a school district follows, the superintendent has considerable influence in creating the superintendent's role.

Efforts to empower staff members in a school district are destined to fail without the support and encouragement of the superintendent. Empowerment demands decentralization. If a superintendent does not advocate decentralization, then there can be no significant empowerment of staff members.

The superintendent must demonstrate a willingness to delegate responsibility and a willingness to share authority. That willingness is quite rare. However, there is an increasing number of superintendents who recognize that empowering others truly empowers them. These superintendents share not only authority but information, which is often called the currency of power. Accountability is also shared, as is the credit for jobs well done (Marburger, 1985).

The superintendent, as the chief administrator of the school district, will be the one person responsible to the school board for administrative decisions. The superintendent is responsible for administering the *entire* system—business matters, personnel, school property, budgets, maintenance, and overall curriculum (Marburger, 1985). Superintendents continue to be responsible for setting and achieving district goals, communicating their vision and shared values, and building district support for the schools in each of the communities within their jurisdiction (Lawson, 1989).

According to Lindelow (1981), for the superintendent the most important job functions are selecting site managers, making as much money for the district as possible, developing standards of service for school programs, district planning, and continuing evaluation of these functions. Superintendents note that the most important task is the selection of principals.

Superintendents become increasingly dedicated to decentralized management once they realize how it can help them meet the responsibilities of their office in a more effective and efficient manner. As the entire system becomes more accountable and responsive to client needs, the job at the top becomes easier and easier (Lindelow and Heynderickx, 1989).

Empowerment benefits superintendents by allowing them to concentrate on long-range planning and the need to communicate vision to everyone outside of the schools who can help make it a reality. Empowerment focuses accountability on decisions, making it clear which individual has ultimate responsibility for any decision. Empowerment increases the quality and quantity of communications among faculty, parents, principals, and superintendents as formal, top-down memos and telephone calls are replaced by more information and face-to-face discussions. Face-to-face communications in a school and district are more likely to cause successful programs to be shared between teachers and principals and principals and superintendents (Lawson, 1989). In the final analysis, greater trust is created for all members.

The message for the superintendent is clear: the aim of the wise is to empower others to use power to help themselves. It is through the diffusion of power that one becomes influential and effective (Marburger, 1985).

PRINCIPAL'S ROLE

The principal's role is most often described in the literature concerning empowerment. Descriptions of the principal's role by superintendents and school board members suggest that the expectations for the principal "to make empowerment work" are high.

Superintendents describe the principal's role in empowerment as being the facilitator or the one who allows others to act. The principal is the creator of a climate conducive to empowerment, a communicator, and a leader.

Facilitator

The principal's facilitator role is multifaceted. The principal's role is as a mentor and resource person, one who pulls together all staff members and asks the question: "What can I do to help you be successful in the classroom?"

The principal is the instructional leader who facilitates and works with staff. An important task for principals is to nurture people as individuals. A principal who is successful at empowering others is one who has developed rapport and stimulates collaborative efforts. The principal is the catalyst who gets faculty to expand their horizons and move in new directions.

To empower others, principals must fully share information with all who need to receive it. The principal must offer opportunities for staff training so that staff feel competent to fully participate. The principal must be willing to work with groups and must be able to build consensus within the staff.

Allowing Others to Act

The principal allows staff to become a part of the decision process.

The principal must be able to receive input in a positive way and then be able to implement that input so that individuals do not perceive the decision process as simply an exercise.

Teachers need flexibility in the classroom role within district guidelines. Principals who empower teachers must trust teachers and their judgment.

The principal's role is to allow staff to think for themselves and come to their own conclusions about how to affect the climate in which they work. Creating a climate for learning is an important task.

In creating a climate for learning, the principal must establish an environment in which teachers know that their ideas will be solicited, given serious consideration, and then utilized as part of the consensus process that best serves students. The principal has to set the climate, develop trust, and spend the time required to achieve success in the schools.

Clear communication is imperative. All staff need to have information for decision making. The principal's role is to keep staff and students informed and at the forefront of decisions. Informed people are empowered people.

Leadership

The principal is a significant member of a team rather than someone who has to "pull people." The principal should be able to say, "I hope to convince and involve you, rather than make you do it."

The principal's role is to be a colleague, rather than a supervisor, one who is supportive of staff. The principal is a leader who facilitates the work of others. This leadership includes developing staff relations and trust. The principal points out problems, generates alternatives and solutions, and then helps to reach consensus.

Being a cheerleader, applauding what the staff is doing, being interested, and reinforcing involvement are parts of the role. The principal needs to study, model, and utilize the concepts of empowerment for the staff as well as provide ownership and a sense of professional worth for everyone.

SCHOOL BOARD MEMBERS' ROLES

Empowerment does not change the role of the school board. The board continues to have *sole* responsibility for setting the education policy for a district. The board then delegates responsibility for implementing that policy (Marburger, 1985). For instance, in districts where empowerment exists, the school board gives responsibility to principals to hire and fire nearly all employees, develop the budget, and decide on necessary support services (Lausberg, 1990).

The board's primary duties, according to Lindelow (1981), are to provide general direction for the district by establishing goals and policy statements, keeping informed about the district's progress toward goals, and acting as a decision maker of last resort.

The school board has responsibility for the quality of education of all students in the district. The members have responsibility for monitoring their administrators and holding them accountable for the implementation of the policies that set forth the means of accomplishing the desired quality. They cannot delegate that responsibility. They are also fiscally responsible to the taxpayers of their district and to the state. They cannot delegate fiscal responsibility. They can, however, delegate some budgetary discretion to the local school (Marburger, 1985).

The school board is a powerful influence on initiating or blocking efforts to empower staff members. For empowerment to truly exist in a school district, the board must do more than merely "go along" with a superintendent's proposal. The board must support the concept of empowerment through its policy-making and fiscal decision-making acts, as well as through the selection and support of a superintendent who is committed to empowerment.

IMPACT ON ROLES

STAFF

Responses to questions about the impact of empowerment on school districts indicated that the area of greatest impact was on the teaching staff, in areas such as their morale, involvement, and effectiveness. Respondents noted that the teaching staff was more viable now because they make decisions and implement them. There is shared responsibility, and all are working harder to achieve goals. The talents of all teachers are utilized as well as the talents of noncertified staff. All benefit from the combined perspectives and opinions of the total staff.

One area of great impact is morale. The outcome of empowerment is higher morale. Individuals are very positive about the work they are doing. They feel important and good about what they are doing for kids. Individuals realize that they can make a difference and that they can share ideas. They are opening up, listening, and becoming comfortable with the process. There is more initiative on the part of teachers and staff to grow professionally and impact change for the benefit of children. Employees feel better about their jobs and themselves because they are participating more and making greater use of the skills they have. The staff are more thorough about what they do, and surveys show that staff feel good about their input. There is more initiative on the part of teachers and staff to grow professionally and impact change for the benefit of children.

Overall empowerment leads to a greater sense of ownership and buy-in to school efforts. There is a greater willingness to risk and try new things. There is a shared accountability for changes that will benefit kids. With empowerment, more people feel responsibility for what's going on. Empowerment addresses the whole issue of ownership. Individuals have more ownership of decisions that impact their environment and they are involved with the implementation of those decisions. With high staff morale and greater involvement of individuals, the net effect is greater effectiveness in achieving organizational goals.

SUPERINTENDENT

Empowerment's impact on the superintendent is in the areas of awareness, time, and developing new skills or behaviors. Superintendents described their increased awareness. They spoke of the need to constantly remember that they must frequently consult with individuals concerning decisions. They repeatedly spoke of the need to talk to everyone involved in a decision or a task.

Empowerment opened communication lines with administration, staff, students, and the public. This open communication provides multiple perspectives on issues, as well as opportunities for the superintendent's point of view to be known. Although the ideal is consensus, even when this is not possible, all benefit from hearing multiple perspectives and from being heard.

Another impact of empowerment on the superintendent's work is the increased time needed to reach decisions. On the issue of time demands, there was universal agreement that acting unilaterally is quicker but does not result in better decisions. The superintendents note that it would be easier and take less time to make decisions unilaterally, but the result would not be the same. Empowerment is less efficient, but the outcomes are much more effective.

The superintendents spend more time waiting to get input from various groups in the district before decisions are made. This requires patience and trust in the process. It may be easier to be authoritarian and more difficult to be collegial.

Empowering staff members requires coordination and organizational skills. From the superintendent's perspective, empowering staff results in more work and more time. There are more meetings, more reports, more communication. Increased communication is time-consuming and labor intensive. The result, however, is that superintendents have more and better information and feel that the decisions being made are better because of this.

In order to empower others, superintendents may need new skills and behaviors. The superintendents interviewed described their need to develop coaching or helping skills as a means of empowering others. They reported being more motivational, rather than "directional." The superintendents often remarked that, in the past, they had been "take charge" or "go ahead and do it" people. Now they find themselves deferring action to others.

Comments reflected the "new me" administrator. The superintendents described themselves as being more democratic. They spend more time and effort gathering input and being involved in committee work. In spite of increased time and effort, they report being happier with their jobs as superintendents. They say that, even though they are working harder now than ever, they are more satisfied with the results of their efforts.

The superintendents note their improved interpersonal and communication skills. They describe the rapport they have established with personnel in the district. Communication is more open and honest. More power is delegated to individuals and groups.

Superintendents become more hands off, allowing staff to try their ideas. Superintendents also report that they struggle to identify which issues should be referred to which individual or group. Using the expertise and time of all individuals appropriately and effectively is a goal of the superintendents.

Superintendents said they are changing their style of administration. Learning to wait is a challenge. Rather than being action people, superintendents must be patient as they allow time for the process of empowering others to succeed.

The impact on the superintendent's role is that the position demands that one be a facilitator, someone who is supportive of change and of others. The superintendent's role changes from being one of a top-down, line authority to one of collegiality. Some trepidation accompanies these changes since district responsibility still rests with the superintendent. Trust is a critical factor for superintendents who perceive their position to be vulnerable and unprotected. Empowering others may appear to be a risk.

PRINCIPAL

When the superintendents and board members were asked to describe the impact of empowerment on the principal's role, they said that there had been no impact because the principals had always empowered their staffs. The principals have shared decisions and allowed decisions to be made at the level most appropriate to the decision. They indicated that communication had improved because of empowerment, and, once again, they stated that empowerment takes time. Continuous conversation and much committee work are required by empowerment. Both an investment of time and good communication skills are essential.

There is a perception that principals are more responsive than they have ever been. Communication between staff members and the principal is constantly improving. There is more control, ownership, and responsibility for programs. Individuals are more willing to take risks and try new things. Figure 9.1 represents the impact of empowerment.

DEFINITIONS OF EMPOWERMENT

Superintendents and school board members provided the following definitions of empowerment.

INVOLVEMENT

Empowerment is the increased involvement of teachers in the decision-making process. It is shared decision making through a solicitation of ideas and a sharing of decisions.

Empowerment is making decisions at the level where they have impact. For instance, custodians are involved in solving custodial problems, teachers in solving classroom problems, principals in solving buildingwide problems, and superintendents in making districtwide decisions (AASA, NAESP, NASSP, 1988). Empowerment is "getting input at all levels."

Empowerment is how much authority teachers have in districtwide decisions. It is the responsibility you give people and hold them accountable for. The superintendents, however, were quick to insert the caveat that time constraints often led to situations in which this ideal of decision making at the level of impact could not, in fact, be implemented.

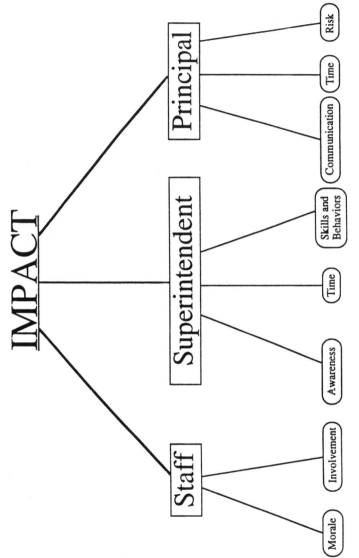

Figure 9.1. The impact of empowerment.

208

OPPORTUNITIES

An extension of this definition is that empowerment is providing opportunities for professional development for staff members. Empowerment is allowing individuals the opportunity to do their own jobs. The superintendents said that implicit in allowing people to do their own jobs is not "second guessing" them. For the superintendents this meant imparting a sense of efficacy to professional employees.

"Empowerment is people being given a job to do and then being left alone to do it," was a frequently offered definition. Empowerment is involving front line people in setting direction for a school.

Opportunities for greater involvement are in areas such as purchasing equipment, deciding curricular issues, or involvement in student affairs. Empowerment is people having a sense of their voice and having control of what's occurring around them in the classroom and in the district.

PROCESS

Empowerment is also a process. Empowerment is the process by which there is an exchange of information and ideas. The exchange may be weekly, monthly, or daily. The exchanges occur between faculty, staff, and administrators. This is full-channel communication. The real key, according to the superintendents, is getting ideas generated.

Authority is broadly distributed (Malen et al., 1990). Individuals are given opportunities to take risks and to compete without repercussions of failure (Lagana, 1989).

Empowerment is a focused process that includes detailed communication and training. It is a process of providing people with the opportunity and resources to enable them to believe and feel that they understand their world and have the power to change it. Individuals have greater autonomy and independence in decision making (Lagana, 1989).

OWNERSHIP

One of the major tasks for administrators is getting staff attuned to being involved in the decision-making process. Staff need to have ownership of what is happening in the district, in the schools, and with the children. Staff members should have ownership over those things that they are responsible for. They should have control and ownership and a part in decision making. Empowerment is giving ownership of deci-

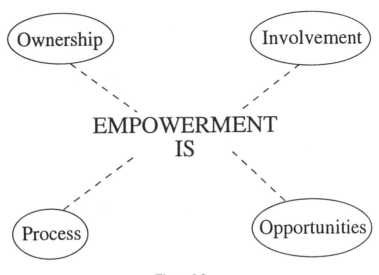

Figure 9.2.

sions and implementation to the appropriate individuals. Empowerment is creating ownership for teachers, staff, and the community. It requires collegiality and listening.

It is a cooperative effort between all staff and administration regarding school concerns. It is cooperative teamwork between and among administration and faculty members.

There are two avenues of empowerment. The first is a management issue. This means the involvement of people most affected daily in the decision process. Ownership is important. When people have ownership in decisions, there simply are fewer problems. The second avenue is that the long-range strategic planning process includes staff, both certified and noncertified, in committees. All staff members are involved in setting objectives that are related to their daily work. Figure 9.2 is a representation of these definitions of empowerment.

RECOMMENDATIONS

There are several key factors that serve as reminders of good practice that superintendents and school board members should keep in mind. First of all, implementing change of any kind takes time. It takes time to implement new procedures, define new roles, and balance these.

Implementing change requires the ability to realistically plan for a future. Planning may be an especially critical issue for educators who have a nine-month perspective on the future. Those who perceive education as simply an August/September to May/June enterprise may suffer from a lack of future orientation. Implementing significant change requires a multiyear plan with clear expectations for each year in the change cycle.

A second factor is concerned with clarity. Roles, responsibilities, goals, and authority need to be clearly defined. Without a clear specification of expectations, chaos and confusion reign. Only when there is clarity can individuals and groups be held accountable for the achievement of goals.

A third factor is the skills needed by individuals who are responsible for empowering others. These skills include group techniques such as conflict resolution, consensus building, brainstorming, nominal group technique, listening, and communicating. Individuals also need planning skills. They must be able to encourage and reinforce others and generally be able to assist with the professional development of a staff. School board members and superintendents may also need to refine the skills that enable them to work together efficiently and effectively.

A fourth factor is that empowerment demands that sufficient resources be invested in preparing staff members for empowerment. This means that resources must be provided for staff development activities. Funding, personnel, time, facilities, and equipment are some of the necessary resources.

A fifth factor is that those who want to empower others must be patient, have faith in the process, and be able to trust others. Empowerment demands a stand-by, stand-back, and stand-off capacity.

REFERENCES

American Association of School Administrators, National Association of Elementary School Principals, and National Association of Secondary School Principals (1988). *School-Based Management—A Strategy for Better Learning.* Reston, VA: NASSP, p. 5.

Delehant, A. M. (1990). A central office view: Charting a course when pulled in all directions. *The School Administrator,* 14, 17–19.

Lagana, J. F. (1989). Managing change and school improvement effectively. *NASSP Bulletin,* 73 (518), 52–55.

Lausberg, C. H. (1990). Site-based management: Crisis or opportunity? *School Business Affairs,* (April):10–14.

Lawson, J. (1989). *Cultivating Excellence: A Curriculum for Excellence in School Administration v. School-Based Management.* New Hampshire School Administrators Association, Durham.

Lindelow, J. (1981). *School-Based Management.* School Management Digest, Series 1, No. 23, Eugene, OR: ERIC Clearinghouse on Educational Management, Burlingame, CA: Foundation for Educational Administration.

Lindelow, J. and Heynderickx, J. (1989). *School-Based Management.* Eugene, OR: ERIC Clearinghouse on Educational Management (ED 309 509) (EA 020 969), p. 109–134.

Malen, B., Ogawa, R. T. and Kranz, J. (1990). Site-based management: Unfulfilled promises. *The School Administrator* (Feb):30, 32, 53–56, 59.

Marburger, C. L. (1985). *One School at a Time. School Based Management: A Process for Change.* Columbia, MD: National Committee for Citizens in Education.

Examples of Empowerment at Work

CHAPTER 10

A Vision of the Future and the New School Principal

JOHN R. HOYLE[1]

INTRODUCTION

Many school principals lack the vision to guide their schools into a complex and troubled 21st century. They talk about effective schools, accelerated schools, and other hot topics on school reform, but principals seem to lack the skills to sell their vision to staff, students, parents, and other stakeholders. Perhaps the daily grind of running a school stunts clear thinking and blocks communications critical to shaping and selling the vision. The following statement by a veteran principal may explain why they lose their vision and suggests a way to regain it.

> Sixteen years ago I broke away from the science class to become a school principal. I recall that I wanted more money and more status and, besides, I had been certified by a state university. I told myself at the time that I would still be a teacher and stay close to the kids. Somewhere along the way, paper work, regulations, board meetings, committees, and reform legislation took their toll; I lost my vision. I grew callous to the requests from teachers for smaller classes with fewer trouble makers. I forgot the exhaustion brought on by the teaching, encouraging, prodding and reprimanding students in warm, dusty classrooms. I lost the sensitivity that once led me to look for the pain in the eyes of a lonely child and try to help. In my quest for higher test scores and smoother waters, I ignored the magic that occurs between devoted teachers and eager students.

[1]Texas A&M University.

In the midst of counting daily membership, checking the cooling system, writing memos, directing the United Way, and counting books, I forgot that teaching and learning and caring are the trinity of education. My zeal for keeping the roof on caused the foundation to crack. My zeal to be an efficient manager of things made me blind to my role in building lives. In my fight with school politics and community brush fires, my heart forgot the peace found in students helping each other.

Yes, I am a school principal. I have the power and knowledge to build a new world by creating a school that is an exciting place to learn. I can work with teachers, students, parents, board members, community to open the doors of the world of opportunity for every child. It is not too late to recall why I entered education. I can still recapture the compassion and the intellectual energy that filled me that first year of teaching. My resolve is to once again place the inquiring faces of students in the center of each task I do. I will strive to empower teachers, parents, and students to help me plan a better school, a more caring community. This will be my vision. (Hoyle, 1990)

Vision has become a catchword for school principals. "If I can just get a clear vision of the goal I want to achieve, then I can make things happen," reasoned a young principal. Being called a visionary principal is considered a high compliment. The question is, how do school principals better communicate their vision to help improve the tarnished image of education? How do principals share their vision and, in the words of Henry Kissinger, "take people where they are and take them to places they have never been?"

VISION—WHAT IS IT?

Vision is a lot like beauty—it is difficult to define, but it is obvious when a principal has it. Some principals are visionaries and others are not. Some have it; others never have it. German philosopher Arthur Schopenhauer realized the limits of a person's vision when he wrote, "Every man takes the limits of his own field of vision for the limits of the world," or as an old track coach told his athlete, "Never build hurdles in your mind because the hurdles on the track are much smaller than the hurdles in the mind." And there is much truth in the words of the old sage who said, "If you believe you can or can't you are right either way."

School principals who seek to improve their vision and perhaps develop a gift of prophecy can learn from the visionaries of history. Joan of Ark had a vision to inspire her armies to chase the British from

French soil. Her vision alone was almost enough until her capture in Orleans. Galileo's visions and astronomical discoveries confirmed Copernicus' theory of the solar system, but he was forced by the Inquisition to denounce his belief that the earth moved about the sun. John F. Kennedy's vision led Neil Armstrong to step on the moon and exclaim "one small step for man and one giant leap for mankind."

Visions have inspired magnificent monuments that have withstood the ravages of time. The pyramids of Giza, the mystical arrangements at Stonehenge, the temples and theaters of the Greeks, the Pantheon and Coliseum of the Roman empire, the cathedrals, castles, and chateaus of Europe had their beginnings in someone's imagination. The World Trade Center, the Epcot Center, and more recently, I. M. Pei's glass pyramid, blending art and technology, had their genesis in someone's vision.

Powerful vision can change the world for good or evil. At Nuremberg, Adolph Hitler's mesmerizing orations of his vision about a thousand-year reign still tears at the heart of Europe because of the millions who died in his twisted dream. The words of Martin Luther King, Jr.'s, vision still linger in the air around the Lincoln Memorial. The words express equality, justice, peace, brotherhood, and sisterhood. Vision holds power. Futurist Joel Barker says it this way: "Vision without action will lead nowhere; vision with action can change the world." Vision with action and faith can truly change schools into places of achievement and creative learning.

REVISION

Vision can also change. Burn Nanus (1992) claims that revision is vital to successful organizations. He asserts that vision can outlive its welcome and lose its power to motivate and change. Nanus singles out Edwin Land of Polaroid fame who tried to create Polavision, a form of instant home movies, and who lost 250 million dollars. He had not taken the video recorder seriously enough. Home movies became a casualty of better technology. Entire industries and education programs can be destroyed or rendered useless by changes beyond their control unless revision becomes an ongoing process. Nanus offers these vital revision points:

- Never get complacent.
- Don't do it alone.
- Don't be overly idealistic.

- Reduce the possibility of unpleasant surprise.
- Watch out for organizational inertia.
- Don't be preoccupied with the bottom line.
- Be flexible and patient in implementing the vision.

Public education and Polaroid have something in common—they have been successful in the past. Perhaps the greatest hurdle is a successful past. United States Secretary of Labor Robert Reich believes, "Great success in the past is one of the major impediments to change in the future."

Thus, if school principals are to succeed in a changing world, they should heed the words of Nanus:

> An important part of visionary leadership for quality therefore is prudence: monitoring change, making the necessary mid-course corrections, and knowing when to initiate a new vision forming process. (p. 20)

This new vision-forming process can lead a school faculty to proactive planning and decision making. The principal is in a position to anticipate and manage the school's future through systematic revisioning. Much time, money, and effort are being spent in restructuring public school education. Principals charged with implementing the newest fad or trend feel the stress of keeping control of numerous administrative responsibilities and trying to convince faculty that site-based decision making, outcome-based instruction, accelerated schools programs, the five correlates of effective schools, and integrated curriculum flavored with total quality management will lift their student achievement to all-time highs. Principals are caught in a restructuring vise between demanding superintendents and reluctant classroom teachers. Therefore, trying to react to and facilitate every major fad that hits the education literature seems to cloud the vision of well-meaning school principals.

Robert Slavin (1989) believes that "faddism" in education is a major barrier to systematic school improvement. He is concerned about harried administrators searching for a "quick fix" for low student performance, who rarely keep a program in place long enough to determine if it is working. They fail to gather hard evidence in any systematic way over an extended period of time and, as a result, become impatient and jump on the next fad wagon. Slavin says that a "gee whiz" story or two about a school that has been "reborn" by a new fad is about all it takes for the system and staff to abandon their current program for another new, untested model. Superintendents and school board members are so desperate for a miracle program to appear in each school to improve student performance and teacher morale that any new "gee whiz" program promising hope is handed to the principal to implement.

Superintendents and curriculum directors hear educational evangelists preaching the miracles of school improvement models proposed by Madeline Hunter, Robert Slavin, Henry Levin, James Comer, or William Glasser and select one or a combination of several and instruct the principal to launch it in three to six weeks. In spite of the principal's reservation about leaping full force into any one miracle model, he/she yields to the pressure and is swept up in group "frenzy" or group tyranny, and the plan is set forth. The inability to manage agreement is common in most organizations. Jerry Harvey (1988) in his "The Abilene Paradox" describes a classic case of group tyranny in a story about himself and three other family members who agreed to drive fifty-three miles from Coleman, Texas, to Abilene in 104 degree heat in an unairconditioned car to eat in a cafeteria that had bad food. Even though no member of the family really wanted to make the uncomfortable trip, they all agreed to go along. Each member of the group gave inaccurate information to each other when they said, "Yes, let's go to Abilene," when, in reality, each family member preferred to stay on the back porch drinking lemonade in Coleman. According to Harvey, organizations often take actions or make decisions ". . . in contradiction to what they really want to do and therefore defeat the very purposes they are trying to achieve. . . . The inability to manage agreement is a major source of organizational dysfunction" (p. 66).

Principals find it difficult to go against the wishes of a superintendent, assistant superintendent, and other principals in the district. Even though they personally feel that a new program or plan sent down from the central office will not work at their school, principals will keep the appearance of being a loyal team player and go along to Abilene. Loyalty is a fine virtue as long as it does not blind the principal to the vision and courage to do the right thing for his/her school and students.

Unless the principal is empowered by the superintendent and board to make site-based decisions about curriculum, personnel, and budget, he/she could risk reprimand or even job loss by failing to implement a mandated districtwide program. If a principal is in such a situation, he/she needs skills in mixed scanning (Etzioni, 1986). Before beginning any new mandated or self-selected school improvement plan, the principal should scan the major ideas in each of the more prominent "gee whiz" reform plans and pick and choose the components that make sense for his/her students and faculty. Chenoweth (1992) scanned and analyzed three of these major reform plans and found several common ingredients. Hoyle (1992) extended the ideas of Chenoweth, which are seen in Figure 10.1.

Principals must use revision to select the best ideas from the many plans and success stories that fill the education literature. It is wishful thinking that all principals will find themselves in completely autonomous schools (Greer, 1993). That is against the nature and history of school bureaucracies. In spite of this, most principals have some "wiggle room" or personal autonomy in which to work with site-based committees and the entire faculty to create school-specific improvement plans. Principals must use this limited freedom by helping the faculty

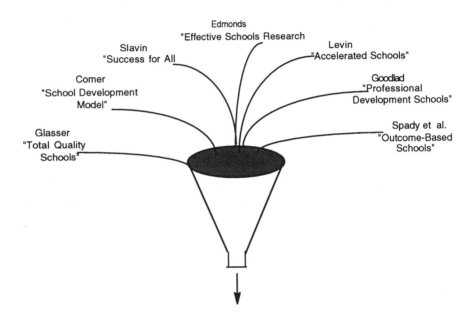

- Higher Expectations

- Empowered Teachers and Staff

- Administrators/Strong Instructional Leaders

- Strong Emphasis on Academic Achievement and Benchmarking Progress

- Rich and Positive School Culture/Climate

- Targeted Staff Development

Figure 10.1.

focus on a set of clearly understood improvement strategies and goals that are guided by a common school vision. For this communication process to work, the principal must make a persuasive, articulate case for the program to engender the needed support from the faculty, community, and the central office bureaucracy.

LEADERS GIVE LIFE TO THEIR VISIONS

School principals who develop a sense of the future and perfect a language that inspires optimism will have success in enlisting others in a common vision. Erika Erdmann and David Stover (1993) claim, "Our future depends on our open-mindedness, critical thinking, and the courage to convert facts – even inconvenient, painful facts – into a solid base for action" (p. 60). According to Kouzes and Posner (1987), "Leaders breathe life into their visions. They communicate their hopes and dreams so that others clearly understand and accept them as their own. Leaders know what motivates their constituents" (p. 125).

Successful school principals have traded the "controlling" mindset for one of shared control by those closest to the cause, problem, or decision. This shared control or efficacy (Fields, 1993), which gives individuals the ability to make their own professional lives successful, is the key to team building. The degree to which each faculty member feels in control of his/her life and teaching role determines the extent to which he/she will contribute to a collaborative effort. Teachers who sense a strong "locus of control" (Rotter, 1971) will be more responsive and creative in task accomplishment. A school principal who will share power and control and articulate a vision of a high-performing school faculty and student body will create the self-esteem and efficacy among the faculty and students to make the vision come true.

THE PRINCIPAL AS FUTURIST

After the school staff and community have been enlisted in a common vision, the next step is to help others bring that vision into a sharper focus. The best way to help others sharpen their mental image of the school of the future is a well designed staff development program on visualization of the future. The focus on future programming is an excellent way to trigger creative juices and intuition among the faculty. Stephen Covey (1991) believes that one way to make "champions of your children is to teach them to visualize to their own potential." He believes that "visualization is based on the principle that all things are created twice: first mentally and then physically. World-class athletes are almost all visualizers; they literally experience their victories in their minds long before they experience them in fact" (p. 48). If a school's faculty, students, and community leaders could visualize and hold in their mind's eye a school where all students and faculty perform at high levels, have respect for each other, and contribute to each others' welfare, then success would follow. The future can be invented, and school principals must be the futurists who cause their inventions.

Janie Hill Halton, principal of Milwaukee Trade and Technical High School and the 1993 National Principal of the Year must be a futurist. She is a hard charging administrator who routinely walks the halls, visits classrooms, and talks with the students about their future. She models what school principals should do to inspire teachers and students to hold on to their futures and make it come true. Milwaukee superintendent Howard Fuller said, "Every child and every parent should be lucky enough to have a principal like Janie Halton" (American Association of School Administrators, 1993).

LEARNING TO BE VISIONARIES

Principal and teachers need training in future studies to help them become the visionaries schools need. Principals and teachers can learn to sharpen their vision through staff development. Site-based decision-making teams could plan a series of sessions that includes training in future trends, methods, and exercises to develop skills in visualization and strategic planning. Working together to create a common vision for their school's administrators and faculty would build a sense of trust and empower them to dream the future and make the future become a reality.

The focus of the inservice is to stimulate the staff to think about the future and to assist in developing a vision reaching beyond what is to what could be. The staff will encounter intriguing ideas, concepts, and challenges for creating a future school. Following is a suggested inservice program to promote a common vision.

Session I: Orientation of the Future and Vision
  Activity: Lecture and videotape on the power of visualization
  Resource: A guest lecturer and a videotape entitled *The Power of Vision* narrated by futurist Joel Barker. Charthouse International Learning Corporation. Burnsvill, MN.
     Time: 2 hours

Session II: School for the Future
  Activity: Future school and student project—Part I. Divide staff into five- to six-member multigrade and subject area faculty.
  Resource: Selected articles from
    • the *Futurist* Journal, published six times annually by the World Future Society, 4916 St. Elmo Ave., Bethesda, MD 20814
    • *The School of the Future* by P. Schlecty, Jossey-Bass Pub.
    • flip chart pad with easels for each group
    • felt tip pens—several colors
  Tasks: Created a school of the future (2005) linked to other human service agencies, business, and local government. Each group will begin by listing the kinds of skills, attributes, knowledge, and values that the faculty would like the students to have when they graduate from their school. The second step is to create the most appropriate learning experiences for teaching those desired attributes.
  Time: 2-1/2 hours.

Session III: School for the Future—Part II
  Activity: Panel of local executives of human service agencies, businesses, churches, and local government
  Task: Each group will gather ideas to include in the future (community) school concept and discuss the best strategies to involve the other community agencies in the final future school project.
  Time: 2 hours

Session IV: School for the Future—Part III
  Activity: Each group will render a drawing of their school on the flip chart pad; the drawing will include the shape and size of the facility, the learning areas and external features, i.e., recreation, community agencies, etc.
  Time: 2 hours

Session V: Future Schools Presentations
  Activity: Each team will present its rendition of a school for 2005 within a twenty-minute time limit. After all presentations, each group will elect a representative to a steering committee to select the best ideas from each presentation

Time:
Activity:

and incorporate them into a shared vision of the school for 2005.

Time: 2 hours plus

Session VI: School of the Future—Shared Vision and Celebration
Activity: A spokesperson for the steering committee will present the shared vision of the school to a combined audience of faculty and community patrons. Refreshments served after presentations.

Session VII: Implications of Shared Visions on School Planning
Activity: Each faculty group will discuss the implications of the shared school vision on current curriculum, teaching, testing, technology, and school organization. Also, the entire faculty would come together to discuss the next steps necessary to build the future school that will produce students with the necessary attributes to make them successful in the 21st century.

The extent to which the shared vision of the future school becomes a reality rests with the enthusiastic support of the superintendent, school board, and the school principal. The faculty will stay focused on the vision only if the leadership is there to constantly encourage them. These suggested staff development sessions will help create a spark of creativity and promote a sharing of new ideas among the entire staff. The leadership of the principal is the most important piece of this picture.

CONCLUSION

School principals must welcome change and create a vision for their schools, faculty, and students. They must picture long-term goals in their minds and articulate them over and over. John F. Kennedy had the ability to translate vision into a set agenda. When he announced the goal of putting a man on the moon by 1970, he rallied an entire nation. Congress raised the funds. NASA hired the top scientists, and the seemingly impossible was accomplished. His goal was specific and clear. If he had said, "We are going to be the world leader in space exploration," there would have been no such organizing focus—the goal would not have been achieved. Being optimistic and accomplishing the vision requires self-discipline and patience (American Association of School Administrators, 1988, p. 13).

Principals need training in the skills of visualization and planning processes. University professors, state certification officers, and other primary stakeholders engaged in the professional development of principals should upgrade their programs to help principals to think holistically, to be creative pathfinders, and to use more vision and imagery. Thomas Payzent (1987), Assistant Secretary of Education, speaks clearly about the importance of vision this way: "As shapers of the future of education, we must be able to transform ideas into action that help schools become places of learning that can make a difference in the lives of children."

The principalship is a demanding position that requires the management skills of a corporate executive, the patience of a tournament bass fisherman, the energy of five year olds, the wisdom of Solomon, and the compassion of Mother Teresa. No one individual can perfect all of the skills needed to create an outstanding school. Only through the use of visualization, sharing both the vision and the power with the staff, and relying on the collective talents of the staff, students, and community will a school ever approach perfection. An African philosopher has said, "It takes a whole village to raise a child." Principals who have the skills and the resolve to rally the entire community for the education of all students will be the visionaries needed to lead schools of the 21st century.

REFERENCES

American Association of School Administrators. (1993). *Leadership News.* Arlington, VA: American Association of School Administrators Pub.

American Association of School Administrators. (1988). *Challenges for School Leaders.* Arlington, VA: American Association of School Administrators Pub.

Chenoweth, T. (1992). Emerging national models of schooling for at-risk students. *International Journal of Educational Reform* 1, 3.

Covey, S. R. (1991). *Principle-Centered Leadership.* New York: Summitt Books.

Erdmann, E. and Stover, D. (1993). Drowning in preconceptions. *The Futurist,* 27(5), 60.

Etzioni, H. (1986). Mixed scanning revisited. *Public Administration Review,* 46, 8–14.

Fields, J. C. (1993). Unlocking the paralysis of will. *The School Administrator* 5(50), 9–11.

Gelatt, H. B. (1993). Future sense: Creating the future. *The Futurist,* 27 (5), 9–13.

Greer, J. (1993). The autonomous school, Paper delivered at the *National Con-*

ference of Professions of Educational Administration, Palm Springs, CA, August.

Harvey, J. (1988). The Abilene paradox: The management of agreement. *Organizational Dynamics,* 17, 17–43.

Hoy, W. and Miskel, C. (1991). *Educational Administration: Theory, Research, Practice* (4th ed.). New York: McGraw-Hill, Inc.

Hoyle, J. R. (1990). A school administrator's vision. *The School Administrator* (March), p. 4.

Hoyle, J. R. (1992, July). "Restructuring for effective schools in the 90's." Paper delivered at the Louisiana State Department Convention, Baton Rouge, LA, pp. 1–16.

Kouzes, J. and Posner, B. (1987). *The Leadership Challenge.* San Francisco: Jossey-Bass Pub.

Nanus, B. (1992). Visionary leadership: How to revision the future. *Futurist,* 26, 20–25.

Payzant, T. (1987). Making a difference in the lives of children: Educational leadership to the year 2000. Paul B. Salmon Memorial lecture, Annual Convention of the American Association of School Administrators, New Orleans, February.

Rotter, J. B. (1971). External control and internal control. *Psychology Today,* 5 (1), 37–59.

Slavin, R. (1989). PET and the pendulum: Faddism and education and how to stop it. *Phi Delta Kappan,* 70 (10), 752, 759.

CHAPTER 11

School Empowerment and Rural Public Schools: A Principal's Dilemma

JAMES M. SMITH[1]
DONALD V. CAIRNS[2]

Within the last decade there has been a gradual movement in all schools and, more specifically, in rural public schools to increase the empowerment opportunities for teachers, staff, and administrators at the building level. This empowerment process is often reified by the implementation of site-based management or school empowerment. Site-based management (SBM) has been instituted by many small districts in anticipation of resolving longstanding problems that exist within the rural school arena (Cawelti, 1989; Gusky, 1990; Martin and McGee, 1990). While this trend appears to hold much promise as a way to correct the deficiencies that still exist within the nation's rural schools, there is also a great danger that SBM may be an inappropriate model to use in many situations. Of equal risk is the fact that SBM may be a correct solution to many of the problems pandemic to rural schools but, if inappropriately applied, will result in consequences not foreseen or anticipated by those initiating the action. There is certainly a clear and eminent danger that, if inappropriately applied, site-based management may become the tool in creating a new "cult of efficiency" mentality by those in rural policy-making positions (Callahan, 1962).

Without question, the industrial model that was adopted by and

[1]West Texas A&M University.
[2]Montana State University.

adapted to the public schools at the turn of the century (i.e., Taylor's Scientific Management) created as many problems as were solved by its implementation. Frightfully, SBM is currently being viewed by many as a similar "fix-all" process. Site-based management or school empowerment is designed to open schools to new ideas and outside influences and to increase overall levels of democratization—clearly, a linchpin in the current wave of the restructuring movement for rural public schools. However, in the frenetic rush to demonstrate that public schools are responsive to demands for increased student outcomes—from impatient politicians and a restless public—it appears that the well-founded concepts of site-based management are in danger of being corrupted by those within and without the profession. Site-based management, as defined by the Educational Research Service (1991), is

> a process in which the school becomes the primary unit of management and educational improvement. This generally occurs through the redistribution of decision-making authority within the district and the school. However, the degree of authority decentralized, as well as the persons involved, vary greatly from district to district. (p. 2)

Few would argue with the conceptual rationality of the previous definition; however, it is the specific application of this concept to the actual school setting that becomes problematic.

This chapter will examine the aforementioned school empowerment issues from the perspective of four differing sets of interactions that surround the organization of a small, rural school. These interactions are situational leadership, effective schools research, sacred and secular societies, and teacher empowerment.

SITUATIONAL LEADERSHIP

Policymakers and professionals have ignored the fact that effective school leadership involves a highly complex set of interactions between the leader, the followers, and the contextual situation that exists within each school. This concept has been expressed best by Hersey and Blanchard (1988) through the use of the formula $ef = f\,(l,f,s)$. The meaning of this formula is simply translated as: the effective leader is a function of the leader him/herself, the followership, and the situation. Indeed, this formula is the very basis for situational leadership theory.

The importance of this situational leadership formula, with respect to SBM, is that the leader's style is generally compatible or incompatible with the followership's level of maturity or immaturity; with the resulting interactions affecting and/or being affected by the total cultural setting of a given school or school district. Therefore, SBM may be either effective or ineffective, depending upon how each of the elements of situational leadership come together. How the various combinations of the above elements mix and match directly impacts any organization's ability to generate and sustain a successful change process. It must also be realized that SBM is highly contextual and operates within a very broad range of organizational factors (i.e., adjoining rural schools can differ as greatly as adjoining urban and suburban schools).

Leaders of schools, as in any other occupation, vary greatly with respect to individual leadership style. However, most leaders fall into one of four distinct categories. These categories, as described by Hersey and Blanchard (1988) are the telling mode (a low people, high task direction), the selling mode (indicated by a high task and high people orientation), the participative mode (reflective of leaders with a tendency to exhibit high people and low task behaviors), and the delegative mode (signified by low task, low relationship tendencies).

Whether the leader is high task oriented, and therefore, very directive in relationships with groups and individuals, is primarily based upon the leader's makeup and personal philosophy. Highly directive leaders are driven by a sense of task accomplishment and, in turn, rely heavily upon telling workers precisely what needs to be done. Those leaders that are both high task and high relationship tend to sell the program, rather than tell the program. While these leaders enjoy people, they have an equally strong commitment to completion of the task at hand.

The leader that exhibits the traits of being able to participate gains more satisfaction from work involving people than from simply completing a task. In contrast, the leader that delegates authority to subordinates receives a great deal of satisfaction from keeping things moving and seeing subordinates solving complex problems successfully; he/she will generally concentrate on the overall picture as compared to merely analyzing minute and intricate details.

Depending upon the maturity level of the followership, each of the previously mentioned leadership styles may be effective or ineffective. A principal with a strong sense of task orientation and a poor grasp of the human side of the organization may be extremely effective when the school site is in chaos. A school in crisis may indeed be in need of a strong leader of the type just described. On the other hand, the school or organization that has had a history of stability (resulting in very little turmoil) and that exhibits a strong sense of maturity on the part of the staff would resent a high task, low relationship leader.

The strong leader may be either effective or ineffective, depending upon the other elements entering into the equation. What is correct in one case is not immediately transferable to another. The leader's ultimate effectiveness is dependent upon an adequate match between his/her style and the followers' levels of maturity, both in the actual sense and in the meaning of a particular skill level. The immature or inexperienced follower will need and require a strong organizational leader to provide direction in order to accomplish the work of the school. In contrast, the mature follower requires a large degree of independence to accomplish the necessary work, thus demanding little guidance from the principal. If the guidance is provided to the mature follower in a highly directive manner, resentment and conflict is often the result. Mature and immature followers represent the extreme ends of a continuum, one that varies both on an individual and organizational basis. School empowerment might be most appropriate and correspondingly successful for mature faculty; however, immature faculty may find this operational style both ineffective and catastrophic.

A leader may be highly effective in a given situation and be a complete and utter disaster in another. Leadership effectiveness is highly dependent upon the individual leader's style in relation to the factors of followership and the cultural situation that exists within the actual school setting. This situational dependency is best expressed by Black and English (1986):

> Staying in power is like learning how to sail. One first has to know which way the wind is blowing. If the wind is blowing against you, one can skillfully tack into the wind and get where you want to go via a zigzag course. Too many administrators have never learned how to tack, let alone view power as going with the wind or skillfully against it. Power is not a force. . . . It is gaining and keeping the momentum of office with and against all of the forces around it. (p. 282)

EFFECTIVE SCHOOLS LITERATURE

Those that are compelled to rush headlong into the SBM model of leadership need to remember that the effective schools research (Brookover, 1981, 1987; Brookover and Lezotte, 1979; Edmonds, 1979; Brookover et al., 1973, 1977) carefully described the effective school principal as one providing a clear vision, exhibiting strong leadership in the areas of instruction, expecting the best of students and staff, and implementing regular and frequent evaluations. Nowhere in the effective schools literature is the principal portrayed as a highly collaborative individual, working with staff and parents through quality circles, or one who empowers teachers. Effective schools literature is replete with descriptions of strong leaders working in the environment of schools that were on the verge of failing their instructional mission. Additionally, much of this research was conducted at the elementary level in inner-city locations. Although critics like Dantley (1990) have argued that effective schools research must be reexamined, others have lauded a symbiotic relationship between SBM and the effective schools findings. This relationship, although often stated, appears tenuous at best. What Dantley (1990) describes in the following passage does not appear to match with what these authors believe SBM to be:

> What is exceptionally evident is that [effective] schools . . . are not arenas of ideas, thinking, and problem-posing pedagogy. The effective leader in this context is thus charged with producing and maintaining an environment that is safe for students to work but not to learn, to walk but not to think, to be but not to contribute. (p. 592)

Additional research conducted by Mann (1989) skillfully demonstrates the power of employing effective schools knowledge toward the reduction of a burgeoning dropout rate in American education; however, only a few similarities exist between this effective schools research implementation and the implementation of comprehensive SBM. Mann (1989) states that "effective principals in effective schools . . . are a visible presence in the school, not for trouble-shooting, but for communicating, supporting and guaranteeing the quality of instruction" (p. 79). It is indeed difficult to disagree with these assertions. Nonetheless, characterizations of this nature are, at best, tangentially related to the SBM notion of a school operating as the primary unit of management and arena for educational improvement. Hanson (1991) skillfully describes the inexact nature of the fit between SBM and effective schools research in the following:

> . . . The literature on loose coupling and the literature on effective schools create an educational dilemma. While the effective schools literature stresses the importance of administrators exerting strong instructional leadership and classroom supervision, the loose-coupling and teacher-autonomy literature suggest that exerting such leadership is not all that easy or perhaps even desirable. (p. 156)

It would appear that those who ardently believe that SBM is a "perfect fit" for all school settings have either overlooked the findings of effective schools research or have taken the liberty of assimilating the effective schools findings with those supporting SBM. It is the fervent belief of authors such as Hanson, Smith, and Cairns that such actions are intellectually and organizationally unfounded. Like those findings generated from effective schools research, some elements of SBM may be appropriate for a given school community, while others might be considered highly inappropriate.

UNDERSTANDING SACRED AND SECULAR SOCIETIES

A third element of the previously mentioned equation is that of the cultural mix of the school and the school community. Pragmatically, this cultural mix may not provide an environment conducive to a democratic leader desirous of opening the organization through site-based management. This obvious conclusion is simply overlooked or merely ignored by many of the SBM zealots. While it is true that the demographics of schools today are changing, it must still be remembered that many of the nation's small and rural schools are sacred societies (Vidich and Bensman, 1968; Iannaconne and Lutz, 1970) and not secular in nature. The sacred society is easily recognized as the society that operates from the notion of the "good old days." Here, the tried, true, and tested is to be relied upon, and often the "new" is to be distrusted. Many new concepts are regarded with deep suspicion and perhaps even contempt. Much that is modern or innovative is simply rejected as "too newfangled." New concepts are often viewed as turning away from the proven, tested, and true methods that have always worked. The words of Smith and Lotven (1991) clearly support this notion of rural schools as a sacred society:

> Rural communities are often resistant to change. They are generally comfortable with the current state of school affairs and prefer that educational innovations first be tested in the "big city." This is repeatedly reflected by research indicating that rural school board members tend to be significantly less progressive than their urban counterparts. (p. 7)

In contrast to the sacred society is the secular society. In the secular society, change is often adopted merely for the sake of change. Much pride is garnered by the constituency of a secular society when the newest and latest trends have been adopted into the operations of the organization, regardless of whether the changes are beneficial. The very latest concept is viewed as positive, uplifting, and secure—even if it is no more than proverbial old wine in a new bottle.

Hence, SBM in the sacred society may have a most difficult time of being effectively implemented. The SBM concept may appear radical to many members of the rural school constituency. Without proper research and staff development efforts, this concept may be doomed from the inception. This does not mean that an infusion of new ideas into the sacred society is impossible; it only means that the methodology and concepts must be approached carefully and properly. While much effort has been expended into standardizing and validating some of the processes necessary to assist a school in achieving SBM, these processes are often not targeted toward those environments with the greatest needs. Larger school districts clearly have greater resources for staff development and institutional research, but, one must ask, are these the places where such research and development are most critically needed?

An obvious example of total disregard for differing contextual environments can be found in the state of Texas. The Texas Educational Agency has provided one of the most clear and absolute directives for the implementation of SBM—that being a mandated process of total implementation for all districts in the state. Texas Senate Bill 1, enacted in June of 1990, requires that each school campus within the state establish academic performance objectives via committee structure, that the board of trustees for each school district adopt a policy to involve professional staff in establishing and reviewing the district's educational goals and objectives, and that professional staff representatives be elected in order to meet with the board of trustees to discuss campus and district concerns (West Publishing Company, 1992, p. 313). Texas House Bill 2885, enacted in May of 1991, further solidifies this mandated action by prescribing specific dates for the development of site-based plans, outlining specific targeted areas for discussion (i.e., goal setting, curriculum, budgeting, staffing, and school organization), and clarifying membership requirements to include not only parents, community residents, and professional staff but also business representatives as well (West Publishing Company, 1992, pp. 332–333). Although waivers and exemptions have been enacted with respect to this legislation, such waivers have definitely not included the replacement of SBM for other similar or dissimilar governance structures.

In keeping with Senate Bill 1 and House Bill 2885, the state of Texas has put forth a manual that outlines how each district will go about the mandatory adoption of SBM. The manual is replete with definite instructions of how, when, what, where, and why to adopt SBM throughout this vast state. This document, entitled *Resource Guide on Site-Based Decision Making and District Campus Planning*, includes such terms as needs assessment, mission statement, strategies, measurable objectives, incremental time lines, assignment of personnel, and evaluative criteria. In the opinion of these authors, this rhetoric sounds much like the business model attempting to impose democracy. As one carefully reads this SBM manual, much of the writing appears analogous to the witty phrase, the beatings will continue until morale improves. The net result of this legislative action and the series of accompanying policy directives is the ultimate organizational oxymoron— bureaucratically mandating local, grass-roots, governance actions.

Texas does not stand alone with respect to such statewide mandated efforts. The Kentucky Educational Reform Act of 1990 (referred to frequently as KERA) likewise calls for the top-down implementation of local decision-making structures, again, providing little to no regard for differences in context (Herman and Herman, 1993). Kentucky's legislation, like that of Texas, specifically outlines dates for the implementation of school-based decision-making efforts, the specific composition of school committees, precise terms for elected council members, and exacting mandates for council activity. Teachers and administrators from both Texas and Kentucky have brought forth serious and strenuous complaints concerning such legislation. Often heard are comments concerning the lack of flexibility with respect to serving individual communities. These concerns are voiced in a particularly ardent fashion by leaders of small and rural schools where SBM once operated effectively via informal structures (i.e., weekly faculty-staff-administration meetings) and has become less successful due to bureaucratic encroachment.

It would appear that the concept of SBM implies that leadership style and philosophy must be adaptable to the followers' level of maturity and, likewise, consider the situation that exists within the total culture of the school. Such interaction should, in turn, result in a more responsive organization. What appears to be occurring in many instances today is a corruption of the basic premises of SBM. By approaching the model in a fashion like that of Texas and Kentucky, SBM is being applied with all the sensitivity that Atilla the Hun demonstrated for the beauty of Rome. Such an approach completely ignores that any analysis of situational leadership be attempted, that adequate training (with concomitant funding) of building-level leadership be initiated, or that SBM be examined with relation to the actual community in which it will be implemented. Sacred and secular societies produce clearly different communities. It would appear that such differences have been lost through the formulation of these mandated legislative acts.

TEACHER EMPOWERMENT AND SBM

A final area of concern regarding the implementation of SBM relates to the obvious absence of a comprehensive discussion of the notion of teacher empowerment. If SBM is to become an effective vehicle for educational reform, a critical element in that process must be the empowerment of instructional faculty. Using Maeroff's definition of teacher empowerment (1988), it is obvious that SBM, in many of its current forms, simply overlooks this highly critical ingredient. Maeroff's definition of teacher empowerment is as follows: "It is the power to exercise one's craft with confidence and to shape the way that the job is to be done" (1988, p. 4).

Many teachers in rural educational communities may be forced to struggle with this definition. Each building faculty may not agree on how they will choose to improve their craft; likewise, they may not agree on how they wish to shape the overall configuration of their job responsibilities. Some faculties may conclude that SBM is simply not appropriate for their institution at this point in time. Other faculties may realize that SBM is not unlike the operational procedures that have been used in their buildings or districts for the past decade. Conceptually, the power of this process rests not with the outcome, but rather with the struggle and debate. To assume that SBM can be procedurally mandated for the rural teaching community (or any educational community) is tantamount to the degree of voicelessness that was created by the autocrats of yesteryear. As Curry (1990) states,

> The authoritarian style of leading and making decisions, which may have worked in the industrial age, is no longer viable in the age of information which requires individuals to think and solve problems. A more collaborative, collegial environment must be nourished in order for individuals in an organization to risk contributing to the decision making process. It is the responsibility of the administrator . . . to provide the time, space, resources and opportunities necessary for teachers to reflect, to think, and to make decisions which impact their professional lives. (p. 17)

A recent model developed by Smith (1993) provides a methodology for discussion and debate like that just quoted (see Figure 11.1). By use of this model, instructional professionals become the center of the SBM process. Teachers, not administrators or state department of education personnel, are considered as the first level of this site-based or school-based process. As teachers struggle to determine what roles they wish to play in this new system, they likewise dismiss other roles that appear less critical. Through an integration process similar to that noted by Follett (1924), ideas concerning participation, structure, training, areas for discussion, areas of concern, and procedures for resolution of conflict become homegrown. The instructional team then transmits

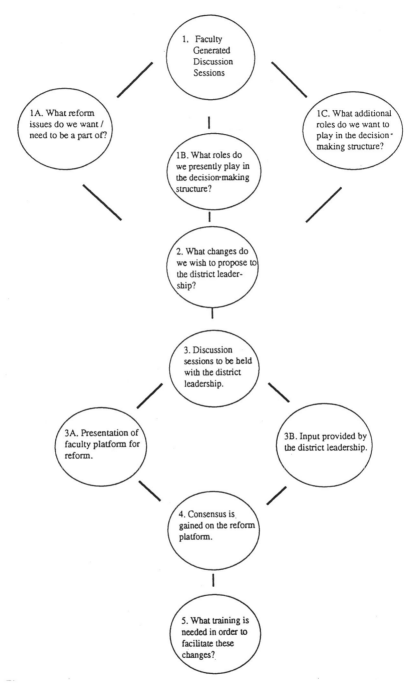

Figure 11.1. A model for teacher empowerment in rural schools.

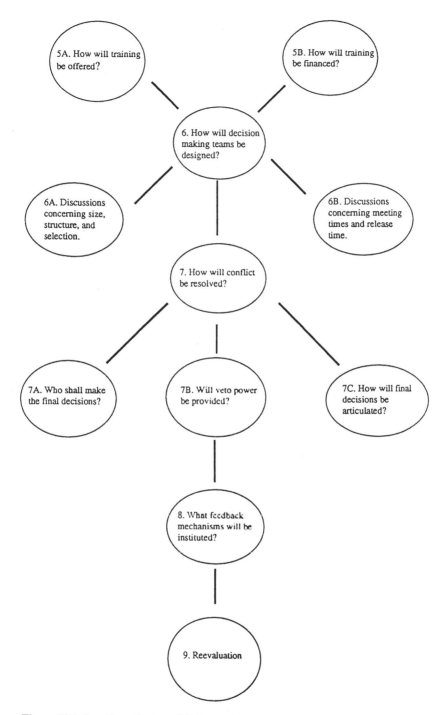

Figure 11.1. (continued). A model for teacher empowerment in rural schools.

these ideas and concepts to the administrative team, where, through dialectic debate, integration again occurs. The final outcome of this process is an SBM system that is designed specifically for a given environment—one where teacher empowerment becomes critical at the beginning, rather than becoming a by-product at the conclusion of such activity.

Although valuable for all teachers and administrators, an empowerment model of this nature is particularly amenable to rural environments, where smaller faculties and administrative teams generally exist. This process may indeed be more complicated and less definable than mandated initiatives. Nonetheless, the struggle for understanding of role, interest, configuration, and procedural action appears to offer much greater promise for actual implementation at the school-site level. As Hoyle et al. (1990) state,

> People will respond to what satisfies their personal needs. School leaders must continue to investigate how staff and students feel about themselves, their tasks, and their school environments. Top performers need an open and supportive climate. This belief is vital in designing, implementing, and evaluating [comprehensive] school ... improvement programs. (p. 20)

This model attempts to bring the factors of interest, perception, concern, and need together in a manner that allows all schools to work toward that top performer status.

ADDITIONAL DILEMMATIC RESEARCH

A cursory review of myriad articles relating to the development of SBM found only one such work related specifically to student achievement. That article presented results of a review of documents from over 200 districts in the United States, Australia, and Canada; in this work it was concluded that SBM alone does not achieve the stated goals of increasing student outcomes, broadening decision making, or changing school policy (Malen, 1990). The Texas Education Agency, however, clearly states that improved student performance is a preeminent goal for mandated SBM: "Site-based decision making will be implemented in a way that ... learning can be improved for all the children and youth in the state of Texas" (Texas Education Agency, 1992, p. ii). Rural school leaders, often chided by their larger school counterparts for ignoring or dismissing research findings, must sense great frustration in situations of this kind. As the research is reviewed, the findings indicate not only a differing perspective on this issue, but offer completely different conclusions. Does SBM bring about improved student learning or not? Although governmental agencies might like teachers and administrators to believe such an assertion, the research simply does not support this stance.

Taliaferro (1991) continues the dilemma by urging the educational community to avoid countless hours of examining such terms as teacher empowerment and school-based decision making and instead to become actively involved in the process of removing barriers to genuine participatory management. It is here that educational professionals are reminded of the fact that power can never be bestowed upon one group by another. Rather, power must come from within. SBM can only be effective if it is collectively determined as appropriate by the faculty, staff, and administration of the given school site.

Fullan and Miles (1992a), in a recent issue of the *Kappan,* carefully describe the many pitfalls that accompany such journeys toward the implementation of genuine educational reform. These authors offer such suggestive caveats as examining resistance, avoiding superficial solutions, accepting problems, and managing change. However, their most powerful comments concerning SBM were in direct accord with a previous section of this work:

> Site-based management . . . also shows problems associated with structural reforms. Daniel Levine and Eugene Eubanks, among others, have indicated how school-based models often result in changes in formal decision-making structures but rarely result in a focus on developing instructional skills or on changing the culture of schools. (Fullan and Miles, 1992, p. 747)

Fullan and Miles continue with their condemnation of unilaterally mandated ventures by stating, "Change cannot be accomplished from afar. . . . Local implementation by everyday teachers, principals, parents, and students is the only way that change happens" (Fullan and Miles, 1992, p. 752).

At this point, hopefully, the basic parameters of this dilemma are becoming clear. Rural school leaders must avoid the dogmatic actions of the past if new learning communities are to be created. However, the design and implementation of complex communities of this nature certainly require more than mandated site-based management efforts. The efforts necessary to create new schools and new school governance strategies may indeed take rural teachers and administrators far beyond what we now consider as SBM.

LOOKING TO THE FUTURE: ERADICATING THE DILEMMA

If rural schools are to successfully educate the children that have been entrusted to their care, then colleges and universities must prepare the rural leader (as well as the teacher) for life within the rural society—one that is often sacred in nature. As has been discussed in earlier sections of this chapter, the leadership requirements of a rural setting are, at times, significantly different from those required of successful urban and suburban educational leaders. Leadership preparation programs must work to illuminate the differences between life in a sacred society and life in a secular society (*Gemeinschaft* versus Gesellschaft). Additionally, colleges and universities need to recognize that administrators, like teachers, go through several levels of concern based upon their own personal growth cycles and philosophies (Parkay et al., 1992). By gaining a clear understanding of these cycles, future rural school leaders will have greater ability to identify movements toward and away from professional actualization.

The five most prominent stages of professional concern are the survival stage, the stage of control, concern for organizational stability, educational leadership concerns, and the stage of professional actualization. The survival stage is characterized by coping with the trauma of leading a complex organization, learning the ropes, and surviving mistakes. This is followed by the leader who, having survived the early stages, concentrates efforts toward organizational control in order to bring sense from seeming chaos. In the third stage of concern, the leader struggles for organizational stability. Efforts are made to routinize problems, to bring sense of stability, or to enhance the veteran status of the position. Educational leadership is the fourth level of new administrative concern and is typified by the new administrator focusing efforts on educational and instructional issues. The fifth and final stage of concern and growth is the professionally actualized principal. Efforts to develop a personal vision, to bring the vision to fruition, and to provide professional growth opportunities to others are the major efforts at this stage of socialization.

It is naive to believe that all principals are capable of becoming professionally actualized within the sacred rural society or that all new principals (or even more experienced ones) are at the same levels of growth at precisely the same point in time. Therefore, colleges and universities need to examine ways to increase the length of time that aspiring administrators are supervised by experienced professors of educational administration; here, the term *experienced* would most powerfully equate with the notion of field experience. Mentor-protegee supervision of this type might be combined with the first few years of actual administrative experience. In this manner, university personnel and neophyte administrators could work cooperatively through the implementation of new ventures such as increasing opportunities for teacher empowerment and implementing new governance structures like school empowerment. Discussions of and investigations into differing levels of maturity within the faculty and administrative team could also be undertaken. Levels of professional growth could, likewise, be carefully examined. University personnel could take the opportunity to network practitioners within similar communities to discuss myriad issues. Through such interaction, practitioners would be provided an opportunity to meet with peers from similar settings but would also be provided with the insight of a scholar to lead them along the scholar-practitioner continuum (Tallerico et al., 1993; Smith, 1992).

Additionally, experienced superintendents and school board members must be made aware of the need to offer unwavering support to those school-site administrators attempting to implement nontraditional empowerment and governance plans. Hanson (1991) states that the implementation of new innovations is prevented primarily in one of two ways: nonimplementation due to indifference on the part of the hosts (i.e., school board and superintendent) or nonimplementation due to indifference on the part of the participants (i.e., principals and instructional personnel). In order to overcome such indifferences, schools need to carefully analyze all elements of the organization in order to determine the desirability of adopting new ventures. Teachers, principals, board members, and central office administrators must be provided time to jointly discuss the many ramifications that surround a complex change in operation as is created by school empowerment style activity. As this time is set aside, all stakeholders in the organization must be alerted to the fact that this process will be lengthy and interactive. In order to move beyond any current operational state, members of the organization must be given abundant amounts of time and freedom to speak their minds. Rural communities often pride themselves on tranquility and equilibrium. As schools begin to investigate new governance procedures and opportunities for increased instructional empowerment, all members of the community must be made aware of the fact that such tranquility and equilibrium will be temporarily shattered.

Comprehensive staff development opportunities must also be made available to rural and small schools attempting to investigate changes in organizational operation. Small and rural schools traditionally have had a more modest staff development budget than have their urban and suburban counterparts (Jess, 1985). Nonetheless, smaller environments often have significantly greater needs for research and staff development to support new programmatic ventures (i.e., to overcome the sacred society). With smaller staff development budgets and virtually nonexistent research capabilities, it would appear that small and rural schools exist, in this case, much like the disadvantaged school children depicted in Kozol's *Savage Inequalities* (1991). Those individuals and/or institutions with the greatest needs are receiving the least assistance.

A clear example of the disparity between need and assistance can be found in the Richardson Independent School District (ISD), Richardson, Texas. Richardson ISD has long been considered a bellwether educational community. Progressive in nature and capable of generating significant amounts of taxable effort, Richardson ISD began investigating the possibilities of SBM implementation in early 1987. By the Fall of 1988, every school in the district had instituted its own site-based planning team, developed a personalized mission statement, determined educational priorities, and produced its own school improvement plan. A document later published under the title of *Site-Based Leadership* (Richardson ISD, 1992) brought together tremendous amounts of research and application data relating specifically to SBM in Richardson, Texas. District offices of Program Planning, Staff Development, and Research and Testing assisted with the compilation of nearly 500 pages of critically important data for teachers, administrators, parents, and community leaders.

Ropes Independent School District, on the other hand, is a small, rural, property poor district located in Ropesville, Texas. The SBM document developed by this district is a five-page pamphlet entitled *Ropes ISD Site Based Decision Making Plan* (Ropes Independent School District, 1993). This document is virtually identical to a model (or template) generated by the Texas Education Agency and contains no supporting research or documentation. Although the latter document meets state-mandated guidelines for the purpose of SBM implementation, it is obviously much less helpful to teachers, administrators, parents, and community leaders.

The purpose of this analysis is not to laud Richardson ISD nor to condemn Ropes ISD. It is to illuminate the vast disparity that exists within two school districts functioning within the same state. The research and staff development capabilities of the first district are clearly superior to those of the latter. However, the needs of the latter district may indeed be greater than those of the former. Students enrolled in each of these authors' graduate classes continually stress that rural schools are offered significantly less staff development than their urban and suburban counterparts. If you have limited exposure to staff development and limited capabilities to generate staff development and research activity, are you not disenfranchised? Although regional service centers and county offices of education heroically attempt to provide such services, these services are not locally designed, nor are they locally controlled. New funding ventures must be undertaken to assure that every school district in every state has the capabilities to function in a manner like that found in Richardson, Texas.

Finally, school-site change, such as that created by SBM, must be viewed as a holistic process, rather than a series of disconnected events having no relationship to expected outcomes. State departments of education must reexamine their role in this holistic process. Are these educational agencies promoting the concepts of SBM in light of current operational philosophies found in various school settings, or are they making such promulgations based on a political mentality? Rather than mandating ventures such as SBM, would progression incentives leading toward other governance models not be more effective? Questions of this nature must not be overlooked. As these questions are pondered, it must also be recognized that mandates from above often result in pocket vetoes, corruption of the vision, goal displacement, and/or a variety of other unintended outcomes.

In light of the data presented throughout this chapter, it would appear only logical for states like Kentucky and Texas to rescind mandated legislation concerning site-based management. Simply stated, ventures of this nature will never provide change like that generated through local action. By rescinding mandated legislation, state legislators could then reallocate funding to grass-roots endeavors that pragmatically have an opportunity to bring about sustained and appropriate change for specific school communities. These locally owned initiatives would certainly more accurately depict the claims of Fullan and Miles (1992) regarding the failure of change from afar and the corresponding potential for success at the local level.

In closing, it would serve the profession well if the concepts of simultaneous loose and tight coupling and school empowerment were to be revisited in light of what is known about situational leadership theory, current research on actualization, effective schools research, sacred and secular societies, and teacher empowerment. As has been discussed throughout the entirety of this chapter, SBM may prove effective in some school sites and ineffective in others. Such success or failure can generally be attributed directly to one or more of the aforementioned factors. By ignoring these factors, practitioners will continue to waste countless hours attempting to comply with models that have been thrust upon them. Obviously, all children do not fit into size five shoes, so why do we continue to believe that all school districts will fit neatly into one governance model? Rural and small school teachers, administrators, boards of education, and community leaders must come together to collectively offer resistance toward efforts to force any one system of governance upon them. In forming such resistance, it would appear that several rather critical issues are at stake. These issues include the potential for loss of outstanding instructional professionals, the potential loss of committed building administrators, and the demise of once responsive rural schools. To acknowledge such a future for rural education is less than palatable for most involved with these schools. If we are desirous of a different future, we must begin creating that future today. Rural principals alone cannot create such a future. Rural teachers alone cannot create such a future. Rural superintendents alone cannot create such a future. All concerned parties must come together to make rural schools of tomorrow the best places they can be. Some of these places may include SBM; others may not. By creating multidisciplinary support for appropriate locally constructed governance ventures, the dilemma concludes. Rationality is, thus, returned to rural schools and rural school life.

REFERENCES

Black, J. A. and English, F. W. (1986). *What They Don't Tell You in Schools of Education about School Administration.* Lancaster, PA: Technomic Publishing Co., Inc.

Brookover, W. B. (1987). Distortion and overgeneralizations are no substitute for sound research. *Phi Delta Kappan,* 69 (3), 225–227.

Brookover, W. B. (1981). *Effective Secondary Schools.* Philadelphia, PA: Research for Better Schools (ERIC Document Reproduction Service No. ED 231 088).

Brookover, W. B. and Lezotte, L. W. (1979). *Changes in School Characteristics Coincident with Changes in Student Achievement.* East Lansing, MI: Institute for Research on Teaching.

Brookover, W. B., Beady, C., Flood, P., Schweitzer, J. and Wisenbaker, J. (1977). *Schools Can Make a Difference.* East Lansing Michigan: Michigan State University.

Brookover, W., Gigliotti, R. J., Henderson, R. D., and Schneider, J. M. (1973). *Elementary School Social Environment and School Achievement.* East Lansing, MI: Michigan State University.

Callahan, R. (1962). *Education and the Cult of Efficiency: A Study of Social Forces That Have Shaped the Administration of Public Schools.* Chicago, IL: University of Chicago Press.

Cawelti, G. (1989). Key elements of site-based management. *Educational Leadership,* 46 (8), 46.

Curry, B. R. (1990). What do you think . . . about teacher empowerment? *Centering Teacher Education,* 7 (2), 16–19.

Dantley, M. E. (1990). The ineffectiveness of effective schools leadership: An analysis of the effective schools movement from a critical perspective. *Journal of Negro Education,* 59, 585–598.

Edmonds, R. (1979). Effective schools for the urban poor. *Educational Leadership,* 37 (1), 15–24.

Educational Research Service. (1991). *Site-Based Management.* Arlington, VA: Educational Research Service.

Follett, M. P. (1924). *Creative Experience.* New York: Longmans, Green, and Company.

Fullan, M. G. and Miles, M. B. (1992). Getting reform right: What works and what doesn't. *Phi Delta Kappan,* 73, 745–752.

Gusky, D. (1990). Without principal. *Teacher,* 1 (6), 56–63.

Hanson, E. M. (1991). *Educational Administration and Organizational Behavior* (3rd ed.). Boston: Allyn & Bacon.

Herman, J. J. and Herman, J. L. (1993). *School-Based Management: Current Thinking and Practice.* Springfield, IL: Charles C. Thomas.

Hersey, P. and Blanchard, K. (1988). *Management of Organizational Behavior: Utilizing Human Resources* (4th ed.). Englewood Cliffs, NJ: Prentice-Hall.

Hoyle, J. R., English, F. W., and Steffy, B. E. (1990). *Skills for Successful School Leaders* (2nd ed.). Arlington, VA: American Association of School Administrators.

Iannaconne, L. and Lutz, F. (1970). *Politics, Power, and Policy: The Governing of Local School Districts.* Columbus, OH: Merrill.

Jess, J. D. (1985). The needs of rural schools. *Illinois School Research and Development Journal,* 21 (1), 6–14.

Kozol, J. (1991). *Savage Inequalities: Children in America's Schools.* New York: Crown.

Malen, B. (1990). Unfulfilled promises. *School Administrator,* 47 (2), 32–59.

Maeroff, G. I. (1988). *The Empowerment of Teachers: Overcoming the Crisis of Confidence.* New York: Teachers College Press.

Mann, D. (1989). Effective schools as a dropout prevention strategy. *NASSP Bulletin,* 73, 77–83.

Martin, J. A. and McGee, M. L. (1990). *Quality Circles/Site-Based Management Implementation in Public School Districts.* Morgantown, WV: West Virginia University (ERIC Reproduction Service No. ED 327 984).

Parkay, F., Currie, F., and Rhodes, J. (1992). Professional socialization: A longitudinal study of first time high school principals. *Educational Administration Quarterly,* 28 (1), 43–75.

Richardson Independent School District. (1992). *Site-Based Leadership: A Plan for Continuing the Implementation of Site-Based Decision Making in the Richardson Independent School District.* Richardson, TX: Richardson ISD.

Ropes Independent School District. (1993). *Ropes ISD Site Based Decision Making Plan.* Ropesville, TX: Ropes ISD.

Smith, J. M. (1993). Teacher Empowerment in Rural Schools: Where Do We

Begin? In *NCPEA: In a New Voice,* J. R. Hoyle and D. M. Estes (Eds.), Lancaster, PA: Technomic Publishing Co., Inc., pp. 312–323.

Smith, J. M. (1992). Reactions of aspiring educational leaders to nontraditional administrator preparation: What are the implications for programmatic change? *California Professors of Educational Administration Journal,* 4 (1), 49–57.

Smith, J. M. and Lotven, B. A. (1991). Teacher empowerment in a rural setting: Fact versus fantasy. Paper presented at the *Annual Meeting of the National Rural Education Association,* Jackson, MS.

Taliaferro, M. B. (1991). The myth of empowerment. *Journal of Negro Education,* 60, 1–2.

Tallerico, M., Burstyn, J. N., and Poole, W. (1993). *Gender and Politics at Work: Why Women Exit the Superintendency.* Fairfax, VA: The National Policy Board for Educational Administration.

Texas Education Agency. (1992). *Resource Guide on Site-Based Decision Making and District Campus Planning.* Austin, TX: Texas Education Agency.

Vidich, A. J. and Bensman, J. (1968). *Small Town in Mass Society: Class, Power, and Religion in a Rural Community.* Princeton, NJ: Princeton University Press.

West Publishing Company. (1992). *Texas School Law Bulletin.* St. Paul, MN: West Publishing Company.

CHAPTER 12

Empowering the School Staff: Legislating New Roles in Kentucky

JANE CLARK LINDLE[1]

In the spring of 1990, the Kentucky General Assembly threw down the gauntlet of radical reform to the commonwealth's principals, teachers, and parents with passage of the 1990 Kentucky Education Reform Act (KERA). Facing possible action by the Kentucky Supreme Court, the legislature was compelled to redesign Kentucky's entire system of public schools based on the Court's declaration that they were unconstitutional (*Rose v. Council for Better Education, Inc.,* 1989). The Court's decision stemmed from a challenge of the state educational funding system by the Council for Better Education, Inc. The Council, sixty-six property poor districts, was joined by seven boards of education and twenty-two students to contest the disparity in funding of school districts. When in July 1989, the Kentucky Supreme Court affirmed a lower court ruling that struck down the public school system for failing to provide a constitutionally mandated "efficient system throughout the state," the stage was set for radical education reform in Kentucky.

Radical reform is neither top-down nor bottom-up. It is both. This has profound implications for empowerment in Kentucky. Empowerment, under conditions of radical reform, is more than a mandate. Kentucky's brand of empowerment is freedom to throw out restrictive state curriculum guides and bureaucratic regulations, but simultaneously,

[1]University of Kentucky.

Kentucky's empowerment is akin to a military charge or mission with the new state Commissioner of Education leading the forces. Within this maelstrom of empowerment forces stands the figure of the school principal. Kentucky's education reform provisions have fundamentally changed principals' and teachers' job descriptions. As many in the state have noted, even veteran educators of fifteen to twenty years' experience are having their first year all over again under KERA.

The purpose of this chapter is to describe the challenges to the Kentucky principal's role in nurturing students, staff, and self. The chapter is divided into four sections. In the first section, the principles underlying Kentucky's education reform are described with particular attention to expectations for student and school performance. The second section lays out the staff and professional development requirements generated by KERA's radical reforms. In the third section, attention is given to the implications of KERA for ongoing principal development, as well as for preparation of future school leaders in Kentucky. Finally, lessons from Kentucky's style of empowerment are delineated for school leaders in the United States and globally.

PRINCIPLES OF KERA

Kentucky has had a consistently undistinguished record in education. Pick any typical national or global indicator of educational excellence, and Kentucky was near the bottom (Combs, 1991). Additionally, Kentucky was facing the same social and economic challenges as the rest of the nation in the 1980's with one of the least educated adult work forces (Bureau of the Census, 1984; Kentucky KIDS COUNT, 1991; Steffy, 1993).

One potent off-shoot of these dismal conditions was the formation by sixty-six property poor school districts of the Council for Better Education in 1985. The Council, along with twenty-two students from seven school districts and their boards of education, legally challenged Kentucky's educational funding system. Although a lower court judge agreed with the plaintiffs that the funding system was "discriminatory," the Kentucky Supreme Court went one step further denouncing the commonwealth's entire educational system as unconstitutional (*Rose*, 1989; Steffy, 1993). In a unique finesse of the separation between branches of government, the court made its ruling in June 1989 but withheld final judgment until the adjournment of the next regularly scheduled session of the General Assembly in 1990. Then-Governor Wilkinson wasted no time in appointing a task force of Kentucky legislators to address educational reform. A wide range of national consultants met with the legislators on a variety of educational matters. Spurred on by support from the Kentucky Education Association (an affiliate of the National Education Association), the Kentucky Congress of Parents and Teachers (a branch of the Parent Teachers Association–PTA), and the Prichard Committee for Academic Excellence (an influential citizens' group) as well as other professional organizations, the General Assembly convened for its regular session in January of 1990 with education reform a major part of the agenda. By March, the Assembly passed House Bill 940, now known as the Kentucky Education Reform Act of 1990, or KERA (Legislative Research Commission, 1990). Governor Wilkinson signed the bill into law in April 1990, declaring the moment "one of the most historic days in Kentucky's history" (Steffy, 1993, p. 3).

The major areas of reforms included finance, curriculum, and governance. Beyond the new formula for allocation of state and local education funds, a deliberate move was made from equity in educational access to equity in achievement (Foster, 1991). The conditions of the work force and the educational system prompted the conclusion that, in the long run, the commonwealth could not afford to "waste" a child. Any dropout rate could not be tolerated. From this, the unifying principle that "all children can learn, and most at higher levels than previously expected" emerged (Steffy, 1993). The state adopted six learning outcomes as follows:

1. Use basic communication and mathematics skills for purposes and situations they will encounter throughout their lives.
2. Apply core concepts and principles from mathematics, the sciences, the arts, the humanities, social studies, and practical living studies to situations they will encounter throughout their lives.
3. Become a self-sufficient individual.
4. Become responsible members of a family, work group, or community, including demonstrating effectiveness in community service.
5. Think and solve problems in school situations and in a variety of situations they will encounter in life.
6. Connect and integrate experience and new knowledge from all subject matters and fields they have previously learned and build on past experiences to acquire new information through various media sources (Kentucky Revised Statues, 1992, Section 158.6451).

Kentucky's education reform is centered on the expectation that no child will be excluded, pushed out, or allowed to easily disengage from the educational system. The opportunities for education were extended into preschool for at-risk three and four year olds and into the summer and after school for older students. The compulsory attendance law was expanded to include pupils up to eighteen years of age. Schools are encouraged to drop pull-out programs for disabled students and to include special education support aides and teachers in regular classrooms (Legislative Research Commission, 1990).

Curriculum reforms include the development of multiaged, developmentally appropriate education, known as primary schools, for children who would have attended kindergarten through third grades. Instead of rigid curriculums and input measures of allocated learning time for various subjects and standardized tests, the curriculum is now outcomes-based, with more authentic tests of student performance. Curriculum frameworks, based on the six learning goals and divided into seventy-five "Valued Outcomes," have been introduced. These frameworks provide more holistic cognitive approaches to learning and more examples of the means by which students can demonstrate achievement through portfolios, performance events, and group work.

One of the most striking reforms has to do with determining educational accountability. Under KERA, the new unit of analysis for test/assessment results is not district-level data, but school building aggregations at fourth, eighth, and twelfth grades. The new assessment program establishes rewards or sanctions at each school, not school district, based on cognitive indicators (test scores on traditional tests, performance events, and portfolios), as well as noncognitive indicators, such as absentee or grade-level retention rates, dropout rates, and attempts by the school to address "barriers to learning." Although the barriers to learning have yet to be fully defined, KERA provided funding for Family Resource/Youth Services Centers as a means of addressing some of the conditions affecting capacities for learning (Russo and Lindle, 1994).

Based on the school-level focus for the rewards and sanctions of assessment, the governance reforms focused on the school (Legislative Research Commission, 1990). School-Based Decision-Making (SBDM or School) Councils were to be implemented on a voluntary basis until the 1995–96 school year. SBDM Councils include principals as chairs, three teachers (or a multiple of three) elected by the school faculty, and two parents (or a multiple of two) elected by the largest parent organizations, usually a PTA or a PTO. The SBDM Councils are legally authorized to make policy decisions in the following areas:

- determination of the curriculum, including needs assessment and curriculum development

- assignment of all instructional and noninstructional staff time
- assignment of students to classes and programs within the school
- determination of the schedule of the school day and week, subject to the beginning and ending times of the school day and school calendar year as established by the local board
- determination of use of school space during the school day
- planning and resolution of issues regarding instructional practices
- selections and implementation of discipline and classroom management techniques, including responsibilities of the student, parents, teacher, counselor, and principal
- selection of extracurricular programs and determination of policies relating to student participation based on academic qualification and attendance requirements, program evaluation, and supervision
- procedures that are consistent with local school board policy for determining alignment with state standards, technology utilization, and program appraisal (Kentucky Revised Statutes, 1992, Section 160.345, j)

In addition, the School Council selects a new principal, in the event of a vacancy, from a list provided by the superintendent who is bound by the Council's decisions. Although the School Council is to be consulted in the hiring of other instructional and noninstructional staff, principals still have the responsibilities of supervision and evaluation of personnel.

At this point it is fair to ask who was empowered under KERA. The answer is probably as complex as the legislation and may seem contradictory to many. Certainly, responsibilities increased at the school level. Principals are less buffered and less buffeted by centralized decisions from local school boards and the state department of education. Teachers are both less isolated and less independent as they become involved in school-level decisions about curriculum and instruction. Parents are less alienated but also less autonomous as they engage in School Council dialogue about the outcomes of education for all children, not just their children. As Kentucky moves into the final two years of implementation, a number of educational issues face the adults and professionals who must interpret and execute this law.

PROFESSIONAL DEVELOPMENT ISSUES

The 1990 Kentucky Education Reform Act was not without provisions for addressing the training and educational needs of professionals. These provisions focused on shifts in delivery, design, and content of professional development as the state's educators had known of it in the past (Steffy, 1993).

Delivery of professional development had been primarily directed at inservice education for teachers, coordinated by regional Professional Development Coordinators (PDC) based at each of Kentucky's seven public universities. Under KERA, regional cooperatives or consortia of local school districts were formed to address common interests and needs, such as coordination of professional development for specialized personnel in several districts or group-purchasing arrangements.

Previously, design of professional development had been left to the idiosyncratic requests of individual districts to the regional PDC. For the first two years of enactment, the legislature required extra inservice days on the specific topics of KERA, including such points as an overview of the law, implementation of primary school, performance assessment, school-based decision making, and motivation of students with diverse cultural backgrounds (Steffy, 1993). For the first time, superintendents were required to receive professional development updates on similar topics. Additionally, professional development requirements for principals were expanded.

The entire approach to professional development shifted from state and district requirements to state mandates and school plans. As schools moved into the third year of implementation, the state shifted content concerns for professional development to the school level. Individual school buildings were required to produce professional development plans using strategic planning techniques. Districts and regional consortia were delegated the task of coordinating the plans and finding resources to support the plans (Kentucky Department of Education, no date; Program Review 93-DSIM-113, 1993).

With individual schools now heavily engaged in activities previously determined by or fulfilled by school district boards and central offices, the role of the principal has been completely redesigned. A number of preparation and professional development issues have materialized that are specific to the principalship.

NEW ROLES FOR PRINCIPALS IMPLY NEW EDUCATIONAL DEVELOPMENT

Defining the new parameters of the principal's role is a necessary step in identifying the types of preparation and professional development needed by principals. Within these roles and new knowledge are embedded issues of empowerment.

WHAT IS THE PRINCIPAL'S NEW ROLE?

There may be as many answers to this question as there are citizens in Kentucky. Principals recognize various symbols of their changing roles. Other referent role groups echo the principals' perceptions and add a few observations of their own.

Fayette County's Morton Middle School Principal Jack Lyons answered the question this way:

> Now principals are more exposed to more groups and their constituencies. The central office does not handle those issues and complaints much anymore. Many of these issues are for School Councils to decide. Especially, during the transition (of implementing KERA) there's also not much central office support because they are not as sure of their role*.

At Henry Clay High School in Fayette County, Principal Michael Courtney made this commentary on the principal's changing role:

> The opportunity for dialogue is often mistaken as an opportunity for aggressive combat. Teachers and parents are empowered constituencies which don't have the background to use their new power. Sometimes issues can't be raised without teachers feeling defensive about the *status quo*. There seems to be a need to defend the way it's been done before you can move on to what might improve it. People aren't really accustomed to the democratic process. They see discussion of issues as a competitive activity rather than a means of learning about new perspectives. I feel like I spend a lot of time trying to keep the peace**.

Lana Fryman, Principal of Bourbon County's Central Elementary, noted that implementing KERA has forced principals to move away from maintenance and routines. She feels she has to encourage nurturing and creativity†.

Principals note longer hours now that so much planning takes place at the school level. Committee meetings are held after instructional hours. Secondary principals are still expected to be visible at the usual student activities such as sports events and dances, in addition to their new SBDM responsibilities.

A recent study of the pilot year (1991–92) SBDM Councils (Lindle, 1992a)‡ found that communication satisfaction was significantly dif-

---

* Personal communication, 1993.
** Personal communication, 1993.
† Personal communication, 1993.
‡ The study was a random selection of principals, parents, and teachers who had served on the SBDM Council during the 1991–1992 pilot year of SBDM Councils. Of 385 possible responses, 211 mailed surveys were returned, yielding a 55% response rate. The following results are more fully explained in an unpublished research report by the author and noted in the citations.

ferent for principals§ as compared to teachers and parent representatives. While principals were more satisfied, a number of factors may have affected teachers' and parents' satisfaction. For the most part, principals were older, had no children in school, and were more predominantly male than were the teachers and parents. Principals, teachers, and parents also made observations about the principals' readiness to assume a role in the SBDM process§§.

From a parent representative, the following comment was made

> My strongest opposition to SBDM Councils is the policy for the principal to be chairperson. He then runs the meetings and intimidates the teachers and parents, although innocently, I believe. It is uncomfortable to ask to write a change in policy for fear of causing hard feelings. I feel the chair position should be elected by each Council.

A teacher representative noted, rather tersely,

> School Council members communicate openly with each other, excluding the principal.

One of the principals also reflected on the new demands for the principal's role:

> This is a worthwhile but time consuming component of KERA. Though I am constantly learning and expanding my knowledge, my training was not geared toward producing a person who had the status of "mini-superintendent." This is at times overwhelming.

In summary, principals and people close to them see a variety of changes in the principal's role. Principals have a higher degree of visibility through the shift to school-level planning and accountability. As they move out of the routines of management of school functions, they find themselves in more contentious arenas of shared decision making. Finding means and substance for supporting teachers who may have done very well in self-contained classrooms but who must now collaborate with other teachers becomes a daily challenge. Many do not feel

---

§ The significant results were found using an ANOVA and a post-hoc Sheffy on the total mean scores of each group. Scores were obtained from a twelve item Likert-scale on Communication Satisfaction developed by the author. Reliability and validity results are available from the author's unpublished report cited in the references.

§§ The comments were volunteered in writing by the participants. Surveys were not coded in order to preserve confidentiality. The writers identified themselves as principals, teachers, or parent representatives in the demographic questions on the survey. Full analysis of the comments are available from the author's unpublished research report listed in the references.

fully prepared for the role shift, which demands more communication, more skills in conflict resolution, more nurturing of adults in conflict resolution, and more nurturing of adults in addressing new discursive activities. Some of their constituents agree. These circumstances suggest a corresponding shift in the knowledge base for principal preparation and professional development.

WHAT DO PRINCIPALS NEED TO KNOW?

In a January 1993 speech to the Kentucky Council for Professors of Educational Administration, Robert Sexton, Executive Director of the Prichard Committee for Academic Excellence, reported a number of requisites for the position of principal based on reports from the field by Prichard Committee members. Sexton's list (1993) included the following:

- the ability to collaborate with other administrators, parents, and the community
- the ability to inspire others to try new ideas and make changes
- the ability to explain policy to teachers, parents, and the community without resorting to jargon, double-talk, or generally confusing anyone
- the ability to manage more with less money (Sexton noted that this last ability is a challenge that business leaders will share with educational leaders well into the 21st century).

Although Sexton and the Prichard Committee played and will continue to play an influential role in KERA's development and implementation, the ultimate authority for revamping the preparation and professional development of principals lies with the new, KERA-mandated, Educational Professional Standards Board (Legislative Research Commission, 1990, p. 9). This board has the authority to establish requirements, review programs of colleges and universities, and determine the eligibility of individuals desiring certification as principals (Kentucky Revised Statutes, 1992, 161.028). At this writing, the board is immersed in revising requirements for teaching. Administrator requisites will be addressed in the near future. Some amalgamation of the observations of principals, teachers, parents, professors, and various organizations such as the Prichard Committee will appear in these future requisites.

In the meantime, a review of the standards being developed for teachers might provide insight into the potential changes for administrator preparation. The Educational Professional Standard Board is currently reviewing a more outcomes-based orientation to teacher education. Beyond an attempt to have teacher preparation focus more fully on the KERA curriculum frameworks, like KERA classrooms, the teacher education classroom is to be more focused on student performance. Along these lines, the board is scrutinizing seven proposed "Educator Outcomes":

1. Designs/plans instruction that addresses Kentucky's Learning Goals and Valued Outcomes for students
2. Introduces/implements/manages instruction that addresses Kentucky's Learning Goals and Valued Outcomes
3. Creates a learning climate that supports student learning outcomes
4. Assesses learning and communicates results to students, parents, and others
5. Reflects and evaluates specific teaching/learning situations or programs
6. Evaluates own overall performance to model/teach Kentucky's Learning Goals and implements a program of professional development
7. Collaborates with colleagues, parents, and others (Council on New Teacher Performance Standards, 1993)

Despite the fact that these seven outcomes were designed with teachers in mind, a quick consideration of these abilities in relation to the challenges faced by principals reveals a number of similarities. In fact, comparisons of these seven outcomes with some of Sexton's points also illustrate commonalities (see Table 12.1).

Even though collaboration was seventh on the proposed teacher outcome list, Sexton's placement of it first and the demands of KERA's new decision-making and instructional formats probably emphasize the essence of empowerment in Kentucky. Collaboration is the driving force among empowerment issues under KERA. While a change in the structural forms of school decision making is specified under KERA as School Councils, the transitional challenge is to attend to the conversion from independent and isolated thinking to collaborative, discursive thinking (Strike, 1993). Much of the empowerment literature has focused on individual teacher efficacy or a definition of professionalism, which allows more room for teachers to exercise their professional judgments (Carnegie Forum, 1986; The Holmes Group, 1986; Maeroff, 1988; Strike, 1993). Kentucky's education reform, based on a judicial and legislative mandate, is far more democratic in its approach to empowerment. Not only are teachers closer to the decision-making process, but

Table 12.1. Common observations concerning
requisite knowledge of principals.

Sexton's Observations	Proposed Valued Educator Outcomes
The ability to collaborate with other administrators, parents and the community	7. Collaborates with colleagues, parents, and others
The ability to inspire others to try new ideas and make changes	1. Designs/plans instruction that addresses Kentucky's Learning Goals and Valued Outcomes for students
	2. Introduces/implements manages instruction that addresses Kentucky's Learning Goals and Valued Outcomes
	3. Creates a learning climate that supports student learning outcomes
	6. Evaluates own overall performance to model/teach Kentucky's Learning Goals and implements a program of professional development.
The ability to explain policy to teachers, parents, and the community without resorting to jargon, double-talk or generally confusing anyone	4. Assesses learning and communicates results to students, parents and others.
	5. Reflects and evaluates specific teaching/learning situations or programs
The ability to manage more with less money	5. Reflects and evaluates specific teaching/learning situations or programs

parents, as proxy for students, and principals are as well. The struggle for efficacy in decision making about schooling in Kentucky can be compared to a clash between professionalism, individualism, and democracy. Or this struggle can be viewed as growing relationships between groups who have not typically collaborated and who have much to learn from each other. It is this opportunity to learn from each other in discourses about educational issues that reemphasizes the educative role of the principal.

The ability to inspire others from Sexton's column, and Educator Outcomes 1, 2, 3, and 6 are linked in the educative role of the principal. Principals are now not merely head teachers as they were historically (Campbell et al., 1987), but also teachers of teachers, teachers of parents, and teachers of the community members now necessary to schooling. More than crises management and conflict resolution, the ability to inspire others to try ideas and make changes is a teaching act. Furthermore, this ability has implications for principals' knowledge of adult development and learning. This ability is also linked to the communication issues raised by Sexton's next point and Educator Outcomes 4 and 5.

Beyond the typical expectations that administrators display competence with the written and spoken word, the ability to communicate with multiple audiences requires a facility of mind. The traditional rhetorical skills of argumentation, debate, persuasion, and reasoning, augmented by instructional expertise, could serve to prepare principals for the demands of a variety of groups. Not only would this knowledge improve principals' capacities to explain policy, but also to report on programmatic results. These improvements would also give principals more tools to accomplish Sexton's final point.

Managing more with less requires proficiency with evaluation, analysis, and projection of resources, and a certain amount of entrepreneurial spirit. With KERA's school-level focus, principals are compelled to access the efficiency of technology and data management, as opposed to waiting for information from the school district's central office or the state department of education. They need to imaginatively leverage resources and promote talents of others. This may mean including business, government, and community in the education process. And the inclusion process brings us full circle to issues of collaboration and communication. By including the broader community, principals must share information to promote the link with other agencies that deal with youth and families.

The implementation of the Kentucky Education Reform Act of 1990 has established a climate where the empowerment accomplished in Kentucky is not as much professional as it is democratic. Empowerment, Kentucky-style, is the essence of collaboration among diverse groups who hold vested interests in schooling. For principals, these conditions require a willingness to engage in discourse, insights into promoting and developing the talents of others, and a facility in communication with disparate audiences using a variety of cutting-edge technology and media in order to leverage the necessary resources. In Kentucky, the role of principal has metamorphosed from that of manager to leader, from caretaker to caregiver, from routines to inventions.

There are lessons in these changes initiated in Kentucky for those wrestling with the meaning of empowerment elsewhere.

LESSONS FROM KENTUCKY ON EMPOWERMENT

Kentucky's primary lesson is in its particular brand of empowerment. This type of empowerment is more expansive than the type that primarily promotes a more professional environment for teachers. Kentucky is unique in guaranteeing parents a say in educational decision making (Epstein, 1987a, 1987b; Chavkin and Williams, 1985; Lindle, 1992b). By expanding the formal decision-making structures to include principals, teachers, and parents, Kentucky embarked on a campaign that democratized schooling further than the typical meaning of local control.

At each school, a cadre of principals, parents, and teachers are grappling with the meaning of their new roles. No ready answers to the perennial issues of democracy are found in KERA legislation. Are the teachers representatives or trustees of the rest of the faculty? Beyond an admonition to include minorities in the SBDM process, added by the legislature in its 1992 regular session [Kentucky Revised Statutes, 1992, Section 160.345(a)], the nature of parent representation and broader parent involvement was not specified. No guidelines for proportional representation of minority or other interest groups was indicated. Like the abundant social issues that dominate the larger social agenda, each school in Kentucky is acting out these debates on a micro-level. The debates are draining for principals, parents, and teachers new to the political arena.

Perhaps an important ancillary lesson from Kentucky's brand of empowerment is that the newly empowered are often ill-prepared to handle either a discursive or a political forum. For a state that is notorious for its political fiefdoms (Steffy, 1993), it is far to easy to adopt SBDM Councils as a political platform rather than a democratic symposium. If Kentucky's schools are to benefit from this democratized style of empowerment, then Kentucky's principals and other participants must become far more adept with and aware of the educative power of discourse (Strike, 1993).

For principals, the implementation of educative discourse requires intellectual growth in their own roles as teachers of communities, as entrepreneurs of resources, and as facilitators of democratic discourse.

When Kentucky made the incomparable vault from last place to first in its redesign of education, it completely overreached common understanding of the meaning of education and perhaps even of democracy. The complexity of the 1990 Kentucky Education Reform Act is no less than the complexity of the concept of democracy.

REFERENCES

Bureau of the Census. (1984). *United States Department of Commerce, Statistical Abstracts of the United States* (105th ed.). Washington, D.C.: U.S. Government Printing Office, p. 135.

Campbell, R. F., Fleming, T., Newell, L. J., & Bennion, J. W. (1987). *A History of Thought and Practice in Educational Administration.* New York: Teachers College Press.

Carnegie Forum (1986). *A Nation Prepared: Teachers for the 21st Century.* Washington, D.C.: Carnegie Forum on Education and the Economy. Task Force on Teaching.

Chavkin, N. F. & Williams, D. L. (1985). Parent involvement in education project. *Executive Summary of the Final Report* (ERIC Document Reproduction Service No. ED 300 908).

Combs, Bert T. (1991). Creative constitutional reform in Kentucky. *Harvard Journal on Legislation, 28,* 367–378.

Council on New Teacher Performance Standards. (1993). *Draft of Proposed Valued Education Outcomes.* Frankfort, KY: Kentucky Department of Education.

Epstein, J. L. (1987a). What principals should know about parent involvement. *Principal,* 66 (3), 6–9.

Epstein, J. L. (1987b). Parent involvement–What research says to administrators. *Education and Urban Society,* 19 (2), 119–136.

Foster, J. D. (1991). The role of accountability in Kentucky's Education Reform Act of 1990. *Educational Leadership,* 48 (5), 34–36.

The Holmes Group, (1986). *Tomorrows Teachers.* East Lansing, MI: The Holmes Group.

Kentucky Department of Education. (no date). Staff note–Item: 704 KAR 3:035 and E, Annual Professional Development Plan. Frankfort, KY: Kentucky Department of Education.

Kentucky KIDS COUNT. (1991). *County Data Book.* Louisville, KY: Kentucky Youth Advocates.

Kentucky Revised Statutes. (1992). *Kentucky School Laws–1992.* Frankfort, KY: Kentucky Department of Education.

Legislative Research Commission. (1990). *A Guide to the Kentucky Education Reform Act of 1990.* Frankfort, KY: LRC.

Lindle, J. C. (1992a). The implementation of the Kentucky Education Reform Act: A descriptive study of the parent involvement provisions. Executive summary of phase 2: Parent involvement and communication satisfaction with the pilot year (1991–92) of School Based Decision Making Councils. Lexington, KY, unpublished research report.

Lindle, J. C. (1992b). School leadership and education reform: Parent involvement, the Education for Handicapped Children Act, and the principal. Occasional Paper #4. Urbana, IL: National Center for School Leadership.

Maeroff, G. I. (1988). *The Empowerment of Teachers: Overcoming the Crisis of Confidence.* New York: Teachers College Press.

Program Review 93-DISM-113. (1993). *The Importance of 1993–94 School Plans.* Frankfort, KY: Kentucky Department of Education.

Rose v. Council for Better Education, Inc., 790 S. W. 2d. 186, Ky. (1989).

Russo, C. J. and Lindle, J. C. (1994). On the cutting edge: Family resources/youth service centers in Kentucky. In *The Politics of Education Yearbook: The Politics of Linking Schools and Social Services,* Louise Adler and Sid Gardner (Eds.), New York: Falmer Press.

Sexton, R. (27 January, 1993). Personal Communication.

Steffy, B. E. (1993). *The Kentucky Education Reform: Lessons for America.* Lancaster, PA: Technomic Publishing Co., Inc.

Strike, K. A. (1993). Professionalism, democracy, and discursive communities: Normative reflections on restructuring. *American Educational Research Journal,* 30 (2), 255–275.

CHAPTER 13

Teacher Evaluation: Communicating the Message of Empowerment

JAMES M. SMITH[1]
CONNIE RUHL-SMITH[1]
MICHAEL D. RICHARDSON[2]

INTRODUCTION

In any evaluation system, "evaluators must confer with teachers" (Stow and Sweeney, 1981, p. 541). Without this dialogue, the documentation collected during the various data-gathering processes is useless. If evaluation is to be meaningful, not only must building-level administrators and teachers confer, but they must genuinely understand one another. Many principals and assistant principals recognize that the evaluation issue is indeed complex. This belief is held for a variety of reasons, one of which centers around the notion that teachers are often more knowledgeable in their subject areas than are building administrators. As Laing (1986) argues, another reason for this complexity is rooted in "vague standards . . . unclear characteristics of what actually constitutes good teaching" (p. 92). For these reasons, the administrator and teacher must communicate explicitly during the preobservation and post observation conferences. Otherwise, any agreed-upon changes in behavior will be rapidly extinguished. According to Laing (1986),

> Teachers rarely make lasting changes unless their own beliefs and values are congruent with the new behavior. . . . Human beings are remarkably

[1]West Texas A&M University.
[2]Georgia Southern University.

resistant to imposed change. Imposed change tends to be exhibited in the presence of the authority and neglected in its absence. When the door closes on the classroom, the teacher is enormously powerful. (pp. 92–93)

Without a clear connection between present actions and desired modifications, the objectives of teacher evaluation will remain unfocused. The observed data may be compared and discussed, but the conference will provide little to no chance for truly altered professional actions.

ADMINISTRATOR COMPETENCIES

Hersey and Blanchard (1988) have postulated a basic competency of leadership, which they have identified as "being able to put the message in a way that people can easily understand and accept" (p. 305). Therefore, principals and assistant principals must have the skills to clearly articulate their supervisory message. When using clinical supervision or some modified form of the clinical supervision mode, there are many skills that an administrator must possess or continually attempt to develop. To be effective in evaluative conferences, all administrators must recognize the importance of the following skills:

1. The ability to clarify the mission, goals, objectives, and purposes for teacher evaluation
2. The ability to establish rapport with the teacher in such a manner that will foster open and frank self-evaluation
3. The ability to establish dialogue with the teacher, which, in turn, facilitates a cooperative climate rather than an adversarial relationship
4. The ability to focus on improvement of present teaching performance, rather than dwelling on prior actions
5. The ability to use nonverbal communication effectively in the conference, thus demonstrating the importance of a teacher both as a professional and an individual

These skills and abilities regarding successful teacher evaluation conferences cannot be effectively implemented without the overarching skill of active listening. Active listening (i.e., paraphrasing, perception checking, relating to personal feelings, and generating feedback) must be pervasive throughout all preobservation and postobservation conferences (Acheson and Gall, 1992; Daresh, 1989). Without the ability to actively listen to the teacher's ideas, thoughts, and concerns, the supervisory conference will be viewed as nothing more than an additional act of bureaucratic entanglement. If properly conducted, teachers will do the majority of all talking in supervisory conferencing, while the principal works to promote and encourage teacher self-evaluation. No rational member of the profession will continue to discuss intimate details regarding the art and craft of teaching if the other member of the dyad is obviously incapable or unwilling to listen. It is for this reason that Thomas (1979) urges the building administrator to "listen attentively, speak frankly and counsel effectively" (p. 42) throughout all supervisory conferences.

Although the administrator may come to the supervisory conference with many of the aforementioned skills and abilities, communication problems still envelop many preobservation and postobservation conferences. These communication problems are generally found when the teacher is uncomfortable or unwilling to communicate honestly regarding his/her performance or perceptions; it may also occur when the teacher attempts to rationalize past performance instead of focusing on future improvement. These problems are often exacerbated by administrator reaction to such situations. These negative counteractions generally include being judgmental, dominating the conversation, and reacting to the individual and not his/her behavior. Each of these counteractions are increasingly detrimental to effective communication and concomitantly provide additional barriers to successful supervision.

As has been stated in earlier sections of this work, the application of any teacher evaluation model requires the administrator to be an effective communicator. Effective communication also forces principals and assistant principals to provide appropriate feedback necessary to facilitate genuine teacher improvement. To illustrate how such feedback might be used with teachers unwilling to honestly evaluate their performance, Pigford (1987) offers some exacting insights. During her first year as principal, Pigford stated that many of the teachers with whom she was working had overinflated perceptions of their professional performance. She addressed this problem by conducting staff development activities that focused on designing clear goals for self-evaluation. She specified that ". . . we needed school objectives so clearly stated that they could not be misunderstood by parents, teachers and students" (p. 141). Through the utilization of a site-based decision-making process, teachers assisted with the development of seven objectives that clearly articulated the vision and direction for their school. These objectives were also utilized as guides for developing individual professional ob-

jectives for classroom teaching. As teachers adopted schoolwide and individual classroom objectives, criteria for teacher evaluation became
increasingly clear. Consequently, there was little opportunity for
supervisory miscommunication between Pigford and the instructional
staff: the teachers knew their objectives and knew that the principal
was available to assist and support them. Communication became
focused on how to meet these objectives in the most professional and
direct fashion. By use of such methodology, Pigford (1987) found that

> the teachers began to regard evaluation as an instructional activity
> designed to improve their performance—not just as a game that princi-
> pals play. (p. 142)

NONVERBAL COMMUNICATION

Buser and Pace (1988) cite several conditions inherent in teacher
evaluation that provide "opportunities for communication, observation,
and coaching that may make a difference" (p. 84). Furthermore, these
same authors contend that even informal, "off-the-record discussions
may result in behavior changes of evaluatees" (p. 85). Few would or
should disagree with such contentions; however, throughout the evaluation process many professionals must be reminded that not all communication is transmitted verbally. Hersey and Blanchard (1988)
describe messages as being delivered in three different ways—through
words (i.e., vocabulary, language, phrases, sentence structure, and sentence clarity), para-language (i.e., rate of speech, diction, tone, rhythm,
volume), and nonverbal behaviors (i.e., gestures, facial expressions, eye
contact, body language, positioning). Obviously, words are of critical
importance and should be carefully chosen, but much more communication takes place during the evaluation process than words could ever
convey. Through voice patterns, the rate and tone of speech, and voice
inflection, principals and assistant principals convey messages of emotion, intent, and purpose. The characteristics of voice and patterns of
speech have, at times, the ability to influence individuals more powerfully than does the selection of words. Nonverbal cues "serve as windows to . . . emotions, desires, and attributes" (Hershey and Blanchard,
1988, p. 309).

Often, the administrator can only imagine or reminisce about the
feelings of apprehension on the part of the teacher and the ramifications
of such apprehension on the entire evaluation process. Samuel Sarabia
(1990) can attest to this fact. As a first year bilingual educator entering

education from the world of business, he was forced to undergo an unusually large number of observations. He eventually became more relaxed but stated, "In the beginning, before anyone would actually come in, I would get very nervous and tense. It would show on the children's faces as well" (p. 49). This nonverbal communication undoubtedly had an effect on Sarabia's evaluation. An observant administrator would recognize such behavior and evaluate it for what it was—an expression of anxiety. An inexperienced administrator might, however, read this as an expression of poor relationships between teacher and students.

The ability to recognize the importance of nonverbal communication in the actual observation period or during the preobservation and postobservation conference is indeed critical. However, it is also critical for the administrator to carefully analyze the setting that surrounds the entire supervisory conference session. If for no other reason, supervisory conferences are uncomfortable because of the differences in perceived position power between the classroom teacher and the building administrator (Daresh, 1989). This degree of discomfort can be diminished with appropriate attention to the following nonverbal considerations: temperature of the conference room, number of external distractions, proximity of the desk and chair to the evaluatee, presence of coffee and/or soft drinks, and appropriate time allotment for discussion of professional issues. Although these actions often are overlooked and, at times, discredited by veteran practitioners, the appropriate setting for supervisory conferences can make the difference between a productive and successful session and a nonproductive session (Wiles and Bondi, 1991).

ETHICS

While principals must be concerned about nonverbal behaviors having an effect on the evaluation process, they must also be aware of the ethical considerations of communication. Clement Seldin (1988) cites an example of common reactions at an informal dinner when a principal was informed by a teacher that the previous year had been very difficult for her family. Illness, layoffs, and other troubles had beset the family. What may have been an innocent communication by the teacher became a questionable comment to the principal in light of the teacher's upcoming tenure decision. Was the comment innocent, or was it meant to elicit sympathy or a favorable rating from the principal? Such ethical communication dilemmas must be handled correctly, or principals will be perceived as untrustworthy and unprofessional by their staff. As Seldin points out, "A teacher is more likely to grow professionally and accept recommendations in an evaluation if the teacher respects the judgement of the principal" (p. 9). For this reason principals need to be extremely careful communicating with teachers because they "may find their reputations tarnished by one instance of questionable behavior" (Seldin, 1988, p. 9). As Barnett (1991) states,

> The competing standards that principals must consider highlight the moral dimension of their roles. In making decisions, they must determine what is right from wrong as well as what is possible. They must consider their own sentiments, beliefs, and values as well as those of the people affected by their decisions. In many situations principals interact with people who have different standards of practice. . . . A principal who is asked to mediate such a situation not only must deal with these competing standards but also must consider his/her own standards for appropriate . . . performance. By coming down on one side of an issue or another, principals must make moral choices and thereby reveal the standards underlying their decisions. (p. 131)

All supervisory communication, whether focused on issues of moral imperatives or simple corrections in classroom technique, must be considered privileged and confidential (much like the communication that transpires between physicians and their patients). A lack of honesty in the evaluation process interferes with the possibility of good, clear communication. Without honesty, the process becomes a game, resulting in little to no professional growth. As Bennis and Nanus (1985) so poignantly state,

> Trust is the emotional glue that binds followers and leaders together. The accumulation of trust is a measure of the legitimacy of leadership. It cannot be mandated or purchased; it must be earned. (p. 153)

If principals and teachers hope to create new schooling structures that advantage rather than disadvantage students, both entities must engage in simultaneous actions of trust, while consistently generating risk-taking behaviors. In keeping with these actions, both parties must admit that risk-taking may result in failure. To admit failure to another professional, trust must pervade the relationship. Without such trust, teachers will never openly discuss the trials and tribulations of their craft and will, therefore, never permit supervisory conferences to affect their professional lives. However, should trust exist and open communication take place, teachers and administrators can begin to discuss critical issues such as empowerment, professional autonomy, student performance, and principles of ethical behavior (Strike, 1990).

TECHNOLOGY

Principals should be meticulous in all aspects of supervisory data gathering and, in turn, must be exacting in the communication of that data to members of the teaching faculty. As a practitioner, Richard Kuralt (1987) found that a laptop computer could assist him throughout various aspects of the supervisory process. By quickly producing a transcript of the classroom observation, the computer helped Kuralt to organize and record observation data efficiently. The transcript was then analyzed by both Kuralt and the teacher observed before the postobservation conference. Kuralt believed this detailed communication resulted in a more "collegial" conference. Kuralt also recorded many exchanges that took place during the preobservation and postobservation conferences. Both of these conferences, along with the observation transcript and the final report, were then sent to the classroom teacher for final review and signature. Kuralt began using the laptop computer to alleviate pencil and paper record keeping, but the real bonus was that "the [computer-assisted observations] enabled the teachers and I to change the patterns of information [exchanged] between us" (p. 72). Kuralt stressed that the use of the computer certainly does not "diminish the need for training and skill in interpersonal relationships" (p. 72). As in all other areas of education, computers can be of tremendous assistance in the facilitation of the communication processes that take place between teacher and principal; nonetheless, such computer-assisted activities cannot replace the need for quality professional interaction. Practitioners and researchers alike must always keep in mind that equipment such as computer hardware and/or software is merely a tool to help the supervisor with the many duties required in assisting professional educators through the growth process.

The use of audio- and videotaping can also be of tremendous assistance to the supervising administrator and classroom teacher. Audio- and videotapes provide an exact account of activities that transpire in the classroom during an actual observation session. These tapes are much more accurate than script taping or other forms of human record keeping. The use of such tapes also provides the supervisor with additional time to analyze questioning strategies, determine room motion, record student recognition and praise, evaluate degrees of modeling, and determine the extent of guided and independent practice. Acheson and Gall (1987) note the importance of such audio- and videotaping exercises for classroom teachers:

> Although video recordings would seem to be a more powerful observational tool than audio recordings, this may not be so. Teachers sometimes are captivated by the image on the TV screen and do not listen to what is being said. Audio recordings have fewer distracting cues, and so it is easier for the teacher to concentrate on the verbal interaction. Research has shown that video and audio feedback are equally effective in helping teachers improve their use of verbal teaching skills. (p. 124)

THE ADDED ELEMENT OF EMPOWERMENT

There are few terms or concepts that have swept the professional literature with the celerity that empowerment has demonstrated. This term can be located in virtually any professional educational journal, text, symposia, or conference that has been published or transpired over the course of the past five years. Multiple definitions for this term exist; however, most appear to focus on the issues of professional enabling, shared decision making, and increased occupational autonomy (Brederson, 1989). Coupled with these fundamental elements is the belief that empowerment cannot exist within the old definition of power as a dominating force (i.e., power over) but, rather, must exist within the context found in relationships of co-agency (i.e., power with). Therefore, for the purposes of this work, empowerment, as applied to educational settings, will be defined as

> the possession and exercise of power, by instructional professionals, in the pursuit of occupational improvement, professional autonomy, and the overall improvement of the educational processes. (Smith and Lotven, 1993, p. 459)

Supervision is inexorably linked to this definition of empowerment. Teachers struggle to improve professionally, as do administrators. Without dialogue that is dedicated to the notion of empowerment and overall school improvement, such struggles will be exacerbated. As principals and assistant principals work with teachers through the various stages of the clinical supervision model, such empowerment dialogue must consciously be included. Although clinical supervision has traditionally been dedicated to the precise analysis of teaching techniques and presentation, such actions must now be broadened to include discussion of issues such as occupational improvement and professional autonomy.

Many teachers are familiar with the research on effective teaching strategies (Good, 1987; Rosenshine, 1986; Brophy, 1981) and clearly understand the various elements of the Hunter Model (1982), the Lesson Cycle (Cartwright and Simpson, 1989), and Bloom's Taxonomy of Educational Objectives (Bloom, 1956). However, these same professionals are frequently dissatisfied with their overall classroom performance. If a supervisor would evaluate the teacher merely on the approved district or state instrument, the ratings obtained by the teaching professional would, in all likelihood, be outstanding. However, the teacher would have gained little to nothing in regard to this professional dissatisfaction.

The observation of classroom teaching is certainly one of the most important aspects of an administrator's job description. After all, schools, in essence, exist for the sole purpose of improving student performance and, therefore, must have a central focus on the consistent improvement of teaching and learning. Nonetheless, to overlook the basic tenets of teacher empowerment while observing or conferencing with a teacher would be as irresponsible as a mechanic merely changing the oil in an automobile when he/she fully realizes that the engine has other substantive damage. Supervisors must create opportunities for the discussion of teacher empowerment throughout the various stages of the evaluation cycle.

As each year begins, teachers and administrators routinely establish goals to be accomplished during the course of the upcoming academic semester or entire school year. These goals are often the replication of material that was written for previous years or are a modification of the goals established by the administrative team or school-based decision-making council. An astute supervisor will encourage those under his/her charge to expand these goals to include ideas or concepts that are larger in scope. For example, the master teacher might compose a set of goals that are specifically targeted to the perfection of previously utilized teaching strategies. A supervisor interested in coupling teacher empowerment with traditional supervision might suggest that this master teacher consider including a goal that focuses on the improvement or inclusion of one or more nontraditional teaching strategies (i.e., service learning projects, case studies, thematic teaching units). As the year progresses, the supervisor and master teacher would discuss progress toward the inclusion of this strategy or concept into his/her teaching repertoire. Classroom observations could be conducted focusing solely on the utilization of this newly adopted strategy. Professional development activities for that particular master teacher might also be tailored to the inclusion of this new strategy or set of strategies. The master teacher would be encouraged to select work-shops to attend that center on this concept. Release time could also be provided by the supervisor to allow the master teacher to visit and collaborate with other teachers expressing similar interests.

Similar supervisory actions could be applied to the neophyte teacher, as well. Because this individual has much less insight into his/her professional strengths or weaknesses, greater degrees of direct supervision would initially be required. However, beginning with the initial clarification conference (Glatthorn, 1990), the supervisor would help the neophyte understand the importance of overall professional development. This discussion would assist the teacher in defining professionalism as both a personal and collaborative endeavor. Throughout the year, the supervisor would assist this younger professional in uncovering resources and ideas that provide an opportunity to further define him/herself as a professional in the classroom and in the overall school setting. By engaging in such discussions early in a teacher's career, this individual is clearly given an opportunity to see the difference between what Sergiovanni (1991) and De Charms (1968) call "Origins" and "Pawns." As De Charms (1968) states,

> An Origin has a strong feeling of personal causation, a feeling that the locus for causation of effects in his environment lies within himself. A Pawn has a feeling that causal forces beyond his control, or personal forces residing within others, or in the physical environment determine his behavior. This constitutes a strong feeling of powerlessness or ineffectiveness. (p. 274)

As an administrator is provided the opportunity to observe classroom presentations, analyze teaching performance, and discuss such activities with classroom professionals, he/she is provided with insights that no other member of the school community possesses. Most classroom teachers work in isolation and, therefore, are unaware of the myriad skills and abilities of their colleagues. Although it seems that everyone knows who the "best teachers" are on any given campus, seldom are individual teaching strengths and weaknesses discussed in formal or informal forums. If genuinely interested in empowering teaching professionals, administrators must carefully examine the data collected from observations and conference sessions to develop committees and teaching teams that will address specific school needs (i.e., parental and community involvement, student motivation, internal and external communication, and effective teaching strategies for at-risk students). Much like university committees, if given the proper charge and provided with sufficient resources and opportunities, these individuals will offer not only a series of valuable solutions to existing problems but also will provide vastly different solutions from those generated by the administration alone.

It is imperative to note that such empowerment opportunities will be successful only if teachers believe that their input and involvement are valued and considered useful in the day-to-day operation of the school. To create site-based councils, teacher improvement teams, or other related committees with no intention of adopting the resolutions/actions created by these units is not only foolhardy, but also destructive to the overall school climate (Ruhl-Smith and Smith, 1993; Smith, 1993). As White (1992) so powerfully found in her interviews with over 100 teachers and administrators from highly decentralized schools and school districts:

> Greater participation in school decision making provided teachers with a greater sense of school ownership. Teachers indicated that their advice was not just given lip service but that their budget, curriculum, and hiring recommendations were actually acted upon. Increased participation in these decisions made teachers feel like active participants, not only in their individual classrooms but also in the development of school policy. Sharing expertise served to build teacher confidence and professionalism and encouraged self-improvement. Teachers realized that they had special talents that other teachers were interested in. Sharing of ideas reduced isolation and fostered cooperation, with a focus on teachers' strong points and on strengthening areas where teachers were weak. (p. 78)

CONCLUSIONS

Through the process of teacher evaluation, administrators can shape the course of instruction within any given building. As Buser and Pase (1988) point out, "Personnel evaluations are a most effective means whereby administrators can communicate the standards, the expectations, and the mission of the institution" (p. 85). Aldrich (1984) states that teachers should "not be allowed to determine their own rules, and the principal should no longer be viewed as a good old boy who managed by dispensing favorable treatment to select employees in return for unquestioned loyalty" (p. 33). By the decisions principals make and the ratings that they provide on evaluations, these administrators are communicating their standards and expectations to the faculty/staff, the students, the central office, and the community.

It is also important to note that teachers are professionals and, in turn, have well-founded perspectives on teaching effectiveness and professional development. These classroom professionals should not be easily coerced into accepting supervisory mandates without appropriate discussion and interaction. The key to supervising professionals is to jointly establish expectations for excellence and work collaboratively in order to see that such excellence comes to fruition. As Daresh (1989) so insightfully states,

> The supervisor who relies solely on formal authority and "pulls rank" to try to make others perform in a particular way will rarely be effective and, with professional employees, will often actually do more harm than good. Teachers who are "told" what to do will often rebel from what they perceive as an effort to manipulate their behavior. (p. 152)

As teachers and administrators continue to struggle with the basic elements of effective supervision, the inclusion of an issue such as empowerment significantly complicates the process. Although many teachers do understand the essential elements of effective teaching and express interest in overall professional development, these individuals have seldom been given the opportunity to engage in collaborative decision-making efforts directed toward overall professional growth. With increased demands for teacher autonomy in school settings, strategies must be developed to provide opportunities for teachers to make key decisions about all of the services they render (Smith and Scott, 1990). These decisions must include, but not be limited to, specific teaching strategies for working effectively with students in varied classroom environments. Discussions of this nature will certainly change the complexion of the supervisory process—such changes appear to be both timely and necessary.

With the many problems administrators face, they cannot afford to be misunderstood. Particularly in the evaluation process, principals need to be clear, firm, and concise. As instructional leaders, principals need to use the evaluation process to improve instruction throughout the entire school. To make such improvements, teachers and administrators must join together in each stage of the supervisory process to discuss effective teaching and the necessary goals to make such teaching become a reality.

REFERENCES

Acheson, K. A. and Gall, M. D. (1992). *Techniques in the Clinical Supervision of Teachers* (3rd ed.). White Plains, NY: Longman.

Acheson, K. A. and Gall, M. D. (1987). *Techniques in the Clinical Supervision of Teachers* (2nd ed.). White Plains, NY: Longman.

Aldrich, H. (1984). All decisions great and small. *Principal,* 64 (1), 31–35.

Barnett, B. G. (1991). The educational platform: Articulating moral dilemmas and choices for future educational leaders. In *The Moral Imperatives of Leadership: A Focus on Human Decency,* B. G. Barnett, F. O. McQuarrie, and C. J. Norris (Eds.), Memphis, TN: National Network for Innovative Principal Preparation, pp. 129–153.

Bennis, W. G. and Nanus, B. (1985). *Leaders: The Strategies for Taking Charge.* New York: Harper & Row.

Bloom, B. (1956). *Taxonomy of Educational Objectives: Cognitive Domain.* New York: Longmans and Green.

Brederson, P. V. (1989). Redefining leadership and roles of school principals: Responses to changes in the professional worklife of teachers. *The High School Journal,* 73, 9–20.

Brophy, J. (1981). Teacher praise: A functional analysis. *Review of Educational Research,* 51 (1), 5–32.

Buser, R. L. and Pace, V. (1988). Personal evaluation: Premises, realities, and constraints. *NAASP Bulletin,* 72 (512), 84–87.

Cartwright, C. and Simpson, T. L. (1989). The lesson cycle: A direct instruction teaching model. *Baylor Educator,* 14 (2), 3–13.

Daresh, John C. (1989). *Supervision as a Proactive Process.* New York: Longman.

De Charms, R. (1968). *Personal Causation.* New York: Academic Press.

Glatthorn, A. A. (1990). *Supervisory Leadership: Introduction to Instructional Supervision.* London: Scott, Foresman and Company.

Good, T. L. (1987). Two decades of research on teacher expectations: Findings and future decisions. *Journal of Teacher Education,* 38, 32–47.

Hersey, P. and Blanchard, K. (1988). *Management of Organizational Behavior.* Englewood Cliffs, NJ: Prentice Hall.

Hunter, M. (1982). *Mastery Teaching: Increasing Instructional Effectiveness in Secondary Schools, Colleges, and Universities.* El Segundo, CA: TIP Publications.

Kuralt, R. (1987). The computer as a supervisory tool. *Educational Leadership,* 44 (7), 71–72.

Laing, S. O. (1986). The principal and evaluation. *NAASP Bulletin,* 70 (493), 91–93.

Pigford, A. B. (1987). Teacher evaluation: More than a game that principals play. *Phi Delta Kappan,* 69, 141–142.

Rosenshine, B. V. (1986). Synthesis of research on explicit teaching. *Educational Leadership,* 43 (7), 60–68.

Ruhl-Smith, C. and Smith, J. M. (1993). Teacher job satisfaction in rural schools: Implications for quality assessment. In *Creating the Quality School: Selected Readings,* E. W. Chance (Ed.), Norman, OK: Center for the Study of Small/Rural Schools, pp. 402–420.

Sarabia, S. (1990). You have to be a scavenger. *Teacher Magazine,* 1 (7), 48–49.

Seldin, C. A. (1988). Ethics, evaluation and the secondary principal. *NAASP Bulletin,* 72, 9–11.

Sergiovanni, T. J. (1991). *The Principalship: A Reflective Practice Perspective* (2nd ed.). Boston: Allyn & Bacon.

Smith, J. M. (1993). Teacher Empowerment in Rural Schools: Where Do We Begin? In *NCPEA: In a New Voice*, J. R. Hoyle and D. M. Estes (Eds.), Lancaster, PA: Technomic Publishing Co., Inc., pp. 312–323.

Smith, J. M. and Lotven, B. A. (1993). Teacher empowerment in a rural setting: Fact versus fantasy. *Education*, 113, 457–464.

Smith, S. C. and Scott, J. J. (1990). *The Collaborative School: A Work Environment for Effective Instruction*. Reston, VA: National Association of Secondary School Principals.

Stow, S. B. and Sweeney, J. (1981). Developing a performance evaluation system. *Educational Leadership*, 55, 539–541.

Strike, K. A. (1990). The legal and moral responsibility of teachers. In *The Moral Dimensions of Teaching*, J. I. Goodlad, R. Soder, and K. A. Sirotnik (Eds.), San Francisco, CA: Jossey-Bass, pp. 188–223.

Thomas, M. D. (1979). *Performance Evaluation of Education Personnel*. Bloomington, IN: Phi Delta Kappa Education Foundation.

White, P. A. (1992). Teacher empowerment under "ideal" school-site autonomy. *Educational Evaluation and Policy Analysis*, 14 (1), 69–82.

Wiles, J. and Bondi, J. (1991). *Supervision: A Guide to Practice* (3rd ed.). New York: Macmillan.

CHAPTER 14

The Classroom with the Empowered Student

DENNIS W. VAN BERKUM[1]

INTRODUCTION

In 1950, Argyris studied long-range planning and group decision making in corporations. During these exploits, he realized that the underlying assumption to which organizations can assess the issues is by determining the appropriate outcomes. Key in this assessment was the value the organization places upon the worth of individual, their values in terms of contributions to the organization, and how the organization can develop its people (Argyris, 1955). When an organization gives priority to the value of people, assessment requires a close evaluation of the organizational goals. Traditionally, schools have been organized in ways that are counterproductive to the well-being of students. They develop a "plastic learner who aquires the skills and information necessary to negotiate a fixed cultural environment" (Vogt and Murrell, 1990, p. 56).

Schools utilize units of command, tight control, and specialization of subject. Schaef and Fassel (1988) describe this as establishing control around a system of autocratic or paternalistic control. Cunningham and Gresso (1993) suggest that people (in this case, students) must be able to discover their abilities to accomplish the greatness they are capable of. This is not easy for students because their maturation has

---

[1]North Dakota State University.

been under the close scrutiny and the controlling eyes of classroom teachers. Thus, students learn to look toward the teacher for direction, "first for safety and later on for the types of actions that get rewards" (p. 199).

Vogt and Murrell (1990) suggest that "the fundamental goal of all educators is empowerment: helping people become capable of setting and reaching goals for individual and social ends" (p. 162). Garman (1989) defined empowerment as "helping people to take charge of their lives, inspiring people to develop feelings of self-worth, and a willingness to be self-critical and reflective about their actions" (p. 2). This appears fundamental to the educational process. Student empowerment offers the opportunity to create an entrepreneurial spirit in students.

However, the current organization of school does not facilitate this process. Student empowerment is the least understood but the most important step in the empowering process of people. Schools tend to be organized in the same manner large private corporations are organized, prompting Block (1991) to state, "One of the failings of our democracy is that our organizations continue to be managed in an autocratic and top-down way despite our espoused belief in the fundamental value of individuals and their right to create paths of their own choosing" (p. xiii). Power over others drives the corporation (schools) to produce specific results.

Power and control of others thus become the meaning of our society and certainty in our lives. As we pursue certainty in education, we too often run the risk of producing rigidity or inflexibility in the teacher and in student learning. Block (1991) suggests that schools that do not empower students will

> become good at manipulating situations and, at times people, managing information and plans carefully to our own advantage, involving the names of high-level people when seeking support for our projects, becoming calculating in the way we manage relationships paying great attention to what the people above us want from us, and living with the belief that in order to get ahead, we must be cautious in telling the truth. (p. 9)

White and Epston (1989) refer to this certainty in therapy as the power of "normalized truths" where discipline is related to a set of beliefs that are rigidly held, tacitly or implicitly self-evident, or unquestioned. These fundamental beliefs consist of regularities or rules of conduct that govern teaching or define our discipline. However, they can also reflect rigidity and a failing to recognize the needs of students.

Educational systems reflect these failings. In our attempts to establish guiding principals for education, we encounter the temptation to use power and certainty to control the learning of others. When teaching does not adequately account for student scores on a standardized test, we often fall prey to the temptation of certainty in teaching. Curricula are set, and instruction is centered on performance on a set of standardized tests that reflect control on valued certainties in education. Poor scores impose corrections on the uncertainties that have developed. Thus, students fall victim to the temptation of power within the classroom.

POWER AND KNOWLEDGE

Teachers instruct and drill for expert knowledge and become blind to the experience the classroom can provide students as they engage in issues that require creative problem solving, curiosity, and empowerment. In addition, teachers control our dependency to become educated. Grades represent a measure of approval from the organization where the emphasis on scores encourages student self-interest, which is defined as seeking dependence and approval of teachers and parents. Grades in the school system cause greater dependence and control by the system, thus increasing self-interest and creation. Block (1991) suggests,

> Our entire experience with institutions has taught us to be successful, we have to please people. Moving through the school system was the most vivid example. The measure of performance in school was our grades. Students get good grades by pleasing their teachers. At times it seems like getting good grades becomes more important than learning. (p. 40)

Shore (1990) offers that all significant inquiry must begin and end in questioning. Although this process may be frustrating at times, it is the price we must pay to open classrooms for exploration—not the relentless interrogations that occur currently to ensure the articulation of the inarticulate parts of life.

Often, teachers unintentionally encourage students to maintain caution and dependency on teachers. Educators and society believe that the survival of student learning is in the hands of the teacher, not the learner. Certainty is supported by the belief that correct answers are the means to measure knowledge, while student creativity is stifled. In a dependence model, the teacher becomes the expert and center of the classroom by exerting power over students using several different methods of instruction. Power and, therefore, control of knowledge is at the fingertips of the teacher, not the learner. Foucault (1980), in a juxta-position of power/knowledge, argues that

> Exercise of power perpetually creates knowledge and conversely, knowl-edge constantly induces effects of power. . . . Knowledge and power are in-tegrated with one another, and there is no point in dreaming of a time when knowledge will cease to depend on power. . . . It is not possible for power to be exercised without knowledge, it is impossible for knowledge not to engender power. (p. 50)

As students become empowered, teachers experience the opportunity to relinquish control over what is learned in the classroom. As the classroom environment recognizes the leadership that students can provide for their learning, the responsibility for learning shifts from the teacher to the student. Sovereignty at the top gives way to a team leadership approach that uses students, teachers, and administrators.

POWER AND CERTAINTY VERSUS EMPOWERMENT AND CURIOSITY

To understand student empowerment is to understand the concepts of power and certainty as compared to empowerment and curiosity. An ex-planation of power and certainty can be found in Bhadha's (1990) "co-lonial discourse" metaphor that describes an approach to power whose "strategic function is the creation of a space for a 'subject peoples'" (p. 75). Key to this concept is that, when the creation of a space by teachers happens, student expertise and specific knowledge run the risk of subjugation rather than liberation. Under the banner of learn-ing, teachers descend upon students in much the same way as colonists descended upon a new land (Kearney et al., 1989). Teachers, even those who have been empowered by the bureaucracy, determine the curricu-lum, procedures, and discipline in the classroom as they view reality.

Under the bureaucratic model, classrooms are created for the purpose of control; surprise is disdained. Consequently, teacher autonomy becomes a way of life where student creativity and empowerment are left unexplored. At such times, students acquiesce, retreat, or even revolt to the process. This sort of colonialization results in unchecked power and certainty of action in the classroom. Students who are malleable to a power/certainty teacher are viewed as ideal and, at times, as an exclusive group of children because they embrace the teacher's view of the world and respond to the teacher's power and dis-courses of certainty. As good students, they readily intertwine their learning with the teacher's expectations. Discarding naive or traditional knowledge, they mimic the language or espouse the expert knowledge of the school system. Borrowing from Block's (1991) "Patriarchal contract," a student who adheres to the teacher submits to authority, denies self-expression, sacrifices for unnamed future rewards, and believes that the above are just.

An averse response may be found among students who "just don't get it." They cannot find a comfortable place within the classroom of a power/certainty teacher. Try as they might, they cannot dismiss their own traditions that allowed them to survive the colonial vision. For these students, repeated attempts to colonize them give a feeling of the "same thing over and over" (Watzlawick, 1978). Teachers view them as problem students with special needs.

Out of this second population, another group has emerged. Students on the edge of the dominate culture run the risk of greater colonization. These students are represented by various groups of diversity, economic status, low-functioning families, or lives that have been organized around a complaint of society. In their pursuit of identity, personal knowledge, their own world, and their past, they either leave school or take on the system. In doing so, they combat the power and certainty a teacher is expecting in the classroom. Teachers view these students as resistant and combative in their search to know their own best interests. Often, the creative thoughts and individual actions of students are unwanted. In doing so, students are trained to look outside themselves to find identity.

Like an underdeveloped nation, students enter the school each year rich in energy, thirsty for knowledge, and willing to conform. They are ripe for colonization. Teachers select those features of the student's experiences that best relate to the teacher's predisposition or expert knowledge and develop positions of power and certainty. Further, this position is supported by the school structure, its need to insure standardized achievement, and the teacher's need to meet the standards of best teaching practices.

CURIOSITY AND EMPOWERMENT

As an antidote to certainty, the concept of curiosity not simply as the sense of interest or even enthusiasm for the lesson, but as tentatively and subjectively (it might be, it could be, it seems to be, etc.) qualified questioning should be considered. To counterbalance teacher power, student empowerment, the sharing of tasks between teacher and student or student and student, or the co-negotiation of solutions is an option. Consequently, the concept of colonialism gives way to one of experimentation and independence. A basic belief held within this newfound experimentation and independence is that students left to their own instincts, their own curiosity, and their own authority become productive.

The classroom where the teacher controls the certainties of correct responses becomes a classroom in which students are allowed to search for answers. The teacher tolerates the outward appearance of confusion and ambiguity without moving on to the next lesson. When students are empowered, they discover exceptions in addition to expert knowledge. Units of learning move more slowly in defining a problem; however, learning is designed with an emphasis on reality. When students do not "get it," questions are asked that will move students to further inquiry of the subject.

This concept insures curricular outcomes but, more importantly, examines the issues from a more problematic view. As discussion among empowered students develops, questioning opens options to many levels of thinking. The empowered classroom operates from a second-order perspective that always considers the teacher-student and student-student relationship first. Questioning strategies look for indigenous knowledge of the student. Great care is taken to identify the strengths of student interaction—not what is wrong in a response to a preconceived question or criterion-referenced test.

TEACHING THE EMPOWERED STUDENT

Teaching that favors power can be juxtaposed with teaching that favors empowerment. While there are times to act decisively and powerfully on behalf of students, these should ultimately move to empowering situations. Engaging methods of teaching that would empower students instead of overpowering them would be preferred. However, this kind of teaching requires a special student-teacher relationship. This collaborative alignment focuses on the student and the teacher teamed against a problem, as opposed to one in which the teacher is almost at odds with the student. Although temptations of power are always ready to manifest themselves in traditional forms of control, an empowering moment may begin by posing a question of whether the lesson or objective to be learned is even appropriate at all. Is there any chance that an error has taken place? Is

*Table 14.1. The teacher powered classroom vs.
the student empowered classroom.*

Teacher Power	Student Empowered
Will be more hierarchical	Tend to be more collaborative
Act as an agent of social control	Consider the consequences of control
Seek to have student respond to methods of teaching	Select teaching method that fits student style and needs
Tend to direct student toward expert knowledge	Calls for special knowledge and competencies of students
Inadvertently causes dependence	Foster independence, a sense of competence, and self-confidence
Use dominant values of society to teach students	Avoids dominant values, instead uses student's language and metaphors
The classroom tends to create a context of passivity.	The classroom tends to create a context of discovery.
When students are unsuccessful, instruction will move toward structure and resort to repetition.	When unsuccessful, instruction moves toward improvisation.
Under the influence of urgency, high test scores, and school policy, unilateral goals are set for students.	Urgency is seen with caution and patience, and constructed solutions are formed with student involvement.

the curriculum presented at this time and in the presented context relevant? How will we know it is useful? Does everyone see the issue the same? If seen differently, how do students understand the problem (Stewart et al., 1991)? These questions offer an opportunity to empower students while freeing teachers from controlling the outcomes of the classroom.

This is not to say that student empowerment is not without structure or specific objectives. Instead of being presumptive, it asks, Who is present? Who is able to participate? What participation is possible? Student empowerment experiments with solutions that, at times, are presumptuous, yet have a tentative place in the problem solving process. The process of student empowerment requires patience and a recognition and acceptance of its own limitations. Student development is of prime importance. Student empowerment also recognizes the receptiveness to change, listening skills and the ability of students to share common opportunities and experiences.

Table 14.1 presents a comparison of a classroom controlled by the teacher to that of one where students are empowered.

LEVELS OF STUDENT EMPOWERMENT

Student empowerment is a developmental process that takes a student from dependency to independence. This developmental process can be found in the works of Wilber et al. (1986). These authors suggest that stages of development occur much as the rungs on a ladder. Each rung on the ladder supports a various phase of development, such as a different self-need studied by Maslow, different self-identities studied by Loevinger, different moral responses studied by Kohlberg, and the cognitive development and the formation of knowledge studied by Piaget. Cunningham (1991) synthesized these constructs into three major stages of development that offer a suggestion to implementation of student empowerment. On the first rung, Selfish Self-Indulgence, students exhibit different emotions. However, these emotions are not identifiable to those of others, particularly their mothers and significant others or teachers. There is the ability to be aware of their needs and their strong self-centered view of life. Students draw no distinction between what is inside and what exists in the external world. Self-gratification is the reward for all things attempted. Students in this environment do not take responsibility for their lives, and they blame others for every problem that develops. As a result of this lack of differentiation and empowerment, students tend to think more highly of themselves and less highly of other students.

On the second rung, Scripted Self-Validation, students become preoccupied with the external world and the roles they are expected to play in the classroom. They seek ways to fit in, please others, and conform to expectations. In addition, students literally follow rules, expectations, and internalize the judgments of others. It is during this period of development that students ascertain a feeling of security, belonging, support, safety, success, and accomplishment while feeling bored, vulnerable or unhappy or have a lack of personal meaning. The results of the lack of empowerment in school result in the incapability of improving.

The highest rung on the ladder, Vital Self-Reliance, is one that allows individual growth and development. Classroom instruction is designed to synthesize and adapt the inner personal nature and the external forces, with a goal of merging the internal self of students with that of the external world. In this type of class, the focus of attention moves from the ego-centered state of conformity to one of balance and unity. In this classroom, individual work is based upon a willingness to trust the student and let go. Students develop confidence where they used to need approval. They accept resources, limits, and responsibilities. Students become internally motivated to act responsibly without reducing self-confidence. They no longer seek any other's approval but maintain a balance with the external world. Mutual benefit is enhanced.

FINAL THOUGHTS

Properly implemented student empowerment may seem to be just basic concepts of quality teaching. Who would want students to respond to problem solving instead of rote memorization of material? The oxymoron that seems to exist is that, while this is wanted, we all, at one time or another, fall prey to either the temptations to exert control for our own purposes or to hold onto impressions and ideas we feel certain are "true."

Too often, empowerment in a school transcends to the principal's office and possibly to the classroom teacher. Students are viewed as consumers or products of the educational process. Student empowerment suggests that students are an integral part of the learning process. The true consumer of education is society itself. Therefore, educators should move from the concept of students as consumers to one where students take an active role in the educational process. They become empowered. This conceptual shift in empowerment will not be without difficulties. Student empowerment is taking empowerment and placing it at the lowest level in the educational system.

The paradox of student empowerment is possibly a self-fulfilling prophecy much like McGregor's idea that managers regard people as either X, needing control, or Y motivated. If teachers view students as needing control and impose limits on student power, they create a dependency for them that requires an X style of classroom management. Teachers who view students as motivated (style Y) will structure classrooms in which students reach agreements on shared responsibilities. The teacher moves from the one whom students depend upon to one who becomes a facilitator of the learning process.

Block (1991) suggests that this view is not a set of techniques one chooses. If we believe that control of the classroom is the teacher's domain, we will not look to empower students. Students will not take control of their lives. Student empowerment seeks to shift the responsibility and control to students who do the "core work of the organization" (p. xv). Classrooms need to move from conventional ways of conducting education that supports conventional politics to one that supports individual thought and expression. Like all self-help programs, they should teach responsibility and self-respect, where the individual develops a strong sense of his/her own competence and independence, whether it be circumstance or substance.

Students become empowered by becoming aware of their own uniqueness, not by becoming something that others prefer. The definition of an
educated person must become more than one of recitation of others'
thoughts and a set of facts. Successful implementation of student empowerment requires a paradigm shift. Individual student learning must
be placed in the forefront. For teachers to empower students, they must
be willing to overcome their own desires for external control of student
minds through the curriculum content they have chosen. Quality, attitude, increased responsibility, and ownership in learning will be the
logical pay-off.

Traditions, policies, and formality tend to explain the way things are
to be. Such actions need change so that new ideas and new experiences
can be realized. Student empowerment offers an opportunity for schools
to improve by recognizing the uniqueness each student brings into the
classroom. Instead of forcing all individuals to follow the same set to
roles, rules, and regulations, schools should try to interchange them to
insure that students become aware of their own talents.

The most promising use of student empowerment may be in the area
of diversity. If students are allowed to become empowered, classrooms
may improve the interpersonal competency of students, effecting a
change in respect for different human factors and feelings. Tension between adversarial groups may become reduced, and an open method of
communication will develop, resulting in fewer efforts for control and
power. Relationships among and within differing groups will rely on
mutual trust, cooperation, shared learning, and advanced problem-
solving skills. Cunningham and Gresso (1993) offer that

> If empowerment occurs individuals become more fully aware of their
> unique abilities, how those abilities can help the organization, and how
> they complement and interfere with the skills of others within the or-
> ganization. Organizations are improved the more individuals learn about
> their own nature. Thus, the key to organizational effectiveness is learn-
> ing how to use individual differences to the fullest. This is the exact
> reverse of trying to force all individuals to follow the same set of roles,
> rules, and regulations in order to try to make them interchangeable.
> (p. 205)

Student empowerment is a flexible concept that is successful only
when the climate of acceptance is appropriate for that of the student
and that of the teacher. Not all circumstances are appropriate for student empowerment. Only those instances that affect students directly
should be considered. We must be careful not to alienate those around
us as we promote student empowerment.

Student empowerment requires that a school clearly state its beliefs about students, its mission in the educational process of students, and its vision for student learning. In doing so, the classroom must create a situation conducive to learning, where student empowerment is viewed as a logical progression of individual development. This classroom should facilitate a flow of communication that indicates a sharing of school expectations with those of students. The teacher participates as the sharer of expertise developed from experience, research, and education, not an instructor who drills expert knowledge. Finally, the empowered classroom should introduce new values that support empowerment in society by establishing a model of behavior in students that allows them to take risks and recognizes their individual strengths and limitations while practicing empowerment.

REFERENCES

Argyris, C. (1955). Top management dilemma: Company needs vs. individual development. *Personnel,* 32 (2), 123–134.

Bhadha, H. K. (1990). The other question: Difference, discrimination and the disclosure of colonialism. In *Out There: Marginalization and Contemporary Culture,* R. Fergeuson, M. Gever, T. Minh-ha and C. West (Eds.), New York: The New Museum of Contemporary Art, pp. 71–87.

Block, P. (1991). *The Empowered Manager: Positive Political Skills at Work.* San Francisco, CA: Jossey-Bass Inc.

Cunningham, W. G. (1991). Empowerment: Vitalizing personal energy. In *Cultural Leadership,* W. G. Cunningham and D. W. Gresso, Needham Heights, MA: Allyn and Bacon, pp. 208–213.

Cunningham, W. G. and Gresso, D. W. (1993). *Cultural Leadership.* Needham Heights, MA: Allyn and Bacon.

Foucault, M. (1980). *Power/Knowledge: Selected Interviews and Other Writings.* New York: Pantheon Books.

Garman, N. B. (1989). Reflection, the heart of clinical supervision. *Journal of Curriculum and Supervision* (Fall): 2.

Kearney, P., Byrne, N. O. and McCarthy, I. (1989). Just metaphors: Marginal illuminations in a colonial retreat, *Case Studies,* 4, 14–32.

Schaef, A. W. and Fassel, D. (1988). *The Addictive Organization.* New York: Harper and Row.

Shore, B. (1990). Indiana Jones blows his mind. *The New York Times Book Review,* (Sept. 8): 37.

Stewart, K., Valenine, L. and Amundson, J. (1991). The battle for definition: The problem with the problem. *Journal of Strategic and Systemic Therapies,* 10, 21–31.

Voght, J. F. and Murrell, K. L. (1990). *Empowerment in Organizations: How to Spark Exceptional Performance.* San Diego, CA: University Associates.

Watzlawick, P. (1978). *The Language of Change.* New York: Basic Books.

White, M. and Epston, D. (1989). *Literate Means to Therapeutic Ends.* Adelaide: Dulwich Centre Publications.

Wilber, K., Engler, J. and Brown, D. P. (1986). Transformations of consciousness. In *Cultural Leadership,* Cunningham and Gresso, p. 208.

The Future of Empowerment

School Empowerment: A Model

MICHAEL D. RICHARDSON[1]
KENNETH E. LANE[2]

INTRODUCTION

The rationale for school empowerment as the process used to facilitate student-centered decisions is based on the proposition that decisions should be made at the lowest possible level (Chapman, 1988; Romanish, 1993). Thus, the school or classroom should be the primary decision-making unit (Bachus, 1991). Many districts that are implementing empowerment strategies are reacting to a perceived need to significantly change educational practice: to empower school staffs to create conditions in schools that facilitate improvement, innovation, and continuous professional growth (David, 1989; Boysen, 1992). The trend toward greater reliance on empowerment, coupled with an increasingly diverse work force (Greinier and Hagler, 1991), has forced many school districts to find new techniques that are substantially different from the individualistic practices they currently employ (Ilgen, 1986). Consequently, *school empowerment* becomes increasingly important as more people (community, faculty, students, etc,) actively participate in the process (Chapman, 1988; Cherry, 1991; Dixon, 1992).

School empowerment requires recognition that, when the impetus and authority for school improvement emanates from outside the

---

[1]Georgia Southern University.
[2]California State University–San Bernardino.

school, it does not produce the responsibility and commitment necessary to sustain improvement (Mojkowski and Fleming, 1988). Research consistently indicates that top down change has rarely been effective; "there will be no effective change in education unless employees at the worksite are involved in making change" (Reed, 1988). Vogt and Murrell (1990) suggest that "the fundamental goal of all educators is empowerment: helping people become capable of setting and reaching goals for individual and social ends" (p. 162).

There are at least three basic philosophical foundations that support school empowerment as an effective management process: 1) change should be student-centered, and, therefore, decisions should be made as close to the student as possible (Chapman, 1988; Herman, 1989; Lewis, 1989); 2) change requires ownership that comes from the opportunity to participate in defining change and the flexibility to adapt it to individual circumstances (Conner and Lake, 1988; Mojkowski and Bamburger, 1990): stated otherwise, change does not result from externally imposed practices (Mercado, 1993); and, 3) knowledge is power (Foucault, 1980)—effective decisions require good and timely information (Hall, 1991). Zander (1977) specifies that group motivation to change is based on several conditions:

> the group repeating a given task periodically (instead of generating a single product and disbanding), the amount or quality of results from the joint product being visible to the members, the members developing some idea about how well the group will do in the future, and each and every member contributing to some degree to helping the group complete its work. (pp. 38–39)

Are the decisions of a group necessarily better than an individual principal? In other words, is the end result worth the effort? Schmuch and Blumberg (1969) speculated that

> Where efficiency depends on continued coordination and interaction of persons, a decision produced by the group to be involved will almost always be superior to one produced by even the most capable of individuals. (p. 89)

School empowerment is the process for releasing the power of the group, teachers, staff, community, and students toward the accomplishment of school goals and objectives (Stimson and Appelbaum, 1988; Cunard, 1989). School empowerment is a *process*, not an *outcome* (Smylie and Denny, 1990). School empowerment is a *means* to an end, not the *end* itself (Short and Greer, 1989; Dagley, 1992; Epp, 1992).

POLICY CONCERNS

Do policymakers tell administrators to empower people or should administrators find ways to make participants in the process feel ownership as they collectively attempt to solve the problems at the point closest to the source? Addressing the issue at the policy table, either at the school or district level (Jackson, 1992), is the only way all participants will become true partners in the process and be knowledgeable of their individual and collective roles (Dagley, 1992). School administrators and teachers both have legitimate roles to play in defining policy. However, policymakers, administrators, and teachers cannot forget that the school board is a crucial link to the community and must balance the roles of policymaker and public servant to ensure that authority and responsibility are appropriately shared (Phillips, 1989). In the development of school empowerment policy, a critical component, crucial to the central administration, the board, and the building-level management, is a clear definition of the parameters of the decision-making process at both the district and the building level (Hoyt, 1991). Before the school board considers empowerment at the school level, it should study extensively what the effect will be on present policy and personnel (Jones, 1992).

Prior to beginning a school empowerment process at the building level, policy should be developed which identifies participants and sets the guidelines for participation (Phillips, 1989). The board should define the respective roles of administrators, teachers, staff members, community and parent supporters, and students who will participate in the decision-making process (Lifton, 1992). Establishing a policy prior to implementation eliminates many problems that result from individuals attempting to negotiate positions during and after implementation (Meadows, 1990; Clark and Greer, 1991).

IMPLEMENTATION

The largest obstacle to school empowerment is how it should be implemented. When the mechanics of school empowerment are fully implemented, some of the participants may be uncomfortable with their changed roles (Lagana, 1989). This phenomenon may be a result of "disturbing the way things are" syndrome or simply fear of the unknown (Fullan, 1991). People often become distressed when structure is altered, even a noneffective structure (White, 1992). Principals cannot say to faculty, "This is the process of teacher empowerment, take it, use it, you are now empowered." Such an action would further the case for bureaucracy, not participation (Mojkowski and Bamburger, 1990). Moeller (1964, p. 140) stated, "Bureaucracy in school system organizations induces in teachers a sense of powerlessness to affect school system policy. The general level of sense of power in a school system varies inversely to the degree of bureaucratization." The failure of some school empowerment attempts can be illustrated through the improper training of the various participants to implement the total process (Neely and Alm, 1993). The administrator must spend the time and develop the expertise to provide staff development, which is necessary to guarantee successful implementation (Short and Rinehart, 1992b). Experience dictates a step-by-step school empowerment process which can be compartmentalized as three separate and distinct steps: conceptual development, role definition, and decision making (see Figure 15.1).

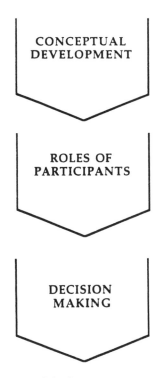

Figure 15.1. School empowerment: a model.

CONCEPTUAL DEVELOPMENT

The first step to school empowerment is conceptual development, which involves the school board, the administration, the faculty, and the community in developing a common sense, a common definition, of what school empowerment really means (Brown, 1987; Bolin, 1989; Bredeson, 1992; Short and Greer, 1993). The terms *teacher empowerment, site-based management, participatory management, decentralization, shared decision making,* and *school-based management* are all included under the general rubric of participatory decision making (Fruchter, 1989; Gomez, 1989; Howley, 1990; Hughes, 1993). But what is school empowerment? What does it mean to the school board, the administration, the faculty, the community, and the staff of the individual school?

Conceptual development implies that all those affected by this phenomenon (school empowerment) must be given opportunity to have input into the meaning of the process (Kirkpatrick, 1985). The definition must be agreeable to all those involved, particularly at the individual school. This definition has no meaning for a school fifty miles down the road or for someone in the state capital or for someone in North Carolina or California. The only limitation is: What does school empowerment mean for the individual school, its faculty, the administration, the school board, students, and the community? There are not commonly agreed-upon definitions of school empowerment; therefore, the participants should explore the boundaries and develop a definition that is meaningful and useful to them (Malen et al., 1990). Unless the interested groups reach consensus on a common definition of what they are working toward, any other attempts to implement the process would be presumptuous (Hughes, 1993).

Two basic beliefs are incorporated in most definitions of school empowerment: (a) those closest to the decision should play a significant role in making those decisions (Lewis, 1989; Mojkowski and Bamburger, 1990), and (b) decisions will be most effective and long-lasting when a sense of ownership and responsibility is developed by participating in the decision-making process (Fullan, 1991; Romanish, 1991). Consequently, when teachers and administrators have developed a clear understanding of their desired expectations, a common belief should emerge: teaching effectively will increase student learning (Hawthorne, 1990). Belief in that commitment and a set of principles could put into motion a positive set of faculty, community, and student expectations. A shared sense of ownership results in shared leadership to create success for students (Chopra, 1989).

ROLE DEFINITION

The second step in the school empowerment process is role definition. Smith and Peterson (1988) define role as "a label for the set of expectations about an individual's behavior" (p. 73). Role definition means that, in an empowered school, roles must be altered. Teachers, staff, students, community, and administration must alter or modify roles they have traditionally expected and accepted from each other (Heller, 1993). No longer can faculty expect, nor should they expect, principals to make all the day-to-day operational decisions. After all, that is what many faculty members want: teacher empowerment, the idea of making decisions about those things that affect them on a day-to-day basis (Short and Greer, 1993).

The roles of all participants must be changed, not just faculty expectation for the principal, but faculty and administration expectations for the community, including parental involvement in the school (Mercado, 1993). For example, how does the faculty and administration in an empowered school propose to involve the 75 percent of the community who do not have students in school (Mannon and Blackwell, 1992)? The school should involve community and parents, although, traditionally, parents have been characterized as apathetic, not caring, uninterested, and not desiring involvement in the day-to-day operation of the school (Cherry, 1991). Teachers and administrators must involve the community and change the community expectation for the school. Community and parental involvement is difficult when a real or imaginary wall has been built up between community and school (Sherer, 1992). Perhaps a more basic assumption should be changed: the school needs the community involved in the school (Delgado-Gaitan, 1991). Purkey and Smith (1983) indicate that "a few studies find parental involvement and support to be a major factor in student achievement" (p. 444).

Student empowerment and the students' role in empowered schools should also be considered (Neely and Alm, 1993). Everyone in the school must perceive that students are empowered and have a social value beyond providing a job for educators (Woods, 1992). Administrators and teachers should be flexible and resourceful in meeting student needs, a supportive environment for student learning should be maintained, and principals should provide facilitative leadership (Short and Greer, 1993). Students should also be actively engaged in the educational process. According to Keedy and Drmacich (1991), student engagement should involve administrators and teachers providing students with ample opportunities for academic success, interesting materials, and social support and facilitating student ownership of the learning and learning process. In addition, school empowerment requires that all students develop cultural sensitivity to the needs of all students and personnel in the school (Nel, 1992).

Many studies have found that role theory leads to understanding the potential for feeling privileged as a consequence of superior status or feeling underprivileged as a consequence of perceived inferior status (Clouse, 1989). Social expectations influence the roles associated with particular positions (Stryker, 1980). Messe et al. (1992) speculate that "in organizations persons with superior status both have an inflated view of their own worth and undervalue the needs and contributions of their subordinates" (p. 209). With empowerment, feelings of superiority must be abandoned and feelings of inferiority must be eliminated (Clinchy, 1992). (See Figure 15.2).

Ilgen (1986) postulated that role theory provides the basic means for linking the individual with the larger organization, without losing either the individual or the system. Current research makes it clear that the empowerment of site-level personnel, especially teachers, through access to decision making and the increased knowledge and status implied in the process, improves both morale and instruction (Maeroff, 1988). Watkins (1986) specifies that administrators must "harbor the growth and support the diverse interest groups who may incorporate a critical element into the decision-making process" (p. 101). However, according to the Carnegie Foundation (1988), teachers

> do not help to select teachers and administrators (only about 10 percent) at their schools, nor are they asked to participate in such crucial matters as teacher evaluation, staff development, budget, student placement, promotion and retention policies, and standards of student conduct. (p. 36)

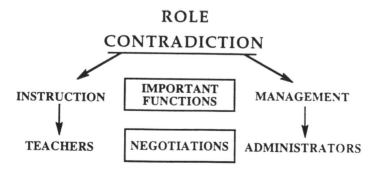

Figure 15.2. School empowerment.

What does the administrator, particularly the principal and superintendent, stand to gain from this school empowerment process? Principals are *frequently* the first line of resistance to site-based decision making, *most often* because of fear or ignorance (Kirkpatrick, 1985; Kahensky and Muth, 1991). Using school empowerment, the principal acts as executive officer, who, by delegated authority, directs instructional improvement and is involved to a much greater degree with the important school functions (Gresso and Robertson, 1992). A pilot program in Dade County, Florida, reported that "principals and teachers in the pilot program reported being tired from the extra work, but thrilled at being part of a revolution in the making" (Dreyfuss, 1988).

The principal who shares instructional leadership with teachers does not give up the responsibility for leadership (Foster, 1990; Eastwood and Tallerico, 1990; Mitchell, 1990; Romanish, 1991) (see Figure 15.3).

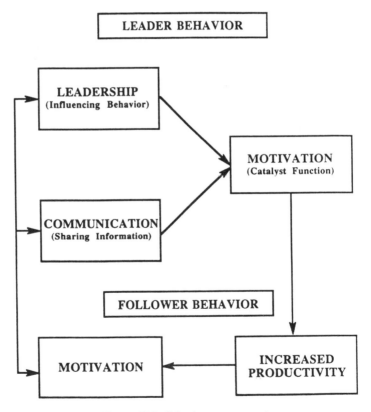

Figure 15.3. School empowerment.

A principal who is able to spend more time preparing schools to meet the challenges of the 21st century because of school empowerment is a more effective leader (Cunard, 1989). Most principals are not comfortable with change that is not clearly defined and leaves the opportunity for unknowns, and most will admit they were not trained to work with empowerment procedures (Stimson and Appelbaum, 1988; Shasin, 1991; Jackson, 1992). Preparing the principal to facilitate the team is no easy task. In fact, Mary Hatwood Futrell, past president of the National Education Association [as quoted in Lewis (1989)] states that "as shared decisionmaking becomes the norm, we hope administrators, far from feeling threatened, will welcome the collegial decision-making process" (p. 81). Similarly, Albert Shanker of the American Federation of Teachers [as quoted in Lewis (1989)] reports that

> one of the greatest assets of any school system is the collective knowledge and experience of its teaching staff—and its untapped potential to acquire more. An effective administrator will, therefore, find ways of activating this asset. (pp. 85–86)

As the source of decision making changes, the roles incumbent in different administrative levels must undergo a similar change. Supervisors will likely have different functions in this new environment. The role of central office personnel will become to a large extent that of support and service to the site, particularly resources and information (Rozenholtz, 1985). Central office personnel will still be an integral part of the educational community because of the need for good, timely information and the importance of some coordination of efforts between schools. However, these positions "could disappear if school systems further decentralize responsibilities to school sites and decisionmaking is flattened in the organizational pyramids of school districts" (Lewis, 1989. p. 100).

The roles of all participants in an empowered school are modified. Parent, faculty, staff, students, and administrators must all critically examine their *needed role,* not their *perceived role.* Although some will be unhappy with their new role and new responsibilities, the needs of the students dictate change from the status quo. Those who are unwilling or unable to change face professional extinction or annihilation (Bolin, 1989).

DECISION MAKING

The third step in the school empowerment process is an examination of how decisions are made. Who makes decisions in school? What kinds of decisions are made? What is the generic process of making decisions? Are there different models for examining how decisions are made, or who needs to make decisions? Decision making at its best is a complex structure with many complicated tasks involved (Lewin, 1947; Hoffman and Maier, 1959; Shaw and Blum, 1965; Hall and Williams, 1970; Newell, 1978; Kanter, 1983; Powers and Powers, 1983; Ilgen, 1986). If the organization is to be efficient where a myriad of decisions are made, people and programs are coordinated, communication channelled, positions allocated, staff recruited, schedules developed, and resources obtained and utilized, then decision making must be shared (Garcia, 1986).

In this segment of the process, administrators and teachers must examine how decisions are made in the school and who is involved and who should be involved in making those decisions (Short and Greer, 1989). Research indicates that one of the real weaknesses of school empowerment is the inability of teachers to understand how decisions are made (Persing, 1989). Teachers make as many as five thousand instructional decisions per day, but instructional decisions are different from administrative or management decisions, which often involve other people, peers, for example (Moore and Esselman, 1992). Instructional decisions are made about such things as "Should I continue to teach addition now or should I stop and go on to language arts?" or "How can I best get this particular student to understand this math concept and what multiplication really means?" or "How can I better help this student understand how to spell phonetically?" All are examples of instructional decisions that teachers make constantly in the classroom (Walberg and Lane, 1989).

With school empowerment, decisions are moved out of the classroom and into peer relationships (Lincoln, 1992). Teachers need training in how to process information, how to collect data, how to examine different alternatives available, and then, ultimately, how to make a decision (Bhasin, 1991; Heller, 1993).

Another problem teachers confront in work groups is a lack of experience with debating issues and building consensus (Malen et al., 1990). Working on group dynamics and the art of compromise early in the transition period from bureaucratic schools to empowered schools may be time well spent and critical to group decision making and consensus (Rummler, 1989). It will be helpful if teachers learn the essential relationship between autonomy and accountability (Kahensky and Muth, 1991). Making decisions can lead to conflict (Scherer, 1992) and mistakes; even when the group finds a solution to a problem, often a new set of challenges appears (Glickman, 1990).

This decision-making process also implies one other important facet: accountability (Hill and Bonan, 1991). If teachers are to be involved in making decisions, then they must be held accountable for those decisions, just as administrators are held accountable (Bredeson, 1992). According to Phil Schlecty [as quoted in Lewis (1989)], "Teachers and principals are only accountable for doing right the things they are expected to do" (p. 102). However, schools are now involved in doing many things that are not the primary prerequisite of instruction and student learning. Schools have become foster parents, surrogate churches, and societal hand-me-downs, often at the expense of what they do well: provide instruction and learning opportunities. School empowerment forces school personnel and their clientele to critically examine the *real* roles for the schools in light of societal expectations (Kuke et al., 1989). School empowerment means that the school should be empowered to do the things that the school does well (Cochran and Dean, 1991). If not, all schools are in serious trouble. In fact, school "survival no longer can be seen as a simple proof of fitness" (Czarniawska-Joerges, 1992, p. 25), but of doing the things that schools do well.

DO TEACHERS WANT TO PARTICIPATE IN DECISION MAKING?

Principals often ask the question: do teachers really want to be involved in making decisions? Teachers talk about empowerment, about making decisions, but do teachers really want to take the time, the effort, and the energy that is required for participatory decision making? Empowering teachers is the key to a new life for American education (Heller, 1993). Frymier (1987) suggested that teachers are locked into a system that blunts teacher enthusiasm and stifles creativity. *Neutering* is the label Frymier used to describe this condition: "Neutered teachers lack physical strength and energy, enthusiasm for their work, and motivation" (1987, p. 12). The answer to the question of teacher involvement in decision making can only be answered at the school level (Short and Rinehart, 1992a).

There may be situations in which teachers do not feel comfortable participating in the process. Teachers should not be forced into empowerment just to be involved (Kirkpatrick, 1985). Rather, the structure for school empowerment "should be flexible enough to allow for varying rates of participation" (Newell, 1978, p. 140). The structure should be appropriate for the task. Different tasks require different structures (Blau and Scott, 1962). Some evidence also suggests that, for some teachers, having the opportunity to participate is more important than actually participating in making the decision (Aronstein et al., 1990). It should be noted that not all teachers desire to participate in this new professionalism, yet they do not wish to be treated as "second-class citizens" (Lewis, 1989, p. 88). Shaw and Blum (1965) also report that "data suggest that group members are more likely to signal their true feelings to the group when this can be done anonymously than when signals are public" (p. 153).

School empowerment implies that decisions are made at the lowest possible level; however, site-based management was mandated by the Kentucky Legislature as a part of their reform effort to be implemented at every school in the state (see Lindle in this volume). How ironic that the concept of local autonomy is actually mandated from the state level. Again, this is a reflection of the top-down mentality that has been so pervasive in most of the educational reform system—which, ulti-mately, led to the downfall of most reform programs because they were mandated without grass-roots level support (White, 1989).

The research sociologist Kurt Lewin (1947) stated that reform can only be meaningful, long-lasting, and beneficial when it springs forth from the grass-roots level rather than being mandated from the top down. Meade (1979) reported that "lasting and significant changes would not occur unless teachers were directly and actively involved in the planning and development of the desired changes" (p. 89).

DO PRINCIPALS WANT TO SHARE DECISIONMAKING?

A fundamental question is: do principals really want teachers and community members involved in decision making? Do principals really believe that school empowerment will be beneficial to them, or do they see it as a threat to their power, their authority, their role, and their function in the school (Richardson and Long, 1991)? Traditional think-ing suggests that power is the ability to make someone do something they would not otherwise do (Dahl, 1963). Filley et al. (1976) examined power as the ability to have social influence over others. French and Raven (1959) examined power from five different perspectives, meaning that people could have power in any of five different ways: reward, coer-cive, legitimate, reverent and expert power. According to a study by Dykes (1968):

> The study findings suggest that the source of much of the tension be-tween faculty and administration is a conviction held by many faculty members that any increase in administrative power and influence must necessarily result in a decrease in their own. . . . The administration and

faculty are seen as adversaries competing for a limited quantity of influence. (p. 405)

Power is given, willingly or by coercion, to the leader by the followers (French and Raven, 1989). Power is not something that can be arbitrarily taken, but it is something that must be given (Stimson and Appelbaum, 1988). The followers must acquiesce to the power of the leader for power to be involved. So do principals want to give up their power? Or, more importantly, do principals have any power? Do they want to give up perceived decision-making power? Blumberg (1969) states,

> The abdication of a traditional hierarchical system, on the part of the principal, in favor of a participative mode does not necessarily mean that he will lose influence over the environment. The results may be, as seems to be the case here, that he attains more influence over matters of substance that are more important to him than matters of procedure. The extension of power within the organization tends to multiply the total amount of power residing in the organization. (p. 51)

School empowerment does not imply that principals give up power (Stimson and Appelbaum, 1988). Empowerment is not a power over, but a power with, concept, meaning that the whole is greater than the sum of the parts (synergy). Principal and faculty can combine their separate power into an organization that is more powerful than the two groups separately. School empowerment becomes power with, not power over or power against. School empowerment reduces the fighting "for power" because each entity must use its power for the organization to be successful (Tranter, 1992), for the school to be effective, not to drive personal agendas. Consequently, each group (faculty, staff, community, parents, students, and principal) must know and understand its role and function in the school empowerment process (Howley, 1990).

But there will be implementation problems in restructuring educational systems to allow for effective school empowerment. According to Blumberg (1969),

> Changes in processes, problems, costs, and benefits develop when the decision-making perogatives in a school are shifted from a hierarchical pattern to a participative one in which the principal shares power with the teachers. (p. 39)

Principals have historically considered themselves custodians of four critical organizational elements: decision making, organizational structure, information, and personnel (Lunenberg, 1992). However, with empowerment these critical elements are more likely to become collegial decision making, consultative frameworks, shared information, and increased group process (Orlich, 1989; Ogletree and Schmidt, 1992).

Training will be necessary to change the perception of principals and teachers toward power and the changed roles in the educational organization (Eastwood and Tallerico, 1990). Some current staff members will be unable or unwilling to adapt to the new management structure (Powers and Powers, 1983). However, these problems are dwarfed when considered in relation to the possible benefits of school empowerment. The possibilities for stimulating the creation of new ideas for instructional programs are exciting (Kahensky and Muth, 1991). The opportunities to truly change the educational service-delivery model are endless. As stated by Kanter (1983), "Involving grass roots employees on participative teams with control over their own outcomes helps the organization to get and use more ideas to improve performance and increase future skills" (p. 241).

IMPLICATIONS

Empowered school decisions, if implemented properly, can improve instruction by creating ownership in those responsible for teaching and learning (Eastwood and Tallerico, 1990). Teacher morale and performance are likely to be higher (David, 1989). Staffing and teaching flexibility will increase (Malen et al., 1990). Teacher and student productivity will increase (Gomez, 1989). As teachers have the opportunity to gain greater insight into school operations, they will have greater status in the organization and will therefore have greater self-worth (Sachs, 1966; Smylie and Denny, 1990). Decision making will improve because of the increased flow of information and additional viewpoints (Lewis, 1989) (see Figure 15.4). In addition, empowered decisions may help teachers learn to share in other areas: for example, instruction and discipline techniques (Brown, 1987; Foster, 1990). The development of collaborative, collegial relationships among faculty is an extra benefit derived for shared responsibilities involved in school empowerment (Smith and Scott, 1990).

School administrators should not be as concerned with "certainties" as with "possibilities" (White, 1989). Consequently, goals are not "givens," but opportunities within which the empowered administrator functions (Perrow, 1982; Bolin, 1989). However, to be empowered, the principal must give decision-making power to the group with all the awareness and honesty the administrator can muster (Malen et al.,

Figure 15.4. School empowerment: changing group behavior.

1990). Blumberg (1969) stated that "if a supportive and honest environment is created, the probability exists that teachers will be eager to take part in changing the traditional bureaucratic pattern of operating a school" (p. 49). As a result, "The practical question is no longer one of whether to use groups, but rather how to use them more effectively in decisionmaking" (Hall and Williams, 1970, p. 40). The question is no longer should schools be empowered, but how should each school develop its own plan for empowerment?

If school empowerment is to be successful and not just another flash in the educational pan, all participants must become accountable for their involvement and contribution to the process (Fruchter, 1989). In the words of James Guthrie (1986), "Unless policies are identified that unleash productive local initiatives, the reform movement seems likely to lose its momentum. And the loss of momentum will end virtually all short-term prospects for sustaining citizens' confidence in the schools and for generating additional public resources for them" (p. 308).

REFERENCES

Aronstein, L. W., Marlow, M. and Desilets, B. (1990). Detours on the road to site-based management. *Educational Leadership,* 47 (7), 61–63.

Bachus, G. S. (1991). The shifting format of administration in small schools: Participatory school decision making (ERIC Document Reproduction Service No. ED 339 571).

Bhasin, K. (1991). Participatory development demands participatory training. *Convergence,* 24 (4), 5–15.

Blau, P. and Scott, R. (1962). *Formal Organizations*. San Francisco: Chandler Publishing Company.

Blumberg, A. (1969). The elementary school cabinet: Report of an experience in participative decisionmaking. *Educational Administration Quarterly*, 5 (3), 39–52.

Bolin, F. S. (1989). Empowering leadership. *Teachers College Record*, 91 (1), 81–96.

Boysen, T. C. (1992). Irreconcilable differences: Effective urban schools versus restructuring. *Education and Urban Society*, 25 (1), 85–95.

Bredeson, P. V. (1992). Responses to restructuring and empowerment initiatives: A study of teachers' and principals' perceptions of organizational leadership, decisionmaking and climate (ERIC Document Reproduction Service No. ED 346 569).

Brown, D. J. (1987). A preliminary inquiry into school-based management (ERIC Document Reproduction Service No. ED 284 331).

Carnegie Foundation for the Advancement of Teaching (1988). *Teacher Involvement in Decision Making: A State-by-State Profile*. Princeton, NJ: The foundation.

Chapman, J. D. (1988). Decentralization, devolution and the teacher: Participation by teachers in the decision making of schools. *Journal of Educational Administration*, 26 (1), 39–72.

Cherry, M. (1991). School ownership—The essential foundation of restructuring. *NASSP Bulletin* 75 (537), 33–39.

Chopra, R. K. (1989). Synergistic curriculum development: An idea whose time has come. *NASSP Bulletin*, 73 (518), 44–50.

Clark, M. and Greer, C. (1991). A culture of politics. *Social Policy*, 21 (3), 53–57.

Clinchy, E. (1992). Choice and the transformation of schools: A superintendent's perspective. *Equity and Choice*, 9 (1), 32–34.

Clouse, R. W. (1989). A review of educational role theory (ERIC Document Reproduction Service No. ED 314 824).

Cochran, M., and Dean, C. (1991). Home-school relations and the empowerment process. *Elementary School Journal*, 91 (3), 261–269.

Conner, P. E. and Lake, L. K. (1988). *Managing organizational change*. New York: Praeger.

Cunard, F. (1989). Sharing instructional leadership—A view to strengthening the principal's position. *NASSP Bulletin*, 74 (525), 30–34.

Czarniawska-Joerges, B. (1992). *Exploring Complex Organizations*. Newbury Park, CA: Sage.

Dahl, R. A. (1963). *Modern Political Analysis*. Englewood Cliffs, NJ: Prentice-Hall.

Dagley, D. (1992). Lesson from the power company. *Journal of School Leadership*, 2 (3), 289–298.

David, J. L. (1989). Synthesis of research on school-based management. *Educational Leadership*, 46 (8), 45–52.

Delgado-Gaitan, C. (1991). Involving parents in schools: A process of empowerment. *American Journal of Education*, 100 (1), 20–46.

Dison, A. P. (1992). Parents: Full partners in the decision-making process. *NASSP Bulletin,* 76 (543), 15–18.

Dreyfuss, G. (1988). Dade County opens doors to site decisions. *The School Administrator,* 47 (7), 12–13, 15.

Duke, D. L., Showers, B. K., and Imber, M. (1989). Teachers and shared decision making: The costs and benefits of involvement. *Educational Administration Quarterly,* 16 (1), 93–106.

Dykes, A. R. (1968). Faculty participation in academic decision making. *Liberal Education,* 54, 394–409.

Eastwood, K. W. and Tallerico, M. (1990). School improvement planning teams: Lessons from practice. *Planning and Changing,* 21 (1), 3–12.

Epp, J. R. (1992). Teacher participation in school government: A central element in educational reform (ERIC Document Reproduction Service No. ED 343 223).

Filley, A. C., House, R. J., and Kerr, S. (1976). *Managerial Process and Organizational Behavior.* (2nd ed). Glenville, IL: Scott, Foresman.

Foster, K. (1990). Small steps on the way to teacher empowerment. *Educational Leadership,* 47 (8), 38–40.

Foucault, M. (1980). *Power/Knowledge: Selected Interviews and Other Writings.* New York: Pantheon.

French, J. R. P. and Raven, B. (1959). The bases of social power. In *Studies in Social Power,* D. Cartwright, (Ed.) Ann Arbor: University of Michigan.

Fruchter, N. (1989). Rethinking school reform. *Social Policy,* 20 (1), 16–25.

Frymier, J. (1987). Bureaucracy and the neutering of teacher. *Phi Delta Kappan,* 69 (1), 9–14.

Fullan, M. G. (1991). *The New Meaning of Educational Change.* New York: Teachers College Press. 313–333.

Garcia, A. (1986). Consensus decision making promotes involvement, ownership, satisfaction. *NASSP Bulletin,* 70 (493), 50–52.

Glickman, C. D. (1990). Pushing school reform to a new edge: The seven ironies of school empowerment. *Phi Delta Kappan,* 72 (1), 68–75.

Gomez, J. J. (1989). The path to school-based management isn't smooth, but we're scaling the obstacles one by one. *American School Board Journal,* 176 (10), 20–22.

Gresso, D. W. and Robertson, M. B. (1992). The principal as process consultant: Catalyst for change. *NASSP Bulletin,* 76 (540), 44–48.

Grenier, G., and Hogler, R. L. (1991). Labor law and managerial ideology: Employee participation as a social control system. *Work and Occupation: An International Sociological Journal,* 18 (3).

Guthrie, J. W. (1986). School-based management: The next needed education reform. *Phi Delta Kappan,* 68 (4), 305–309.

Hall, J. and Williams, M. S. (1970). Group dynamics training and improved decision making. *The Journal of Applied Behavioral Science,* 6 (1), 39–66.

Hall, R. H. (1991). *Organizations: Structures, Processes and Outcomes* (5th ed.) Englewood Cliffs, NJ: Prentice-Hall.

Hawthorne, R. D. (1990). Analyzing school-based curriculum decision making. *Journal of Curriculum and Supervision*, 5 (3), 279–286.

Heller, G. S. (1993). Teacher empowerment–Sharing the challenge: A guide to implementation and success. *NASSP Bulletin*, 77 (550), 94–103.

Herman, J. (1989). A decision-making model: Site-based communications/governance committees. *NASSP Bulletin*, 73 (521), 79–84.

Hill, P. T. and Bonan, J. (1991). *Decentralization and Accountability in Public Education*. Santa Monica, CA: Rand.

Hoffman, L. R. and Maier, N. R. F. (1959). *The Use of Group Decision to Resolve a Problem of Fairness*. Ann Arbor: Willow Run Laboratories, University of Michigan.

Howley, A. (1990). Teacher empowerment: Three perspectives (ERIC Document Reproduction Service No. ED 328 991).

Hoyt, K. B. (1991). School board members, secondary school principals look at reform. *NASSP Bulletin*, 75 (537), 82–87.

Hughes, L. W. (1993). School-based management, decentralization, and citizen control–A perspective. *Journal of School Leadership*, 3 (1), 40–44.

Ilgen, D. R. (1986). Small groups in an individualistic world. In *Interfaces in Psychology: Organizational Psychology and Small Group Behavior*, R. McGlynn and R. George (Eds.) Lubbock: Texas Tech University Press, pp. 149–169.

Jackson, S. E. (1992). Team composition in organizational settings: Issues in managing an increasingly diverse work force. In *Group Process and Productivity*, S. Worchel, W. Wood & J. A. Simpson (Eds.). Newbury Park, CA: Sage, pp. 138–173.

Jones, R. R. (1992). Setting the stage for change. *Executive Educator*, 14 (3), 38–39.

Kahensky, M. and Muth, R. (1991). The mutual empowerment of teachers and principals (ERIC Document Reproduction Service No. ED 332 377).

Kanter, R. M. (1983). *The Change Masters*. New York: Simon and Schuster.

Keedy, J. L. and Drmacich, D. (1991). Giving voice and empowerment to student engagement: A school-based interactive curriculum (ERIC Document Reproduction Service No. ED 356 516).

Kirkpatrick, D. L. (1985). *How to Manage Change Effectively*. San Francisco: Jossey-Bass.

Lagana, J. F. (1989). Managing change and school improvement effectively. *NASSP Bulletin*, 73 (518), 52–55.

Lewin, K. (1947). Group decision and social change. In *Readings in Social Psychology*, T. M. Newcomb and E. L. Hartley (Eds.) New York: Holt and Company, pp. 330–344.

Lewis, A. (1989). *Restructuring America's Schools*. Arlington, VA: American Association of School Administrators.

Lifton, F. B. (1992). The legal tangle of shared governance. *School Administrator*, 49 (1), 16–19.

Lincoln, W. (1992). Shaping good decision makers. *Learning*, 21 (1), 63–65.

Lunenberg, F. C. (1992). Introduction: The current educational reform movement—History, progress to date, and the future. *Education and Urban Society,* 25 (1), 3–17.

Maeroff, G. I. (1988). Teacher empowerment: A step toward professionalization. *NASSP Bulletin,* 72 (511), 52–54, 56–60.

Malen, B., Ogawa, R. T., and Kranz, J. (1990). What do we know about school-based management? A case study of the literature—A call for research. In *The Practice of Choice, Decentralization and School Restructuring,* W. H. Clune and J. F. Witte, (Eds.), London: The Falmer Press, pp. 289–342.

Mannan, G. and Blackwell, J. (1992), Parent involvement: Barriers and opportunities. *Urban Review,* 24 (3), 210–216.

Meade, E., Jr. (1979). *Philanthropy and Public Schools: One Foundation's Evolving Perspective,* New York: Ford Foundation.

Meadows, B. J. (1990). The rewards and risks of shared leadership. *Phi Delta Kappan,* 71 (7), 545–548.

Mercado, C. I. (1993). Caring as empowerment: School collaboration and community agency. *Urban Review,* 25 (1), 79–104.

Meese, L. A., Kerr, N. L., and Sattler, D. N. (1992). "But some animals are more equal than others": The supervisor as a privileged status in group contexts. In *Group Process and Productivity,* S. Worchel, W. Wood, and J. A. Simpson (Eds.). Newbury Park, CA: Sage, pp. 203–223.

Mitchell, J. E. (1990). Coaxing staff from cages for site based decisions to fly. *The School Administrator,* 47 (2), 23–24, 26.

Mojkowski, C. and Bamburger, R. (1990). Developing leaders for restructuring schools: New habits of mind and heart (ERIC Document Reproduction Service No. ED 330 078).

Mojkowski, C. and Fleming, D. (1988). School site management: Concepts and approaches (ERIC Document Reproduction Service No. ED 307 660).

Moeller, G. H. (1964). Bureaucracy and teacher's sense of power. *The School Review,* 72 (2), 137–157.

Moore, W. P. and Esselman, M. E. (1992). Teacher efficacy, empowerment, and a focused instructional climate: Does student achievement benefit? (ERIC Document Reproduction Service No. ED 350 252).

Neely, R. and Alm, D. (1993). Empowering students with style. *Principal,* 72 (4), 32–33.

Newell, C. A. (1978). *Human Behavior in Educational Administration.* Englewood Cliffs, NJ: Prentice-Hall.

Ogletree, E. J. and Schmidt, L. J. (1992), Faculty involvement in administration of schools. *Illinois Schools Journal,* 71 (2), 40–46.

Orlich, D. C. (1989). Education reforms: Mistakes, misconceptions, miscues. *Phi Delta Kappan,* 70 (7), 512–517.

Perrow, C. (1982). Disintegrating social sciences. *Phi Delta Kappan,* 63 (10), 684–688.

Persing, T. E. (1989). Your staff must learn decision processes. *The School Administrator,* 46 (3), 21–23.

Phillips, P. R. (1989). Shared decision making in an age of reform. *Update,* 20 (3), 30–37.

Powers, D. R. and Powers, M. F. (1983). *Making Participatory Management Work*. San Francisco, CA: Jossey-Bass.

Purkey, C. S. and Smith, M. S. (1983). Effective schools: A review. *Elementary School Journal*, 83 (4), 430–444.

Reed, C. J. (1988). Site-based decision making: An implementation experience. *Collective Bargaining Quarterly*, 1 (3), 1–6.

Richardson, M. D. and Long, P. K. (1991). Restructuring school reform. *Clemson Kappan*, 10 (1), 14–15.

Romanish, B. (1993). Teacher empowerment as the focus of school restructuring. *School Community Journal*, 3 (1), 47–60.

Romanish, B. (1991). Teacher empowerment: The litmus test of school restructuring. *Social Science Record*, 28 (1), 55–69.

Rozenholtz, S. J. (1985). Effective schools: Interpreting the evidence. *American Journal of Education*, 93 (3), 352–388.

Rummler, R. L. (1989). Turn to your teachers for curriculum improvement. *Effective Educator*, 11 (4), 30–31, 37.

Scherer, M. (1992). Solving conflicts – Not just for children. *Educational Leadership*, 50 (1), 14, 17–18.

Schmuch, R. and Blumberg, A. (1969). Teacher participation in organizational decision. *NASSP Bulletin*, 53 (339), 89–95.

Shaw, M. E. and Blum, J. M. (1965). Group performance as a function of task difficulty and the group's awareness of member satisfaction. *Journal of Applied Psychology*, 49 (3), 151–155.

Short, P. M. and Greer, J. T. (1993). Empowering students: Helping all students realize success (ERIC Document Reproduction Service No. ED 355 670).

Short, P. M. and Greer, J. T. (1989). Increasing teacher autonomy through schared governance: Effects on policy making and student outcomes (ERIC Document Reproduction Service No. ED 319 096).

Short, P. M. and Rinehart, J. S. (1992a). School Participant Empowerment Scale: Assessment of level of empowerment within the school environment. *Educational and Psychological Measurement*, 52 (4), 951–960.

Short, P. M. and Rinehart, J. S. (1992b). Teacher empowerment and school climate. (ERIC Document Reproduction Service No. ED 347 678).

Smith, P. B. and Peterson, M. F. (1988). *Leadership, Organizations and Culture*. Newbury Park, CA: Sage.

Smith, S. C. and Scott, J. J. (1990). *The Collaborative School*. Eugene: University of Oregon.

Smylie, M. A. and Denny, J. W. (1990). Teacher leadership: Tensions and ambiguities in organizational perspective. *Educational Administration Quarterly*, 26 (3), 235–259.

Stimson, T. D. and Appelbaum, R. P. (1988). Empowering teachers: Do principals have the power? *Phi Delta Kappan*, 70 (4), 313–316.

Stryker, S. (1980). *Symbolic Interactionism: A Social Structural Version*. Menlo Park, CA: Benjamin/Cummings.

Tranter, W. H. (1992). The new principal. *Executive Educator*, 14 (2), 29–31.

Vogt, J. F. and Murrell, K. L. (1990). *Empowerment in Organizations: How to Spark Exceptional Performance*. San Diego, CA: University Associates.

Walberg, H. J. and Lane, J. J. (1989). *Organizing for Learning: Toward the 21st Century.* Reston, VA: National Association of Secondary School Principals.

Watkins, P. (1986). From managerialism to communication competence: Control and consensus in educational administration. *Journal of Educational Administration,* 24 (1), 86–106.

White, P. A. (1992). Teacher empowerment under "Ideal" school-site autonomy. *Educational Evaluation and Policy Analysis,* 14 (1), 69–82.

White, P. A. (1989). An overview of school-based management—What does the research say? *NASSP Bulletin,* 73 (518), 1–8.

Woods, P. (1992). Empowerment through choice? Towards an understanding of parental choice and school responsiveness. *Educational Management and Administration,* 20 (4), 204–211.

Zander, A. (1977). *Groups at Work.* San Francisco: Jossey-Bass.

CHAPTER 16

The Autonomous School*

INTRODUCTION

An issue related to reform and school change has not been frequently discussed in the literature. Yet the need for individual school autonomy appears to be an absolute prerequisite for site-based management or school-based change projects.

Explored in this chapter is the concept of school autonomy. In one sense, it seems ironic to even argue the case for building autonomy because our country's longest standing educational tradition is local (school district) autonomy. Though not the original reason for centering education finance and control at the community level, the rationale for local system autonomy that has emerged over the centuries is that local autonomy enables each child's educational needs to be addressed. No such claims can be made for centralized educational systems found in other nations throughout the world.

It would seem that, as communities across the nation become more and more heterogeneous, local school systems would see that the "better meet the educational needs of each child" argument could also be applied to the individual schools of the district. Such is not the case.

*This chapter is based on a paper delivered at the *Annual Conference of the National Council of Professors of Educational Administration,* Indian Wells, CA, August 12, 1993.

[1]Georgia State University.

Evidence that building autonomy remains a myth is not hard to find. Illustrative are two studies recently completed with support from the Danforth Foundation and other agencies (Greer and Short, 1988; Greer et al., 1990). The first was a three-study of the empowerment process utilized in nine schools throughout the nation. The second was a seventeen-school project in Arizona where multiage, multigrade classrooms were studied in grades K–12.

In these studies, it was found that local building autonomy was more myth than reality, in spite of assurances and guarantees given by school district leaders at the initiation of each project. For example, in the Arizona Project, a principal learned that the multiage, multigrade classroom two teachers were planning for the fall would not be permitted. This surprising decision was given by the superintendent even after the superintendent had attended the project's initiation conference the previous summer. At the conclusion of the initiation conference, the superintendent had publicly given permission to the principal and teachers of the school to proceed with the experiment during the coming year. The reason the superintendent gave for reversing the decision was that an outside curriculum consultant had advised that the schools of the district were not ready for multiage, multigrade classrooms.

A second illustration of the absence of building autonomy is taken from the empowerment project. A high school, through the insight and knowledge of the principal, became "bombproof" because of its relationships with the business community and citizen leaders. The attendance area and the school became unified as all stakeholders within and outside the school worked to redesign the school to make it more responsive to the needs of the students attending the school. The school was allowed to operate its program independently of school system curriculum guidelines for more than three years. Eventually, however, the school system reasserted its dominance over the school through a series of leadership personnel decisions that went against the recommendations of the school's advisory committee.

Similar examples can be found time and again in the literature on school leadership and system governance. In nearly every case, when individual building autonomy is absolutely essential to the success of a change project, school district officials have moved to deny the school the required freedom.

Why? That is the issue explored in this chapter. Particular emphasis has been given to boards of education and their members, the superintendent, and central office professionals. At the building level, the spotlight is focused on the principal and the teachers. Addressed in a less direct way, only because of space limitations, are the attitudes and values of the citizens of the community and the state.

The final introductory comment is that the problems related to school autonomy have been cast in a teacher empowerment context. Other issues could be used, but empowerment, with its emphasis on shared governance decisions, seems particularly well-suited for a discussion of school autonomy. In essence, it is absurd to think about teachers participating in making basic decisions of the school if the school system insists that such decisions be (a) approved by the central office or (b) similar to those made in other schools of the system.

THE BOARD OF EDUCATION

Board of education members are the policymakers in public school districts. The history of lay school boards hearkens back to the colonial days of the country and revolves about the community's responsibility to provide basic education to the children of the community.

It has been noted that the typical board member has changed over the years. At one time, board members were likely to be the intellectual, moral, and social leaders of the community. Many were professionals who accepted positions on the board as a part of their community responsibility. Their primary concern was that all the children of the community be educated.

In recent times, board members have reflected more diverse backgrounds. While many professionals continue to serve on boards, there are now additional players. Today, it is not unusual to find blue collar workers, homemakers, political aspirants, retired persons, members of fundamental religious sects, and representatives of right-wing political groups serving on boards of education. It should come as no surprise that the behavior of such diverse board members is unpredictable. Some board members are interested in making themselves highly visible so that their political futures are assured. There are those who serve because the salaries they receive supplement their regular income (and in some cases, the board salary represents the member's only income). Still others serve on the board to insure that their personal religious or political viewpoints are given full treatment in the classrooms of the district. Such persons are the "single-issue" board members referred to in the literature. The interesting thing about diverse board members is that, regardless of background and beliefs, almost all have a commitment to centralized control of the school system. Even those "educational statespersons" whose board membership represents a commitment to the youth of the community possess a sense of "stewardship" regarding their service. Stewardship for such persons means insuring equity for all students, and "equity" translates into equal programs, faculties, facilities, and so on. Said another way, these board members want only the best, but the best must be available to all students.

"Political" board members fight for their constituents as members of the board. They insist that whatever programs and services are available to any of the systems' students also be made available to the students in their own ward or voting district. The appropriateness of such programs is not so important as their availability. This insistence of program equity is very appealing to the voters and, in turn, reinforces the politician's desire to continue as the champion of the ward's students. The long-term result of the politician's behavior is the favorable disposition of the voters should the board member choose to run for higher office at some future date.

The "single-issue" board member also buys into a centralized system of administering the school system. Only when all of the teachers of the system are using the same textual materials can the "single issue" member hope to influence all of the students regarding the member's particular religious or political perspective.

Board members not falling into one of these three categories tend to accept the leadership of the others when questions of centralized control of the school system arise. In part, they accept centralized control of the schools because systems have always been governed that way.

WRITTEN BOARD POLICIES

The instrument boards of education use to enforce centralized administration of the school system is the written policy. The policy is considered a guide for discretionary action that is interpreted and implemented by the professional educators of the system.

Viewed as a significant step forward in school administration when it was introduced in the 1950s by Daniel R. Davies and Henry M. Brickell, the written policy enabled boards to insure that their wishes regarding the purpose and direction of the school system would be realized. Policies became the vehicles for school boards to establish and practice local system autonomy.

Today, most school systems have rather elaborate manuals of school board policies. The entire array of policies is designed as a management system that regulates nearly every aspect of school system operations.

Policy systems, however, work to make the realization of autonomous schools difficult, if not impossible. Either new policies would have to be written, or exceptions to existing policies would have to be granted to enable individual schools to depart from the standard programs and instructional arrangements of the system. Yet without such relief from existing policies, schools wishing to begin programs of teacher and student empowerment or other reform programs are barred from success before even beginning their change efforts.

THE SUPERINTENDENT

It is little wonder that a board of education made up of members representing diverse interests and purposes would appoint a superintendent who felt as it did about centralized control of programs, facilities, and staffs. Furthermore, the literature reflects that boards are quite willing to rid themselves of superintendents who depart very far from their ideas regarding system governance.

Added to this control mandate from the board (and backed by the board's written policies), superintendents themselves have been trained as decisive, "take charge" types of persons who run the schools. The powerful "CEO" superintendent is the model for superintendents-to-be during their years of teaching and early administrative experience.

Thus, what exists at the leadership level of public school systems throughout the country is 1) a board of lay persons with diverse backgrounds and interests, all interested in centrally controlling the activities of the system; 2) a system of written board policies that affirms the policy-making responsibility of the board, the board's legal obligation to appoint a superintendent, and the principle of centralized control; and 3) a superintendent who, by training and experience, views the superintendency as a powerful executive position and runs the school system in accordance with the directions established by the board.

THE CENTRAL OFFICE STAFF

As in most bureaucracies, the education professionals who make up the staff of the central office are the stabilizing force of the system. Boards of education and superintendents come and go, but the central office staff goes on forever.

Composed of assistant and associate superintendents, directors, supervisors, and similarly titled individuals, the central office staff's role is to assist the superintendent in administering the school system in accordance with the policies of the board of education. In actuality, however, the staff far too often serves as the preserver of the status quo. Observers of central offices describe individuals who engage in monumental turf battles whenever their personal job responsibilities are threatened. Each high ranking administrator who is added to the staff from outside the system is viewed as a person with potential for reorganizing people out of their jobs.

Is is little wonder that reforms such as teacher empowerment and site-based management, with their emphases on basic educational decisions being made at the school site, would be alarming to the central staff. If indeed it might come to pass that individual schools could make the program and instruction decisions related to the students attending their individual schools, then what might happen to the coordinator's and supervisor's jobs?

There is ample evidence that the above description of central office staff fears is more than idle speculation. In the mid-1980s, this writer submitted an experiment in participative decision making (the precursor of teacher empowerment) to the executive committee of a large metropolitan school system. The plan called for autonomy to be given to three experimental elementary schools so that the staffs of the three schools would be free to make the program and instruction decisions that best helped the students of each school learn. The plan further called for the schools to be free of the system adopted curricular programs and from the usual supervisory assistance given by central office personnel to the schools of the system.

The experiment was generally supported by the executive committee although there were a few dissenters. The telling comment, however, was delivered by an area superintendent who said, "I think the experiment will work, but I believe it cannot go forward without the approval of the board. If the experiment is a success and the plan is adopted by other schools, a lot of central office people will lose their jobs." The meeting ended shortly after this "death knell" comment was made. The writer, some eight years later, is still waiting for a decision to be communicated to him regarding the system's disposition of the request to experiment in the schools.

BUILDING LEVEL

In this exploration of impediments to local building autonomy, the focus has been on the board of education and the professional staff at the central office. A different set of impediments exists within the individual schools of the system.

THE SCHOOL PRINCIPAL

The school principal, like the superintendent, views the principalship as a power position. As one principal in the empowerment study said, "I've spent four years studying for my doctorate just so I could make the decisions in this school."

Administrative styles may differ among principals, but a bedrock belief exists among them that, if anything goes wrong, they are responsible. Viewed from a different perspective, this belief encourages the principal to be the final arbiter of all things that are going on in the school. Over and over again, one finds, in descriptions of the principal's work day, statements that reflect up to 80 percent of the principal's work day is spent in conversations of less than two minutes duration. Many principals find such a working day far from unwelcome. By having members of the staff constantly asking for advice, the principal's leadership position in the school is affirmed.

Although this is an accurate description of the work and decision-making activities of principals, it does not tell the whole story. One of the reasons the principal is able to make decisions in such rapid fire order is that the decisions are either 1) routine decisions that the principal makes over and over or 2) simple invocations of decisions already made by the board of education or central office staff.

Such is the life of middle managers. Their primary responsibilities are to carry out the wishes of the system leaders and to refer unique decisions and problems to their supervisors for settlement.

Independent action is very risky for the principal. Even when such action results in some benefit to the school and the students, the principal is subject to criticism from the central office staff for "going it alone" or, even worse, being a "loose cannon."

The worst possible scenario is the situation that results when a principal takes independent action and is wrong. The memory of such mistakes haunts principals throughout their careers. Some mistakes are considered so bad that the principal is reassigned to another school or to a "no responsibility" central office job. Other less critical mistakes are brought up and used against the person as promotions to new schools or system directorships are considered.

Thus, the principal in today's school is likely to be a person who carries out central office directives, is careful to check or refer any new situation to a superior, and is careful not to bring any criticism to herself or himself or to the school.

Such a "leader" would seem to be a very colorless person, and this description generally fits. In fact, if those responsible for choosing principals were totally honest, they would admit that such persons are precisely what they are looking for as principals. They are "safe" and very unlikely to embarrass the school system.

These comments probably appear to be criticisms of today's principals. Really, they are not criticisms of principals but criticisms of school systems that are so bureaucratized that such colorless people are considered ideal buildings principals. Said another way, school systems are generally much more concerned with coordination and standardization than they are with specialization. It is this fact that makes autonomous schools so problematic.

If it is agreed that few existing principals would care to lead truly autonomous schools, the question then becomes, "What sort of person would lead an autonomous school?" The key ingredient that emerges from the two studies mentioned at the beginning of this chapter is the belief that all instructional efforts of the school should be focused on the students attending that school. It should not matter what other schools in the system are doing regarding instruction for their students. What is important is the learning needs of that particular group of students.

In one sense, the autonomous school should be able to operate as do good private schools. The College School of Webster Groves (Missouri) is such a private school. The school has established a national reputation because of its attention to the learning needs of its students. It has resisted programs in vogue in other schools. Instead, the director and her faculty have created and developed programs and learning activities because of their usefulness to the students currently attending the school.

A second quality of an autonomous school leader is a belief that all of the resources of the school should be utilized in helping students. Such a person resists making singular decisions but encourages and facilitates all of the staff members to share in the basic decisions of the school.

One technique used by Richard Tranter, the Principal of Murray (Utah) High School, to help encourage teachers to join in the decision-making process was to simply refuse to answer questions. When a teacher asked him a question, he would simply say, "What do you think we should do?" Richard would then put the teacher's solution into effect whenever possible. After a relatively short period, the teachers began to realize their opinions did matter and that they could have a voice in the decisions of the school.

A final quality of an autonomous school principal would be a person who forms partnerships with parents and other members of the school community. The effect of such an effort is to erase the dividing line that exists between the school and its community. The community members are viewed as stakeholders whose insight and advice are vital to the success of the school program.

An example of such a principal is Christine Johnson during her years as principal of Abraham Lincoln High School in Denver. Christine began her effort to make the community a part of the school by including business and higher education leaders from the attendance area in the "think tank," a group of teachers and administrators created to define the school's mission. Very quickly, the group was expanded to include parents and additional teachers. Out of a year-long planning effort, the school programs and structure were modified to better serve the different groups of students who were attending the school.

Today, Lincoln is a unique high school in the school system. Its programs are serving the students attending the school, its "school within a school" structure gathers together students with similar needs and interests, and all of the stakeholders in the community regularly contribute to the school's success. It is an automonous school.

The conclusion of this section related to the principal is that most principals serving in the schools of the nation see themselves as occupying the central leadership positions in their schools. They enjoy the status of the position, and most would not wish to change their roles even if offered the opportunity. The primary responsibility of the position in their eyes is to carry out the programs and mandates of the central administration.

The leadership responsibilities of principals in truly autonomous schools where the emphasis is on the learning needs of the students attending the school would appeal to few current school principals. The school would largely be "going it alone," there would be no central office established "roadmaps" to guide the principal and staff, and most program and instructional decisions would be both unique and consensual.

THE SCHOOL FACULTY

School faculties are diverse collections of individuals. It is nearly impossible to generalize about their attitudes toward school reform. In the empowerment project, the faculties readily agreed to participate in the project. Once the empowerment process was underway, however, these same faculties became less enthusiastic. Majority participation became a difficult attainment in several schools and an impossible objective in others.

Studying the observational data provides several clues about faculty participation in empowerment projects. It seems clear that initial enthusiasm results from the concept of "shared governance." What teacher would not like to have a hand in determining how a school is organized and run? What is not recognized, however, is that sharing the governance responsibilities very likely exposes a faculty member to value conflicts with other teachers. Furthermore, discussions regarding the direction a school should take or an instructional decision it should make seem to go on forever. It does not take long for many faculty members to decide that shared governance is potentially dangerous, takes too much time and energy, and is best left to others.

The result is that, if the empowerment project is to be carried forward, it will be done by a small group of "true believers." Additional believers do join over time, but it is a long, slow process.

A second characteristic of faculties noted in the empowerment and Arizona studies is that faculties are sustainers of their school's culture. These observations support similar findings of ethnographers starting with the precedent study by Cusick (1973). Sustaining the school culture means that the faculty tends to support relationships, rules, and other "ways of doing things" that have "always" existed. Furthermore, the experienced faculty members will take it upon themselves to teach the school's "way of doing things" to the new teachers.

Sustaining the school's culture appears to make the faculty like the central office staff in that it is interested in maintaining the status quo. In the empowerment and Arizona studies, maintaining the status quo was part of the culture in some schools but not in others.

In the schools that made the most progress in empowering teachers and students, change, innovation, and reform seemed to be expected. These values were part of the schools' cultures. The faculties in these schools expected to be involved in shared governance activities and in other innovative programs.

In the other schools, exactly the reverse seemed to be true. Changes did occur from time to time, but only after sustained effort by the principal and other school officials. In these schools the prime cultural value appeared to be the preservation of the status quo.

One final characteristic that affected faculty participation in empowerment efforts was the faculty members' perceptions of their roles as teachers, their places in the general organization of schools, and the resources they expected in their work as teachers. Marie Hughes, a pioneer in the field of teacher-student interaction analysis, frequently used to say to her students at the University of Arizona. "The best way to predict how a teacher will teach, is how she (or he) was taught." This conclusion, based on her research, reflects that faculty members bring to the school setting traditional perceptions of principal/teacher relationships. They also bring traditional expectations of teaching techniques and of working with students in isolated classrooms.

This characteristic was reflected in the empowerment data over and over again as teachers expressed 1) the desire to "just be left alone" 2) fears that their innovative work with students might not be acceptable to the central office, or 3) a discomfort with school policy discussions in which the principal participated. Such feelings served to curb the enthusiasm of faculty members toward empowerment and to limit their willingness to participate.

The conclusion of this section related to faculty participation in empowerment projects and other innovations requiring building autonomy, in that such participation is problematic. The faculties of the schools selected for the empowerment project first voted to participate in the project, and, even then, many individuals had great difficulty in joining the effort. It is safe to assume that faculty members, without the opportunity to volunteer, would be even more conservative in their enthusiasm for such innovations.

A CONCLUDING STATEMENT

School reforms that require significant decisions to be made at the building level will probably never be successful. The difficulty rests in allowing individual schools the independence they require to implement innovations such as site-based management, teacher and student empowerment, and so on. The problem is that all of the major players believe in a strong, bureaucratic school system.

The arguments that school officials use to defend the system's autonomy are lost when building autonomy is discussed. The fact that system data reflect great disparities among the system's students and their learning needs has little impact on the board members, superintendents, central office staff members, building principals, and teachers of school systems. There appears to be an assumption that a system's singular curriculum and instructional arrangements are appropriate for all students of the system.

So why are we talking about teacher empowerment and site-based management?

REFERENCES

Cusick, P. A. (1973). *Inside High School: The Student's World.* New York: Holt, Rinehart & Winston.

Greer, J. T. and Short, P. M. (1988). *The Empowered School District, A Grant Request to the Danforth Foundation.*

Greer, J. T., Allen, P., and Slawson, A. (1990). *Arizona Restructuring Project, A grant Request to the Danforth Foundation.*

CHAPTER 17

Moving Beyond Traditional Notions of School Empowerment

PEGGY C. KIRBY[1]

INTRODUCTION

The literature is replete with examples of "empowered" schools, teachers, parents, and students. Unfortunately, most accounts suffer from lack of operational or conceptual definition of the term. Close examination usually reveals association of empowerment with participation in decision making. While this certainly is a necessary component, it is clearly insufficient to create and maintain systemic changes in schooling. Yet, while we can lament the imprecision in our language related to school restructuring, we cannot overlook the importance of at least starting somewhere. Thus, decision participation is a necessary component of empowerment. In this chapter, it is proposed that empowerment must now move beyond mere decision participation to include responsibility by decision makers, support by administrators at all levels, and expanded inclusion in decision processes.

EMPOWERMENT WITH RESPONSIBILITY

Principals can attempt to move beyond top-down Wave 1 reforms with their emphasis on accountability and minimum standards, and they

---

[1]University of New Orleans.

can dream about bottom-up Wave 2 reforms emphasing school empowerment. There is little guidance, however, on how to bridge the gap between these two efforts (Styron, 1993). Not surprisingly, therefore, moves toward school empowerment usually begin with changes in the structure of school governance. After all, there are numerous models for democratizing decision-making processes [see, for example, Hallinger and Richardson (1988)]. Absent, however, are explicit models for increasing individual and collective capacity for decision making and ownership of decisions.

The popular rhetoric claims that teachers will take responsibility for decisions that they are involved in making. Yet we often find that the kinds of decisions teachers choose to address do not directly impact instruction. Housekeeping and other mundane issues consume an inordinate amount of time allotted to shared decision making (Kirby, 1992; Styron, 1993). While such experience can serve to assure teachers of commitment to empowerment, systemic change will not occur unless decision makers move beyond concerns about working conditions to concerns about teaching and learning. The future of teacher empowerment depends upon teachers' willingness to assume responsibility for decisions about children.

Rosenholtz (1989) found that, for some teachers, empowerment may mean giving them freedom *from* the boredom and frustration of their everyday work conditions, rather than freedom *to* grow and develop. Thus, under traditionally limited structural assumptions, empowering these teachers might mean allowing them to withdraw or to become stuck in perfunctory exercises in trivial decision making. Under future assumptions, it must mean involving the entire school in meaningful change through frequent opportunities for collaboration and continued learning. Voices in decision making must be accompanied by responsibility.

In describing teacher leadership, Barth (1988) shied away from formal structures for collective decision making. Instead, he called for the creation of a "community of leaders" wherein teachers would assume responsibility over issues of importance to them. Let teachers take responsibility for decisions to which they are passionately committed, he claimed, and the outcome would be effective leadership: "Teacher leadership is less a matter of according trusted teachers responsibility for important issues than of ensuring that all teachers are given ownership of a responsibility about which they care deeply. One person's junk is another person's treasure" (p. 139).

Too often, teacher empowerment takes the form of representative democracy. A group of teachers is elected to represent the views of their peers. This may accomplish the immediate task of involving teachers, but it suppresses the larger goal of engendering responsibility. As Barth (1988) and others (e.g., Midgley and Wood, 1993) have realized, the efficacy of teacher empowerment is contingent upon the willingness and ability of teachers to take responsibility for schoolwide decisions.

Levin's Accelerated Schools Process [see Hopfenberg et al. (1993)] includes additional direction for creating empowerment with responsibility. Core values of accelerated schools include experimentation, discovery, and risk taking. As one participant explained, "a natural part of it is reaching outward for information and help[ing] to try and solve the problem, so the responsibility is shared, as well as the rewards" (p. 53).

Unfortunately, teachers rarely solicit information when making schoolwide decisions. Kirby and Bogotch (1993) discovered a general devaluing of information among teachers involved in school governance. They studied schools that had implemented a deliberate process for schoolwide decision making. Teachers in these schools reported that they made decisions on the basis of their own existing knowledge, without seeking additional resources. Experiences with past choices took precedence over any external source of information. Further, teachers and principals rated external sources of information as less useful than internal sources. Thus, even restructuring schools appear to reject the possibility of learning from the experiences of others. Professional journals, conferences, consultants, and data base information systems clearly are underutilized. While some may argue that these sources are ignored due to cost, it is clear from the Kirby and Bogotch study that educators dismiss the professional knowledge of their field as irrelevant to their individual schools. Empowerment with responsibility presumes a change in such attitudes, attitudes that serve to perpetuate the status quo.

We suggest that these two pieces of the empowerment puzzle—matching problems to decision makers on the basis of interest and information utilization—have been missing from past reform efforts. Whereas much deliberation has gone into the democratic sharing of decision authority, little attention has been paid to the kinds of decisions considered and the appropriateness of the decision-making body to attend to these issues. More flexibility in decision participation is warranted to assure that those empowered with decision authority want such authority and are genuinely passionate about the outcome. The intent of Wave 2 reforms was not to transfer all decision authority from administrators to teachers, but to expand decision authority in areas of direct concern to teachers. Issues that teachers consider mundane or trivial are best left to the discretion of others. One lesson from efforts thus far is that professionalism is not equivalent to decision authority unless that authority is over issues of direct interest to teachers and directly impacting the core technology—teaching and learning.

The second missing piece has been the expansion of information resources in decision making. Attention to who makes decisions without concomitant attention to how (and on what basis) decisions are made has guaranteed a perpetuation of the status quo. Teachers view their own experiences as useful to their planning, but they reject the lessons of others. Thus, each school feels compelled to reinvent each problem and each solution. It is ironic that the devaluing of others' experiences and expertise characterizes a reform movement that emphasizes improvement through increased involvement. A change in attitude in this area is not likely to come easily. Decision makers will need guidance in how to locate and use existing resources. More importantly, they will need administrative support for increased information usage. This support must come in the form of information valuing and increased access. This leads to the second major thesis regarding the future of empowered schools.

ADMINISTRATIVE SUPPORT FOR SCHOOL EMPOWERMENT

Early discussions of the role of administrators in teacher empowerment debated the distribution of power. It is now generally accepted in the management literature that power shared is an infinite resource, not a zero-sum game. When more people are committed to educational improvement, more resources (in terms of expertise, time, creativity, etc.) are amassed to fuel the endeavor. In order to sustain the effort, however, the support of school administrators at all levels is required.

Researchers have long recognized the importance of the principal's support of educational change (Berman and McLaughlin, 1977; Mann, 1978; Sarason, 1971). Indeed, the principal's acceptance and active support of school improvement projects may be crucial to the eventual institutionalization of the innovation. The school administrator, therefore, must remain actively involved in participative school governance. Teacher empowerment must be viewed as an expansion of responsibility rather than an abdication of authority.

Arends (1982) synthesized the literature on administrative support in an attempt to define specific ways in which administrators demonstrated their support of a project. He found that administrators supported projects by providing public verbal endorsements, role clarity, and consistent governance structures; defending goals and activities against dissenting voices; and giving something of value to organizational members. Arends found this last manner of displaying support to be the most effective. Both material and non-material rewards were perceived as supportive. Teachers valued extra time, space, money, status, and affection.

Blase and Kirby (1992) found that effective principals were adept at "leading by standing behind" (p. 64). These principals provided essential resources for teacher-directed projects and tangible incentives for teacher leadership. In many cases, resources included such basic necessities as paper, textbooks, and access to copiers. Time for joint planning was also a key element of support. Some principals released teachers during the school day, while others freed them from unnecessary paperwork and meetings. In addition, principals demonstrated their support for change by encouraging professional growth and exploration of other school change projects. For example, they provided funds and time for teachers to attend professional conferences or visit other schools.

Andrews and Soder (1987) also noted the importance of the principal's role of resource provider, citing higher gains in student achievement in schools where principals were perceived as more supportive. Kirby and Bogotch (1993) added that this role includes providing access to information for decision making and modeling a valuing of information use. Principals can demonstrate this valuing through encouraging and funding professional development activities. They can scan professional journals and disseminate relevant articles to their teachers. Allowing teachers to visit one another's classes and classes in other schools provides additional access to information.

Principals' support of teacher empowerment also must include a building of capacity for shared decision making. Too often, there is an assumption that, if teachers are granted authority over school decisions, they will somehow know how to work together, creating appropriate structures for decision making and selecting issues that will lead to improved learning outcomes. There is seldom much attention to group development and decision processes. Often, the efforts are abandoned in frustration because participants fail to understand the natural evolution of groups. To avoid conflict—an inevitable stage in group development—they retreat to the former safety of noninvolvement or settle for less creative compromises. Deliberate instruction in group processes can help prepare teachers for greater involvement. Networks of schools engaged in similar reform can serve to reassure participants that conflict is natural and even desirable, forcing the careful deliberation of issues before implementing ill-conceived proposals.

Finally, principals support teacher empowerment by serving as liaison between the school and the central office. In some cases, this becomes a buffering role. When district administrators are reluctant to change authority structures, the supportive principal protects the school's initiatives from district interference. Roles are clarified with the superintendent, as well as teachers. Teachers are clearly informed of the domain of their authority and publicly supported in their decisions.

In other cases, district administrators are brought into the process. Where the relationship between the district and school is secure, the expertise of district personnel can greatly enhance school-level decision making. Consultants can be mobilized to help with group development, resource acquisition, grant writing, and networking with other schools.

The nature of the relationship between school and district has direct impact on the success of school-initiated change. Under ideal conditions, district and school administrative support of the change effort enhances the likelihood of success. Yet even when districts verbally support reform, principals play a pivotal role in communication between the district and school. They must keep actors at both levels informed of plans, limitations, and progress.

The role of the school administrator under participative governance, thus, expands substantially. It becomes more fluid in that the setting influences the kind of support that will be most effective. Principals must be astute scanners of the environment in order to best allocate their own energies. They must remain abreast of all developments and be prepared to defend the collective decisions of their teachers.

Though often overlooked in school change efforts, a systematic evaluation plan can be of tremendous benefit to the principal in his/her buffering role. Formative evaluation provides the data needed to convince a superintendent to allow a project to continue or to persuade teachers to rethink their strategies. Objective, ongoing evaluation need not be the principal's responsibility, but, as the principal's instrument of defense and support, it should be built into any improvement model.

Styron (1993), a first-year high school principal, attempted to locate his role in a restructured high school. He found support to be a key theme in his daily activities. Opportunities to support teachers arose throughout the school day, at board meetings, and in meetings with parents and students. He also learned that support sometimes means not making decisions. Too often, teachers took their problems to him and, as had been their previous custom, waited for his solution. He learned that support for teacher empowerment is intricately connected to teacher responsibility. By reflecting questions back to the teachers rather than providing answers, he demonstrated his belief in their capacity for problem solving.

Empowerment with responsibility and administrative support present two challenges to the future of school reform. Without either, little enduring change is likely. A third, perhaps more radical, issue for future reform efforts concerns the role of other members of the school community, including parents, students, homeowners, business, and government.

INCLUSIVE EMPOWERMENT

A third issue already impacting school reform is the expansion of control. Board members are elected to represent the views of their constituents, and parents are expected to express their concerns to school personnel. In earlier times this may have been a workable arrangement. Boards had considerable power, and schools were responsive to the demands of the public. Under conditions of school empowerment, however, control is largely vested in personnel at the school site. With the erosion of the neighborhood school concept and with the gradual acceptance of school-based management, the arena of actors involved at the school level will have to be expanded if the views of voters, parents, and elected officials are to be represented. Public voice, if it is to be heard, will have to transfer from the district level to the school site.

Many schools still enjoy significant parental involvement, and, in some cases, school empowerment has included parents in decision making. In other cases, parents demanded greater voice through school choice or vouchers. The increasingly favorable sentiment toward choice is indicative of the need to include parents as formal members of school teams. In fact, parent involvement in change processes is one of the most effective ways of engendering support.

Some reform models are quite explicit about the role of the family in school empowerment. In the accelerated schools process, for example, schools are urged to invite families to accelerated schools training sessions. They are encouraged to include students and parents in creating the school's vision and to include families in their school meetings and celebrations (Hopfenberg et al., 1993).

Community involvement also extends beyond the families of children in the school. The astute administrator will solicit the participation of business leaders, social service agencies, politicians, senior citizens, and universities. Not only does this expand the resources available to the school, but it helps students see the connection between what they do in school and the world outside. As Hopfenberg et al. (1993) propose,

> In traditional education, a separation has often existed between schools and the world in which skills and knowledge are used. Instead of encouraging this isolation, the accelerated schools philosophy and process emphasize active and challenging learning experiences that are relevant to the students' current life challenges, interests, and cultural values, (p. 292).

Inclusion has become the overarching goal of special education. When separated from their peers or singled out for special treatment, children are less likely to reach their full potential. Similarly, schools are less likely to achieve their optimal goals when they isolate themselves from the larger communities in which they thrive.

Not unexpectedly, few schools have grappled with the specific details of how to include the larger community in key schoolwide decisions. Empowerment is still in its infancy; most teachers remain uninvolved in meaningful schoolwide improvement. Where involvement has been expanded, issues of governance, relationships with administrators and district personnel, and limitations on control may require years to evolve to a level of stability that will allow for purposeful reform. Inclusion is the next step in this evolution; it will enhance efforts by supplementing resources, and it will sustain efforts by expanding the base of support.

CONCLUSION

Three themes emerge as critical to the continuation of school empowerment: responsibility, administrative support, and community inclusion. Teacher empowerment has been associated with teacher voice in decision making. While this is arguably a necessary first step toward school empowerment, alone it is insufficient to create and sustain positive school change.

In exchange for decision authority, teachers must be given and accept responsibility for their actions. Although little guidance has been offered in this area, responsibility is more likely when teachers are involved in issues they identify as most critical and when they have access to resources that allow for *informed* decision making.

Administrative support for school empowerment is provided through increased access to information and other key resources and through negotiation with the central office to accept new forms of governance, curriculum, instruction, and alternative uses of resources. Finally, empowerment must be inclusive of the larger school community if it is to survive public scrutiny. Further, expanded inclusion makes schooling more meaningful and relevant to children.

REFERENCES

Andrews, R. L. and Soder, R. (1987). Principal instructional leadership and school achievement. *Instructional Leadership*, 44, 9–11.

Arends, R. (1982). The meaning of administrative support. *Educational Administration Quarterly*, 18, 79–92.

Barth, R. (1988). School: A community of leaders. In *Building a Professional Culture in Schools*, A. Lieberman (Ed.), New York: Teachers College Press, pp. 129–147.

Berman, P. and McLaughlin, M. W. (1977). *Federal Programs Supporting Educational Change*. Santa Monica, CA: Rand Corporation.

Blase, J. and Kirby, P. C. (1992). *Bringing out the Best in Teachers: What Effective Principals Do*. Newbury Park, CA: Corwin Press.

Hallinger, P. and Richardson, D. (1988). Models of shared leadership: Evolving structures and relationships. *Urban Review*, 20, 229–245.

Hopfenberg, W. S., Levin, H. M., and Associates. (1993). *The Accelerated Schools Resource Guide*. San Francisco, CA: Jossey-Bass.

Kirby, P. C. (1992). Shared decision making: Moving from concerns about restrooms to concerns about classrooms. *Journal of School Leadership*, 2, 330–344.

Kirby, P. C. and Bogotch, I. (1993, April). Information utilization in restructuring schools. Paper presented at the *Meeting of the American Educational Research Association*, Atlanta, GA.

Mann, D. (1978). *Making Change Happen*. New York: Teachers College Press.

Midgley, C. and Wood, S. (1993). Beyond site-based management: Empowering teachers to reform schools. *Phi Delta Kappan*, 75, 245–252.

Rosenholtz, S. J. (1989). *Teachers' Workplace: The Social Organization of Schools*. New York: Longman.

Sarason, S. B. (1971). *The Culture of the School and the Problem of Change*. Boston: Allyn & Bacon.

Styron, R. (1993). *The Introduction of Shared Governance by a First-Year Principal*. Doctoral dissertation, University of New Orleans.